"You Seem to Like Your Money, and We Like Our Land"

A Documentary History of the Salish, Pend d'Oreille, and Kootenai Indians, 1875-1889

"You Seem to Like Your Money, and We Like Our Land"

A Documentary History of the Salish, Pend d'Oreille, and Kootenai Indians, 1875-1889

edited by
Robert Bigart
and
Joseph McDonald

published by
Salish Kootenai College Press
Pablo, Montana

distributed by
University of Nebraska Press
Lincoln, Nebraska

Publication of this book was made possible through the generosity of the Oleta "Pete" Smith Endowment Fund of the Montana Community Foundation.

Cover design: Corky Clairmont, artist/graphic designer, Pablo, Montana.
Cover illustration: Chief Arlee, Peter Ronan, *Historical Sketch of the Flathead-Indians from the Year 1813 to 1890* (Helena, Mont.: Journal Publishing Co., 1890), p. 78.

Library of Congress Cataloging-in-Publication Data:
Names: Bigart, Robert, editor. | McDonald, Joseph, 1933- editor.
Title: "You seem to like your money, and we like our land" : a documentary history of the Salish, Pend d'Oreille, and Kootenai Indians, 1875-1889 / edited by Robert Bigart and Joseph McDonald.
Description: Pablo, MT : Salish Kootenai College Press, [2020] | Includes bibliographical references and index.
Identifiers: LCCN 2019042548 | ISBN 9781934594261 (paperback)
Subjects: LCSH: Salish Indians--Montana--History--19th century--Sources. | Kalispel Indians--Montana--History--19th century--Sources. | Kootenai Indians--Montana--History--19th century--Sources.
Classification: LCC E99.S2 Y68 2020 | DDC 978.6004/979435--dc23
LC record available at https://lccn.loc.gov/2019042548

Published by Salish Kootenai College Press, PO Box 70, Pablo, MT 59855.

Distributed by University of Nebraska Press, 1111 Lincoln Mall, Lincoln, NE 68588-0630, order 1-800-755-1105, www.nebraskapress.unl.edu.

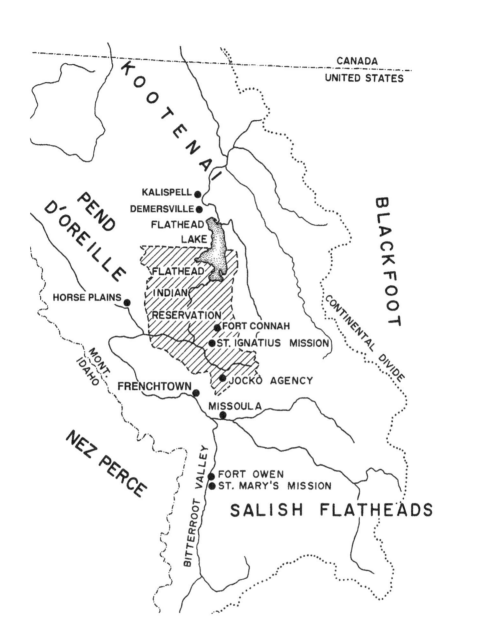

**Flathead Indian Reservation
Showing Tribal Territories
and Surrounding Towns**

Table of Contents

Detailed Table of Contents

Introduction

In the middle of the nineteenth century, the Salish, Pend d'Oreille, and Kootenai tribes had navigated a world of military struggles with enemy tribes in alliance with the newly arrived tribe of white Americans. By the last quarter of the century — 1875-1889 — the paradigm had shifted, as the tribes worked to keep the peace with the white man while struggling to preserve tribal rights and assets from the onslaughts of the growing white population.

In just fifteen years, the Flathead Reservation tribes careened from dramatic efforts to stay out of the 1877 Nez Perce War to seeking ways to get the white justice system to punish white men who murdered Indians. In 1889, the Missoula County Sheriff was actively pursuing Indians accused of murdering white men. Whites responsible for killing Pend d'Oreille Chief Michelle's relatives and Kootenai Chief Eneas' son went unpunished.

In 1882, the Salish, Pend d'Oreille, and Kootenai leaders negotiated terms for the sale of a railroad right of way through the reservation. Over the 1880s, Chief Charlo worked to secure the right of the Salish to remain in the Bitterroot and, if possible, to obtain enough government aid to help the tribe establish a self-supporting Salish community in the Bitterroot Valley.

Cautions, Biases, and Selection Strategies

The documents of Flathead Reservation history in this collection were selected because they offered valuable information about the tribes. However, because they were written records, they also reflect the biases and bigotry of the white men and women who wrote the records. The readers need to look beyond the bigotry to see the specific incidents being described.

The editors have given preference to statements by individual Indians or chiefs or descriptions of specific activities. The documents chosen needed to be readable and make sense on their own. Normally historians often rely on many small, short references in diaries or newspaper articles which do not tell a full story.

The documents have not been edited to remove all bigoted words or references. However, an offensive term describing Indian women has been rendered as "s...."

The editors have tried to use "sic" as conservatively as possible. It is usually only used when we felt the reader might be confused about whether the mistake was in the transcription or in the original manuscript.

The most important sources for tribal history are the oral traditions of the elders. The written sources contribute towards telling history, but they do not give the history. Hopefully, the documents reproduced here will supplement the oral tribal histories currently being collected and written by the Salish–Pend d'Oreille Culture Committee in St. Ignatius and the Kootenai Culture Committee in Elmo, Montana.

Complementary Sources

Readers of Salish, Pend d'Oreille, and Kootenai Indian history between 1875 and 1889 will want to also look at some other books of historical sources published by Salish Kootenai College Press. Of particular interest would be the two volumes of Agent Peter Ronan's letters that were published in 2014: Peter Ronan, *"A Great Many of Us Have Good Farms": Agent Peter Ronan Reports on the Flathead Indian Reservation, Montana, 1877-1887*, and Peter Ronan, *Justice To Be Accorded To the Indians: Agent Peter Ronan Reports on the Flathead Indian Reservation, Montana, 1888-1893*. Selected Ronan letters describing the views and actions of tribal members have been reprinted in this volume of documents, but the full Ronan collection included much information about other reservation events not covered in this book. Robert J. Bigart, editor, *A Pretty Village: Documents of Worship and Culture Change, St. Ignatius Mission, Montana, 1880-1889* (2007) included much more detailed information and description of the 1880s at St. Ignatius Mission than has been reproduced in this book. Hopefully, the present volume can serve as an introduction to the broader world of written evidence about tribal history between 1875 and 1889. The citations for the source of each document in this volume will allow readers to do follow up research and learn more about the context of the events described.

Echoes of the Past

The historical sources for the 1875-1876 period include a number of topics that were important in earlier periods. For example, Agent Charles Medary's annual report for 1875 indicated how some Pend d'Oreille were beginning to make progress in expanding their farms (Document 4). A Helena newspaper article from 1875 (Document 5) indicated that a Pend d'Oreille buffalo hunt on the Blackfeet Reservation had to be quickly abandoned after some young Pend d'Oreille lassoed a wife of the senior Piegan chief. Two letters from Agent Medary in August 1875 (Document 3) and December 1876 (Document 9) emphasized the limits of the agent's authority to keep Indians on the reservation in the face of opposition from the chiefs. The chiefs and other leaders constantly complained that the government had not kept the promises made in the 1855 Hellgate Treaty (Documents 7 and 10). In a famous speech from 1876, Chief Charlo complained bitterly about Missoula County taxes and the failure of some whites to treat the Bitterroot Salish fairly (Document 8).

Intertribal warfare slowed but continued for some years after 1875. Felix Barnaby's account describing his father's raid on Sioux horses in 1875 was one of the most detailed surviving accounts of a Salish war party (Document 6). Two newspaper accounts from 1883 (Documents 48 and 56) refer to Salish willing to take Piegan and Crow horses. The Piegan horses (Document 48) were actually white men's horses the Salish ended up trying to return to the original owners. In the 1880s Salish–Pend d'Oreille horse raids dropped off dramatically.

The Nez Perce War

Problems of keeping the peace with the whites exploded in 1877 when the hostile Nez Perce retreated through Montana. In particular the Bitterroot Salish tried to remain neutral. There was some evidence that Duncan McDonald met the Nez Perce on the Lolo Trail and offered to guide them north to Canada, avoiding the white settlements (Documents 14 and 27). The Nez Perce headed for the Crow country instead, and suffered several bloody battles.

Before the Nez Perce arrived in Montana, Charlo sent Chief Adolph to Missoula in July 1877 to reassure the whites of the peaceful intentions of the Bitterroot Salish (Document 15). That same month, Charlo and the reservation chiefs pledged neutrality in meetings with Flathead Agent Peter Ronan and the Fort Missoula commander (Document 18). An unusually detailed account of peaceful Indian-white social interactions in the Bitterroot Valley in 1877, was Will Sutherlin's description of Indian guests at a Fourth of July celebration in the valley (Document 17).

When Joseph and the hostile Nez Perce entered the Bitterroot Valley, Charlo admonished them to not rob or harm the white settlers (Documents 21, 23, and 29). In fact, a number of prominent Bitterroot Salish joined the army troops and white volunteers at Fort Fizzle in an unsuccessful effort to prevent the Nez Perce from entering the valley (Document 19).

Many western Montana whites applauded the protection settlers received from the Bitterroot Salish (Document 20). The only reward the Salish received from the government was to be included in an ammunition sales ban. The Salish were officially bared from purchasing the guns and ammunition they needed to hunt for food and protect themselves (Documents 22, 23, and 28).

In 1878, when a band of hostile Nez Perce slipped through western Montana and were accused of murdering whites in Rock Creek and elsewhere along the way, several prominent Bitterroot Salish joined the soldiers and white settlers in pursuit. According to one account, Francois LaMoose, Narcisse, Louis Vanderburg, and Martin Charlo joined the white men chasing the Nez Perce out of Montana (Document 30).

Dealing with the White Montana Justice System

Another crisis confronting the Salish, Pend d'Oreille, and Kootenai Indians between 1875 and 1889 was dealing with the biases of the Missoula County justice system. The Missoula Sheriff was much more anxious to find and punish Indians who killed white men than white men who killed Indians.

One of the first cases was the October 1881 murder of Cayuse, a Bitterroot Indian, by Howard Preece and James Morris in a drunken gun battle on the streets of Stevensville. Chief Charlo demanded Preece and Morris be turned over to him for punishment, but the two men were arrested and jailed in Missoula (Document 39). The courts muddled through, but Preece died in custody and Morris was jailed for at least eight months before being found innocent of murder.

Another case a year later illustrated significant differences between Indian and white views on punishment for murder. In June 1882, Koonsa killed Frank Marengo in a drunken fight on the Flathead Reservation (Document 42). Both were mixed-blood tribal members. Koonsa surrendered to Chief Michelle and Chief Arlee, who decided to fine Koonsa a number of horses, some of which were to go to Marengo's family. Agent Peter Ronan arrested Koonsa and charged him with murder in the United States Court in Deer Lodge. Much to Ronan's chagrin and the outrage of many white Montanans, Koonsa was released and the charges dismissed. The federal court found Koonsa had already been tried and punished for the murder by traditional Indian justice, and no one could be charged twice for the same crime in the United States. Many Montana whites were also outraged by Chief Arlee's argument that the white man who sold Koonsa the alcohol was responsible for the murder, not Koonsa who committed the crime while under the influence.

Two Salish Indians returning from a visit to the Crow Indians were murdered in April 1884 near Bozeman (Document 61). Despite a reward offer for $300, apparently no one was tried or convicted of the murder.

In March 1886, the Montana Governor pardoned three tribal members who had been convicted of assaulting whites in Missoula County while intoxicated (Document 69). Bendois, one of those pardoned, was arrested for stealing two horses from one of the Finleys at the Jocko Agency in October 1887 (Document 73).

The final cascade of problems between tribal members and the Missoula County Sheriff was triggered by the capture of Larra Finley, an accused murderer, by Al Sloan in Choteau County on the Great Plains. Larra Finley had been blamed for a number of crimes over the years, but was always released for lack of evidence (Document 79).

After Larra Finley was captured, he made a statement accusing two other Indians, Pierre Paul and Lalasee, of murdering two white men in the Jocko Valley two years earlier (Document 81). Finley's statement inspired Missoula Sheriff Daniel Heyfron to call out a white posse and invade the reservation to arrest Pierre Paul and Lalasee. Unfortunately, neither the sheriff nor any of the posse knew what Paul or Lalasee looked like. Consequently, the white posse took the railroad to the reservation and accosted any Indian they met. One Indian saw the white men approaching with guns drawn. He ran and the posse shot him. The Indian murdered by the posse was innocent, and the death enraged many tribal members (Document 81). The posse then took a train off the reservation and no one was prosecuted for the murder of the innocent Indian. The conflict over the accused Indian murderers came to a head in 1890, and four Indians were hung in Missoula in December of 1890.

In July 1889, two mixed bloods, Joe Finley and Baptiste Matt, were cleared of murdering Seven Pipes or Benoit on grounds of self-defense (Document 82). The Missoula justice system could handle Indians killing other Indians and was very motivated to punish Indians accused of murdering white men.

Unfortunately, the sheriffs showed little interest in finding and punishing white men accused of murdering Indians. Sometime during the winter of 1888–1889, some relatives of Chief Michelle were murdered east of the mountains and white men were suspected (Document 83). In the summer of 1889, Kootenai Chief Eneas' son, Sam, was murdered in Demersville, probably by a white man. The Missoula County Sheriff never found or arrested the killers (Document 85). Needless to say, Agent Ronan and many tribal members were angry about the lack of fairness in the white justice system.

Government Negotiators

The 1880s were the occasion for a series of government officials negotiating with the Flathead Reservation tribes for a railroad right-of-way and the move of the Bitterroot Salish to the Jocko Reservation. Fortunately, we have transcripts or detailed accounts of the statements by the chiefs at these negotiations.

Joseph McCammon met the reservation chiefs in August and September of 1882 (Document 45). The chiefs met together before McCammon arrived, so they could decide on a unified strategy to present to the government negotiator. The chiefs' first choice was for the railroad to avoid the reservation. When that proved impossible, they asked for a million dollars. They finally settled for $16,000 to be paid in cash — not annuities — and a promise of free rides for Indians on the trains. In September 1883, the chiefs again met ahead of time to coordinate strategy in meeting Senator G. G. Vest and Representative Martin Maginnis. The tribes agreed to welcome the Bitterroot Salish if they moved to the Jocko Valley (Document 53).

Senator Vest wrote a detailed account of his 1883 negotiations with Charlo over the Bitterroot Valley. Charlo refused to move, but did agree to go to Washington, D.C., to present his case directly to higher officials (Document 52). Charlo went to Washington in 1884, but he still refused to remove to the reservation (Document 59). Finally in 1889, General Henry Carrington and a punishing drought forced Charlo to agree to move (Document 88). According to Carrington's account Charlo succumbed to Carrington's persuasion and logic. We do not have Charlo's version of his negotiations with Carrington.

In June 1889, Kootenai Chief Eneas met with Agent Ronan and an agent of the United States Justice Department to discuss means to protect the Kootenai from whiskey sellers. Eneas complained about government meddling which forced the reservation chiefs to give up whipping as a punishment (Document 80).

These negotiations only give brief windows into the views and values of the nineteenth century chiefs. Despite the language and cultural barriers, the transcripts show leaders who were determined to look out for the interests of their communities despite great odds.

Economic Role of the Tribal Members

Several sources give glimpses of the role of the Salish, Pend d'Oreille, and Kootenai in the western Montana economy in the 1880s. One writer noted the importance of the Salish as customers when they visited Helena on their way to and from the plains in the early 1880s (Document 57). They sold buffalo robes and skins, and then spent the money at Helena merchants. A January 1884 article noted an Indian couple employed cutting firewood for a white Missoula resident (December 58). William Wheeler noted in 1885 that reservation farmers sold their surplus grain crop in Missoula (Document 66). In his 1885 annual report, Agent Ronan included a list of the larger farmers on the reservation (Document 67). Three years later in 1888, Indian Inspector E. D. Banister included another list of farmers in his report to the Secretary of the Interior (Document 75). In 1889 a Flathead Reservation Indian was hired as a guide to a white hunting and fishing party on the reservation (Document 86).

Conclusion

The Salish, Pend d'Oreille, and Kootenai Indians navigated treacherous waters between 1875 and 1889. Strong leaders guided them successfully through the crisis of the Nez Perce War and its aftermath in 1877 and 1878. Somehow, they were able to keep the peace and do what they could to protect Indian rights against a biased white justice system. The chiefs also stood up for tribal rights and interests in negotiations with government officials from Washington, D.C. Many events were stacked against the tribes, but they had capable leaders and survived to fight another day.

Robert Bigart
Joseph McDonald

Chapter 1

Documents of
Salish, Pend d'Oreille, and Kootenai
History Between 1875 and 1879

Document 1

New Police Force Created for Pend d'Oreille and Kootenai
February 1, 1875

Source: Peter Whaley, Flathead Indian Agency, to Hon. E. P. Smith, Commissioner of Indian Affairs, February 1, 1875, St. Ignatius Mission File, Bureau of Catholic Indian Missions Records, series 1-1, box 10, folder 10, Marquette University Special Collections and Archives, Milwaukee, Wis.

Editors' note: Note that in 1875 the police force on the reservation was controlled by the chiefs rather than the agency. At this time government rations were only issued at times of special need.

Flathead Indian Agency,
Montana Territory,
Feb. 1st, 1875.

Hon. E. P. Smith
Commissioner of Indian Affairs
Washington, D.C.
Sir;

I have the honor to submit monthly report for January 1875. The Indians have been as before, peaceful and no report has reached me within the past month of any serious misdemeanors committed either among themselves or against their white neighbors.

The Pend d'Oreille and Kootenai chiefs have established a system of police to prevent crime and immorality on the reservation, by promptly punishing offenders. I sincerely believe these two chiefs to be determined to try and better the habits and condition of their people.

The Indians absent on the buffalo hunt are reported as returning with good supplies of meat and robes. From the commencement of the month until about the twenty-fifth, the weather was severely cold; the thermometer indicating from 20 degrees to 40 degrees below zero; and this great depth of snow, made many of the Indians dependent upon the Agency, and any great suffering was prevented by furnishing them with such supplies of food and clothing as I felt myself authorized to procure with the money at my command.

The last few days it has been turning warmer, and the Indians are preparing to start on a hunt for elk, deer and such other game as the reservation and neighboring country affords. Owing to the severe cold, it was for a time impossible to run the mills but the employees were steadily occupied in the shops making repairs etc. or cutting and hauling fire-wood and saw-logs.

Deeming the affairs of the Indians and of the Agency in a prosperous condition at present.

I am very respectfully
Your obedient servant
Peter Whaley
U.S. Ind. Agent.

Document 2

Chief Arlee and Father Philip Rappagliosi

April 14, 1875

Source: Father Philip Rappagliosi, *Letters from the Rocky Mountain Indian Missions,* ed. Robert Bigart, by permission of the University of Nebraska Press, Lincoln, copyright 2003 by the Board of Regents of the University of Nebraska, pages 55-58.

Editors' note: By the spring of 1875, Father Rappagliosi was stationed at St. Ignatius Mission on the Flathead Indian Reservation. The chief he wrote about in this letter was Chief Arlee, who lived in the Jocko Valley and was chief of the Bitterroot Salish Indians on the reservation. Rappagliosi was visiting the church at the Jocko Agency. No record has been found to give Chief Arlee's version of the interactions Rappagliosi described. Some footnotes have been omitted. This letter from Father Rappagliosi was originally published in a German Catholic mission publication, *Katholischen Missionen,* in 1876.

Dealings with an Indian Chief

[Another letter of Philip Rappagliosi from April 14, 1875, makes us familiar with the difficulty which missionaries among the Indians must face frequently, namely the moodiness, touchiness, and small-minded vanity of the chiefs. The ability of the Father to appease and to win over the offended chief and the picture of Indian ways of life that is presented to us at this occasion leads us to submit this letter to our readers. — 1876 editor of *Katholischen Missionen.*]

Since I wrote my last letter, I spent two weeks in another Indian camp to teach those who were making their first communion. The chief of that camp had been angry at us for some time. He is a very eloquent (in Indian terms) and extremely proud man; some Whites and Protestants or Catholics (in name only) used this to change his mind about us. As a result of recent contracts between the government of the United States and his tribe, he received much money since part of the Indian land was ceded. This caused him to become conceited so that he became demanding and unmalleable. Therefore my trip had two purposes: I wanted to teach the children about the Catechism, and to win back the heart of that stubborn Indian and his people. When I arrived at the camp he was not there; but I knew that he would have to return the

Philip Rappagliosi, S.J.
Source: Filippo Rappagliosi, S.J., *Memorie del P. Filippo Rappagliosi,
Missionario Apostolico Nelle Montagne Rocciose* (Rome:
Tipografia di Bernardo Morini, 1879), frontpiece.

day after and this was exactly what happened. Our first talk was rather cold, especially in the beginning. When I got off my horse in front of his cabin, he was by coincidence standing by the door and looked at me as if he did not know me. I went over, shook his hand, and welcomed him back. He turned his head away and gave no answer. Pretending not to have realized, I continued: "I am coming to visit you." Then he waved me over into his house and said:

"Come in!" I entered and saw two women who offered me a big wooden chair. I believed that this was the throne of the ruler of the Indians, who was still standing angrily outside. Therefore, I only took a seat on a little bench. After some minutes the chief came in too and immediately sat down on the big armchair. I was very happy that I had left it free. Then I told him that I had come to teach those who were making their first Communion, and that I was going to stay in the camp for a couple of days. He did not pay attention to this and started right away to express his anger about something that had happened to him with one of the Blackrobes. I already knew about the whole story and had expected this eruption. That's why I patiently let him speak and, when I realized that he was about to get to the end of his expressions of anger, I calmly said: "I appreciate your opening your heart to me; but maybe we should talk about it another time. I will come back. Today I just wanted to come for a short while and now I will head back to the one who offered shelter to me for tonight." And, putting my hand on his shoulder, I whispered into his ear as if he were my best friend: "I want to stay and eat with you too a couple of times for as you know I do not have a residence here." He answered calmly, "Oh!" which meant good. This "Oh" was not unimportant to me, but being content with my first visit, I climbed up on my horse with the hope that the "Oh" would be followed by what still needed to be said.

Two days later I was back and the reception was much friendlier. He shook my hand, had me sit down on his chair, and passed me the pipe — the strongest sign of friendship among the Indians. Then he said to me: "Philip, I love you," and added a flattering compliment about my knowledge and pronunciation of the Indian language. I used this moment of good humor to tell him that I had not eaten since the early morning. At once he had a good meal prepared for me. In order to honor me he wanted me to eat by myself, but I realized that he would rather eat with me. Then he took a seat next to me and called for three or four others of the best educated to join us. After the meal we sat down around the fireplace again. Quietly and ceremoniously we lit the pipe and passed it around in the circle. As soon as the first clouds of smoke had begun dancing in the air the chief interrupted the silence and spoke: "Blackrobe, when the Indian has finished a meal with his friends he smokes, and when he smokes he talks about what he wants." I saw what this whole introduction was aiming at. I answered: "Oh!" and he repeated the whole of his angry speech from two days before. The thing was like this: At Christmas a Mission had been completed for the Indians which ended at Epiphany or Three Kings Day. Because the Indians were still on the hunt it was impossible to gather them earlier. On Christmas Eve, as usual, a long ceremonious service took place with many Indian participants. The Father who held Mass, however, recommended they postpone Communion until the end of the Mission, although he allowed people to take Communion during this Holy Night if they wished. My chief arrived just the night before Christmas and went to the Father in order to confess and take Communion. The Father gave him the Sacraments but then he made the comment that all the other chiefs had preferred to wait until the end of the Mission to prepare themselves more fully, and that he would have done better to wait as well. Haughtily he went away swearing about everything.

When he started complaining to me, he asked why Christmas had not been celebrated with the tribe of Saint Ignatius this year. I replied to him and said that it had been celebrated and that I had gathered the people at midnight, decorated and lit up the church, and that there had been a Christ Child on the altar, etc. Hypocritically he threw in that Christmas had not been celebrated because there had not been any Communion. I responded: "Everybody who wanted to could take Communion." He answered: "But the Father refused to give it to me." "The Father did not refuse," I said, "but he told you what he told everybody else as well, namely, to wait until the end of the Mission to become more fully prepared." He did not know what to say now and seemed to be satisfied. Then he started to ask me other random questions which were not his own ideas but had been taught to him in an evil manner by the Whites. I slowly answered all of them, and when he had nothing else to say anymore I spoke to all the bystanders and reminded them to keep the faith. When I had finished they said all together: "We agree." Since it was already nighttime we prayed and everybody went to sleep. Early in the morning I went away to hold Mass in the cabin of a sick man as I had promised. I, nevertheless, informed the chief of the fact that I would celebrate Mass at his place next Sunday and that's where the Indians should be gathered. That placated his ego quite well, and I took the chance to offer him the Sacrament of Confession. During the week I continued teaching Catechism. On Saturday I returned to the chief; he received me in a friendly fashion and confessed as did several others after him. The conversation during the evening went on very amicably and no angry word was said. On Sunday morning the Indians gathered and the chief and the others took Communion. When I said goodbye the chief shook my hand, affirmed his contendedness to me, and promised to come to the mission church at Easter — a promise that cheered me up and gave evidence of the fact that I had won him back completely. He kept his word and visited the other Fathers also. All the ones whom I had prepared for their first Communion came with him. They all received their first Communion at the biggest feast of the ecclesiastical year.

Document 3

Treaty Rights to Leave Reservation

August 14, 1875

Source: Charles S. Medary, U.S. Indian Agent, to B. F. Potts, Governor of Montana, August 14, 1875, U.S. Office of Indian Affairs, "Letters Received by the Office of Indian Affairs, 1824-1880," National Archives Microfilm Publication M234, reel 502, fr. 643-649.

Editors' note: Bureaucrats in Washington, D.C., assumed Indian Agents had total control over the reservation residents. On the Flathead Reservation, the tribes were not getting government rations, and the chiefs insisted on their treaty rights to hunt, fish, and gather off the reservation despite the regulations of the Indian Department.

Flathead Ind. Agency
Montana Territory
August 14th, 1875

His Excellency B. F. Potts
Governor of Montana
Helena, M. T.
Sir,

I have the honor to acknowledge the receipt of your letter of 6th inst. relative to certain Flathead Indians belonging to this Agency roaming over the settlements of the Territory in violation of the orders of the Ind. Department, etc. In reply I have to inform you that all the Indian chiefs here were made acquainted with the contents of the order on the subject, issued by the Department December 17th 1874. They insist on having the right under the Stevens Treaty, to leave the reservation at pleasure.

Article III of that treaty with these Indians says: "And provided, That, if necessary for the public convenience; roads may be run through the said reservation; and, on the other hand, the right of way with free access from the same to the nearest public highway is secured to them (the Indians); as also the right in common with citizens of the United States to travel upon all public highways.

"The exclusive right of taking fish in all the streams running through or bordering said reservation is further secured to said Indians; as also the right of taking fish at all usual and accustomed places in common with citizens of the Territory, and of erecting temporary buildings for curing, together with the privilege of hunting, gathering roots and berries, and pasturing their horses and cattle upon open and unclaimed land."

Notwithstanding the Article quoted, I have used every effort at my command to restrain them from absenting themselves without leave; but owing to the failure of their crops on account of a late spring, and no provision being made for this Agency by the Government to subsist them, they are in a measure compelled to leave the reservation in search of game and berries. No escort of soldiers is available here at present, and without military aid I am powerless to enforce the order of the Department. In connection with this, I cannot too strongly urge the necessity of the early establishment of a military post in the vicinity of Missoula, not only for the protection of citizens in this remote part of the Territory but also for the ultimate advantage of the Indians who deprived of their roving facilities will have to assume industrial habits at home.

As in your communication the Flatheads are especially referred to, I must state that most of those Indians belonging to the reservation are at home. The majority of that tribe have taken up land and reside in the Bitter Root Valley under the Garfield Agreement; they should in my opinion be looked upon and treated as citizens.

Regretting very much that any of the Indians of this Agency should have given cause for complaint, I will at once submit the matter to the Department for such instructions as will enable me to act promptly and satisfactorily.

Very respectfully
Your obt svt
Charles S. Medary
U.S. Ind. Agt.

* * * * * * * *

[Enclosure:]

Helena, Montana
August 6" 1875

Sir,

Flathead Indians from your Agency are roaming over the settlements of the Territory, in violation of orders of the Indian Department. A band of them is reported to be engaged in firing the grass and timber on the upper Big Hole river in Deer Lodge and Beaverhead Counties and a band caused a great fright in Meagher Co. a few days since. As hostile Indians are committing depredations in several localities of the Territory the presence of your Indians in any of the settlements without escort will cause fright and may result in a collision between the settlers and Indians which we would all very much deplore. A few Flathead Indians were here yesterday but I did not learn their destination.

An enforcement of the orders not to allow the Indians to leave their reservation without escort is now necessary to prevent trouble.

I trust you will take such actions as will avoid trouble.

I am Sir your obedient svt.

B. F. Potts

Governor

Document 4

The Flathead Agency in 1875

September 13, 1875

Source: Charles S. Medary, U.S. Indian Agent, to E. P. Smith, Commissioner of Indian Affairs, September 13, 1875, U.S. Commissioner of Indian Affairs, *Annual Report of the Commissioner of Indian Affairs* (Washington, D.C.: Government Printing Office, 1875), pages 304-307.

Editor's note: Medary's condescending and racist attitude shows through clearly in his annual report of 1875. He also included some useful information about the economic progress the tribes were making in preparing for the loss of hunting resources, especially the buffalo. His efforts to get the government to honor the Garfield Agreement must be noted, as well as his efforts to get Chief Arlee to establish a tribal police force for the reservation Salish. He displayed the common white opinion that hunting, fishing, and trapping did not require special skills, knowledge, and hard work.

Flathead Indian Agency,
Montana Territory, September 13, 1875.

Sir:

In compliance with instructions I submit the following report in regard to the condition and affairs of this agency.

Having assumed charge as late as the 1st of July last, I am therefore unable to furnish much desirable information from personal experience and observation, and the report must necessarily be incomplete in many particulars.

The statistics accompanying were partly compiled from the meager records in the office and such estimates as were deemed most reliable.

This agency is located near the head of a pleasant valley, on a small tributary stream of the Jocko River, in the southeast corner of the reservation and distant about twenty-eight miles from the town of Missoula. The country intervening between it and the settlements, owing to its mountainous character, is uninhabited for fourteen miles, and the road leading to the agency from that direction is almost impassable for wagons.

The present site of the agency was located by former agent, C. S. Jones, in 1871; but nearly all the Government buildings were erected as late as 1873, and are therefore new, but in an unfinished condition. The old agency, (situated one mile below the new one, and in existence since 1860,) consisting of a few dilapidated houses and the best farm, so far as land is concerned, in this valley, was abandoned to Arlee, the Flathead chief, and a few of his people, in the winter of 1873. A new site might have been more wisely chosen in one of the adjoining valleys, nearer the habitations of the majority of the Indians, where more available land could have been found, and in larger tracts; although the Jocko Valley cannot be excelled anywhere for grazing, timber, and water-privileges. What little there is of fertile land along the Jocko and its tributaries is occupied and cultivated by Indians and mixed-bloods; and it is altogether impossible to find and break up another large and suitable farm for Government purposes in close proximity to the agency.

The Indians belonging to this reservation are —

First. The Upper Pend d'Oreilles, who have occupied the soil since and before the treaty; they number, as near as can be estimated, about 850 souls. A large majority of them live in the neighborhood of Saint Ignatius Mission, some few near the mouth of the Jocko, and their chief, Michelle, with a few followers, resides on and cultivates a small farm four miles west of the agency. Some of this tribe have made laudable and successful efforts to become self-sustaining by the labor of their own hands in agricultural and other pursuits. The greater number, under the second chief, Andree, who is chief in all but drawing a salary from the Government, make regular annual excursions to the east side of the Rocky Mountains on their accustomed buffalo-hunts.

Second. The Kootenais, numbering about 350 souls. One-half of these, with their chief, Eneas, live on both sides of the line near the center of the Flathead Lake; occupying themselves with some little effort at agriculture, but chiefly with hunting, fishing, trapping, &c. The remainder of the tribe comprises the destitute, aged, blind, cripples, and prostitutes. Many of the helpless rely upon the Government for support, while the balance infest the neighboring towns, pandering to their own low passions and to those of depraved whites. For want of horses, but few join in the annual hunts. Generally speaking, the Kootenais are willing and able to work at manual labor, but their ardor for gambling prevents them from accumulating property.

Third. The Flatheads removed here from the Bitter Root Valley, under the Garfield agreement of August 27, 1872. A census was taken of them by me on the 7th instant, in order to correct the pay-roll; and I find them to consist of twenty heads of families, numbering in all 81 souls. They reside in the immediate vicinity and within two or three miles of the agency, in houses constructed for them two years ago. Nearly all of them may be said to be civilized, only a few of the young men joining parties in the hunt or other pursuits off the reservation. They are chiefly occupied with agriculture, and cultivate the old Government farms (100 acres) and several small patches besides. In consideration of their removal from the Bitter Root Valley, the Government appropriated $5,000 per annum for ten years, which sum has been regularly paid to them, and the money, so far as I can ascertain, has, with few exceptions, been wisely expended.

Arlee, their chief, is very anxious for the fulfillment of the agreement entered into between General [James] Garfield and himself, and he should be encouraged to that end. In several interviews with me he complained that 600 bushels of wheat, guaranteed to be delivered to his people the first year after removal, have never been provided. By referring to the second article of the agreement it will be found that the then superintendent of Indian affairs for Montana was to furnish the wheat in question. Why it was not furnished I have no means of ascertaining; but if the Indians are entitled to it yet, I think it would be a wise policy on the part of the Government to appropriate means to obtain it for them. Indeed, the small sum of money requisite for the purchase of 600 bushels of wheat is trifling in comparison with the good which it might accomplish. The strict fulfillment of all obligations will not only encourage those Flatheads already removed to persevere, but will have a great influence on the ultimate removal of the remainder of the tribe from the Bitter Root Valley. There are yet between 300 and 400 Flatheads living in that valley, adherents of the chief Charlos, who so far have refused to listen to any counsel for removal, and hold no communication with the agency whatever; having apparently abandoned all relations with the Government, believing that the Garfield treaty will never be fully carried out. However, as an order has been issued by the county authorities for the assessment of their property with a view of collecting taxes, the majority of them will, if the Garfield promises are kept in good faith before them, probably remove to the Jocko within another year. I wish here to state that Adolfe, the second chief who signed the agreement, has failed in every particular to comply with its provisions, and his name has therefore been stricken from the pay-roll transferred to me by my predecessor.

All of the Indians belonging to this reservation have ever been friendly-inclined toward the whites; but complaints reach this office, from time to time, of missing horses alleged to have been stolen by them; of setting fire to timber and grass in distant parts of the Territory, and other like offenses. The crime of killing a white person has only once been laid to their charge, and the murderer, a Pend d'Oreille, was promptly surrendered and suffered death by hanging. Upon going to the annual hunts they associate themselves with large bands of Nez Percés, Spokans, Coeur d'Alénes, and other Indians coming over the mountains from Idaho; and offenses alleged to have been committed might have been perpetrated by members of other tribes. Unprincipled white men will sell them liquor, and an intoxicated Indian will, if he does not commit some outrage, cause fright. Under date of August 6th last, the governor of Montana complained that certain Flatheads were roaming over the settlements, without escort, causing fright and committing depredations; the whole correspondence on the subject was submitted to the Department for instructions, under date of August 16. I believe the establishment of a military post in the vicinity of this reservation to be an urgent necessity. An outbreak on the part of the strange Indians coming over the mountains annually, has long been feared by the citizens; and although the Indians belonging to my agency are considered peaceable, it is not known at what time they may enter into a combination with the non-treaty Nez Percés, Spokans, &c., and cause serious disturbance, as has been the case with other equally peaceable tribes. But setting aside all danger of hostility, I still believe a company of soldiers to be a necessity, to keep roving bands of Indians from leaving their reservations, and thus exercising a salutary influence toward their civilization. An Indian will naturally work rather than starve, and confined within the limits of his proper country he would have to turn his attention to some industrial pursuit.

Of the crimes committed by one Indian against another, the generality of cases are adultery. This offense among the Pend d'Oreilles and Kootenais is punished by severe flogging and confinement. I cannot countenance the whipping, which in nine cases out of ten is administered to the women only. It is barbarous, and I have advised the chiefs to try and adopt some other mode of punishment — for instance, work for the benefit of all. There has been one case of murder reported, when one Pend d'Oreille killed another; the causes were women and whisky. The murderer is now confined in the Indian jail, but as the killing was done through strong aggravation and partly in self-defense he will probably be acquitted. The Flathead chief, at my suggestion, will organize a police force, and punish offenders among his people with work and fines, for the benefit of the poor and destitute.

The Government should give the Indians of this reservation more assistance in the way of providing tools, &c. About 60 plows, 60 double harnesses, 10 or 12 wagons, and some edged tools would be applied to excellent use. As the field and garden crops are very short this year, owing partly to a late spring, grasshoppers, and ruinous rains after the grain was cut and shocked, some of the poorer should be provided with seeds by next season. I find here about 90 small packages of garden-seeds, from the Agricultural Department, which should have been issued last spring, but will be held for issue next year.

The educational affairs are in the hands of missionaries, three Sisters of Charity being the teachers. The schools are at Saint Ignatius Mission, and consist of one boarding and one day school. The boarding-school is attended by twenty-eight female scholars, who have made excellent progress in the common English branches, house and needle work, &c., and the school must be considered a decided success — for girls. But a boarding-school for boys also is indispensable for the future welfare of the Indians. The education of girls alone might be of greater benefit if it were not certain that they would finally marry ignorant Indians and soon lapse into semi-barbarism, or, at least, forget, practically, all that had been taught them at school. If boys alone were instructed they would make better use of their acquirements, and if they should marry uneducated girls they would take pride in imparting their knowledge to them, or would at least teach them the English language and civilized manners and customs. Yet the training of boys alone would not produce the desired result. Both sexes should be educated, and at the same time. The boys will not go back to Indian habits, and when they marry they will select their equals in intelligence, if they are to be found. Thus will the next generation have become English-speaking and well-informed beings. Then would we have English-speaking chiefs instead of our now ignorant ones; this of itself would go far toward improving the condition of all. I believe that five years of schooling for both sexes will be of greater benefit to the Indian tribes than ten years devoted to the boys, or twenty years to girls, alone. I hope, therefore, that the Government will at once see the propriety and necessity of establishing an additional boarding and industrial school for boys, leaving their training in the hands of the worthy missionaries now controlling the educational interests of the reservation, and that a sufficient sum will be appropriated therefor at an early day. The small sum necessary for establishing such a school would, in a short time, more than balance the amount which will otherwise have to be expended on the same children if allowed to grow up in ignorance and in their usual wandering and non-productive life. The honorable Commissioner is well aware of the fact that, under ordinary circumstances, a "boarding and industrial school" is the only practical kind for Indians.

Arlee, chief of the Flatheads, is very desirous of trying a day-school at the agency for the children of his tribe; but I consider it decidedly impracticable, as the experiment at the mission, for the past two or three years, has been a failure. Indian children, when they can come and go at pleasure, cannot be induced to attend regularly or take much further interest in book matters than the first novelty of being taught.

I desire to call the attention of the Department to the fact that the employé force of this agency is inadequate. It is utterly impossible to find men out here who would willingly work for the wages now paid them and subsist themselves. As it is, I have to arrange my appropriation for "pay of employés" in such a manner that I can have only a few indispensable hands, who must be subsisted out of the same fund; and besides subsisting these, there are many persons who come here on business for whom it is impossible to refuse accommodations. In my opinion, the whole amount appropriated for employés should be paid in salaries; this would give me two or three additional hands. An extra appropriation should be made for subsistence, especially this year, when nothing has been produced at the agency.

Under date of July 19 last, I made a special report in regard to the condition of the public property received from my predecessor. A great many of the tools are broken and unfit for use, and all the animals, with one or two exceptions, are fit only to perform half service. I have purchased such articles as were immediately necessary, as far as the means at my command would allow; and the employés have been kept steadily busy on improvements of the agency when not occupied on Indian or other current work; but much remains to be done to give the buildings a decent appearance outside and have them comfortable within. I am trying to be as economical as possible, and have purchased articles of every description at the lowest market-rates by paying promptly, but may yet be obliged to make a special requisition for shops, mills, and buildings. The mills are doing fair work, but a new smutter for the grist-mill must be purchased very soon.

In my estimate for funds for third and fourth quarters, 1875, I requested $5,000 to be expended on roads. The roads on this reservation, and leading from here to the settlements, are the worst in this Territory, and the amount asked for should be appropriated; which, if judiciously expended, will be a benefit to all concerned, and ultimate save double the amount in the wear and tear of Government wagons and teams, and also of those of the Indians.

The sanitary condition of the Indians will compare favorably with other tribes, and the medical service is in charge of an experienced and competent physician; the only drawback being the want of a hospital and medicines. A liberal supply of the latter was shipped by the Department over a year ago, but was never received, the loss of which is severely felt. The fault for non-delivery lies with the contractors for transporting Government freight, and I reported the fact to the Department under date of August 7, 1875.

Accompanying I furnish a map of the reservation, believing it to be the most correct that has yet been made.

Believing that, with proper attention, this reservation and the people belonging to it can be brought to a good state of prosperity within a reasonable time by the assistance of the Government in carrying out my suggestions, I am, very respectfully, your obedient servant.

Chas. S. Medary,
United States Indian Agent.

Hon. E. P. Smith,
Commissioner of Indian Affairs, Washington, D.C.

Document 5

An 1875 Buffalo Hunt Meets a Quick End

November 5, 1875

Source: "Indian Troubles," *The Helena Independent* (daily), November 5, 1875, page 3, col. 3.

Editors' note: Little Plume was an important and powerful Piegan chief. The exuberance of a few young warriors put the entire Pend d'Oreille camp in danger. Needless the say, the Pend d'Oreille were no longer welcomed to the Blackfeet Reservation to hunt the diminishing herds of buffalo.

Indian Troubles.
A Daring Attempt by Pen d'Oreilles to Lasso Piegan Women.
The Blackfeet Agency.

For some months past a good deal of trouble has been experienced at the several Indian agencies by roving bands of savages intruding upon the reservations of other tribes and making difficulties between the Indians. A few days since a band of Pen d'Oreilles left the new agency and came down among the Blackfeet. While there two of their braves discovered the wife of Little Plume and a young girl some distance from the agency

And lassoed them.

It was the evident intention of the Indians to drag them into the brush near at hand and perpetrate some outrage upon them.

The act was, however, observed by some white men, who immediately interfered and procured

The release of the women.

When the circumstance was reported to Little Plume, that chief was greatly incensed, and hostilities between the tribes would have been unavoidable but for the prompt withdrawal from the reservation of the Pen d'Oreilles — an event procured by the good offices of

Mr. Rainsford,

of the Blackfeet agency.

The military appear to be quite unable to prevent the intrusion of

These Roving Bands,

and the only way of preventing difficulties lays in the diplomacy of the agents.

Document 6

An 1875 Horse Raid Against the Sioux

1875

Source: Excerpt from "Kutenai Notes," Claude Schaeffer Papers, Glenbow Archives, Calgary, Alberta, folder 161.

Editors' note: This story of an 1875 horse raid against the Sioux was related to anthropologist Claude Schaeffer in 1934. Presumably the story was told by Felix Barnaby, Joseph Barnaby's son. Barnaby's account is remarkably detailed. Note the aid the white woodcutters gave to the Salish horse raiders.

About 59 years (1875) Joseph Barnaby was with the Salish on the plains along the Musselshell river. One night some Sioux Indians raided the camp's horses, leaving only a yearling, a mare, a colt and a 2 year old.

The chief was Charlot.

In the morning when it was announced that over 50 horses had been driven off by the Sioux. It was in January and there was no snow at that time. A pursuit party was organized. Some of these returned.

At noon a young man was sent for a black stud, which had not been stolen. Joseph said that he would set out himself and prepared himself with dry meat, moccasins, a rifle and a revolver with lots of cartridges.

His wife asked him, "what he was going to do & where he was going?" He said he was going to pursue the Sioux & get his horses, or else, get other horses. Charlot told him that the camp would move further down the Musselshell next day, as firewood & grass was getting scarce there and the camp would stay there awhile.

Joseph told Charlot to wait eight days for him and after that, they could move away. Joseph shook hands all around and left. Felix watched him until he was out of sight.

Joseph in the evening ~~went on top of a small hill but~~ then crossed a level plain, rather than passing through some hilly ground. So he would see any enemies approaching. Joseph heard a sound as he approached the hills and he looked around to see some Indians pursuing him. There were more than ten of them.

He got off his horse and got ready to receive them, and was ready to fire underneath his horses neck. All he could see was horses, as the Indians were lying behind them, and charging. He knew he would have a chance to shoot them, as they came up and turned.

They were within 50 yards when the Stud neighed and the leader raised his hand for Joseph not to shoot and all raised up from behind their horses. Joseph then saw that they were some of the Salish who were pursuing the Sioux.

The Salish got off and all had a smoke. They advised him to return as his horses were far off. He refused to return and said that he was now on a raid. Antoine Arlee, and another man named Felix decided to accompany him. Felix ? [question mark in original] had a poor horse, was nearsighted and had no weapon at all. Joseph told Felix that he'd better not accompany him but Felix wished to go. (Felix and Joseph were close friends, so the former wished to be with him.)

The three started out and rode until late at night, when they slept for awhile. Early in the morning they started and rode all day. In the evening they climbed a hill and saw the Missouri river, at a big bend. They moved down and came upon a log cabin with four white men who were cutting firewood for the river boat (steamboat). The whites were friendly and cooked a good meal for them. They then rode on. They had told the whites that they were on a raid and the whites volunteered to help them, in any way they could, if the raiders would return by that way.

They crossed the Missouri over the ice. There were large herds of buffalo on the other side but they rode right through them. They stopped for the night and started out early in the morning. They travelled for three days more and reached a country sloping towards the east. They stopped for the night. They took off their saddles but did not picket their horses, as they would not stray off. (They slept in the way described previously.)

While they were sleeping, Joseph had a dream and was told, "Look at me" and Joseph saw that this one was looking directly at him. "Do your best to get possession of me. If you do, look at my children and they will be yours." Joseph looked and saw behind the brown mare, with a bald face, with a big belly touching the ground and a whole string of horses behind her. She said, "If you fail to get me, there will be much trouble ahead of you." Joseph awoke and knew that it was only a dream. He looked and saw a horse about 10 yards away and he thought it was the one who spoke to him but he soon saw it was his own horse.

He awakened the others and they started traveling. He told his companions of his dream. It soon became daylight. They travelled until noon when they came to a high bench, which they climbed and looked around the country.

Away ahead of them was a deep gulch in which a creek ran, lined with poplar trees (they had a spy-glass with them). The only living thing to be seen were large herds of buffalo on the prairies. Near the gulch they saw another bench.

Joseph filled up his pipe to smoke while Antoine looked through the glass. Joseph watched Antoine and saw that he was excited at [as] he looked through the glass at one spot. Antoine saw some Indians near the creek bench and these were moving with pack horses. Then Joseph took the glass and saw 20 horses, with four Indians driving them. Then another party with 20 horses came in sight, with four driving them and some with packs. When Joseph looked closer, he saw that the pack horses, only had pack saddles on, and no packs, and he knew that they were coming over to chase buffalo.

The Salish watched them until they reached the creek, and they soon saw smoke rising from along the Stream. A little later on, they saw four riding off and these began to chase & kill buffalo. The other four came over to help them skin and cut up the buffalo and soon all returned to the creek with the meat.

Joseph then told the others that they would ride towards the creek and that they would be there by sundown. The Salish moved and kept out of sight. By twilight they were close and stopped for a time. Joseph thought there were about 50 horses in the party.

They approached closer after nightfall and again stopped. Felix was told to remain there with the horses. Joseph left his rifle with him and told him if he heard shooting, to ride off. Felix refused to do this but said he would come to help them, if they were discovered. ("He felt he would starve or be killed, if he were left alone.") The others crossed the river on the ice. The night was dark and no moonlight.

Antoine and Joseph approached the camp from opposite directions. Joseph followed a little trail though clumps of thorn bushes, expecting to see the camp at any moment. He continued to advance in the darkness. A wind suddenly blew the poplar camp fire into light and he saw the that the dark spot were men sleeping and he was very close. He walked backward very slowly and then heard his partner coming up the trail behind him. Antoine buckskin leggings were making considerable noise against the briar bushes but Joseph could not warn him. Joseph reached and found a stick which he threw at Antoine. The latter stopped and then retreated backward and Joseph followed him. (The stick hit Antoine on the breast and Antoine knew it was his partner who had done this.) They met and talked it over and decided the horses were above the camp. They continued looking but couldn't find them. So they turned back and went down the river where the horses were found grazing.

They gathered up the horses and Joseph looked around for the brown mare but she was not in the band. Joseph told Antoine that they had better continue to look for the others as there were more than 50. Antoine didn't want to do this but Joseph continued the search. (Antoine said no the horses are all yours anyway.)

Antoine then drove off these horses. Joseph found the remainder of the horses and among them was the brown mare, with the bald face who had spoken to him in the dream. He drove them off and joined his partner and the other band. They crossed the ice which was slippery, so they scattered gravel on the ice for the horses. Joe caught the brown mare and mounted her, and all the other horses followed her, strung out in a string. They reached Felix and found him waiting. Their own horses were turned loose and they mounted some of the fresh horses, and went off.

Joe took the lead and the other two drove the horses and they travelled until daylight. (The Indians were Sioux). They could still see the creek & camp site at daybreak.

When the sun was way up, Antoine hollered at Joseph that they might as well leave the horses as he was afraid that they might be pursued and caught. Joseph refused saying "If you wish you can pick out a horse. you & Felix and ride on but I wont leave the horses."

Felix refused to do this. Joseph had given Felix his revolver. Antoine took a fresh horse and rode off leading a horse. Joseph and Felix continued to drive on, with the horses.

Towards evening Joseph saw one person ahead of them & thought this might be the Sioux, who had circled around them & were waiting for them. Joseph said the only thing to do was to continue on, as they had been seen. They continued and saw that it was Antoine waiting for them. He turned loose his spare who went in among the herd. Antoine said "the reason why I waited here, was that I thought of what I would say to the Salish when I reached camp. That I had left you because I was afraid. I will stay with you now until we reach home."

They crossed the Missouri at day break and went to the cabin of the whites. When they got there, they were welcomed and invited to stop and eat. Joseph refused saying they might be overtaken at any moment. He asked for some food to eat while they travelled. They were given bread & meat and they continued traveling.

Soon after they had to cross some ranges. The Sioux meanwhile reached the white's cabin soon after and the latter told them that the Salish had passed through the previous night and were far away by this time. The whites invited the Sioux to get off and eat and finally prevailed upon the ~~Sioux~~ to stop and eat. The white *slowly* started to get a meal, to give the Salish more time to escape. They ate & left but several hours later they returned to the cabin, saying that the Salish were too far away to be overtaken.

The Salish continued traveling until sundown and then stopped and rested, as they were almost exhausted.

They started the next morning, rested & smoked at noon. Then Joe asked Antoine, "how many horses of the band he wanted." Antoine said, "If you wish, you can give me one. You are in need of horses more than I as yours have all been taken." Joe then gave Antoine the brown horse that he had led off. He then asked Felix who said he only wanted one. Joe gave him a mare with a colt and gelding. They believed themselves safe at this time, so this is why they divided the horses.

Meanwhile at the camp, after Joe left, Charlot announced that camp would be moved farther down the Musselshell, where they would wait for Joe. He asked the people for extra horses with which to move Joe Barnaby's family.

Not far from the camp was a high ridge. They stayed here for seven days and the next was the one that they were supposed to break camp, not waiting for Joe any longer.

Then Felix B & his brothers were awakened some time during the night, to see a big fire burning. They said their morning prayers. They were told by their mother that she had a dream, "in which she was told to cook whatever food she had left and you invite the Chief & old people for breakfast here at your tipi. If you do this, again you will see your raider (husband) here at your home and you will be glad & happy at his return. If you fail to do this, you will fall into more sorrow & distress." She awoke and knew it was a dream. She saw before her a dark shadow which she saw was their own black dog, Bull. She wondered if the dog had spoken this to her. She waved to Bull to go away.

Joseph Barnaby, meanwhile, travelled all day and came to a level basin, across which was a deep creek, with high banks. He decided to stop all night but was looking for the place to ford it. Then he thought that there might be enemies waiting for them at the ford. As he thought of this, he was seized with the chills (a warning). He stopped and waited for his companions. They then drove all the horses further down, to spend the night there. Antoine asked why this was done and Felix reproached him for always questioning Joe for reasons for his actions, as Joe was the leader. Felix laughed. They unsaddled and spent the night there.

At day break, they arose and started out and finally found a place to ford the creek. ~~They could see the high ridge from here.~~

As Felix B mother was through cooking, he & his brother were sent around each side of camp circle to invite Charlot & the old men to eat. These just filled the tipi and the food was spread out, just as the Sun came up. When they were finished with grace, they heard three shots and the tipi quickly was cleared of people. Felix B understood then that Joseph was just arriving and he watched them approaching, from the ridge near camp.

Felix B was sure that the whole camp wished Joseph to be successful in his raid and the entire camp was out waiting for him, to shake hands and congratulate him, on the horses he had captured.

Then Charlot, the old men and the three raiders went in and finished the ~~breakfast~~ meal prepared by Felix's mother.

(The day before, at the place where Joe had the chills, four Blackfoot escaped from the Crows and were waiting in ambush for Joseph's party. If the latter had proceeded across the ford, he would have been attacked by the Blackfoot. The latter waited a long time for them at the ford on the trail, and finally started to look for them but they failed to reach their camping place. This was told a year later, when the Blackfoot and Salish were friendly and the former inquired who was so wise, as to elude them, at that time. Joseph later met one of the four white men in the Bitterroot valley. The brown mare was kept until she died and she had a lot of colts. Bull was the one who had talked to Felix B mother as he wouldn't have been standing there, otherwise. The Sioux awakened in time, to see all of their horses being driven off. One of them went on afoot (15-20 miles) back to the main camp and organized a pursuit party and this is the one that nearly caught up with Joseph, at the Missouri. This was told to the Blackfoot who told it to the Salish.)

Document 7

Failed Treaty Promises and the Bitterroot Salish

February 19, 1876

Source: Chas. S. Medary, U.S. Indian Agent, to J. Q. Smith, Commissioner of Indian Affairs, February 19, 1876, U.S. Office of Indian Affairs, "Letters Received by the Office of Indian Affairs, 1824-1880," National Archives Microfilm Publication M234, reel 505, frames 212-221.

Editors' note: Medary outlined the failure of the government to keep the promises made in the 1855 Hellgate Treaty. Charlo and the Bitterroot Salish recognized the government failure and were probably also skeptical of Medary's ability to keep his promises to rectify the situation.

Flathead Indian Agency
Montana Territory
February 19th, 1876

Hon. J. Q. Smith
Commissioner of Indian Affairs
Washington, D.C.
Sir,

I have the honor to make a special report, in regard to the general condition of the Indians under my charge, their wishes and necessities, and to offer suggestions calculated to bring about all the results desired by the Government.

In a communication of Febr. 9th, 1876 to the Honorable Board of Indian Commissioners (sent through the office of the Hon. Commissioner of Indian Affairs,) I had occasion to mention several facts, relating to the condition of the Indians here, which I stated would be reported more fully to the Department.

The complaints made from time to time, in regard to the non-fulfillment of the Treaty, are well founded. The hospital, houses for the Chiefs, breaking up 10 acres of land for Chiefs, Employment of Tin-smith, Asst. Miller &c — With the limited number of Employés allowed me, it is not possible for me to do much work for the Indians, which could be done by *Laborers* — If the full amount provided by the Treaty for Employés at this Agency could be given me, so that I could employ two or three laborers, much could be done towards their improvement and benefit.

I have several times referred to the effect such neglect on the part of the Government, would have on the Indians at Bitter Root Valley, who refused to accept of the terms of the Garfield Treaty, believing that the promises would never be fully carried out. I have understood that this question of the removal of the balance of the Flatheads from Bitter Root, was one of great importance to the Government. If so, I must right here recommend that the first act towards that result, be the strict fulfillment of the Treaties. Other steps can then be taken which will undoubtedly solve the question.

It is a delicate and difficult question, but I am confident that with the prompt and fullest aid from the Government, I can accomplish the desired result. When I assumed charge here in July last, I was assured by those best informed, that I could *never* get Charlot, and his band to remove from the Bitter Root, but my treatment towards the Indians of this Reservation since that time, and the manifest interest I have taken in their welfare, and the fact that I have never made a promise that I have not fulfilled to the letter, has given them confidence in me, and this confidence has reached Charlot at Bitter Root. Now, the same parties who had previously given up all hopes of their removal say that they believe these Indians may eventually remove, if I will continue in my present course of action. But I must have timely assistance from the Government, and to that end I must request the fulfillment of the Treaty. The removal or suspension of Arlee (who is disliked by all his tribe on account of his selfishness and dishonesty as reported in my communication of Jany. 28th, 1876) and the appointment of say, Istach Partee a popular Flathead now on the Reservation, and a warm personal friend of Charlot. He was strongly talked of for Flathead Chief at the time of the Garfield Treaty, and if an election had been held, he would have been chosen, but Arlee was *appointed* by former Agent [Daniel] Shanahan.

This would prove very satisfactory to all the Flatheads now here, and to Charlot and his band who all dislike Arlee. — Arlee's position here as Chief is one of the greatest drawbacks to the removal of Charlot and his people from the Bitter Root.

Last week Charlot with eight of his men visited me. He spoke of Arlee in unmeasured terms as an unjust man &c, and stated that he was not a Flathead, and should not be Chief of that tribe. He appeared very sad, and referred to the injustice of imposing taxation on him, and his people. Enquired the reason for stopping annuity goods, and complained that the Treaty had not been fulfilled in other particulars. It was a trying position for me under the circumstances, and especially since I was as much in the dark upon some of these points, as he was. And as his complaints were in a measure just I could scarcely approach him on the subject of removal.

In regard to taxation, I told him I had no jurisdiction over civil proceedings, and that so long as he had refused to remove to the Reservation but had accepted "nolens volens" the condition of citizenship he would be subject to all the laws governing white men; that now there was a wall between us, and that I could neither advise nor assist him. If he should conclude however, to remove here with his band, I would promise to do all in my power for them, and should strongly urge the Government to not only fulfill all the provisions of both Treaties, but to secure other benefits not named in the Treaties, to the end that all his people should become self-supporting. In conclusion, I told him that I had advised the County Commissioners to go slowly in regard to taxation, and that if they should decide to force it, to do so in a manner which should make it as little of a burden as possible, viz: to demand but 20% of the full tax the 1st Year, 40% the 2nd, 60% the 3rd, 80% the 4th and full tax the 5th Year.

I promised him, too, that if he should decide to remove to the Reservation before July next, that I should myself pay all the taxes then due from himself and band. With all this, he was much pleased, and he went away with a lighter heart. His father was a brave and good man, the Chief of the Flatheads, and Head Chief of the Confederated tribes, and I promised that *he* should be the same here. I have the greatest sympathy for him and the people now with him in the Bitter Root Valley and shall use every effort to lead them out of their present trouble and poverty. He loves that Valley and reveres the memory and words of his father, who it is stated told him never to remove therefrom, that if he should ever be forced to remove, to go towards the rising, and not the setting of the Sun. He is not satisfied, but that in a few Years he may again be driven farther West, if he should now remove to the Reservation. The Indians at present on the Reservation are growing more anxious to become self-supporting, especially the Kootenais, who reside near the Lake and who are very poor. All are beginning to see the necessity and importance of work, but as they are too poor to provide themselves with the necessary tools and implements to till the soil, they are left helpless.

To have the means and health to work without the will is one thing, but to have the will, without the means is sad indeed. There can be nothing more demoralizing to these helpless children than to feel their dependence and have the desire to work, and to get no assistance from their Great Father, whom they consider rich enough to assist them all without feeling it. And these facts are still more unjust in their eyes when they Know the millions of money that are spent by that same Father to feed, clothe, and aid the Sioux, and other bands who are continually waging war, destroying property, and taking the lives of the Whites. When we ourselves are unable, to see the justice or consistency of this, it is not reasonable to expect these poor ignorant people to do so.

There are upwards of over one hundred Indians now ready and anxious to abandon the hunt, for the farm, and are only waiting to be supplied with the requisite implements. The number will increase very rapidly each year judging from the past six months. — If the Government will furnish Wagons, Plows, harnesses, scythes &c sufficient for these 100 deserving Indians — say 2 Wagons, 2 Plows, and 2 double sets of harnesses to every ten, with other implements in proportion, I think I can safely guarantee, that all three of the Confederated tribes, will be self-supporting by the expiration of the Stevens Treaty in 1879; a consummation greatly to be hoped for.

I cannot agree with the policy of making Treaties, (and especially Indians of this class) in such a manner that a large sum of money shall be paid in annual installments during a long term of years, nor indeed in giving money at all. Had the Stevens Treaty, in addition to providing Saw and Grist Mills, a Wagon & Plow Makers Shop &c, erected a certain number of houses each year as needed, devoted sufficient funds for the purchase of Plows, and Wagons &c, as desired and established a boarding and industrial School, these Indians might, today, be in a very prosperous condition. The sums of money expended yearly for the last 16 Years under that Treaty have done little else good than to keep them from starving. They are scarcely better off today than when the Treaty was made.

If a larger sum had been expended each year for a shorter term of years and in a manner similar to that I have alluded to, beneficial results would soon have shown themselves. Now is the time to encourage these Indians while they are in the spirit of independence, and are ambitious to adopt the customs and comforts of civilization, through industry. I have satisfied them, that the hunt secures simply a bare living, while industry, will make them happy, supply them with the necessaries, and comforts of life, and provide a home and subsistence in old age. To cut them off now, would be to discourage them forever.

I respectfully invite your attention to Articles IV & V of the Stevens Treaty, which show that these Indians are not at present receiving the full benefits promised them by said Treaty.

Very respectfully,
Your obedt. Servant,
Chas. S. Medary
U.S. Indian Agent.

Document 8

Chief Charlo's Anger Over Taxes

April 26, 1876

Source: Chief Charlo, "Indian Taxation," *The Weekly Missoulian*, April 26, 1876, page 3, col. 3-4.

Editors' note: In this angry speech, Charlo laid out the injustice of taxing the Bitterroot Salish Indians. The Missoula County government wanted the tax money to avoid bankruptcy, but also hoped the taxes would force the Salish to leave the Bitterroot Valley. Charlo's anger was obvious, but the reader must be careful, because the *Missoulian* editor probably made changes to the transcript. The speech has been reprinted and quoted many times over the years.

Indian Taxation.
Recent Speech of a Flathead Chief, Presenting the Question
from an Indian Standpoint.

Yes, my people, the white man wants us to pay him. He comes in his intent, and says we must pay him — pay him for our own — for the things we have from our God and our forefathers; for things he never owned and never gave us. What law or right is that? What shame or what charity? The Indian says that a woman is more shameless than a man; but the white man has less shame than our women. Since our forefathers first beheld him, more than seven times ten winters have snowed and melted. Most of them like those snows have dissolved away. Their spirits went whither they came; his, they say, go there too. Do they meet and see us here. Can he blush before his Maker, or is he forever dead. Is his prayer his promise — a trust of the wind? Is it a sound without sense? Is it a thing whose life is a foul thing? And is he not foul? He has filled graves with our bones. His horses, his cattle, his sheep, his men, his women have a rot. Does not his breath, his gums, stink? His jaws lose their teeth, and he stamps them with false ones; yet he is not ashamed. No, no; his course is destruction; he spoils what the Spirit who gave us this country made beautiful and clean. But that is not enough; he wants us to pay him besides his enslaving our country. Yes, and our people, besides, that degredation of a tribe who never were his enemies. What is he? Who sent him here? We were happy when he first came; since then we often saw him, always heard him, and of him. We first thought he came from the light; but he comes like the dusk of the evening now, not like the dawn of the morning. He comes like a day that has passed, and night enters our future with him.

To take and to lie should be burnt on his forehead, as he burns the sides of my stolen horses with his own name. Had Heaven's Chief burnt him with some mark to refuse him, we might have refused him. No; we did not refuse him in his weakness; in his poverty we fed, we cherished him — yes, befriended him, and showed the fords and defiles of our lands. Yet we did think his face was concealed with hair, and that he often smiled like a rabbit in his own beard. A long-tailed, skulking thing, fond of flat lands and soft grass and woods.

Did he not feast us with our own cattle, on our own land, yes, on our own plain by the cold spring? Did he not invite our hands to his papers; did he not promise before the sun, and before the eye that put fire in it, and in the name of both, and in the name of his own Chief, promise us what he promised — to give us what he has not given; to do what he knew he would never do. Now, because he lied, and because he yet lies, without friendship, manhood, justice, or charity, he wants us to give him money — pay him more. When shall he be satisfied? A roving skulk, first; a natural liar, next; and, withal, a murderer, a tyrant.

To confirm his purpose; to make the trees and stones and his own people hear him, he whispers soldiers, lock houses and iron chains. My people, we are poor; we are fatherless. The white man fathers this doom — yes, this curse on us and on the few that may yet see a few days more. He, the cause of our ruin, is his own snake, which he says stole on his mother in her own country to lie to her. He says his story is that man was rejected and cast off. Why did we not reject him forever? He says one of his virgins had a son nailed to death on two cross sticks to save him. Were all of them dead then when that young man died, we would be all safe now and our country our own.

But he lives to persist; yes, the rascal is also an unsatisfied beggar, and his hangman and swine follow his walk. Pay him money! Did he inquire, how? No, no; his meanness ropes his charity, his avarice wives his envy, his race breeds to extort. Did he speak at all like a friend? He saw a few horses and some cows, and so many tens of rails, with the few of us that own them. His envy thereon baited to the quick. Why thus? Because he himself says says [sic] he is in a big debt, and wants us to help him pay it. His avarice put him in debt, and he wants us to pay him for it and be his fools. Did he ask how many a helpless widow, how many a fatherless child, how many a blind and naked thing fare a little of that little we have. Did he — in a destroying night when the mountains and the firmaments put their faces together to freeze us — did he inquire if we had a spare rag of a blanket to save his lost and perishing steps to our fires? No,

Chief Charlo
Source: Montana Historical Society, Photograph Archives,
Helena, Mont., 954-526.

no; cold he is, you know, and merciless. Four times in one shivering night I last winter knew the old one-eyed Indian, Keneth, that gray man of full seven tens of winters, was refused shelter in four of the white man's houses on his way in that bad night; yet the aged, blnded [blind] man was turned out to his fate. No, no; he is cold and merciless, haughty and overbearing. Look at him, and he looks at you — how? His fishy eye scans you as the why-oops do the shelled blue cock. He is cold, and stealth and envy are with him, and fit him as do his hands and feet. We owe him nothing; he owes us more than he will pay, yet he says there is a God.

I know another aged Indian, with his only daughter and wife alone in their lodge. He had a few beaver skins and four or five poor horses — all he had. The night was bad, and held every stream in thick ice; the earth was white; the stars burned nearer us as if to pity us, but the more they burned the more stood the hair of the deer on end with cold, nor heeded they the frost-bursting barks of the willows. Two of the white man's people came to the lodge, lost and freezing pitifully. They fared well inside that lodge. The old wife and only daughter unbound and cut off their frozen shoes; gave them new ones, and crushed sage-bark rind to put therein to keep their feet smooth and warm. She gave then warm soup; boiled deer meat, and boiled beaver. They were saved; their safety returned to make them live. After a while they would not stop; they would go. They went away. Mind you; remember well: at midnight they returned, murdered the old father, and his daughter and her mother asleep, took the beaver skins and horses, and left. Next day, the first and only Indian they met, a fine young man, they killed, put his body under the ice and rode away on his horse.

Yet, they say we are not good. Will he tell his own crimes? No, no; his crimes to us are left untold. But the Desolator bawls and cries the dangers of the country from us, the few left of us. Other tribes kill and ravish his women and stake his children, and eat his steers, and he gives them blankets and sugar for it. We the poor Flatheads, who never troubled him, he wants now to distress and make poorer.

I have more to say, my people; but this much I have said, and close to hear your minds about this payment. We never begot laws or rights to ask it. His laws never gave us a blade nor a tree, nor a duck; nor a grouse, nor a trout. No; like the wolverine that steals your *cache*, how often does he come? You know he comes as long as he lives, and takes more and more, and dirties what he leaves.

Document 9

Agent Chas. Medary Fights with Flathead Reservation Leaders December 8, 1876

Source: Chas. S. Medary, U.S. Indian Agent, to J. Q. Smith, Commissioner of Indian Affairs, December 8, 1876, U.S. Office of Indian Affairs, "Letters Received by the Office of Indian Affairs, 1824-1880," National Archives Microfilm Publication M234, reel 505, frames 698-705.

Editors' note: Agent Medary's lack of diplomacy and inability to get along with Flathead Reservation leaders eventually forced him out of office, and he left Montana in disgrace. There is no way to tell how much of the opposition stemmed from T. J. Demers, the white trader married to a Pend d'Oreille woman, and how much flowed from Duncan McDonald and Chiefs Arlee and Michelle.

Flathead Ind. Agency
Montana Territory
December 8, 1876

Hon. J. Q. Smith
Commissioner Ind. Affairs
Washington D.C.
Sir,

It has become my duty to make a special report in regard to certain matters at this agency, to which I respectfully call your earliest and particular attention.

I have heretofore reported the Flathead chief Arlee, for his frauds etc. as being totally unfit for his position. He is now continually annoying me with threats, because I will not pay the Flathead money in bulk to him instead of paying it to each individual head of family as I am instructed to do and as I have done heretofore.

The reasons for wishing to be "Disbursing Agent" can only be to rob his people. When former Agent [Peter] Whaley was here, Arlee tried to enter into an arrangement with him by which the Flatheads were to receive but a small portion of their pay, and the balance was to be divided between the agent and himself. Of course Mr. Whaley objected to any such fraud, but was after all imposed upon to enter on his pay roll as Flatheads, persons who were not not [sic] entitled to a cent.

Arlee being afraid to ask me to become an accomplice in this robbery, his only recourse is to try and browbeat me into paying the before mentioned money into his own hands. In this he has failed and his anger knows no bounds. A week or ten days ago he called Michelle, Chief of Pend d'Oreilles, and Duncan McDonald, now trader at the agency, and several Indians — and proceeded to Frenchtown, where they had a conference with T. J. Demers (Store Keeper) and whisky seller. The result was a determination to put me and my employés off the reservation at an early day, by violence if necessary.

Demers now has cattle on this reservation in violation of law, and in August last I reported the fact to the U.S. Dst. Attorney, and suit has been brought against him. I am fully convinced of the fact that he has for years been selling whisky to the Indians of this reservation and still continues to do so; and every intelligent white man in the county is morally certain of the fact: but so far, I have been unable to get sufficient proof to convict him. He does more to create dissatisfaction amongst the Indians and to make them rebellious against the agent and the Government than all the rest of the white men in the county. I shall at once consult a lawyer with a view to indict Demers for conspiracy. He, with several other white men (Some of them former employés of the agency — and s.... men) have been trying for some time to incite the Indians to violence, telling them that if they would make a row and Kill the agent etc. the Government would make a better treaty with them, and would give them plenty of clothing, rations, tobacco, etc. just the same as given to the Sioux and other hostile tribes. And as these Indians are fully aware of the general truth of such statements they are apparently ready to act whenever the occasion may arise.

Arlee is, strictly speaking, not a Flathead, but partly Snake and partly Nez Percez, having been adopted into the tribe years ago. His admixture of blood gives him some influence with the roving Indians from Idaho. This chief was *appointed* to his position by former Agent [Daniel] Shanahan and not elected by his people. He is a miser, a *chronic grumbler*, and a lazy and unpopular chief. Several times the Flatheads have tried to get me to remove him or to have an election held that they might have another chief. He hates religion, turns a deaf ear to the good advise of the agent, and scorns the good example of the Kootenay chief "Eneas," in regard to generosity and the care of his people.

Michelle, the Pend d'Oreille chief, is a cripple and lives near the agency, 16 miles from his people, who reside at the mission under charge of the second chief Antillè, a worthy and good Indian. Arlee and Michelle are therefore drawing pay, as chiefs, which they are not entitled to, as they perform no service to the Indians nor to the Government: on the contrary they are nuisances and bad examples. I therefore ask for *orders* to pay the salaries of these two chiefs from this time forward to Antillè, second chief of Pend d'Oreilles, and to any Flathead that I may in the meantime decide upon. I understand that at some other agencies, the agent has the power to make and to break chiefs. I think this proper, as it is the only way to assert the authority of the Government and to discipline the chiefs. I would also ask for such authority at this agency.

A garrison may be established near Missoula next spring, citizens and agents have applied for military protection again and again. The Indians Know of these efforts; they also Know that the Government does not own a single gun or pistol at the agency and that the few employés, living in the scattered houses would be entirely at their mercy in case of an outbreak.

Under existing circumstances I have deemed it my imperative duty to make application to General John Gibbon for an officer with 15 or 20 men, to be stationed here for the protection of life and property: (Copy of letter herewith enclosed). The halfbreed alluded to in the letter to Gen. Gibbon is one Duncan McDonald, Son of Angus McDonald, formerly a factor of the Hudson's Bay Co. This halfbreed has a fair education, and I assisted him in every way possible — he desiring to enter into trade — and hoped that he would eventually become a useful man. However I must consider him the most treacherous and dangerous of all the halfbreeds. His education and admixture of white and Nez Percez blood give him great influence — and he uses it for the worst purposes in trying continually to raise a sedition against me and the Government.

Arlee and Michelle are now absent in Deer Lodge (without my authority and without asking my permission to go) as witnesses, I believe against the Government in the Demers case. If it be true that they are *his* witnesses of course they are there to testify that they gave him permission to have his cattle on the reservation. They must therefore perjure themselves, as they, twice at least, denied to me that they had given him authority, and indeed, Arlee several times complained that Demers had cattle here in violation of law. In conclusion I would respectfully ask the following questions:

1. If an Indian or Halfbreed on the reservation conspires against the agent or brings into discredit the authority of the Government or creates dissatisfaction and discord amongst the other Indians or among any of them, is he not punishable the same as a white man under Sec. 2111 & 2112. Rev. Statutes?

2. Does the law now require an Indian or halfbreed to get a license to trade? and if so, has an agent any power to regulate the sales of such an Indian or Half-breed.

Very respectfully
Your obt svt,
Chas. S. Medary
U.S. Ind. Agt.

Document 10

Treaty Promises Not Fulfilled

January 30, 1877

Source: Duncan McDonald, "From Jocko Reservation," *The New North-West* (Deer Lodge, Mont.), February 9, 1877, page 2, col. 8.

Editors' note: Duncan McDonald, a mixed blood tribal member and trader, pointed out the failure of the government to fulfill the 1855 promises to provide the Flathead tribes with a school, hospital, shops, and other services.

From Jocko Reservation.
A Member of the Confederated Tribes Makes Some Pertinent Remarks.

Editor New North-West —

Permit me through the columns of your paper to correct a few of the erroneous assertions concerning the difficulty in this section, manufactured principally by the agent and harped upon by the *Missoulian*. For the benefit of the public generally I shall respectfully refer to the treaty concluded between Isaac J. Stevens and the tribes, known as the Flatheads, Pen d'Oreilles and Kootenais; dated July 16, 1855.

Article V.

"The United States further agree to establish, at suitable points, within one year after the ratification hereof, an agricultural and industrial school, erecting the necessary buildings, keeping the same in repair and providing it with furniture, books and stationery, to be located at the Agency and to be free to the children of the said tribes, and to employ a suitable instructor or instructors. To furnish one blacksmith shop to which shall be attached a tin and gun shop; one carpenter's shop; one wagon and plow-maker's shop; and to keep the same in repair and to furnish with the necessary tools. To employ two farmers, one blacksmith, one tinner, one gun-smith, one carpenter, one wagon and plow-maker, for the instruction of the Indians in trades and to assist them in the same. To erect one saw mill and flouring mill, keeping the same in repair and furnished with the necessary tools and fixtures, and to employ two millers. To erect a hospital, keeping the same in repair and provided with the necessary medicines and furniture, and to employ a physician; and to erect and keep in repair and provide with the necessary furniture the building required for the accommodation of the said employees. The said buildings and establishments to be maintained and kept in repair as aforesaid, and the employees to be kept in service for the period of twenty years. And in view of the fact that the head chiefs of the said confederated tribes of Indians are expected and will be called upon to perform many services of a public character, occupying much of their time, the United States further agree to pay to each of the Flathead, Pen d'Oreilles and Kootenai tribes five hundred dollars per year for the term of twenty years after the ratification hereof, as a salary for such persons as the said confederated tribes may select as their head chiefs, and to build for them at suitable points on the reservation a comfortable house, and properly furnish the same, and to plough and fence for each of them ten acres of land. The salary to be paid to and the said houses to be occupied by said head chiefs so long as they may be elected to that position by their tribes, and no longer, and all of the expenditures contemplated in this article of this treaty shall be defrayed by the United States, and shall not be deducted from the annuities agreed to be paid to said tribes, nor shall the cost of transporting the goods for the annuities, but shall be defrayed by the United States."

Of the above article of treaty we find $7,400 allowed as a salary per year to these mechanics. We also find one miller and one carpenter filling these various positions at a salary of $1,200 each per annum; and, according to evidence given by the Agent's Clerk before the Grand Jury, the Agent's private servant (a gentleman of African persuasion) is carried on the pay rolls as blacksmith. During the past summer the government employees at this place devoted the principal part of their time to herding cattle, horses and hogs (private property of the Agent) and were paid out of the government funds. I now ask, in all candor and sincerity, has this portion of the treaty been fulfilled, or is it anything miraculous that the Indians should try to have this fraud investigated? All this talk of a probable outbreak, is a manufactured falsehood, no one having heard of it before it appeared in the columns of the *Missoulian*. Why does it not state by whom was this intended plot discovered, and who or how many were connected in this conspiracy? and if such is the case, let justice take hold of the guilty parties. Why shield it any longer from the public? But it seems that upon this point it prefers to remain neutral. What the Indian wants is an Agent that will either give them what the treaty calls for, or show in what way this money is expended, also, let him be honest, sober and upright —

* * * * * * *

Respectfully,
Duncan McDonald.

Flathead Agency, Jan. 30, 1877.

Document 11

Piousness of Flathead Indians

March 6, 1877

Source: "Flathead Indians," *The Helena Independent* (daily), March 6, 1877, page 3, col. 3.

Editors' note: The pious conduct of the Bitterroot Salish Indians during an 1877 visit to Helena impressed this Helena journalist.

Flathead Indians.

Last week there arrived in this city a large party of Flathead Indians, returning from their annual hunt on the Yellowstone. Being Catholics, they stopped over Sunday to attend Divine service at the Church of the Sacred Heart, and after service they took occasion to visit Saint John's Hospital. Miles Daily, who had been a patient in that institution several years, had died on Saturday night, and his remains were laid out in the Chapel of the Hospital preparatory to receiving the last religious rites. When the Indians observed the corpse they made inquiries concerning it, and after consultation, their Chief giving a signal to the men, placed himself in position, and, followed by them, marched slowly and solemnly around the bier several times. Halting, they kneeled very reverentially, and the Chief recited the Catholic prayers for the dead in the Flathead language, the responses being given by the party. Rising, they left the Chapel, and the Flathead women, led by the wife of the Chief, entered the room, and, kneeling around the corpse, she recited the litanies for the dead, of the blessed Sacrament and of the blessed Virgin, the other women joining in the responses, all in the Flathead language. This done, they arose, and in sweet voices full of melody, intoned a hymn to the blessed Virgin, also in their own language. These Indians are from Missoula county, and they are among the first charges of that renowned Indian missionary, Rev. Fr. [Pierre] De Smet.

Document 12

Sketches of Flathead Reservation Leaders

1877-1893

Source: Mary Ronan, *Girl from the Gulches: The Story of Mary Ronan as told to Margaret Ronan*, ed. Ellen Baumler (Helena: Montana Historical Society Press, 2003), pages 182-186, 188-189.

Editor's note: Mary Ronan was the wife of Peter Ronan, Flathead Indian Agent from 1877 to 1893. Her descriptions of Flathead Reservation leaders reflect her prejudices, but also include personal observations missing from the official documents. Some footnotes have been omitted.

Indians, Customs, and Religion

An interesting character of whom I saw much was Arlee, a Nez Perce, whose Indian name, translated into English, was Red Night. He had married a woman of the Salish tribe, settled in the Bitterroot Valley, and agreed to government terms. To the bitter and never-ending indignation of Charlot, the hereditary chief of the Flatheads, Arlee moved to the reservation with a following of Flatheads whose war chief he had long been. Arlee came from a long line of fighting men. His father had been killed by the Blackfeet in 1817 when Arlee was only two years old. While he was still a young man, Arlee had achieved a great reputation as a "brave." In carrying out the family tradition, no less than three of his sons were killed fighting against Crows and Blackfeet.

Arlee was sixty-three years of age when we came to the agency. He was a fat and pompous monarch and fashionable with his fringed buckskin shirt and leggings, fantastically beaded vest, belt, pouch, and moccasins, and bright-colored blanket folded around his protruding stomach. Topping all this magnificence, he always wore a brass dog collar around the crown of his hat. I never saw him without an eagle's wing in his hand. This he carried with a grandeur that endowed it with all the symbolism of a scepter.

My observation led me to the conclusion that when an Indian was chief he was so by virtue of being a chief among men. This was true of every chief I knew well personally. It was especially true of Eneas (the Indian pronunciation of St. Ignatius), the Kootenai chief. . . . . His Indian name was Big Knife. He was tall, handsome, clean, and commanding in his brilliant striped blanket and weasel skin pendant.

I shall say a word about one other of our interesting neighbors. In 1877-78 Duncan McDonald, then a handsome young man of twenty-eight, was conducting a trader's store just outside of the agency square. We saw a good deal of him and also of his father, Angus McDonald. The elder McDonald was a splendid, intelligent old Scotchman who came to Montana in 1838 and established a trading post for the Hudson's Bay Company on Post Creek, about halfway between St. Ignatius Mission and Flathead Lake. He remained on the reservation after the company had abandoned the post by right because his wife belonged to the confederated tribes through her father, an Iroquois, and her mother, a Nez Perce. So devoted a friend was he that once, when I made a trip to California, he rode horseback the thirty-five miles from his home on Post Creek to the agency just to bid me good-bye and wish me a happy journey. Another time he presented me with a gold nugget shaped like a harp, and so, he thought, particularly appropriate.

Duncan, much sought after by those who studied the tribal customs, history, legends, and language of the Salish, was not aware of the advantage of capitalizing on his Indian ancestry and inheritance. He was anxious to appear to be a pure-blooded Scotchman like his father. As his father had done, so he took an Indian wife and was, so long as she did live, a devoted husband to her. In Louise's veins ran the blood of the Salish, Nez Perce, Kootenai, Iroquois, and French forbears. Her Indian name was Queel-soo-ee, meaning Red Sleep. According to Duncan, one of the peaks in the Bison Range near Dixon has been given her Indian name.

Our third son was the first white child born on the Flathead Indian Reservation on November 1, 1878. We christened him Matthew James for his two grandfathers. When the baby was a few days old, Michelle, chief of the Pend d'Oreilles, stalked into the sitting room just off my bedroom where Mr. [Peter] Ronan was seated. The chief was accompanied by five or six important tribesmen, dressed in their brightest blankets, and by the agency interpreter. The Indians squatted in a semicircle and brought forth the pipe of peace. Michelle took a long-drawn puff and passed it on, and it went around until it reached the White Chief. He too, took his long-drawn puff, thus completing the circle of peace.

Michelle broke the long silence, speaking solemnly in Indian. When he ceased the interpreter translated. The Indians had heard of the birth of the white papoose. They rejoiced for now they knew that their friend the White Chief had, indeed, established his home among them. It had been agreed in council that if the papoose were to be adopted into the tribe and to take the

Indian name of Chief Michelle there would be perpetual peace and friendliness
between the family of the White Chief and the Salish and their allies. Mr.
Ronan ceremoniously requested that he be excused to inform me of the honor
which they wished to bestow upon our son.

The Pend d'Oreille chief had been named Michelle when he was baptized
by a Jesuit missionary. His Indian name was Whee-eat-sum-khay (Plenty
Grizzly Bear), a name to be proud of because the grizzly bear is the most
respected, feared, and emulated of all the animal kingdom. To say "he has
the heart of a grizzly bear" was the greatest compliment that could be paid a
brave. Michelle's Indian name had not been earned in combat with grizzlies
but had been bestowed upon him as a tribute to his acknowledged courage
by the Lower Kalispels, the name of whose hereditary chief had been Plenty
Grizzly Bear.

How we laughed! Such a beautiful baby — blue eyes and soft brown curls
— and to be called Plenty Grizzly Bear! Major Ronan returned solemn faced
to the council. In my name as well as his own he accepted the honor proffered.
Each member of the delegation expressed individually his gratification; the
interpreter repeated each speech. The long ceremony closed with a request to
see the papoose. The savages filed respectfully through my bedroom and passed
the dainty blue and white crib of little Whee-eat-sum-khay. As each looked
into the crib, he voiced his approval saying, "Shay!"

"And now," said Michelle sadly as he took his departure, "I have no name."

Mr. Ronan was puzzled but found the explanation the next day when he
went with the interpreter to Michelle's camp. The Pend d'Oreille chief was
sitting in his tepee in dejection, his head bowed and covered by his blanket. He
wore s.... leggings. In answer to Mr. Ronan's question he told that his fringed
leggings, arms, and pony had been taken from him because he had made himself
nameless in giving his name to the white papoose the day before. As long as
he remained unnamed he must be in this dejected and reduced state. When
Mr. Ronan protested that they could remain friends without this sacrifice on
his part, Michelle replied proudly that he made the sacrifice of his name with
a big heart, that relief would come presently, for the Indians had that morning
dispatched two runners to the camp of the Lower Kalispels whose principal
chief had lately died, and whose name, interpreted into English, was the Man
Who Regrets His Country, requesting that Michelle be permitted to assume
the dead chief's name.

Within a few weeks the answer came from the Lower Kalispels that if the
Pend d'Oreilles and Flathead would send them six ponies in payment for six
which had been stolen from them by members of the one or the other of these
tribes, some eight years before they would look favorably upon the request for

the loan of their dead chief's name. The ponies were sent and the transaction was terminated in a satisfactory manner.

On Christmas Day in 1878 Mr. Ronan was summoned to St. Ignatius Mission, and amid much form and ceremony the proclamation was made before the confederated tribes of Flathead, Pend d'Oreille, and Kootenai that henceforth the son of the White Chief should be a member of the confederated tribes and bear the name Plenty Grizzly Bear, and that Michelle, the chief of the Pend d'Oreilles, should henceforth be called in Indian the Man Who Regrets His Country. . . . .

The most beloved of our Indian neighbors was Michel Rivais, the blind interpreter who was officially appointed to that position and came to live within the square during our second year at the agency. He was a born linguist, with a remarkable command of Canadian French and many of the Indian tongues. Michel's English translations were quaintly phrased. His natural intelligence and gift for language had been cultivated by the Jesuit missionaries.

Michel Rivais was born in 1837. He was the son of Antoine Rivais, a French Canadian trapper and Emilia, a Pend d'Oreille s..... Michel's wife was a clean, kindly Nez Perce s..... They had lost two children, and were devoted to the son and daughter that remained. Before he was forty-five years of age, he became totally blind as a result of rheumatism. Everything that medical science could do was done at government expense, through the efforts of Mr. Ronan and Senator G. G. Vest of Missouri, to restore Michel's eyesight. He could see dimly enough to grope his way to the office when he first became interpreter but within two years was in total darkness. He was quite helpless in his blindness and always had to be led. He walked stumblingly, timidly. Ironically enough, his Indian name was Chim-coo-swee, The Man Who Walks Alone. His devoted wife usually guided him about, for his fine-looking son and daughter died within a short time of one another when they had reached young man- and womanhood.

Michel's wife and children were always the most picturesque and beautifully dressed of the Indians around the agency. Mother and daughter did beautiful bead and handwork. Most of Michel's salary as government interpreter went for the purchase of gay blankets and shawls, silk handkerchiefs, and a most vivid and varied assortment of velvets and silks for Indian tunics and leggings.

I enjoyed listening to Michel talk in his quaint way. He related to me many legends of Coyote, a sort of tutelary spirit, and other tribal stories, which always I was intending to set down verbatim and never did so. Best of all he liked to tell how the Flathead were the first Indians in Montana to embrace Christianity and civilization. He would grow so eloquent and his fervor would send such a light into his eyes that they seemed to regain their lost sight.

He told the well-known story of the expeditions that were sent to St. Louis, Missouri, in search of the black robes, of the arrival of Father [Pierre] De Smet, their accomplishments at St. Mary's Mission, and how the black robes had befriended him and taught him from the time he was little more than a baby.

Michel was about medium height, slender, with the fine features of his French father and bronze color of his Indian mother. His straight black hair he wore in a long bob we associate with a page or herald of medieval times. His costume was quaint and all his own. It was neither the dress of the white man nor that of the Indian, but a nondescript assortment of the two modes.

The Jesuits had taught Michel to sing and to play the violin. He had a fine old instrument; where he got it I do not know. On summer evenings he used to sit on the sill of his open doorway and play softly and plaintively, sometimes improvising. Michel's voice was melodious and true. At church he led the Indians in the congregational praying and singing. They sang simple Masses in Latin; the praying was in Indian.

Mary Ronan
Source: Toole Archives, Mansfield Library, University of Montana,
Missoula, photograph number 83-138.

Document 13

Bishop O'Connor Visits the Flathead Reservation and Meets Tribal Leaders June 21, 1877

Source: James O'Connor, "The Flathead Indians," *Records of the American Catholic Historical Society of Philadelphia*, vol. 3 (1889-1891), pages 88-97, 102-110.

Editors' note: O'Connor was the Bishop of Omaha, Nebraska. This account is freely laced with his viewpoint and bigotry in addition to relating details of his June 1877 visit to St. Ignatius Mission and the Flathead Reservation.

The Flathead Indians

After a ride of twelve miles through the Missoula valley [June 21, 1877], we turned into a canyon just wide enough for the road and the bed of the mountain torrent, then a small stream, that sweeps through it in the rainy season. Ascending this canyon over rocks and boulders for a distance of about four miles, we came on a stretch of meadow land, a mile wide, brilliant with prairie flowers, and fringed with pine trees. On either side rose the mountains to a height of several thousand feet, and from their opposing summits stretched an awning of light clouds, giving to the valley the general appearance of a vast hall or temple, though of a temple not made with hands. On the skirt of the woods, to our right were several tepees, and out on the meadow the Indians were digging their favorite "bitter root" [camas]. Digging the bitter root! Alas, it is a quest in which too many are engaged all over this beautiful world.

This was the first time I had seen the Indian on his native heath, entirely removed from association with the white man, and engaged in a pursuit peculiarly his own.

Those bare-headed figures, in their bright blankets, moving through the tall wet grass, in search of a wretched esculent in a scene so subline, so isolated and lonely, made a profound impression on me, and an impression sad as it was profound. They were men, but how little they had in common with other men. They were savages, but savages the misery of whose lot had been made intolerable by civilization that surrounded them. They were the lords of the soil, but were being driven from it by the rapacity of men who know neither justice, nor pity, nor remorse. Who with the ordinary instincts of humanity could see them thus engaged on a soil that, but for the injustice of the white man, would now yield them golden harvests, and not be touched with compassion for them, and not think it a reproach to belong to the race that oppressed them? These at least were my thoughts as we passed through this glorious entrance to the home of the Flatheads.

A drive of about five miles brought us into the Jocko valley, one of the most beautiful in Montana. It is perhaps fifteen miles long, by about four wide, and completely encircled by high mountains, which rise as they recede till some of their pure white peaks look into it from a distance of twenty miles or more. Away to the right of us are the Agency buildings, and due north, some cabins and tepees occupied by the Indians.

We stopped for dinner at the Agency, where Mr. [Peter] Ronane, the newly appointed agent, gave us a most hospitable reception. And here, I must say, for the information of those not conversant with the subject, that Indian agents are appointed by the President of the United States, with the advice and consent of the Senate. Their term of office is for four years and their salary fifteen hundred dollars a year. Their duties, as prescribed by the Revised Statutes of the United States, are: "To manage and superintend, within the Agency, the intercourse with Indians agreeably to law, as may be prescribed by the President, the Secretary of the Interior, the Commissioners of Indian Affairs, or the Superintendent of Indian Affairs." These Statutes further provide that, except as to crimes, for the punishment of which express provision has been made, "the general laws of the United States as to the punishment of crimes committed in any place within the sole and exclusive jurisdiction of the United States, except the District of Columbia, shall extend to the Indian country." This provision, however, is not to be construed so as "to extend to any Indian committing any offence in the Indian country, who has been punished by the local laws of the tribe, or to any case where, by treaty stipulations, the exclusive jurisdiction over such offence is, or may be secured to the Indian tribes respectively." Indians must live on the reservations they have chosen or to which they have been removed, and cannot leave them or transact business or hold communication with whites or other Indians without permission of their agents.

From these statutes it is evident that the powers of Indian agents are, perhaps unavoidably, vague and undefined, though restricted in some places more than others by treaties and local laws and customs of particular tribes. However, I do not see why, practically, they should not be regarded as absolute and entirely arbitrary.

For what redress has the Indian for an abuse of authority on the part of an agent? The experience of long years has shown that he has none whatever. No adequate supervision of the agent is provided for by law. He is alone with his tribe, or tribes, and literally, "monarch of all he surveys." There is, it is true, a physician, there is an interpreter, there are farmers and mechanics, there may be teachers on the reservation, but they all depend on him or his friends for the positions they hold, and are therefore more likely to screen than to expose his irregularities. Who, then, is to interfere between him and his helpless wards should he see fit to oppress and fleece them? It is only cases of the most aggravated and cumulative wrongdoing that can ever reach the Department or the Commissioners of Indian Affairs, and even then what is the remedy? Why, at best, the removal of the agent and the appointment of another who will be sure to walk in his footsteps.

Irresponsible authority of this kind is very trying to the virtue of ordinary men. To the dishonest and the depraved it affords opportunities of practising [sic] every species of injustice. And who does not know that the incumbents of this office have, with only a few exceptions, belonged precisely to these classes? What wonder, then, that they should have administered it solely with a view to their own aggrandizement and that their heartless inventive rapacity should have driven the poor savage to utter hopeless despair.

The true, the only remedy for this state of things, it seems to me, will be to put the administration of Indian affairs entirely into the hands of the military. The officers of our army understand the Indian better than any other class of men in the country; they appreciate his good qualities, make proper allowance for his faults, sympathize with him, admire him, and do not despair of the possibility of elevating him from his present degraded and helpless condition. I heard an officer, high in command, say this summer that in the thirty-eight years he had been in the army, most of which time he had spent on the frontier, he had never known the Indians to have been in the wrong in any difficulty they had had with the Government or the white settlers. I heard another of equal rank asset that if he were Sitting Bull, the last thing in the world he would do would be to "come in," for that he and all others of his race had been most outrageously treated by the Government and people of this country. A third, who had spent eight years in the Yellowstone country, told me that if detailed to make the attempt and furnished with the necessary means, he felt certain he could succeed in civilizing the Indians of that region within ten years. Of course he underestimated the difficulty of such an undertaking, but I give his statement only as going to show the opinion entertained of the Indian by military men.

No one doubts the capacity of our army officers to administer Indian affairs efficiently. Their integrity is happily above suspicion. Why not then entrust these affairs to them? They would thus be left not to irresponsible individuals, but to an organization in contact with the savage, trained to methodical habits and under the strictest possible supervision.

Were the Indians allowed to occupy their ancestral homes or hunting grounds, or to live on the reservations assigned them at a proper distance from military posts, with missionaries of their choice, and under their own tribal laws and customs; were supplies furnished them through the nearest quartermaster and traders forbidden to deal with them or even approach them, except once or twice a year at the posts, and under the supervision of the local officers; were the local commanders instructed, as in the British possessions, to require them to keep the peace amongst themselves and with surrounding tribes, and to protect them against the white settlers, the Indian question, I am quite sure, would soon find an easy and a satisfactory solution.

Having visited the different offices and work-shops at the Agency, we continued our journey northwards. At some points the rich soil of the valley was overlaid with sand and stones swept down from the mountains by rains, but even these spots were covered with flowers of startling brilliancy. Whenever the conversation flagged a sense of loneliness and isolation stole over me. The only sounds were made by our wheels and the hoofs of our broncos. The only living thing visible on the landscape was a small herd on the foothills to our right, but whether of elk or domestic cattle we could not tell even by the aid of a glass. Beyond those hills wolves and "catamounts" and bears, black and brown and grizzly, roamed in numbers and in safety, but none of them put in an appearance. Even the graceful antelope, that on most other western highways feeds or canters within view of the traveler, was nowhere to be seen. The mountain labyrinth that extended for hundreds of miles on all sides of us made me, at least, feel completely shut out from the world beyond.

Passing through this sublime scenery one is, indeed, often led to exclaim: "O, ye mountains and hills, bless the Lord; praise and exalt Him above all forever," but of merely mundane associations it is suggestive not at all. Above you is a sky as beautiful as that of southern Italy, looking down on valleys fairer to see than the Vale of Cashmere, as described by the poet, or the fabled home of Rasselas, on crystal streams flowing through flowery meads and dark frowning glens, on mountain peaks, surpassing in height and rivalling in grace and beauty of outline the Rhigi, the Jungfrau, or the Matterhorn. Yet mountains and streams and valleys unsung and unnoticed by poet or traveler, without a history, without associations, and even without name.

But we are at the gate of exit from the Jocko. Before and near it is a ranch kept by a half-breed, guarded apparently only by a half dozen Indian dogs that come bounding towards us, and bark and snarl at us with præter-canine fury. We enter the canyon, dark with pine and a thick undergrowth, and so narrow that there is barely room for the road and a stream that sweeps through it. The road is in a shocking condition, but the worst mires are being filled with brush and dirt by a band of Canadians and half-breeds. We plunge, however, into some frightful holes of uncertain depth, not knowing in what plight we shall get out of them. But our hardy team are used to such ventures, so in due time they bring us into the bright sunshine and on to a very passable roadway. We turn south, ascend the foothills of the range we have just passed to a height of some fifteen hundred feet, from which we get our first view of the St. Ignatius Mission. The scene is one of surpassing beauty and grandeur. Before us is a narrow valley sloping gently on either side to the river that drains it. It stretches away to the east and northeast, widening as it recedes for a distance of forty miles to Flathead lake, a feeder of the Columbia. It is inclosed on the south by a chain of mountains that rise as abruptly as a wall to a height of ten thousand feet above the plain and fourteen thousand above the level of the sea. They are covered with perpetual snow. Here and there passing clouds cast their shadows upon them or hang around some of the higher peaks, leaving the others brilliant in the evening sunlight. From a lake near the top of this range a waterfall descends perpendicularly a distance of a thousand feet and then pursues its downward course at a lesser angle as a foaming torrent, till it reaches the valley. Had not my attention been directed to it I should not, I confess, at the distance we were from it, have distinguished it from the snow drifts that seam the side of the range, east and west of it. When the unfortunate Thomas Francis Meagher, whilst Governor of Montana, visited St. Ignatius he "christened" several peaks of this range; but no record was made of the names, and they are now forgotten. Midway in the valley is the Mission — its log-cabins, tepees and even the church and parsonage dwarfed into toys by the mighty mountains that overshadow them. We descend at a rapid pace and in half an hour are in the village.

Our first visit is to the church, which is a much finer building that one would expect to find in such a place. It is a frame, 90 x 40 feet, with a good stone foundation, and is in the Roman style, with clere-story, columns and apse. It was designed by Father [Anthony] Ravalli, and built about fifteen years ago by the Indians under the superintendence of another father. It has side altars, statues and pictures, but the decorations are rather gaudy, though on that account all the better adapted to the taste of the worshipers. A platform eight or ten feet square takes the place of the pulpit, and on it stands a wooden crucifix, carved by Father Ravalli, and of rare merit, I should say, for an amateur artist. Before the platform in the nave is a bier on which rests a small coffin that looks not unlike an orange box, but a little narrower at one end than at the other. There is no mistaking its contents. An infant form is there hastening to decay, and Mother Church will lay this waif from the wilderness in the ground as tenderly and with the same ritual as if it had been destined to wear a crown. As we look for a few moments at the rude casket, we reflect that earth has a little less misery and heaven more joy than they had a few days before. As we leave the church we are met by a Father and some fifty Indians — men, women, and children who, having heard of our arrival, have come to see and welcome the first "red-gown" that has visited their mountains. I find a hundred bright, inquiring, honest eyes turned upon me, and feel that I am sitting for my portrait. Young and old crowd around me and take my hand with a word of greeting which I regret to say I have forgotten. Their joy is as demonstrative as it is simple and sincere. All wear blankets of various colors, leggings and moccasins. They are bareheaded, their long black hair falling loosely over their shoulders. I am struck by the regularity and beauty of countenance of the men and by their erect and stalwart figures. Among them is an octogenarian in a white blanket who attracts my particular attention. He is the only one with a head gear, a loose velvet cap, with a band of beaver fur. He is short-necked, deep chested, and straight as an arrow, and his broad, brown face is furrowed into ropes of muscles. The fire of his pagan youth still burns in his eye, but Christian faith and piety have thrown a halo around a countenance that without it might be terrible to see. As I gaze at him I cannot help asking myself the question: What would not a Rubens or a Vandyke have given to be permitted to sketch you?

Among the women there is, alas! not one that would make a heroine for even a dime novel. In their faces I see a trace, but only a trace, of that woe-begone expression which woman wears in all pagan lands. Here, indeed, she is not the drudge she is among the pagan tribes. Here all her higher rights are held sacred, but a drudge she would be thought even here by her more favored sisters in "the States."

Little papooses stare at me in wonder over their mothers' shoulders, and as their gazelle-like eyes and the beauty and innocence of their faces, as well as the novelty of such a situation for young America, draw from me some exclamation of pleasurable surprise and attract me towards them, the mothers are both pleased and amused, and the men laugh outright. I make a little address of thanks which is translated into Selish, and we retire to the residence of the Fathers.

In about twenty minutes the church bell rings to summon the villagers to evening prayers. I stand at the parlor window to see them come. As they arrive from different directions, old and young, tall men and little children, and mothers with their papooses on their backs, approach the mission cross in front of the church, kiss this sign of their redemption devoutly, and enter the building. Whilst they are at their devotions I am informed that they assemble at half past six o'clock every morning for prayer and Mass. After Mass they are instructed in the catechism for a quarter of an hour. The women and children attend another instruction of the same kind in the forenoon. In the evening about sun-down all assemble for evening prayer in the church, which is preceded or followed by a third instruction. On Sundays they have High Mass and a sermon at nine o'clock in the morning and they assist at Benediction of the Blessed Sacrament or the Way of the Cross and an instruction in the afternoon. The great majority of them approach the sacraments once a month, and many once or even oftener than once a week. Of the twelve hundred at the Mission not more than five or six neglect this duty altogether, and these only because in practice at least they have returned to polygamy. They are especially fond of going to confession, and some of them, if allowed, would do so more than once a day. A Father told me that when with them on the buffalo hunt he had more than once been approached in the middle of the night by a scrupulous Indian who, taking him by the toes, would waken him and ask him to hear his confession. This, I submit, is a little more than many more favored believers of the white race are accustomed to do. Yet of these same Indians Father [Nicholas] Point, an early missionary among them, wrote in 1848: "Not a quarter of a century since, the Cœur d'Alenes were so hard-hearted that, to paint them to the life, the common sense of their first visitors found no expression more just than the singular name which they still bear. Minds so limited that while rendering divine worship to all the animals that they knew they had no idea of the true God, nor of their souls, nor, consequently, of a future life. In fine, a race of men so degraded that of the natural law there survived among them only two or three very obscure notions, which few, very few, of them attempted to reduce to practice. Yet it must be said to the credit of the tribe that there were always in their midst elect souls who never bent the knee to Baal. I know some who, from the very day the true God was preached to them, never had to reproach themselves with shadow of infidelity." [Ind. Sketches, page 16.] The most warlike perhaps of all Rocky Mountain tribes, the piety of the Flatheads has not diminished their bravery; for since their conversion, as well as before, they have been more than a match for their neighbors, the Sioux and the Blackfeet.

Again I am at the parlor window, this time attracted by a melancholy chant of many voices outside. A procession is filing out of the church and singing what I take to be the *Miserere*. It is, however, I am told, a dirge these Indians, whilst yet Pagans, used to sing at the funerals of their dead warriors, arranged by one of the early missionaries and adapted to the Christian hymn to which I am now listening. The men go first, the women follow. Then comes the bier

we had seen in the church borne by four men, its light burden covered with a
black pall. After the bier walk a cross-bearer and acolytes, one of whom carries
a vase of holy water, and last a priest in cap and cope. Slowly and reverently
they advance towards the graveyard, some five hundred feet distant, singing
as they go, till they are out of sight and hearing. The frail form in its final
resting place, the mourners return in groups, and, as the Angelus bell rings,
I am struck by the suddenness with which they cease conversation, assume
devotional postures and retain them, statue like, till the prayer is ended. . . . .

The Fathers at the St. Ignatius Mission get no assistance whatever from
the Government or from any other quarter. They support themselves by their
farm, stock and mills. They give employment to twenty Indians, and many
others would be willing to work if they could be employed. The community
consists of two priests and four lay brothers. The brothers work themselves
and superintend the Indians engaged on the farm and in the mills. There are
in the village a grist mill, a saw mill, run by water power, and a printing press.
Father [Joseph] Giorda is preparing for publication a dictionary of the Selish
language of about eight hundred pages which will be printed at St. Ignatius,
and a pamphlet of narratives from the Sacred Scriptures of one hundred and
forty pages in Selish, from this press, was presented to me on the occasion of
my visit.

There is also here a convent of the Sisters of Providence from Montreal,
established twelve years ago, with boarding and day schools for girls. In this
school the ordinary branches of a plain education are taught. The "ologies,"
thank goodness, are excluded, but particular attention is paid to embroidery.
All the scholars are taught housework and gardening, and to each is allotted
a piece of ground to till. They took great pride in showing me these little
gardens, and insisted on my trying their strawberries which were the largest and
most luscious I had ever seen or tasted. Every one accustomed to visit convents
knows the neatness with which they are kept, but the order and cleanliness of
this house surpassed anything of the kind I had ever seen. Besides teaching, the
sisters also visit the sick in and near the village, and supply them with medicine
at their own expense. The Father told me that plain though the education be
that is given in this institution, it elevates the girls so far above the condition of
their families that several become dissatisfied with their state of life when they
return home. This evil they truly remarked would be avoided, could the boys
receive the same advantages as the girls, but this, with the limited resources of
the mission is at present impossible.

St. Ignatius is not laid out in streets, owing, I was told, to the fact that
the Indians insist on locating their cabins so that they may be able to see the
church from their doors. They visit it frequently during the day for private

prayer, but when not in it they take great pleasure in being able to look at it. "Where a man's treasure is there also is his heart." The cabins as a general rule are about fifteen feet square, well built of pine logs from the neighboring mountains, and are both clean and comfortable. With the exception of one or two bedsteads, I saw nothing that could be called furniture in any of them. The inmates sit or rather squat on the ground or recline on the robes or skins that serve them for beds. Sacred pictures and crucifixes are fastened to the walls, and kettles and other cooking utensils stand on the open hearths or hang from hooks or andirons. The tepees are furnished or unfurnished in the like manner only that in them the fire is in the centre of the floor and the smoke escapes through and opening above it. Outside one of the cabins, women were drying beef or buffalo meat over a slow fire. The meat was boned, cut into long strips and laid on an arch of wooden bars about two feet above the fire. Every cabin and tent had its contingent of savage dogs, who recognizing the habit of the Fathers allowed us to pass if not graciously, at least unchallenged.

We visited the prison, resolving on the way to ask for the liberation of the captives but we found it empty. It is a square building of stout logs with loopholes near the ceiling and divided into four cells with hallway through the centre.

We arrived at the Mission on Friday evening. All day long, Saturday, Indians continued to arrive from the surrounding country. They called in bands, and singly, at the pastoral residence, which, and every part of which, they are accustomed to enter unbidden, and without knocking at hall or room doors. The Fathers told me that they can have no privacy from them, except by locking themselves in their rooms. At their suggestion I took this precaution before going to bed, the night of our arrival. It was well I had done so, for going out of my bed-room at six in the morning I found a young gentleman in a blue blanket leaning against the jamb of the door who, had it not been locked, would, I presume, have invited himself to be present at my toilet.

Among the notables who honored me with a call was Anteli, local chief of the Kalispels. He was converted in 1849, is 74 years of age, and of a rather sad expression of countenance. He said all his children, seventeen in number, and his brothers were dead and over there in the graveyard. Another was Michelle, chief of the Pend d'Oreilles, a good man, I was told, but weak and easily led. Then there was Ignace, chief of the Kootenays, who said he had come seventy miles to meet me. He is a man of noble mien, and, unlike the other Flatheads, wears his hair cut short. He stands, I should say, about six feet four in his moccasins. He has a reputation for great sanctity of life, and, certainly, his noble face wears the expression peculiar to persons much given to spiritual contemplation. When chosen chief he found his tribe greatly demoralized, but he has made it one of the most exemplary in the mountains. He spends on his people his salary and every thing he can save.

Red Night, a noble looking man of about sixty, told me he lived at the Agency, but, having heard of my visit to the Mission, he had come to see me. He wore a white Kossuth hat and a blue blanket, and an eagle's wing hung at his girdle. Obesity had taken all grace from his figure, but I thought I had never seen a finer head or face than his. I could hardly take my eyes off him. He reminded me of the portraits of Benjamin Franklin with which we are familiar, but he had greatly the advantage of the philosopher in the beauty and the brilliancy of his dark eyes. As is the case with all these Indians, his hands and feet were almost disproportionately small. He asked me if he might smoke, and on my requesting him to do so, he handed his pipe to an Indian to light, and, having taken a few whiffs himself, passed it to the others, of whom there seven or eight in the room. It went the round several times before all were satisfied. The Indians, I noticed, treated this man with respect, but showed great reserve in his presence, owing, I was afterwards told, to the fact that he was one of the few who had left the Bitter Root valley for the Agency.

Baptiste the Lean, a kind of assistant chief to Anteli, and his *locum tenens* when absent, said he "came to thank the great Blackgown for his visit to the Indians, and to ask him some questions." Then took place the following dialogue or "interview," which, as you will perceive, involved some rather knotty questions, but which I give as taken down at the time:

"Some of the white people, I am told, talk against our custom of whipping Indians. Our chief, at the Bitter Root, told us last year not to whip them, but to put them in prison. What, then, are we to do? All the chiefs have given up whipping, but I continue to whip bad Indians. I have learned from the priests, from the beginning, that it was right to whip them, and I shall never give up doing so. Many are opposed to me because of this. Having once taken God's hand, I will not let it go. I am sure the priests approve of my whipping bad Indians. I have always done the priest's bidding, even at the risk of my life, because I loved the Church. I am not afraid of my priests. That's all."

"For what crimes do you whip?"

"For adultery, abandonment of a wife by her husband, lying, stealing, slander, disorderly conduct at church or prayers, gambling, drunkenness and violent anger."

"You should not whip, since your chief has forbidden you to do so."

"Are not all these things sins?"

"Yes, but it is not necessary to punish all sins with the lash."

"Should not these offences be punished?"

"God will punish them, if not repented of."

"Is not the whip good?"

"Yes, when used by the proper authority and in proportion to the offence."

"Can I continue to whip?"

"Not till you become chief, or get the chief's authority to do so."

"Must, then, the whip be abandoned?"

"Yes, if the chief require it."

Baptiste here looks sad, but says resignedly: "Then whipping is at an end." But, a bright idea occurring to him, he immediately adds: "When put in prison, Indians will lie, profess sorrow for their offences, be pardoned and then do the same things over again."

"Don't believe what they say a second time."

"Well, then, I shall give up whipping."

But still he has another plea for his favorite mode of punishment.

"Must I obey the head chief, and not obey God?"

"When you obey the chief in matters of this kind, you obey God."

"I have opened my heart to you, but I have another question to ask. The two highest chiefs of our people have told me to act no more as chief, the local chief, here at the Mission, wishes me to act as such in his absence. Whom should I obey?"

"The highest chiefs."

"If these men should go astray, am I to follow them?"

"Not when you are certain that what they ask you to do would be a sin?"

"But they did wrong in abandoning the whip."

"You are mistaken, for everybody knows that the chief is at liberty to whip, or not, as he thinks best."

"But if the whip be abandoned, the people will become bad, and the priests will the sorry."

"That may or may not be so, but you must not disobey your chief, even though you think the people may become bad in consequence. You cannot do evil that good may come of it."

The Penal Code of the Flatheads provides for only two kinds of punishment, whipping and imprisonment, and these for the offences already mentioned. I asked Baptiste how murder was punished in the tribe. He looked puzzled for a moment, then said no one charged with the crime had ever been brought before him. The Fathers, however, informed me that retaliation, or compensation, are the usual modes of redress resorted to by Indians in this case. The custom of whipping has existed among the Flatheads from time immemorial. They consider it a necessary atonement for offences committed and they often present themselves voluntarily to the chief and ask to receive it for even private transgressions. When pagans they believed it wiped out the guilt of the action

for which it was inflicted and made full satisfaction for it, and long after their
conversion it was no easy matter to convince some of them that they were
obliged to confess the sins for which they had thus been punished. Not long
ago a Cœur d'Alenes took to himself a wife who was not superior to all the
failings of her sex. The very evening he brought her home, she was found to
be in no amiable mood, for she commenced, as they say in Montana to "make
it hot for him." She complained of the food set before her, spat it out of her
mouth with an expression of great disgust, and told him, among other delicate
compliments she paid him, that if she had not taken him, he never would
have been able to find a wife. This was more than he could bear, so leaving
the cabin instantly, he abandoned her, went to a distant part of the Territory,
married another woman, and lived with her two years. He then returned to the
Mission, presented himself to the chief to be whipped for what he had done,
and, having received the punishment, went to his wife and asked her if she still
entertained the opinion of his matrimonial prospects she had expressed on the
night of their marriage. She took it all back, and they have lived very happily
ever since.

Some time after the interview with Baptiste, given above, he brought me a
variety of Indian curiosities, and among them bear's claws, and other amulets
worn by the Flatheads, when yet pagans, and two Blackfeet scalps taken by him
in one of the last wars with that tribe.

There is a police force of about thirty men at the Mission. The chief, with
two of his men, called to see me on Saturday afternoon. He offered me an
escort home, but when told that it was seventeen hundred miles away, by the
road I had traveled, and more than two thousand by that by which I indended
to return, and was made to understand what these distances meant, his surprise
was amusing, and he declared that if any of his men were to accompany me
they would never be able to find their way back.

One of the Fathers told me that some years ago this man, returning from
a scouting expedition to the Blackfeet country, had traveled seven days and
seven nights in the snow without tasting food, and that on the seventh day,
meeting a horse he killed it and, having eaten some of the flesh raw, continued
his journey. Another still living in the village had traveled and fasted for a week,
with nothing to sustain life but a small piece of raw hide he found on the road.
These facts will give one an idea of the extraordinary physical endurance of the
Indians, and of the great advantage he has in this respect over white troops in
frontier warfare.

Late on Saturday evening a scout arrived from the Bitter Root, bringing
an exaggerated account of the rising of the Nez Percés in Idaho. The news was
evidently as unexpected as it was unwelcome to the chiefs and others who heard

it. They said little, but looked very thoughtful, and even sad. Their manner more than their words satisfied me that the Flatheads had had no knowledge of an intended outbreak by their friends and allies, and that they would take no part in it. The event proved that I was not mistaken, for not only did they not join the hostiles, but they even told Joseph that if in passing through the Bitter Root and neighboring valleys he committed any depredations on the whites, they themselves would join in the pursuit of him. And Joseph would seem not to have forgotten the threat.

On Sunday morning I said early Mass in the church. A great number went to communion. It was a novel sight to me to see the Indian mothers approach the altar rails with their papooses on their backs. But, after all, was it not a touching and beautiful one and pleasing to Him who said, "Suffer the little children to come unto me and forbid them not?" I assisted at the High Mass. The singing by the choir, composed of the sisters and their pupils, was good, but truth compels me to say that the congregational singing, however edifying to those who participated in it, was to me simply shocking. It sounded as if at least a dozen harmonious wolves were scattered among the congregation and were doing their best to prove they had not been taught the gamut in vain.

I preached to a large congregation, of whom only about fifteen were white. Among the latter was the new agent, whom I was happy to be able to introduce to my hearers as one who antecedents entitled him to their respect and confidence. My remarks were interpreted by Father Bandini, who, indeed, rendered me this service in nearly all my interviews with the Indians.

With the Mass closed, I may say, this, to me, ever-memorable visit to the pious Flatheads of St. Ignatius. Immediately after dinner we left the village accompanied by the agent and his interpreter, and over the same hills, across the same streams and along the same valleys, by which we had passed before, we returned to Missoula.

We found the inhabitant greatly excited over the Indian "scare." Several white families had already come into the little town from the Bitter Root, and the rest were expected to follow. All, however, felt greatly assured by what we had to tell them of the dispositions of the Flatheads, whom they knew to be the most intimate friends and allies of the Nez Percés and who, they feared, would be the first to join them in the general rising that was expected.

Early next morning we met Captains [Charles C.] Rawn and [William] Logan going into Missoula in advance of their command. They had left Fort Shaw three weeks before with portions of their companies to establish a small post in the Missoula valley. I had made the acquaintance of Captain Logan at Helena, so we stopped to tell him what we knew of the situation. As he left us he said: "Well, if the Flatheads only keep quiet I think we shall be able to take care of the Nez Percés ." He little dreamt that he was to be one of the first to fall in the very first encounter with those savages. . . .

Document 14

Duncan McDonald Offers to Guide Nez Perce?

July 1877

Source: Camille Williams to Mr. McWhorter, June 21, 1937, Lucullus V. McWhorter Papers, Manuscripts, Archives, and Special Collections, Washington State University Libraries, Pullman, Washington, box 12, folder 84.

Editors' note: Williams, a Nez Perce historian, recorded a Nez Perce tradition that Duncan McDonald offered to guide the Nez Perce hostiles directly north from the Lolo Trail to Canada, avoiding the white settlements. No record has been found of McDonald admitting his possible offer to help the Nez Perce flee to safety in Canada. Some periods have been added.

Kamiah Ida. 6/21 – 37

Mr. McWhorter:

I visited Philip Williams yesterday. I talked to him in regard to making a trip to Big Hole battle ground in July. in reply he said he was not able to stand travel as he was feeling weak, but he thought that he will be alright in one month, may be month of August. Philip did look weak. I was told that Philip Evans was too old to make a long trip, and he is the only one that has a car. Philip Williams don't have a car any more because of weak sight of his son. I did not buy mine because of sickness of my wife.

I also met another old man that was with waring band. I asked him about Looking Glass's trip to Crow reservation, he said that Looking Glass was never in Crow settlement, the Nez Perces met some of the Crows prior to Canyon fight. Crows promised the Nez Perces in the fight they (Crows) will fire their guns in the air and they did. the Crows also give amunition to the Nez Perces. they also told them that there were some Bannock Indian scouts with the soldiers and that their horses were getting weak and they will be easily picked off of their horses whenever they are driven back in the fight, but after the canyon fight one Nez Perce was Killed by the Crows, and one wounded. they also stole Nez Perce horses. and about a day or two after one old man and his wife were Killed their grand child taken. The boy growed till he was about 14 yrs when he died. these two old couple mentioned dropped out, because of no horses, it wasnt Known by the head man, Lean Elk till a few days after. Looking Glass did not see the Killing. so he never took the dead body along. Looking Glass told the Nez Perces, when in Flat Head reservation, that Crow Chief told him if he ever is in trouble with the whites to come over and that they Crows would help them (Nez Perces). so Looking Glass insisted in going to Crow reservation.

reason he told his people this because some of the Chiefs or Kol-Kol-smin wanted to accept the suggestion of Duncan McDonald a half breed Nez Perce son of Mr. [Angus] McDonald of Hudson Bay Co. the last named, send his son Duncan, to go and meet his people the Nez Perces and him Duncan to lead them to Canada, as Duncan Knew the trail. so if majority of the Nez Perces would had accepted McDonald help they whole band would had arrived in Canada without a loss of a man. so the understanding the whole band was, that they were going to join the Crows in their country, meaning in their own Nez Perce country, as Nez Perces owned a large tract of country west of Crow country, but instead, they had to go on to Canada which was not their goal because different bands of Indians were also fighting them.

these old warriors dont mention any one trying to burn soldiers out of their dugout or hole they were in as no logs, or not enough dry wood to burn, all green wood.

well I just dont Know where we could get a car, we need one with a trailer to carry our blankets and camp but we will manage it some way.

I am yours truly
Camille Williams

Document 15

Chief Adolph Sent to Reassure
Missoula Whites
July 1877

Source: "Making Medicine," *The Weekly Missoulian*, July 13, 1877, page 2, col. 4; *The Weekly Missoulian*, July 13, 1877, page 3, col. 2; "Honor to the Flatheads," *The Helena Daily Herald*, July 17, 1877, page 2, col. 3.

Editors' note: This is the remarkable story of Bitterroot Salish Chief Adolph visiting Missoula to assure the white people of the peaceful intentions of the Salish during the Nez Perce War. While Adolph was camped at Missoula some irresponsible white men took to the bridge overlooking Adolph's camp and started taking pot shots at the Salish. Fortunately, Adolph complained to the local authorities rather than shooting back, and the leading citizens of Missoula were able to calm the situation.

Making Medicine.

Adolph and Eneas, two Flatheads, upon receipt of Poker Jo's story, came into town for a medicine talk. Adolph said: Look at me. My hair is white. I have seen white men ever since I was seven or eight years old, and never harmed one. I like all the whites, and if I had wanted to fight I would have commenced long ago. When Victor died he told his people to be peaceable with the whites all their lives. I talk but one way, and that is friendship for the whites. Charlos sent me word when he heard the Nez Perces were fighting, for me to keep the young men peaceable. All the Flatheads will do as Charlos and I say. A white chief on Sun river (probably Gen. [John] Gibbon) told me when I was on the buffalo hunt last winter that all Indians were going to fight this summer, and I told him the Flatheads would not fight the whites. The white chief gave me ammunition. Charlos is head chief at home, and I am head chief when my people are hunting. I have a grudge against the Nez Perces. Forty years ago they were at war with the Flatheads, and killed my brother. I have a good heart for the whites, and will help them if they cannot whip the Nez Perces. Adolph expressed the opinion that the Nez Perces would try and escape by Snake river, and not come into Montana.

Eneas spoke in the same vein, and declared his devotion to the whites.

On Monday, a Flathead giving his name as Stel-is-lass, came down from Charlos' camp to meet his family which had been at Camas prairie. Coming right from Charlos, he was anxious to express his devotion to his white brother, and sought an interview. He said: Charlos has sent me to talk to the Indians and tell them to do right. Charlos says the Flatheads will not help the Nez Perces fight the whites. They will be neutral. Nez Perces runners have not been at Charlos' camp; he will not talk with them. Charlos says he wants all the Flatheads to come home and be peaceable.

At the request of the Governor Maj. [Peter] Ronan and Capt. [Charles C.] Rawn visited Charlos camp in Bitter Root valley Sunday. They found him at mass, in Stevensville, and was assisted in their conference by Father [Jerome] D'Astie. Charlos expressed himself rejoiced to meet these representatives of the government. He expressed unalterable friendship for the whites. He said he would not join the whites to make war on the Nez Perces — he would be neutral.

There can be no doubt that the sentiment of the Flatheads is friendly. They would so express themselves if they were on the eve of an outbreak; but their solicitude concerning the attitude we attribute to them, and the alarm they express and seem to feel lest the Nez Perces may invade this country give evidence of their sincerity. To any questions as to whether there will be any of our Indians who will join the Nez Perces in case of an invasion they reply that there are bad Indians as well as bad white men.

* * * * * * * *

Some commotion was occasioned among the Indians Saturday by some parties going on the bridge and practicing with their rifles, the balls whizzing by not far from Adolph's lodge on the other side. Adolph promptly reported the matter to military authorities and to leading citizens in town, and an investigation showed that no harm was intended. People can not be too circumspect in their actions at times like these, and they should avoid everything that has an appearance of unfriendliness.

* * * * * * * *

Honor to the Flatheads.
To the Editor of the Herald:

Notwithstanding the sensational stories circulated by persons who would wish to injure the Flatheads and inflame the minds of the whites against these reservation Indians whose home is in the Bitter Root valley, the most reliable information comes now from Maj. [Peter] Ronan and the Jesuit Fathers that these people are loyal and give the most undoubted proofs of their friendship and determination to protect the whites by scouting the mountain passes, and spreading the first signs of approaching danger. That figure of language was strong indeed that was used the other day at the council of the Fathers and Agent Ronan by "Charlos" the original Flathead chief whom they saw on Sunday the 8th inst, attending mass with his family at Saint Mary's Mission. This "Charlos," is the chief, whom the Secretary of the Territory officially reported as wandering in parts unknown, but who has not been away from his farm, and at the time mentioned he was engaged in making hay. Being questioned in regard to the whites "Charlos" said: "My father's name was Victor, who was the head chief of this nation, and made the treaty with Governor Stephens [Isaac Stevens] eighteen years ago. It was my father's boast that the blood of a white man never reddened the hand of a single Indian of the Flathead tribe. My father died with that boast on his lips. I am my father's son and will leave that same boast to my children. If danger threatens, I will send runners to inform the settlers and the Captain of the soldiers and you the Agent. I will do all in my power to defend the whites and their homes." Machel, Andra and

Chief Adolph
Source: Drawing by Gustavus Sohon, National Anthropological Archives,
Smithsonian Institution, Washington, D.C., #08502500.

other chiefs of the Pen d'Oreilles, Kootenais and Flatheads all give unqualified assurance of their loyalty to the Whites.

And while we are assured on the part of the Flatheads of their present and past fidelity, let there be great care, lest in the zeal and excitement of the present Indian campaign, some heedless recruit or citizen soldier, with a desire to try one of Uncle Sam's new guns, kills some friendly Indian in the hope that he can prove that it was an accident. Each one of the volunteers in Missoula county carries the lives of many citizens upon the action of his cool, deliberate judgment. There should be no mistake, and no excited soldiery led unawares upon a friendly camp, which is destroyed without a word of explanation, as in the case of Red Owl, a friendly Nez Perce chief, with fifteen lodges, who, a few days ago, had sought a place of shelter among the whites, where they encamped, feeling secure, but where the soldiers "fell upon them and killed them all." A disaster of this kind to a family of Flatheads, or other friendly Indians, would sound the tocsin of a bloody and exterminating war upon the whites, the end of which no man could anticipate. It has been said, I believe, by the *New North West*, that one of the objects of the government in locating the post at Missoula, was to aid the authorities in the collection of taxes, etc., from the Indians. For the benefit of those who would jeopardize the peace of the whole Territory for the small pittance that might be forced from the Indians in the Bitter Root, as taxes upon a few ponies, I will venture the assertion, that if this one of of [sic] the objects of the new post had been made known at Washington, the location of a post at Missoula would not have been made. And at this day, if it is known at Washington that these troops are to be used principally for the enforcement of taxes, and not for the peace and protection of the white people, they will be withdrawn before the snow flies. The enforcement of taxes from these friendly Indians is a serious question, and cannot be productive of any good, but may result in the estrangement of these people whom we now recognize as friends in need. The most prudent vigilence should be exercised by all commanding officers of citizen troops, lest some one in the heat of other excitement than that which prompts true patriotism, should fire an unguarded shot into some friendly camp. A case in point: Four young men in Missoula, on Friday the 6th inst., went out upon the bridge to try their new guns, and took for a target a pole about twenty feet from the lodge of Adolphe, a friendly Indian, encamped on the opposite bank of the river. He cried out and made all possible demonstrations of alarm, and believes to this day that his lodge was the possible target. This was carlessness [sic], at least, in the young men, and might have resulted in much harm. "An ounce of preventive is worth a pound of cure."

Caution.

Document 16

Bitterroot Settlement of Salish Indians

July 3, 1877

Source: Will Sutherlin, "West Side of the Bitter Root — Sweathouse Farmers," *Rocky Mountain Husbandman* (Diamond City, Mont.), August 16, 1877, page 2, col. 2-3.

Editors' note: Will Sutherlin gave a short description of the Salish farms in the Bitterroot Valley and Chief Charlo's two-story house.

West Side of the Bitter Root — Sweathouse Farmers

On our return from Corvallis to Stevensville, when in sight of that point, we turned aside and visited a number of farmers upon Burnt Fork creek, among which we remember John Robertson, C. A. McKinney, Napolean Darmontzer. These gentlemen have good houses and farms and enjoy the prospect of fair crops.

At Stevensville we met Thomas Harris, P. Whaley, J. Silverthorn, and Rev. T. W. Flowers. Mr. Harris has a most beautiful home and farm upon Three Mile creek out at the foot of the mountains, about eight miles from Stevensville. He is one of the oldest white settlers of the valley, having located here in '62. His home was selected by himself, and given to him at a treaty with the Flathead tribe.

Mr. [Peter] Whaley has served a term as Indian agent of the Flatheads, and, unlike other agents, he is still regarded by them as their friend. He is the only agent that we remember who ever returned any government funds which could not be expended advantageously.

Mr. Flowers is the Methodist minister of this section. His home is now at Stevensville, but he has recently located a choice farm on Burnt Fork creek, which he is improving.

From Stevensville we crossed over to the west side of Bitter Root river, and turning southward, traveled along its beautiful bank, passing first upon our right W. E. and Dudly Bass' farm. Determined to call upon them on our return, we pushed on several miles through magnificent timbered land, which extends from the river back into the mountains from two to three miles. The land in some places is gravelly and unfit for farm land, but as a rule the soil is good, all of it producing an excellent growth of bunch-grass.

Three miles further up we passed a settlement of Flathead Indians, numbering six or seven families. They live in log houses, and have small farms of growing grain. Some of these locations are very desirable, but their improvements do not amount to anything. They own horses and cattle, and earn a living by working. Charlos, the Flathead chief, has a home in their midst. His dwelling is a two-story log house with four rooms, and his farm which covers over a pretty little park before his house, encloses seven or eight acres, upon which there is a good growing crop of wheat.

Leaving the Indian settlement we passed through a grove of timber, and coming out upon a little prairie, we beheld one of the prettiest farms and homes we have ever visited. The prairie is nearly circular in shape with beautiful timber standing around it. Through this level prairie, whose gentle grade pitches off from the foot of the mountain towards the river, runs a babbling rivulet, while in the centre stands the pleasant home and farm owned by Monroe Fulkerson. In his garden we picked some delicious strawberries, and saw as fine a young orchard as we have noticed in the country.

Passing through a skirt of woods we again came out upon a most beautiful garden spot. Here the prairie, which is surrounded with the finest article of pine timber we ever saw, is much larger than the one in which Mr. Fulkerson resides; and at intervals, around the prairie, are circular glades fenced off with timber. In these glades or parks, and around the main prairie, are to be found the thriftiest farmers and most desirable homes in Montana, of which we remember: M. B. Liter, W. L. Emmett, B. F. Tudor, Robert Nelson, R. S. Fowler, J. P. Martin, A. S. Blake, W. N. Smith, John Vincent, Oscar Clarke and F. A. Ess.

This settlement is known by the novel name of the Sweathouse settlement, taking its name from a very beautiful stream which runs there, and which furnishes an ample supply of water for the farms. It would be difficult to give a separate description of the farms, as they are so near alike and located in sight of each other, but we can say that we have nowhere seen more promising fields of grain, prettier gardens and young orchards, and more hospitable farmers than we met upon Sweathouse. Many of them are old settlers, and are well-to-do in a financial way. Their homes, though not gothic mansions, are comfortable, while for beautiful natural surroundings they have few superiors. Nearly all of the settlers here have families. They are members of the Fort Owen Grange, which has a splendid hall, a fine organ, large library, and a good membership.

Will.

July 3d.

Document 17

Salish Indian Guests at
Fourth of July Celebration
July 4, 1877

Source: Will Sutherlin, "Fourth of July on the Bitter Root," *Rocky Mountain Husbandman* (Diamond City, Mont.) August 23, 1877, page 7, col. 1-2.

Editors' note: Sutherlin's description of the Fourth of July celebration in the Bitterroot showed the success of Salish efforts to coexist peacefully with their white neighbors.

Fourth of July on the Bitter Root.

Being loath to leave the valley, it was no hard matter to be persuaded to stay one day longer. So in company with newmade friends, I turned aside to spend the fourth in the enjoyment of a picnic with the Sweathouse people and their neighbors. The grounds selected were a few miles below Sweathouse creek, and about a mile from the home of Charlos, the chief of the Flathead Indians, in a grove of large pines near a clear babbling brook, which meanders laughingly down from St. Mary's mountain across the bench land and into the Bitter Root river. A more suitable place could not have been selected. The ground was level and thickly covered with a growth of grass, and the pines were very large and straight, running up probably a hundred feet without a limb and spreading out with bushy green tops, nearly touching each other, making a pleasant shelter from the sunshine. From the hour of nine until eleven, vehicles loaded with men, women and children were continually arriving until nearly half of the residents of the valley were upon the grounds. For a while they scattered in clusters about the grove, but as the day grew older they become more sociable, and by noon the whole party had congregated in a circle, and were passing the time upon the topics of the day. Finally, the preparation for the feast began, and in a short time a large table had been spread. Baskets were brought from the several wagons and their contents emptied upon the table until it fairly tottered with its heavy load of good things. There were light bread, boiled ham, chickens and turkey; there were currants, gooseberries, raspberries and strawberries, pies, great piles of them, doughnuts, cookies, jelly cakes, confectioneries, and great stacks of pound cakes, whitened and coated, carved and trimmed as neatly as if designed for a queen's table. Besides these, there was a great variety of nicknacks which were palatable. The desert was large dishes of strawberries and cream. When all had eaten until satisfied, there remained enough to supply a meal for as many more. This was left upon the table, and some seventy or eighty Indians who had recently arrived, and were standing about the grounds, were invited to partake of it. This was a somewhat romantic scene. The ladies and gentlemen stood back while the Indians, little and big, old and young, came forward and feasted. When all were seated, in company with an acquaintance and an old residenter [sic] of the valley, I took a stroll along the table. Flathead Brown, a farmer, occupied the seat I had formerly used, while next by his side sat Delaware John, an Indian who served in the Federal army in time of the rebellion; while by him sat Plenty of Bear, a cunning looking halfbreed Nez Perce and Flathead. He wore a stovepipe hat with a pretty feather in it. Further down the table sat some half dozen fine looking young Indians some of whom were friendly Nez Perces. These young fellows were all painted and rigged up in fancy style. Next to them were a younger lot and some old men and s....s. Opposite Plenty of Bear were seated a row of young damsels, some of whom showed a considerable of the mingling of races, the Caucasian almost predominating. Their names as told to me were, Anna, Ann, Malta, and Mary Lumphey. The last named is represented to be the daughter of the wealthiest man in the Bitter Root valley. She is probably eighteen years of age. Her features are finer than most Indians, and her eyes were a sharp brown. She was dressed in Indian attire, except a lady's shawl, which hung over her shoulders. Her hair was rather coarse but long and wavy, and, though braided, it reached nearly to her waist. One of our party said she was pretty, but the writer is not a judge. I was told considerable about her relations of which there were some familiar and distinguished names connected; but lest I should fail to get it correct, I leave this bit of history for some other fellow. When the Indians were about through, Charlos, the Flathead chief, and his family arrived, and were treated to cake and pies and made to feel welcome. It may seem strange to some who read this, that Indians should be treated in this manner by the white people. But when they learn more of the Flathead tribe and their friendliness toward the settlers, they will have concluded that they are deserving the respect shown them.

Charlos and his father before him have always boasted that they and their people never have shed the blood of a white person. His band who live under him, are and have been peaceably disposed. They have lived here ever since the valley was first known. They are friendly to the people. Many of them have little farms of their own, and some of them have considerable property in horses and cattle, and are following the footsteps of the whites by laboring for a living and improving their knowledge. It is the custom of the good people along this valley to give the Flatheads an occasional feast, and the Fourth of July is as well remembered by them as by most white people.

After the feast, Mr. J. D. Baggs, Mr. Moon and some other gentlemen, rigged a large swing between two trees and the party amused themselves at swinging and jumping the rope, while the little boys and young Indians run several foot races, which added to the pleasantries of the day.

The afternoon was well advanced when the crowd dispersed to their homes, and I went on my way with treasured thoughts of the national holiday, its pleasant incidents, and the hospitable people of Sweathouse neighborhood.

Will.

Document 18

Salish and Pend d'Oreille Efforts to Stay Out of the Nez Perce War July 10, 1877

Source: Peter Ronan, *"A Great Many of Us Have Good Farms": Agent Peter Ronan Reports on the Flathead Indian Reservation, Montana, 1877-1887*, ed. Robert J. Bigart (Pablo, Mont.: Salish Kootenai College Press, 2014), pages 17-19.

Editors' note: Agent Ronan and Captain C. C. Rawn, the commander of army troops at Fort Missoula, sounded out tribal leaders about their intentions to stay out of the Nez Perce War. The Flathead Reservation Indians wanted peace, but they wanted to get paid if they worked as scouts for the whites. Chief Charlo described the annual cycle which incorporated planting and harvesting into the hunting and gathering schedule.

Missoula, M. T.
July 10th 1877

Hon. B. F. Potts.
Govr. Montana
Helena, M. T.
Sir:

On the 5th day of July I received your letter of June 29th, requesting that I, with some of the most influential Fathers, seek the Flathead Camp — Charlos' band — and have a talk with the Indians, and to counsel peace, and alliance with the Whites; also, to gain whatever information I could and report to you.

On the day of the reception of your letter Capt. [Charles C.] Rawn, in command of the Military Post near Missoula, arrived at the Agency for the purpose of gaining some knowledge of the Indians of this Reservation, and before proceeding to Charlos' camp, I concluded to hold a council with the Chiefs and head-men of the Confederated Tribes of my Agency, and for that purpose, in company with Captain C. C. Rawn and John Sheehan, taking with me an Interpreter we proceeded to the Mission.

On our way to the Mission we met Michelle, head chief of the Pen d'Oreilles, returning from a visit to his sister at the Lakes, who agreed to talk with me at the Agency on my return. On the morning of the 6th, André

Second Chief of the Pen d'Oreilles, called into the Council representatives of the three confederated Tribes, viz: Flathead, Pen d'Oreill[e]s and Kootenais. Father [Leopold] Van Gorp and Father [Joseph] Bendini were also present. The Indians gave us unqualified assurance of their loyalty to the Whites, and stated that upon emergency they were ready to go to War with any tribe or confederation of tribes who might attempt to make war upon the settlers of Montana. Capt Rawn asked for Indian scouts to guard the passes, but the Indians were unwilling to go into service unless the Captain or myself could give them assurance of payment, a proposition neither of us would accede to, without instructions from our respective Departments, and we were both unwilling to make any promises that we could not fulfill to the letter.

The Indians, therefore, would not agree to act as scouts unless fully assured of payment but said, upon the reception of any news of danger, they would immediately dispatch messengers to the Military Post at Missoula, and to the Agency. After the conference we returned to the Agency where we met Arlee, Chief of the Flathead reservation Indians, who denounced, as false the intimation that he ever stated that any of his people had any intention of Joining the hostiles. He stated that they were peaceable and friendly to a man and would defend with their lives, if necessary, the Whites. Michelle, the Pen d'Oreille Chief, expressed himself in the same terms. Feeling fully satisfied of the peaceful intentions of the Reservation Indians, I proceeded to Charlos' Camp, up the Bitter Root Valley, in company with Captain Rawn and my official Interpreter, Baptiste Marengo, and on Sunday July 8th arrived at St. Mary's Mission, where we met Charlos, who with his family, was in attendance at Mass. Father D'Asti [Jerome D'Aste, S.J.], in charge of St. Mary's Mission, arranged preliminaries for our talk with the Chief.

Charlos greeted us in a frank and manly way and stated that his heart was glad to meet us, as bad stories had been put in circulation about himself and his people, and he hoped now he would have a chance to have the truth told of him to his White friends. In answer to my question "Where are your people?" he said: "This broad Country is our home — it is usual every year, after my people put in their crops, for them to go to the different Camas prairies, for the purpose of digging those roots for winter use, and while the s....s and Children perform that duty, the young men hunt and fish —

When the crops begin to ripen they return to their homes — They are on their ways home now, as I am informed by one of my young men, and twenty lodges are encamped near Missoula, the rest will soon follow." I then asked him how he felt in regard to the Whites, and he answered: "My father's name was Victor — he was the head Chief of this nation; he made the treaty with Governor Stephens [Issac I. Stevens], eighteen years ago; It was my father's boast that the blood of a Whiteman never reddened the hands of a single Indian of the Flathead tribe. My father died with that boast on his lips — I am my father's son, and will leave that same boast to my children."

In answer to my question "Will you join the Whites, with your warriors, and make war on the Nez Perces?" he stated "If danger threatens I will send runners to inform the settlers and the captain of the soldiers, and you, the Agent, I will do all in my power to defend the Whites and their homes, but I cannot send my young men out to make war on the Nez Perces. When my old enemy, the Blackfeet, came here to redden the Valley with my people's blood, the Nez Perces assisted us and, helped to drive them away. No, I cannot send my young men out to fight them, but I will help to protect the Whiteman's home."

I then asked him the news, and he said he was sorry to state that Red Owl, a Nez Perce Chief, and father of Louison, a Half-breed Flathead, who lives at my Agency was Killed by the Whites, on the head of the Clearwater River, together with fifteen lodges of his people. Red Owl was friendly to the Whites and asked the White people to designate a safe place for him to camp, with his people, which was done, and the Chief went into camp feeling that he was safe from the Whites. In the meantime a company of soldiers arrived in the vicinity of Red Owl's camp, where they captured one of Joseph's band, and they promised him his liberty on condition that he would guide them to Joseph's Camp. The Indian agreed to the proposition, but instead of taking them to Joseph's camp, he guided them to Red Owl's lodges, and the Whites fell upon this friendly band and Killed them all. This news, Charlos stated, he got from reliable sources and as Red Owl was known in Montana, he sent Messengers to different Indian camps to tell the truth concerning the death of Red Owl, and to say that the whites deplored the treachery and the snare that they were led into by Joseph's renegade.

On our way up the Bitter Root, we met Eagle-of-the-Light, formerly Chief of Joseph's band of non-treaty Nez Perces who was driving a band of loose horses, and we were informed that he was going up the Lo Lo Pass to bring back the Nez Perce camp, which left Missoula some three weeks ago with the intention of going over to the Nez Perce country, but who were met by a runner who informed them of the uprising of Joseph's band against the Whites and they went into camp and sent Word to their friends here of the trouble and asked advice. Eagle-of-the-Light advised peace and the return of the tribe to Missoula, there to camp in the vicinity of the Military post until peace was made, and for that purpose he was going out with fresh horses to assist them in; this was the Indian statement, and of course I give it as repeated.

There are a number of wild stories afloat in regard to Indian massacres lately perpetrated, but I cannot trace them to any reliable source and will refrain from making any mention of them. I feel perfectly confident, however, of the good faith of Charlos, the "original" Flathead Chief, and his band as well as all of the confederate tribes under my Jurisdiction but of course this will not prevent me from taking every precaution to guard against danger or surprise.

The only danger I apprehend at present is from the Indians of the Snake and Columbia rivers, as far north as Colville, who may possibly be influenced to Join the hostiles, in that case, if they come through this country it seems to me that the Chiefs, no matter what their influence may be in their tribes, will be unable wholly to restrain their young men, as there are restless and adventurous spirits among the Indians, as well as among the Whites who would be only too glad for an op[p]ortunity for plunder and rapine.

Very respectfully
Peter Ronan
U.S. Ind. Agt.

Document 19

Salish Indians Protect Bitterroot Whites in 1877

Late July 1877

Source: The Confederated Salish and Kootenai Tribes of the Flathead Reservation, Montana, vs. The United States of America, Docket 61, "Depositions: Before the Indian Claims Commission," October 1952, Records of the U.S. Indian Claims Commission, RG 279, Docket 61, Exhibit A-2, vol. 2, National Archives, Washington, D.C., pages 30-31, 40-42; [Michael A. Leeson], ed., *History of Montana, 1739-1885* (Chicago: Warner, Beers & Company, 1885), page 149.

Editors' note: This testimony by Eneas Granjo was compiled as evidence in the tribes' case in the U.S. Indian Claims Commission. The roster on page 149 of Leeson's *History of Montana*, gave the names of the Salish Indians who took part in the 1877 Nez Perce War and received federal pension payments in 1881.

Direct Examination by Mr. [George] Tunison:
Q. State your name.

A. Eneas Granjo.

Q. What's your age?

A. Sixty-nine, seventy, somewhere around there.

Q. Where do you reside?

A. Arlee.

Q. Is that on the present reservation of the Confederated Tribes?

A. Yes, sir.

Q. Are you a member of the tribal council of the Confederated Tribes?

A. Yes, sir.

Q. Have you been chairman of that council?

A. Yes, sir.

Q. How many years have you been on the council all together?

A. Oh, about 16, 18 years. . . . .

Q. What about the Nez Perces, did they come into the Flathead country [in 1877]?

A. Just only when — the only thing that I know of, when they come over to wipe out all white people. That's the only thing I know of.

Q. This is the time of Chief Joseph?

A. Ya, Chief Joseph.

Q. And what did the Flatheads do?

A. Well, they went to see Chief Charlo, Bear Claw, and Chief Joseph he told them, he says: "I am going to wipe out all white people starting from Lolo."

Q. From where?

A. From Lolo. Charlo said, "No, white man is my friend, and I don't want no blood shed on my reservation. You better move out of here," and he says, "I want you to get out right away." "No,["] Chief Joseph says, "I am going to start from here wipe out all white people." Well then, Charlo told him, he says, "If you do that, you got to wipe me out too." So then — now, the reason I know this, I am telling you this story because I have done interpreter here for Joe Lamoose and all these Indians that was scouts at that time, because we got pension for Joseph Lamoose; it's in the record in Washington too, this, what I am telling you. So then Charlo says, "All right." So then he gathered up quite a few Indians and he told these Indians, "Now you go over to the soldiers and make them give you white handkerchiefs and they will give you ammunition and you go and tell Chief Joseph to move out right away; if not, fire." So then they went over to the — there was quite a few of them — Big Pierre's father was in, and Paul Charlo's father was in the bunch, and my father was in the bunch, and a lot of Indians was. I know lot of them; of course, they are all dead. And so they went over there and they got white handkerchiefs and they got ammunition from the soldiers; they chased the soldiers back — the soldiers were afraid of Chief Joseph. So then they put Alec Matt at Captain; he was Captain. They appointed him as captain of these Indians, Flathead Indians, so then when they got there, Alec Matt told Chief Joseph, "We want you to move right away." "No," he says, "we are going to wipe out all white people." Well, Alec Matt told him, he says, that "We are here to protect the white people, and if you do that, you got to wipe us out." And they keep talking, you know and the tribe — the Flathead Tribe says, oh, quit that nonsense, says, let's fire, let's shoot. The same way with the Nez Perces, they were telling that to Chief Joseph, on both sides, because some of them understands that. Paul Charlo's father understands little, just few words you know, and of course he knowed what they were saying, and some of the Nez Perces, I guess, they knowed what Alec Matt was saying, so they says, quit that non sense, let's fight. So finally, they talked there and then Chief Joseph says, "All right, I will move." He says, "I won't do no harm." That's when he moved, he went towards Big Hole country.

Q. He got out of the Bitter Root country, did he?

A. Yes, he got out of there.

* * * * * * * * *

Captain Matt's Company No. 9, July 6 to August 6, 1877. — Alexander Matt, Baptiste Matt, Cozack Matt, Louis Carron, Grand Joe, Louis Pierre, Delaware Jim, Pierre Jim, Ottawa Jim, Otzack, Jos. Lamoise, Eneas Francois, Antoine Moses, Enos Foreshids, Shoner Jack, Antoine Nimpipe, Antoine Cœur de Lion, Medicine Pierre, James - - - - , Francis Kiser, Prudurn, Martin Charlo, Joseph Dishon, Mattische, Charles L'amour, Antoine (L'amour). Of the above named volunteers, Cœur de Lion, Medicine Pierre, James - - - - and Joseph Dishon were reported dead in 1881. To each of the surviving volunteers the sum of $30 was granted, together with a like amount to the heirs of the four deceased members of the company, bringing the total payment, on account of Matt's company, up to $780.

Eneas Granjo
Source: Carling Malouf Papers, MS 640, Toole Archives, Mansfield Library, University of Montana, Missoula, box 79, folder 7.

Document 20

Whites Applaud Salish Protection of Settlers in the Bitterroot August-September 1877

Source: *The New North-West* (Deer Lodge, Mont.), August 10, 1877, page 2, col. 1; *The Weekly Missoulian*, August 10, 1877, page 3, col. 3; "Our Sham Indian War — Noble Conduct of Catholic Indians," *The Catholic Sentinel for the Northwest* (Portland, Or.), September 20, 1877, page 4, col. 1-2.

Editors' note: Montana whites expressed their appreciation for the protection of the Salish during the Nez Perce War. Their Bitterroot neighbors gave the Salish a feast of thanks.

— The Flatheads have earned another credit mark and stood true through circumstances trying their fidelity to the utmost. They are largely intermarried with the Nez Perces, have been on friendly relations with them many years and occupy a most exposed position in case of hostilities with them. These circumstances, and their indisposition to pay the taxes levied on their property, created an apprehension of them and fears were entertained by many in Missoula county that in case of trouble they had most to fear from their own tribes. Their actions and attitude in learning of affairs in Idaho were by no means assuring. It further appeared to be credibly reported on their authority that if the Nez Perces come fighting they would help resist them but if they wished to go through peaceably they would assist them in that purpose. But when Capt. [Charles C.] Rawn entrenched the Flatheads went into the rifle pits with him and volunteered to assist in repelling them on his terms that they must surrender or fight. We have since been advised that even succeeding the passage of the Lo Lo they were irreconcilable to the presence of the Nez Perces and wanted to fight them. It is also stated Charlos' warriors will co-operate with [John] Gibbon although they declined to go under officers. If the Flatheads maintain this good faith through these troubles their fidelity deserves more than passive recognition, and should be rewarded substantially. This attitude probably changed the whole course of events in Missoula county, and the faithfulness of a friend is more deserving of reward that the concessions of a foe. This should not be forgotten when peace is established.

— *The New North-West*

* * * * * * * *

L. R. Maillet, who came down from Bitter Root valley Thursday morning reports that the people of the valley gave to Charlos and his people a feast Wednesday. The people of Bitter Root are deeply sensible of the assistance rendered by the Flatheads, while the Nez Perces were passing through, and believe that the Nez Perces would have ravaged the country if they had not been restrained by fear of the Flatheads. Charlos made a speech, recounting the past friendship of the Flatheads for the whites: urging his young men to always live in amity with them, and showing them how much better off they were than the Nez Perces who are now being pursued as outcasts in the earth.

* * * * * * * *

Our Sham Indian War — Noble conduct of Catholic Indians.

Of all the burlesques that were ever perpetrated by an intelligent people, the present so-called Indian war is the most ridiculous. It had its origin in dishonesty, and its conduct has been marked by such incompetency as would — in any country in Europe — cause those in command of the troops to be cashiered in disgrace.

How people in other portions of the civilized world must laugh at the spectacle presented when they behold an army of more than a thousand regular troops — assisted by innumerable volunteers and Indian scouts — engaged in watching, chasing, intercepting, but never catching — two hundred Indians! Here we have all the available troops of a great nation brought into the field under command of Major Generals, Brigadiers, and Staff officers without end, aided by the influence of the civil authorities of several states and territories, and supplied with the munitions of war by the general government. Yet these doughty warriors are unable to arrest the progress of two hundred Indians on a march of two thousand miles.

It is a singular fact — but nevertheless true — that the Indians engaged in this so-called war are the proteges of the Protestant churches, whose members — under the peace policy inaugurated by President [Ulysses S.] Grant — were made Indian Agents.

The Catholic Indians are not only peaceable but they have also proved their fidelity to the teachings they have received by refusing to join the hostile Nez Perces and also by driving them out of Montana.

Prior to the conflict in which the Nez Perces are engaged, a message was sent from Joseph's band to the Cœur d'Alene Indians — under charge of the Jesuits at the Sacred Heart mission, Idaho — asking them to join the forces of

Joseph in a war against the whites. But these good Catholic Indians answered the hostiles that they were Catholics who could take no part in murdering innocent people, and, as they had no grievances to revenge, hence they could not participate in the proposed war. And how nobly these Catholic Indians have preserved not only their own good name but also the lives of the whites, we may learn from the Lewiston *Teller*, which pays the Cœur d'Alenes this well-merited tribute: — "The Cœur d'Alene Indians," says the journal in question, "throughout the present difficulty have acted nobly. When, at the first outbreak, the citizens of Pine Creek had fled to Colfax, Seltis, the chief of the Cœur d'Alenes, sent his warriors to patrol around the farms deserted by the settlers, in order to prevent any other Indians from plundering the premises." In addition to this honorable and heroic action, Seltis waited upon Father [Joseph] Cataldo, S.J. the priest in charge of the mission, and told him to write to the white people, that the Cœur d'Alene Indians were not only peaceable but they would also defend the American settlers against the attacks of any hostile Indians that dare invade their country. In response to this friendly missive the settlers throughout Whitman county replied by a vote of thanks signed by upwards of a hundred settlers.

We earnestly hope that some suitable testimony may be presented by the general government to the honorable chief of the Cœur d'Alenes as a memento of his true and tried allegiance. The action of Seltis also had great influence in preserving the loyalty of the Spokans and their adjacent tribes. To the honor of Seltis it must also be told that not a single member of his tribe followed the fortunes of Joseph.

Another evidence of the friendliness of the Catholic Indians may be found in the fact that when Joseph and his band of warriors reached Montana and encamped on the banks of the Missoula river, they were compelled to move their camp by a body of Flathead Indians who are under the spiritual charge of the Jesuit Fathers of St. Mary's Mission, the oldest missionary station on this coast. On learning that Joseph and his band had reached their vicinity, the Flathead chief Charlot assembled about fifty of his warriors and went forth to meet the hostiles in order to warn them not to commit any depredations in that neighborhood. This warning had the desired effect and neither murder nor robbery was committed in that region. We are credibly informed that when the chief of the Flatheads entered the tent of Joseph the latter approached to take him by the hand, but Charlot motioned him back, addressing him at the same time in these memorable words: "Chief of the Nez Perces, I am a Catholic, and, as such, I cannot take your bloody hand." Here, then we have two very remarkable incidents of the beneficial influence of Catholic teaching upon Indian tribes, who are thus rendered friends of the whites at a time when every appeal of consanguinity is made to them to join the enemies of the whites in their warfare. Let us hope, therefore, that the facts thus developed will have a beneficial result in proving to the Administration the necessity of again restoring to the Catholic Church the Indian Missions of which she has been so unjustly deprived, and also that they may tend to open the eyes of those in authority to the fact that it is cheaper to maintain peace with the Indians by means of Catholic missionaries than by any other method.

The present Indian trouble — insignificant as it is — has already cost many valuable lives and millions of money, all of which could have been saved if even one honest man had been sent to treat with Joseph for the Wallowa Valley, which was his legitimate property by all the laws known to humanity and justice. Unfortunately, however, for both the country and the Indians, those who pretended to represent the American people thought they could achieve a little cheap glory by precipitating an Indian war which they vainly imagined they could crush in a brief campaign. How sadly their foresight was thwarted, and how disgraceful the whole conduct of the campaign has been, those who read the telegrams from the hunting grounds, and the list of the killed and wounded, can well attest.

Document 21

Salish Protection of Bitterroot Whites
Noted Again
August 31, 1877

Source: "Trip to Stevensville," *The Weekly Missoulian*, August 31, 1877, page 3, col. 3-4.

Editors' note: This reporter gave significant credit to Chief Charlo and the Bitterroot Salish for protecting the whites from the hostile Nez Perce. The writer also mentioned the gathering of the Salish at St. Mary's Mission for mass.

Trip to Stevensville.

Last Saturday afternoon we accepted an invitation from Con. Kohrs, the cattle king of Western Montana, to take a seat behind his steppers and head toward Bitter Root valley. Con. went up to see if he could find hide or hair of some forty or fifty cattle that had escaped from a band that he had bought last year. We went up for — we will say health.

In and about Stevensville the uppermost topic of conversation continues to be the passage of the Nez Perces through the valley. It is remarkable, when we think of it, upon what a brittle thread the lives and destinies of these people hung during the week the Indians were in the valley. It is a feather in the cap of old Looking Glass, and one that should entitle him to favorable consideration in any subsequent disposition of these Indians, that he restrained the lawless and made the entire tribe keep their faith with the whites. They boldly announced their intention of trading, and if the people would not sell to them that they would help themselves. So a virtue was made of necessity, and they bought what they wanted, with the exception of butcher knives and ammunition, which were cached in advance of their arrival. The last day the Indians were at Stevensville some lawless whites sold them whisky, and it looked pretty squally for the settlers for a while; but Looking Glass sent the drunken home as fast as they appeared, and the citizens got together and talked seriously of putting those who had so little regard for the public welfare in a position that they could not get their feet to the ground. It is the prevalent belief that the chiefs hurried the Indians away from the liability of collision, and that they would probably have remained in the valley if they had been unable to get whisky, and would have been that much nearer to their pursuers. Aside from this whisky episode all parties bear uniform testimony to the general good behavior of these hostiles.

All speak, too, in the highest terms of the honorable conduct of Charlos, the Flathead chief, during the whole of this critical period. Charlo is half Nez Perces on his mother's side, and is a near relative to Looking Glass; but he would hold no communication with them, and gave them to understand that he would fight them if they committed any depredations in the valley. The Nez Perces were probably induced to a better course of conduct from a knowledge of Charlos' determination.

A visit to the venerable Father [Anthony] Rivalli, who has labored in this region for thirty-five years, could not be neglected upon the occasion of being at Stevensville. His health has been feeble, but he is now stronger than he has been for a year past. In answer to an inquiry why he did not seek some place where he could spend the evening of his days in more comfortable quarters and enjoy the society of his friends, he arose with alacrity and led the way to his drugstore, his machine shop and his furnace. Here are the scenes of the triumphs of his vigorous manhood, and here he lingers in the hope that, he may still serve his fellowmen. While ever having a zealous care for the spiritual welfare of mankind, he had neglected no means, within his power to promote their comfort and temporal welfare. An accomplished physician and surgeon, he has ever responded to the call of suffering, and his shattered health can now be traced to exposure upon such errands of mercy. When his course of usefulness shall have ended, no man will be more sincerely or deeply mourned by all classes and conditions of men of whatever creed — white or Indian — than this self-denying, philanthropic and liberal-minded Father.

While at the Mission, the Flatheads, to the number of about 100, assembled from all parts of the valley for mass. The correctness of the performance of their duties of worship and of their responses shows the pains that have been taken to instruct them. The conviction is irresistible upon attendance at these exercises that great good is being accomplished among this unfortunate people. It is hard to instruct a people in the ways of religion while they lead the lives of savages. The impressions that it has taken years to form are obliterated in one season of mingling in bands and roaming about the country in search of game. Many of them have adopted the pursuits of peaceful life, and more of them would do it if they were aided in a way of life they know nothing of. A conference with Father [Jerome] D'Astie, in charge of the mission, discloses some of the difficulties in the way of any departure from the traditional habits of the Indian. If he is deprived of ammunition and his arms taken from him, he must starve. The government will manifestly have to support him until he has learned to support himself in a new way of life. The Father appreciates the difficulties in the way of civilizing and Christianizing the Indian while he remains a vagrant, but a feeling of mistaken kindness can not reconcile him to the idea of any restraint being put upon his conduct.

The past season has been one of peculiar hardship to Bitter Root valley. First, the grasshoppers destroyed the entire crops in the upper end of the valley; second, the Indian excitement, causing men to abandon their homes and fort up during the whole of July, entailed great loss upon every settler in the valley and caused many crops to suffer for want of timely irrigation; and, lastly, the hail-storm in the later part of July destroyed almost everything on the west side of Bitter Root. It is estimated by competent judges that there will not be more than enough raised in the valley to bread the inhabitants and furnish seed for another year.

Document 22

Peaceful Salish Indians Denied
Ammunition to Hunt
October 1877

Source: *The Helena Daily Herald*, October 20, 1877, page 2, col. 1; *Rocky Mountain Husbandman* (Diamond City, Mont.), October 25, 1877, page 2, col. 1; "The Flatheads," *The Helena Independent* (daily), October 26, 1877, page 3, col. 2.

Editors' note: As a reward for their faithful protection of the Bitterroot whites, the federal authorities prohibited the sale of ammunition to them for hunting. The Salish were faced with starvation and possible injury from enemy tribes as their reward for defending their white neighbors.

The Flatheads are here and want ammunition to hunt buffalo. They are peaceable, their crops are deficient, and they have to get meat, steal or starve. Give them the ammunition.

—*The Helena Daily Herald*

* * * * * * * *

We learn from parties direct from Helena that Charlos, with 22 lodges and about 200 of his people, were encamped near there on their way to hunt buffalo in the Muscleshell and Judith countries. These Indians are endeavoring to purchase ammunition for their hunt, but thus far, we are told, have been unsuccessful. This is certainly unjust, and a poor return for the service rendered by this chief and his warriors to the settlers of Bitter Root valley during the invasion of the Nez Perces. Hearing of the approach of the hostiles, Charlos summoned his warriors about him, and was ready and anxious to oppose their entrance, and it is a well-known fact that their peaceable transit through the Bitter Root is due in a great measure to the presence of his warriors. We cannot see why any one should entertain any antipathy for this band of Flatheads. They are not government pets, but are non-treaty Indians, and have, we believe, never received anything from the government except a title to their lands on the Bitter Root, which is their birthright, having been in their possession long before the white man had tracked the American plains or even scaled the heights of the Alleghanies. They live there upon their own resources, and are accustomed to take an annual hunt for the purpose of getting a supply of meat for the coming year, which, in connection with what vegetables, etc., they can raise, enables them to live without pillaging. The Crow Indians, a far more treacherous tribe, are furnished annuities, and ammunition to hunt in this region, and we see no reason why the Flatheads, who have never been known to take the life of a white man, should not be allowed to purchase ammunition when hunting is their main source of living.

— *Rocky Mountain Husbandman*

* * * * * * * *

The Flatheads.
They Must Have Ammunition or Steal Cattle.
General Sherman's Opinion.
If they Don't Have Buffalo they will Starve.

Gen. [William T.] Sherman, in writing from Missoula to the Secretary of War in regard to the condition of the Flathead and confederate tribes of Indians, truthfully says: "Had there been four companies here last year, the Nez Perces would not have dared to revolt. There remain of the same class the Flatheads, Pen d'Oreilles, Spokanes and Cœur d'Alenes, all of whom claim the right to go where they please through Montana to the buffalo region at the headwaters of the Missouri. The agent of the Flatheads came to see me last night with a most intelligent Catholic priest, who has charge of the mission of St. Ignatius, forty-two miles north of this. They describe the Indians as numbering 1,700, disposed to peace, and who refused to go in with the Nez Perces, but offered to fight them in their own way. The agent has not a dollar and no authority to promise them meat. They won't work or lay in a stock of winter food. They say there are buffalos near — that is, 300 or 400 miles to the northeast, and are bound to go after them. They promise to keep well to the north to avoid the white settlemente [sic], but once out and hungry they will steal tame cattle, and the next thing will be shooting and war. They complain because the traders are forbidden to sell them ammunition. They have forgotten the use of the bow and arrows, and all want powder and caps. These they cannot get, and discontent is natural. The agent said he had tried to dissuade them from this hunt at this time, but without effect. Some have already gone. I told the agent that I could not meddle with his business when he could go to Deer Lodge and represent the state of affairs to the Commissioner of Indian Affairs by telegraph and obtain instructions. These Flatheads are friendly, but they must go for buffaloes or starve. If they go for buffaloes they may come in contact with white settlers, who know not the difference between the Nez Perces and Flatheads, and trouble may result.

I instance [sic] this case to show why we need more than one small company here. A company can defend itself in a block house, and afford a rallying point for settlers; but this is not the only office of troops. They must defend the post and furnish protection to threatened points.

Document 23

Salish Friendship and White Perfidy

October 23, 1877

Source: "Rocky Mountain Correspondence," *McGee's Illustrated Weekly* (New York, N.Y.), vol. 3, no. 1 (November 24, 1877), page 3, col. 1-2.

Editors' note: Another account of the frustration of the Bitterroot Salish after they had stood in defense of the white settlers and were rewarded by a ban on ammunition sales when they needed the ammunition to defend themselves on the plains and kill buffalo to support themselves.

Rocky Mountain Correspondence.

Helena, M. T., Oct. 23d, 1877.

At this season Montana appears in her most at[t]ractive aspect, and with the smoky haze that fills the atmosphere under her bright suns and blue skies, are unrolled each day pictures of beauty and loveliness whose effect no artist could rival or approach. If Bryant had lived in Montana in autumn, he never would have sung —

"The melancholy days have come,

The saddest of the year."

but might have said, "It is now the time when slumber seems to hover on the air, and the veil of Indian summer floats blue, thin, and silent, lovely as a dream."

As if to compensate for the dark cloud of hostiles that lately passed over some of the sparsely-settled portions, Montana dons her loveliest garb of peace and tranquility, and the savage Joseph and his murderous band are prisoners in the hands of our great Indian fighter and gallant soldier, General [Nelson A.] Miles. The severe punishment inflicted upon these non-resident cut-throats, first by General [John] Gibbon, and then by the hero of Bear Paugh Mountain, will hereafter deter any other band from a neighboring territory from ever again attempting a raid on white men in this. The friendly Indians of Montana are just paying our city their annual visit on their way to hunt the buffalo, and for a week past have been on our streets in hundreds, selling horses, making purchases, and laying in their supplies for the journey. Their camp of sixty lodges is a mile from town, and each day they visit us with new faces in red, crimson and yellow.

On Sunday last, on the occasion of the funeral of Professor Deitrich, who was killed two months ago by the Nez Perces, about one hundred Flatheads (Catholic Indians) came in mounted and dressed in plumes and paint, as curious spectators of the solemn scene. Yesterday Charlos, the noted Christian chief of the Flatheads, in a conversation with one of the Fathers, repeated the warning he had given last July to Joseph, saying: "I watch you in the Bitter Root Valley; and if you harm any person or steal a horse, we will destroy you all." The order prohibiting the sale of ammunition to all Indians is very perplexing to the Flatheads, who come to Helena with money, skins and furs, as well as their memorable unbroken treaty of friendship, to purchase powder and lead for their fall hunt. The Governor, United States Marshal, and leading citizens of Montana, have telegraphed to authorize the sale to them. The order should be modified so as to discriminate in favor of the Flathead Nation, who would be sure to use the privilege for the legitimate purpose of killing game for their subsistence, and to prevent it from falling into the hands of doubtful or hostile Indians. They can be trusted with more confidence than those white men now in the brush selling contraband goods to all Indians alike. Yesterday I witnessed the sacrament of baptism of an Indian child in the Catholic Church; the sponsors were adults, and other Indians were present and joined in singing the Pater Noster and Credo in their own language. The Black Gowns are the only ones who baptize and Christianize Indians in this country — all other apostles come among the red men for trade and traffic, and are called "bad medicine."

The annual Territorial Fair at Helena, after a six days' exhibition, was lately closed, after one of the most successful efforts of the kind ever held in Montana. About ten thousand dollars were the receipts, and nearly that amount was paid out for premiums, for the races and expenses. The display of agricultural products was very great in variety, and the excellence of all kinds of grains and vegetables could not have been surpassed anywhere. In Missoula County another fair was held from the 11th to the 13th of October, where fine products and fine stock of the Jocco Valley only could be exhibited. Missoula is the only county in Montana that has yet paid much attention to culture of apples, melons and other fruit. In the article of flour Montana has this year made an over-product; and notwithstanding the great demand of the Government for the supply of troops and Indians in this Territory, the price remains firm at five dollars per sack, or ten dollars per barrel, thus giving a nice cash margin to our farmers here, and a great saving to the Government in the item of transportation. In the matter of fresh beef on the block, the Helena

Military Post (six companies of the Third Infantry) is supplied with the best in the world at $3.70 per hundred pounds. The mining season (placer washing) is about over, as the water recedes at the approach of cold weather. The quartz mines are still busy, and will continue their work through the winter to supply the various mills and smelters. But no camp in Montana has made such rapid progress the last year in mines, mills and men, as the City of Butte, Deer Lodge County, which has doubled its population to near three thousand people within a twelvemonth.

The Montana Company, at Jefferson City, a large and expensive concentrating works, has just received a telegram from New York, saying, "Thirty-five thousand dollars to your credit to pay wages and expenses." The outlook for the winter of the quartz mining camps of both gold and silver from Philipsburg, Butte City, Ten Mile, Pony, Jefferson, Gregory, Iron Rod, Vipond, Highland, Silver City, Clarke's Fork of the Yellowstone, is very encouraging. On Sunday last a Catholic church of fine proportions and creditable workmanship, lately erected at Butte City, was dedicated by Father De Rickery [Remigius De Ryckere], pastor, assisted by Rev. Father Paulin [Cyril Pauwelyn]. The attendance was very large, partly of Protestants, who came to witness the ceremonies, and to hear again the fine music rendered in concert the night previous by the Helen[a] Choir who travelled ninety miles by coach to aid the good work of their friends in Butte, and help them pay for the erection of their church. It is not so hard to build churches here as in older communities. It is the rule in Montana to give liberally to all public improvements, and especially to Catholic churches.

Not until after all All Saints' do we begin to look to our stoves and wood-piles; about that time good fires will be in order, and then is inaugurated the good cheer and social enjoyments that carry us through the colder winter months. Since the 1st of September the weather has been calm and pleasant, and so inviting are the out-door amusements at this season, that the people of Helena had a pic-nic, on last Saturday, on the top of Mount Helena, six thousand feet above the sea. Most of our sportsmen, in parties, are now encamped in the woods for deer-shooting and every day we have black tail on our streets by the wagon load. A particular friend, William H. Ewing, Esq., a farmer and stock-grower in the valley, brought in last week fourteen deer from a party of three, all killed within twenty miles of Helena. The subscriptions in Montana to your excellent *Illustrated Weekly* will increase in proportion as the circulation becomes general in camps where a canvass has not been made for subscribers.

Pioneer.

Document 24

Agent Ronan Investigates Indian-White Friction at Horse Plains January 2, 1878

Source: Peter Ronan, *"A Great Many of Us Have Good Farms": Agent Peter Ronan Reports on the Flathead Indian Reservation, Montana, 1877-1887*, ed. Robert J. Bigart (Pablo, Mont.: Salish Kootenai College Press, 2014), pages 35-37.

Editors' note: Ronan interviewed Indians and whites in Horse Plains, west of the reservation, and received conflicting accounts of recent friction between the races.

Flathead Agency, M.T.
January 2d, 1878

To the
Hon. Commissioner of Indian Affairs
Washington, D.C.
Sir:

Pursuant to arrangements made with "Simon," 2d Chief of the Lower Pend 'Oreilles or Kalispels, and brother of "Petah" head-chief of that tribe, information of which was given to you in my special report bearing date December 10th, 1877, I met that chief at St. Ignatius Mission, on the 26th day of December. All the Indians who make Horse Plains their home, when not hunting, consisting of some thirty warriors, accompanied "Simon," and several of the White settlers of that place, including Charles A. Lynch, the complainant, were also present.

Having called the parties together I stated, through my interpreter, that complaints had been forwarded to Washington against the Indians by the White settlers of Horse Plains, claiming that the Indians were committing depredations in throwing down their fences, Killing their hogs and cattle, ruining their crops by driving their herds to graze upon them, and other offences; and that I was directed to inquire into the matter, and to take prompt measures to protect the settlers against such outrages.

Simon replied that the general home of the Lower Pen d'Oreilles was far to the West of Horse Plains, on the Columbia river, but the Indians who I saw before me, deeming Horse Plains an Indian country, and better adapted to their wants as it was in the vicinity of game and fish, and also a good grazing country, made it their home. Of late years several White men settled among them — he did not dispute their right to do so — but there were wrongs Committed on both sides, and as the Whites made their statements he desired that the Indians should now make theirs.

From the various grievances stated by the Indians against the settlers from poisoning their dogs to altering stallions, I will cite one as it related directly to Mr. Charles A. Lynch, the complainant, and was not denied by him, and as showing that the Indians have also their grievances.

An old Indian rose in his turn and said, "One day I came up to this Mission and my heart did not feel easy — at last a raven or a crow or something else whispered in my ear 'go home to Horse Plains' — I went back and found Charla (meaning Mr. Lynch) had my horses caught up and was using them to thresh his grain. The horses looked bad and I felt bad. I demanded five dollars Charla said he would give me three — I did not like to take three — but when I thought it over I took three dollars because I always think it is better to take half a cup of coffee if I cannot get a full one."

From all the information I could gain I am led to believe that offences have been committed on both sides, but no serious trouble has yet occurred; but in an isolated place like Horse Plains, where the settlement consists of only six families, it is a matter of surprise to me that greater offences have not been committed by the Indians, when it is reflected that the Indians occupying the vast region extending from the Flathead reservation to the Columbia river are under no treaty stipulations, have no reservation and receive no aid from government. In his remarks Simon said: "Our people had a talk last summer with a man sent by the Great Father to Spokane bridge to meet us — there were six tribes present — we did not understand all he wanted of us, but our people thought he wanted to put us into Coralls instead of reservations. Tell the Great Father in Washington we like the country around Horse Plains and I think our people would like to have their reservation to take in that country — I do not say this for sure, but I think so." Here I would remark that I consider it a great misfortune, both for the Indians and the Whites, that a settlement was made upon Horse Plains as the place is situated some ninety miles west of Missoula, the nearest white settlement to the east, and to the West stretches that vast Indian country to the Columbia river only occupied by Indians.

There are no inducements for settlement west of Horse Plains, and to the East the Jocko Reservation precludes settlement, so that little valley is now, and to all appearances must remain, an isolated settlement of six or eight families in the heart of an Indian Country. Under those circumstances if I might be permitted to make a suggestion, it would redound to the interest both of the Whites and Indians that Horse Plains either be included in the Jocko reservation, or be set aside as a reservation for the Lower Pen d'Oreilles.

I finally settled all past difficulties between the settlers and the Indians, in a seemingly satisfactory manner to all concerned by suggesting that both parties were, in a measure to blame and it was desirable that the past should be forgotten, and that in future they live in peace to-gether. I stated to the Indians that if any depredations were reported to me in the future I would have the guilty party arrested and punished, and that the settlers would be treated in like manner. Simon said he would remain all Winter at Horse Plains and would arrest and punish any of his people who might do wrong, but in case they resisted his power he would call upon me to aid him.

The settlers feel perfectly assured that no trouble will occur while Simon remains on the Plains, but fear the worst when he returns to the lower country. Some inducement should be held out to Simon to remain at Horse Plains, as it would be a cheaper and better mode of providing against trouble than by stationing military there for the purpose of protecting six or eight settlers, who are disappointed and chagrined at the delay of the North Pacific Railroad company in building their road through the country as was supposed would be the result when the land was occupied by them, and thus afford an outlet and a market.

No doubt some of the Indians of Horse Plains are overbearing, disagreeable, mischievous, and tantalize the Whites by their petty thefts and depredating proclivities, but no serious difficulty has yet transpired.

I trust, as they do not belong on this reservation, that special instructions be given me if I am supposed to be accountable for their future behavior.

I have the honor to enclose complaints from one of the settlers, — who failed to attend the meeting, — prefering to put them in writing.

Very respectfully,
Your obdt servt,
Peter Ronan
U.S. Ind. Agent.

Document 25

The Adventures of Pete Matte

February-March 1878

Source: "Horse-Stealing, Again," *The Weekly Missoulian*, February 15, 1878, page 3, col. 2; *The Weekly Missoulian*, February 15, 1878, page 3, col. 2; "Lynching of Pete Matte," *The New North-West* (Deer Lodge, Mont.) March 15, 1878, page 3, col. 2.

Editors' note: Pete Matte was accused of being an equal opportunity horse thief, stealing both Indian and white owned horses in the Bitterroot Valley. He was lynched without trial soon after.

Horse-Stealing, Again.

Our dissertation last week on the subject of horse stealing, and the further fact of horses constantly disappearing from their accustomed ranges, has had the effect of calling attention to a matter in which it seems that the joke is being carried a little too far. Sheriff [M. M.] Drouillard started up to Stevensville Tuesday night, with the avowed purpose of placing Pete Matte where he would do the most good — in the penitentiary. He was seen Tuesday riding a horse belonging to I. A. Robinson (if any evidence were necessary to convict him of horse stealing) and it is now said they have the dead wood on him. Indeed, it could not be regarded as an open question for years that Pete was a horse thief, if not worse. Over four years ago he was in the Missoula jail for some time for being concerned with the Gash boys in the murder of a man named Goodwin in Idaho, and they only escaped merited punishment at that time from the failure of the Governor of Idaho to send a requisition for them. A reward has been hanging over his head since that time, and no one has seemed to want money bad enough to claim the reward. The most remarkable thing in connection with this matter is, that a murderer and horse thief should be allowed without molestation in any community. The effort now being made for his apprehension must not fail: he will be more dangerous to the community being banished and returning on accasional [sic] marauding expeditions than he is at present. His death by violence is only a question of time: at the time of the Big Hole battle he was found by the soldiers hovering about the Nez Perces' camp in company with A. K. Gird, with the apparent design of stealing

Indian horses. Gird has since died a violent death. There have been numberless occasions in the last four years when two resolute men could have arrested this outlaw — one to pinion and the other to disarm him. He has, no doubt, confederates — both white and Indian — to give him notice of approaching danger, and to aid him in his nefarious work. The nature of the case requires that every orderly person in the country constitute himself a policeman for society, to ferret out and punish these outlaws.

* * * * * * * *

Francois, an Indian living near Stevensville, who is fully up to the average citizen anywhere, came down Tuesday on business connected with putting a stop to the horse stealing business. He believes that there have been fully fifty horses stolen out of Bitter Root valley this winter. Pete Matte, after an absence of eight or ten days, returned to Stevensville last Saturday. He was probably engaged in driving up the canyon the horses mentioned in last week's paper. Francois mentions that Pete Matte once before stole from him twenty-seven head of horses, which he luckily got back because some Indian friends who knew the horses, were camped on Big Blackfoot, and took them away from Pete.

* * * * * * * *

Lynching of Pete Matte.
He is Captured and Hung in Bitter Root Valley.

For several years Pete Matte has been one of the worst characters in Montana. He with an accomplice undoubtedly murdered a man in Snake River Valley for his money. Pete escaped from the Missoula jail before getting his deserts for that offense. Before and since that he has made horse-stealing his profession and was so adept at the business that probably several hundred head of horses have been stolen by him and his "pals" from citizens of Deer Lodge and Missoula counties. Laterly [sic] the thieving of Pete and his crowd has become so extensive that unusual exertions were made to capture them, but until Saturday last unavailingly. On that day, however, he was caught, and on Sunday morning paid the penalty of his crimes on a pine tree in the valley above Stevensville at the hands of, it is supposed, citizens.

The circumstances as related to us by Mr. Robertson, a cattle dealer from Utah, who saw his body Sunday morning after it was cut down, were as follows: Matte was captured on Saturday morning at Goodwin's ranch, something more than twenty miles above Stevensville in Bitter Root valley. The arrest was made by Sheriff Drouillard and two deputies. The accounts differ immaterially as to to [sic] the manner of capture. The officers say they surprised him very early in the morning while he was passing between the house and the barn; that they ordered him to throw up his hands and he did so, becoming a prisoner without resistance. Pete's wife says the officers came into the house, took him by surprise and captured him there. She says that she and Pete had been camping out for some time on the mountain side; that Goodwin told Pete it was a shame to keep his wife out that way in the mountains, and that he had, therefore, brought her in only the evening before.

Matte was forthwith brought to Stevensville, where the party stopped for the night. Our informant understands that the Sheriff slept with the prisoner — both shackled together that there might be no possibility of Matte's escape. Between 12 and 2 o'clock the officers report a number of masked and armed men came into the room, removed the shackles and took Matte away with them. His body was found the next morning suspended to a tree about one and one-half miles from Stevensville. He had been hanged by the neck until dead. Although Matte was a criminal, doubtless guilty of murder, and an outlaw by that and his nefarious business; although he had proven by a record of years that he would cut a throat or steal a horse at any hour, his hanging by summary process remains a violent infraction of law and unjustifiable taking of life. He had been captured; was in the hands of a *posse* of officers of the law sufficiently strong to place him in prison, and have him tried and punished by the legally constituted tribunals. It is only when there is no adequate law or the Courts are proven inadequate, insufficient or corrupt in the administration of the laws that a resort to Vigilantism is justifiable, and no such condition exists in Missoula county. An infraction like the above works no good to a community.

Document 26

Tribal Law Enforcement on the Reservation

March-April 1878

Source: "Why Indians Abandon the Reservation," *The Weekly Missoulian*, March 29, 1878, page 3, col. 3-4; "The Indian Side of the Question," *The Weekly Missoulian*, April 12, 1878, page 3, col. 3-4; Omar G. V. Gregg, "An Open Letter," *The New North-West* (Deer Lodge, Mont.), April 26, 1878, page 3, col. 6; *The Weekly Missoulian*, May 3, 1878, page 3, col. 2.

Editors' note: Local whites and the United States government tried to impose white concepts of justice on tribal leaders on the Flathead Indian Reservation.

Why Indians Abandon the Reservation.

O. G. V. Gregg, writing from Flathead Agency, upon a subject of which he has had abundant opportunities to become well informed, sends a lengthy communication upon this subject, from which the following extracts are taken:

"Much has been said of late regarding the continuous camping of Indians belonging to the reservation in and around Missoula. To any one versed in Indian nature this does not seem strange, as it is the height of an Indian's nature to make a living for himself and his family as easily as possible. Were it not for the inducements that they receive from the different villages throughout the Territory, doubtless they would have to devote more time to hunting and fishing. The treaty framed between the U.S. Government and themselves grants them the privilege of hunting and fishing throughout the Territory; that is, as long as they observe the treaty.

"One small party, belonging to the confederated tribes, seldom, if ever, comes on to the reservation, for fear of being punished in a most brutal manner. Flogging, carried into effect by one of their petty chiefs, has caused many to abandon their homes and seek refuge from the hands of tyrants in other localities. A little over one year ago, the U.S. Grant Jury, then convened at Deer Lodge, ordered flogging abolished, since which time it has been practiced in the dead hours of night.

"It may be necessary here to state that there are only two crimes that are punishable — fornication or adultery. The punishment that now awaits the perpetrators of the above crimes is to be confined in a small log cabin, dark as a dungeon, to be placed in a lying position, tied hands and feet, to subsist upon a scanty allowance of bread and water for weeks at a time, whilst those that have committed theft, and those who have murdered their wives and daughters, are permitted to roam at large.

"That the Indian would be better off if he were to remain upon his reservation, and that there should be some mode of punishment inflicted upon all that are guilty of crime, all will admit, but, whatever the punishment is, let it be accordance with the customs of civilized nations."

The communication in regard to the punishment of offences among Indians may be construed as an intimation of censure upon the authorities at the Agency. It cannot be properly so regarded. It is merely the opening up of one of the great questions where the Indian policy is radically at fault, and discloses the fact that, under that policy, Indians are amenable to no law. An Indian can commit murder or steal anywhere in the Territory, and the probabilities are that, if his punishment is attempted by the civil authorities, he will be demanded by the government. The government pursues a manifestly vicious policy in allowing Indians to deal with their own offenders in their own way. The whole theory of Indian jurisprudence is a compelling of recompense to the party injured. We ought to be persuaded that it is dangerous to allow a people who have but faint ideas of what is necessary for the welfare of society to administer laws for the good of society. We ought to be persuaded that barbarians, who are allowed to continue the practices of barbarians, will forever remain barbarians. They should be taught better things, and be taught them by the strong arm of the law. If an Indian is convinced that he will be punished for wrong doing, he will not be long in finding out the expediency of doing right. They should not be allowed to make and execute their own laws, but should have them framed and executed by a people of superior civilization. Republican institutions among savages are not wholesome. The only punishment, according to our correspondent, is that designed to enforce a conviction of the sanctity of the marriage relation among Indians. Their ideas are loose upon this question. The original Indian idea made a wife a purchasable article, value computed in ponies, and to be put away at will. The eradication of this idea cannot be accomplished in one generation, and the teachers who have been among the Indians are entitled to much credit for the advanced state of the inculcation of this idea of our religion. The opinion that the Indians possess superior traits of character in many respects has frequently been expressed in these columns. Take the same number of the white race, and let them become vagabonds in the country, spending their time in idleness, and deriving their subsistence as they can, and they would speedily degenerate into outlaws and fall to cutting each other's throats. But it does seem possible that Indians can be made better, and one important step in this direction is to encourage them to quit their nomadic habits and adopt the habits of civilization, in their domestic relations and in their methods of subsistence, as speedily as possible.

— *The Weekly Missoulian*

* * * * * * * *

The Indian Side of the Question.

The question of Indian cruelty assumed a tangible shape two weeks ago. An old Indian woman was circulating disparaging reports, and appealed to the citizens to interfere in behalf of humanity. In no spirit of officiousness, but as friends of the Agent, and well-wishers for a correct administration of affairs upon the reservation, two citizens of this place joined in a letter to the agent. Here is the letter, and the proceedings thereon:

Missoula, Montana, April 2, 1878.

Maj. Ronan:

Dear Sir — This old woman says her daughter has been in the Indian jail twenty-one days; that her wrists have been tied with cords until her hands are fearfully swollen. For the credit of the Agency, it seems a case requiring your investigation, and, if the case is as reported, you out to stretch your authority to see that she has better treatment.

— — — — — — — — —

Gentleman:

Your letter of April 2d reached me by messenger on the same date, and on the 3d I repaired to the Mission, taking with me the bearer of the letter and my official interpreter. I was much pleased that the opportunity arose, through your letter, to set the good people of Missoula and elsewhere right upon the matter referred to, as interested parties, as my investigation proves, have foully and wilfully [sic] misrepresented the conduct of Indian laws and discipline upon this reservation.

Andra, one of the head men and chief of Indian police, immediately upon my arrival, called his policemen together in council, and I told my interpreter to carefully interpret your letter, as I read it, word for word, to them, and ask if it contained the truth.

Andra made the following reply to it:

"I am now sixty-eight years of age — I never committed a cruel act in my life. The daughter of this woman, who brought that letter to you, is in jail under sentence of 26 days; her time will expire on Sunday morning, when she will be let out, and her lawful husband will be here to take her to his lodge. Her

husband is an older man than I am, a chief in our tribe; his name is 'Big Lance.'
She deserted him, and ran off with a young Indian of the Spokane tribe. I
heard of it, and sent out my police and overhauled them at Horse Plains, and
brought them back. The Spokane Indian I will keep in jail for 30 days, and
then send him back to his people, who will again punish him — perhaps not
so much, but he will be punished. The woman, on next Sunday, I will give to
her husband, who will be here to take her to his lodge. Is there anything wrong
in this?"

Agent — "The letter says the woman's wrists are tied and lacerated."

Andra — "Your government built the jail; no separate rooms are made. I
keep a guard about the jail nearly all the time. When we have a pair of adulterers
in jail, we must keep them separate. When my guard goes away, they are tied to
keep them apart, but never to hurt them."

Agent — "The letter says the woman is starved to a skeleton."

Andra — "The letter lies. Three times a day the prisoners are fed everything
that my people and family have to eat themselves; and three times a day they
are taken out to walk in the air and sun — all day Sunday they are allowed out
under a guard."

Agent — (to the woman) — "Have you seen your daughter, and are you
satisfied with her treatment?"

Woman — "I have seen her, and she is sorry for what she has done; she is
not badly treated."

Agent — "Why did you bring me such a letter?"

Woman — "A young Indian told me a lie at Missoula."

Agent — "Are you satisfied with what Andra says?"

Woman — "Yes; Andra told me to live and eat with his family until Sunday,
when he will let my daughter go back to her husband's lodge, and I will stay
and visit her, and try to make it up between them."

Agent — "Then you are satisfied."

Woman — "Yes."

Agent — "It has been written to Missoula, and printed in the paper, that
you whip prisoners in the dead hour of night."

Andra — "Indians are not cowards; if we had any whipping to do, we
would do it in the day-time."

Agent — "Then you do not whip prisoners."

Andra — "For over a year that law is changed, and no one is whipped; nor
has any one been whipped for any offense. I try to keep my Indians good. The
most of them are good; but it takes force to keep some in the straight road."

Agent — "What crimes are punishable?"

Andra — "Every wrong that is done: stealing from each other, gambling, adultery, drunkenness, or anything else that is wrong. You white men have a law to send your people to jail for many months for giving whisky to Indians. Now, I can send any one of my young men to Missoula, and give him something to trade, and he will come back with all the whisky I want; but I do not let them trade for whisky; they go to jail if they do — it is our law. In Missoula, they can get drunk and get whisky. You have a law against it, why is it not enforced. Why do not the white people drive our bad Indians away from their town. They hide bad people when I send for them. White men would not like to have me hide their bad people here. You said it was printed in the paper that my prisoners were whipped in the dead of night. Who is my enemy that told such a lie?"

Agent — "It will do you no good to know."

* * * * * * * *

An Open Letter.
How the Flathead Police Administer Punishment.

To the Editor New North-West:

The question of Indian brutality as published a short time since in the *Missoulian*, led to a partial investigation on the 9th instant. It is not necessary to repeat the full proceedings of the council held, only suffice it to say that it has not changed public opinion in the least. It could reasonably be expected by all persons of intelligence that it would be denied by Chief Andra and his police force. Had the investigation alluded to been held with those who have shared in this punishment, or even with spectators, things might have borne a different aspect. But it stands today just where it has for years, unmolested. Over one year ago the U.S. Court, then convened in Deer Lodge, ordered flogging abolished; but it seems that afterwards it was kept up for a short space of time. Determined to not get foiled in their fiendish mode of punishment Chief Andra and his advisers adopted another method more brutal because of its long duration, viz.: The prisoners to be confined in a small log cabin and to be tied with cords for weeks at a time. Often is it the case that for weeks after the prisoners are given their liberty the prints of these cords are quite noticeable. Andra's report as published in the *Missoulian* regarding the kind treatment prisoners receive at his hands is a manufactured falsehood, gotten up in order to exhonorate [sic] himself and shield from further comment his tyranical advisers undoubtedly premeditated several days prior to having this interview. He gives for an excuse, that tying is his only method of keeping separated two adulterers. Has he forgot that the log building referred to contains five separate apartments, or does he think for a moment that no one outside of an *Indian* has knowledge of the fact? His statement, contradictory to flogging, may or may not be true, as my informant may have testified falsely, but positive evidence can be produced that he did flog after receiving orders to stop it. As before stated, women have been arrested at midnight in the town of Missoula for prostitution and taken to the Reservation and punished severely, whilst murderers and thieves are allowed to run at large, thus bidding defiance to both Territorial and Indian law. One thing quite noticeable regarding the crime they utterly detest is that certain parties even bid defiance to their law, living in adultery for years at a time under their observation, and simply because Andra and his police force know quite well they would resist being arrested, do not make an effort to meddle with them. Whence this change from brutal to kind treatment? Will some one rise and explain? When was this jail building altered so as to contain only one room? Dark as a dungeon, with scarcely ventilation enough to sustain life, the prisoner there remains to serve out the sentence pronounced upon him by his tyranical judge. Have not their cries been heard the whole night long? Whether it is better for the people of Missoula to tolerate the continual camping of these Indians around their town, or to see that they be allowed to return to their reservation unmolested; or, if punishment is necessary to check that crime, to see that it is done according to the laws and customs of the United States, time alone will prove.

Omar G. V. Gregg.

Flathead Agency, April 18, 1878.

* * * * * * * *

Omar G. V. Gregg, well known in this county, and who has secured the title of "Jocko Missionary," from his connection with the Flathead Mission, as printer for the Fathers, was ordered off the reservation by Agent [Peter] Ronan on Tuesday — a few minutes after the receipt of the last *North-west* at the Agency.

Document 27

Duncan McDonald Wrote Indian History of Nez Perce War April 1878

Source: Duncan McDonald to L. V. McWhorter, February 1, 1928, box 8, folder 40, Lucullus V. McWhorter Papers, Manuscripts, Archives, and Special Collections, Washington State University Libraries, Pullman, Washington.

Editors' note: Most of this letter describes McDonald's efforts to research the Indian side of the Nez Perce War, including his 1878 trip to Canada to interview Nez Perce Chief White Bird and other survivors. His history was published in the *New North-West*, a Deer Lodge, Montana, newspaper, in 1878 and 1879. McDonald suggested he had no contact with the hostiles in 1877, which does not agree with some Nez Perce traditions recorded by Camille Williams, a Nez Perce historian. Note McDonald's comments about feeling caught between the Indian and white communities because of his mixed blood heritage. Some of this letter was very hard to decipher. It is rendered here as accurately as possible. Some periods have been added.

Dixon February 1st 1928

L. V. McWhorter
Yakim'a Wash.
Dear Sir
    Yours of the 16th Ult. was received and note of what you say about pay regarding Chief White Bird. The very man I wanted to meet across the line while he and Sitting Bull were camping together. I made the trip at my own expense no one influenced me to take the undertaking. only I wanted to know the facts and not beliefs. My reason, I was asked by Cap James Mills who was publishing the New North West in Deer Lodge. he wanted to write up the cause of the war from the Indian point of view and by asking who he could get the information from Indian side. By inquiring he was told to give the job to Duncan McDonald living on the Flathead Indian reservation. This man is the writer. Mr Mills was the owner of the newspaper. at same time was the Secretary of the state of Montana. I agreed to him I will do the best I can, but I never told him that I was leaving for Canada to see Chief White Bird. he never new where I was until I wrote him from Canada That I was with White

Duncan McDonald
Source: Montana Historical Society, Photograph Archives, Helena, 943-624.

Bird. he sent me papers to whom it may concern and enlightning them of my business. You ask how far I was from Big Hole battlefield. I was about four miles west of Missoula when I met the volunteers going back to Missoula. I asked them where are the hostiles. They told me that they are out of the Lo Lo or Capt [C. C.] Rawns Fort and moved up the Bitter Root Valley. In getting this information I changed my notion and returned to Missoula. I was calculating to go right into the hostile camp, since they got out Lo Lo I quit.

I was home when the battle took place at Big Hole. You know if every or warrior will tell you he will tell only his experience. for my part I would not bother asking only the leaders. White Bird & Looking Glass refused Chief Joseph point blank to surrender after Chief Joseph told them that the Army officers offered good promise & he will surender. Shortly after Looking Glass was Killed shot through the head & fell at the feet of his brother Task Alex-see mae, he was the last man Killed in battle near Bear Paw Mountains. you mention of a good narrative of the wife of Chief AlaKats wife. I dont understand as I Knew her personally. one of the pretties women of the tribe and was badly wounded at the battle of Big Hole & died shortly two or three days later. AlaKat Twat-we-toat & Looking Glass were all Killed at Bear Paw battle.

I am not anxious to bleed any one in this matter but I am not in a position about ready cash and I am at a loss to say how much I want.

As I understand you wanted to Know from first hand getting Chief White [Bird] to go to Fort Walsh & there meet an american officer to make arrangements to to [sic] surrender. And how it happened I was in the ring as an interpreter. And how did he consented. Bear in mind I fell in with Col. [Acheson G.] Irvine with a bunch of Mounted police. It seems he was detailed by Col. McLeod [James F. Macleod] who was the senior officer at Fort Walsh. The bulk of the force was stationed for short time as the America Capt [George William] Baird he would not take any chances regarding his scalp to go to Sitting Bulls. Chief White Bird camping together & a noted of Little Bear Nez Chief is the man that Col. McLeod feared. he stands about as Big as Sitting Bull, very threatening & restles. Poor White Bird I guess he thought by remaining with Sitting Bull that he was safe. Col. McLeod was very anxious to get rid of Sitting Bull and White Bird. so there was much scheming to get rid of American Indians peaceably if possible.

White Bird & Looking [Glass] never met Gen [Nelson A.] Miles or Gen [Oliver O.] Howard at the battle ground only Chief Joseph & Yellow Bull acted as messenger to Looking Glass & White Bird. at one time Joseph was with troops when they were fighting Lieut Jerome was with the Indians. So far my letter will be understood my Knowledge of the Council & Fort Walsh.

I remain yours truly
Duncan McDonald

You suggest if I want to read a little pamphlet "Crime against the Yakama's" you would send me one. I would be pleased to have it. Did you every make friends with any white man when you can prove that he was telling a big lie. I made enemies among the whites because I corrected them about their story and I need not worry about their feelings towards me. It is a long ago since the Nez Perces war took place, but some of my writings in the New North West are still in the Historical library of Montana at the Capital Helena. I am in the same box as the Kaisar of Germany. the germans [curse?] him that he was too much of pro British because his mother was british and the british hate him that he was too much of a German, because his father was a German. this is my predicament.

Document 28

Flathead Reservation Chiefs Complain About Ammunition Ban May 1, 1878

Source: "Tales of the Times," *The Anaconda Standard*, April 30, 1893, page 9, col. 1-2.

Editors' note: The three principal chiefs of the Flathead Reservation tribes complained in 1878 about the unfairness of withholding ammunition and guns from peaceful tribes. The Indians needed guns and ammunition to feed themselves and protect them from enemy tribes on the Great Plains.

Tales of the Times.
True Stories and Fanciful Yarns Illustrative of Modern Life and Character.
Written for the Standard.

The following letter was dictated nearly 15 years ago by Arlee, chief of the Flatheads, Michel, chief of the Pend d'Oreilles, and Eneas, chief of the Kootenais. The two latter chieftains are living still, but Arlee has gone to the happy hunting grounds. The station near the Flathead Agency was called Arlee in honor of this Flathead chief, and his burial place is in the Indian burying ground, near the church at the agency:

Flathead Agency, Mont., May 1, '78.
E. A. Hoyt, Commissioner of Indian Affairs, Washington, D.C.
Honored Sir:

We cannot read words but from those we hear spoken from our agent, and others we feel that you have a good heart for the Indian, and whenever it is in your power, you will try to do him justice and smooth his rough road. For over 30 years we have had Catholic missionaries among us, who teach us the gospel, and try to point out the trail which will lead to the white man's road. Some of us have houses to live in — have good farms fenced — have crops now planted — have families growing up around us; and our laws forbid that we have more than one wife. We never have had war or trouble with your people, and during all our lives, until last summer we could go to traders and buy guns and ammunition. While the Nez Perces were on the warpath we did not care to buy ammunition or guns as it might look bad to the whites, as that tribe of Indians has always been our friends and allies in our wars against the

Blackfeet, the Sioux and other enemies. War is over now and our young men after laboring in the fields and gathering in their crops, thought it hard when the agent told them they could not buy ammunition with which to hunt. We know his advice is good to stay at home and cultivate the land and take care of one's crops, as in the near future the disappearance of game, as the whites advance upon our hunting grounds, will compel us to rely upon the earth to produce food from our toil to support our children. But our crops are planted, and the buffalo are only a short distance from us across the mountains on the east side, over a trail that leads through no white settlements. They are plentiful and our young men desire to hunt them and procure meat while the old people stay at home and take care of the crops until they ripen, when all will return from the hunt and help to gather them; but our agent tells us we cannot buy ammunition except powder, ball and caps. Such ammunition is of no use to us as we have no muzzle loading guns, nor could we buy them if we had the money, as they are not now for sale that we know of. We cannot throw our good guns away — they cost us very much money. We have forgotten the use of the bow and arrow. We are told it is your wish that we stay at home; this is good advice; we are doing our best to bring our children up to work, but when the crops are planted and nothing to do, we feel that it would be a great wrong to force our young men to stay at home when they so much love to hunt the buffalo, and return the time work commences, cheerful and happy and well supplied with meat and furs to gladden the hears of the old people. We who address you are the head chiefs of the tribes — the time is fast coming when we will be in our graves, for we are three old men; we love our people, and we hope you will not refuse us the only source of great pleasure we have in our lives, the opportunity to have guns and ammunition with which to kill game. The Great Spirit knows we do not want them for war, for when the white people were few in our country we always treated them as friends. The great war chief of the soldiers. General [John] Gibbon, was here lately, and he knew us and most of our old men. He was willing that we should have metallic ammunition, good to hunt with, but our agent says that he must obey the orders of a greater peace chief, who gave the order that fixed ammunition must not be sold to Indians. Now we will await anxiously to hear your written words, and hope our prayer will be granted.

Arlee, (his X)
Head Chief Flatheads.
Michel, (his X)
Head Chief Pend d'Oreilles.
Eneas, (his X)
Head Chief Kootenais.

Interpreter, Michel Revais.

Witness to marks, N. A. Lambert.

Hardly 75 years have passed since the foregoing letter was dictated by the Indians chiefs of the Flathead reservation, and for several years past not a vestige of those magnificent wild animals are to be found upon the former hunting ground, or in fact anywhere in the boundaries of the United States. A herd of nearly 100 head are now owned by two half-breed dwellers on the Flathead reservation. This herd came from the natural increase of one yearling bull and two heifers driven by an Indian from the vicinity of Fort Shaw, or Sun river, across the Rocky mountains and over the Cadot pass about 11 years ago to the Flathead reservation. The increase of this herd has averaged about the same as a herd of cattle. Several of the males have been slaughtered, and their meat disposed of in the Missoula butcher shops, while the heads and skins have brought fancy prices. This slaughter of male buffalo was necessary in order to decrease their number in conformity with the number of cows running in the herd. It is understood that the herd will be placed on exhibition at the world's fair, as a resident of Butte has been negotiating with the owners to give bonds for the safe return of the buffalo on the range on the Flathead reservation or a stipulated value of any animal that may not be returned. Twenty thousand dollars was the amount stipulated to be paid to Charles Allard and Michael Pabolo, the mixed blood owners of the herd, for their use for exhibition at the world's fair for six months, the full bond to be put up, is said to be in the neighborhood of $400,000. It will be a great disappointment if anything should occur to prevent the exhibition of this magnificent herd of Montana buffalo at Chicago.

Document 29

Salish Friendship vs. White Hostility

May 6, 1878

Source: Jerome D'Aste, S.J., to Rev. and Dear Father, May 6, 1878, *Woodstock Letters*, vol. 7, no. 3 (1878) pages 179-184.

Editors' Note: The Bitterroot Salish protected the whites despite hostile actions of the whites towards the Indians in 1877. Father D'Aste also recounted the losses the Salish suffered because they were not allowed to purchase ammunition for the buffalo hunt after their crops had failed while they were protecting the white settlers in the Bitterroot Valley.

St. Mary's, Montana Ty., May 6th, 1878.

Rev. and Dear Father,

P. C.

To give your Reverence some idea of this mission among the Flat-Head Indians of St. Mary's Valley, or as the whites now call it, Bitter-Root Valley, in Montana Territory, I must make some remarks about their relations with the Government and with the whites. You must not imagine that we are here in a wilderness, far apart from the civilized world. No, we have, in this valley which extends about sixty miles, a populous settlement of whites.

Formerly, indeed, this valley was an Indian Reservation, and according to Governor [Isaac] Stevens' treaty, made in 1855, with the three united tribes of the Flat-Heads, Pen-d'Oreilles, and Koote-nays, no white man should have been allowed to pass an established temporary boundary, until the Government would decide whether another valley, that of the Jocko, the actual Reservation of the Pen-d'Oreille Indians, would be more fit for them. But little by little the whites, some with permission of the chief of the tribe, others without it, began to pass the established boundary, and when a few years ago the Bitter-Root Valley was opened for settlers, it was already taken up by whites.

Our Indians are now in a very precarious condition. The Government, in consequence of the misrepresentations of the money-seeking officials, regards the Flat-Head tribe as having given up their tribal relations, and patents have been issued by the Land Office for the fifty-two families which are supposed to be willing to become citizens, the other families being regarded as having removed to the Jocko Reservation. But the Indians continue to go on as before; they still consider their chief as their principal authority, and few only are living on the farms surveyed for them, and for which the patents, though issued two years ago, are not yet delivered. The only difference is, that for the last six years they have not received a cent from the Government. A few of the Flat-Heads, about six families, moved to the Jocko Reservation, and it is among these few families that are divided the five thousand dollars which were promised these Indians for ten years, besides the annuities, granted by the treaty made with Gen. [James] Garfield, about six years ago. While the whole of the tribe here in Bitter-Root Valley, about three hundred and fifty in number, in recompense for their historical fidelity to the Government and the whites have to support themselves as best they can. To aggravate their condition they are now forbidden to buy ammunition, though most of them have paid high prices for their breechloading guns. Moreover very few of them have any seed, so that, next summer, their condition will be worse. The only means of subsistence left to them, at present is the buffalo-hunt. But this, besides the inconvenience of detaining them for about eight months in the year, far from the mission, is now full of danger; their horses and lives being exposed to the greediness of a multitude of hostile Indians, who are well armed. In fact, last winter our Indians lost many horses on the buffalo ground.

In proof of the fidelity of these Flat-Heads to the Government, and of their friendship to the whites, notwithstanding the ill treatment they have experienced at the hands of government officials, and of many whites, I will give you a brief account of their behavior during the late Nez-Percés war, from which also your Reverence will see the influence our holy religion has over the passions of these savages, and that our work among them is not altogether fruitless.

Early last summer, as soon as the tidings of the hostility of a band of Nez-Percés in the lower country, reached Bitter-Root Valley, and there appeared some possibility that the hostile Indians might take refuge from the soldiers in this valley with whose passes they were familiar, the whites here became alarmed. There are two Indian trails leading into this valley from the Nez-Percés country in Idaho Territory; one, called the Lo Lo (Laurence) Fork's trail, enters at the lower end of the valley, the other, at the head of the valley. Both trails are very rough, and though many of the Nez-Percés used to follow them to the buffalo hunt, it was generally thought impossible for them to enter by either, burdened as they were with women and children and over one thousand horses. But as soon as the rumor spread that the soldiers were driving the Indians towards these trails, most of the Bitter-Root Valley settlers, many of whom were already prejudiced against the Flat-Heads, chiefly on account of their being Catholic, began openly to show their feelings; and the more so because a few of these Indians are intermarried with Nez-Percés, and some Nez-Percés families lived in the valley. The alarm grew to such an extent that they sent for arms, built three forts, and *some weeks* before the hostile party arrived, left their farms and shut up themselves and families in the forts. The newspapers of the county had frequent spicy articles full of calumnies against the Flat-Heads, and exciting in the settlers feelings of fear and distrust. Every movement of the Indians was watched; in their most innocent actions hostile intentions were discovered by the alarmed people; no powder nor ammunition was allowed to be sold to them. It was of no use for me to tell the people that they had no reason to suspect the Flat-Heads; that by acting in so distrustful and cowardly a way without the least foundation for it, they were provoking the Indians and exciting them to revolt. The settlers would not believe me and some went so far as to say that the Fathers were urging the Indians to get rid of the white settlers.

At last the official news came that the hostile band, driven by the soldiers, was entering Bitter-Root Valley by Lo Lo Fork's trail. The excitement then grew intense. Many people were talking of killing all the Indians. The intentions of Chief Charles [Charlo], son of the famous Flat-Head Chief Victor, were sounded by the Indian Agent and the commanding officer of the recently established military post in Missoula. Charles answered that he and his people would remain neutral, if not provoked by either party. About twenty-five soldiers and all the volunteers that could be gathered together, about two hundred, fortified themselves at the mouth of the Lo Lo Forks' defile, by which the Nez-Percés were coming. The exact number of their warriors was not known, but it was reported that they were well armed and had plenty of horses. Their armed men must have been three hundred or three hundred and fifty, under four principal chiefs, the most notorious of whom was Joseph, now a prisoner in Leavenworth. Some half-breeds, and some whites, friends of our Indians, with the intention of reconciling them with the settlers, persuaded some to follow the volunteers. They went, moved rather by curiosity than by the desire of fighting. It was by them that Charles, in order to avoid fighting, sent word to the hostile party to take some other trail to the buffalo country. The commanding officer, distrusting the courage of his volunteers, many of whom were of the opinion that the hostile Indians should be allowed to pass unmolested through the valley, had two parleys with the enemy who refused to surrender on the severe and, it seems, unreasonable conditions offered to them. A last intimation was therefore given to them, that unless they surrendered by noon of the next day, they would have to fight their way through. They then held a council, in which it was proposed to make a night attack upon the soldiers and volunteers. Had they acted upon this, a regular butchery of the soldiers and whites would have been the result. But their scouts reported that Flat-Heads were in the volunteers' camp; and fearing to be obliged to fight not only the whites but also the Flat-Heads and their allies, the Pen-d'Oreilles and Kootenays, they took the bold resolution of getting out of the defile by way of the hills. So, early in the morning they broke up their camp, and climbing up a steep hill which it was thought impossible for them to ascend, encumbered as they were with about two thousand tired horses and a multitude of women and children, and in sight of the soldiers and volunteers, they emerged from the defile in splendid order and marched up the valley without a shot being fired on either side, and encamped about five miles further upon the road.

Next day, Sunday, they again decamped and were to pass about a mile from our Mission, on the opposite side of the river. Charles, who did not like the idea of being slighted by the Nez-Percés, gathered around the Mission all his Indians, about seventy in number, many of them without arms or ammunition, and went out to see them pass, ready to fight them had they showed any such inclination. He had told his men before to pray with fervor at the Mass I said for them early in the morning, When the Nez-Percés passed by, all well armed, Charles, with true bravery, refused to shake hands with their chiefs, or to have any communication with them, because of the murders committed by them in Idaho Territory.

For the next two days, the settlers, whose love of money overcame their fear of the hostile Indians, began to trade with them. They were destitute of provisions, though they had plenty of money. To give you an idea of the booty they had accumulated in Idaho Territory by the destruction of several large stores and by robbing a large party of Chinamen, I will say that they had rolls of gold coin, heavy bags of gold dust and a quantity of greenbacks. In the small village of Stevensville, near our Mission, they spent over one thousand dollars, and would have spent more had they not been hurried off by the news that [Gen. O. O.] Howard was close behind them with a large force.

The sight of these Nez-Percés, all well armed, boasting of their exploits in Idaho Territory, and almost masters of the country, was a great enticement for our Indians. Yet not one joined them. What a contrast to the good behavior of our Indians was that of some whites who, for the sake of making a few dollars, sold whiskey to the savages, thus exposing the whole settlement to ruin. To the praise of our Indians, be it said, that after the Nez-Percés went out of the valley according to their promise, without molesting the settlers, Charles, in accordance with the neutrality he professed, refused even a scout to the General.

Among the Nez-Percés that passed here there were no Catholics, with the exception of a few women who were forced to follow the camp.

Such a proof of fidelity on the part of our Indians should have convinced the government officials that they had nothing to fear from our Catholic Indians; and yet they are forbidden ammunition for hunting purposes. May God reward them for their uprightness and relieve them from the distress which it has brought upon them.

Your humble servant.

J. D'A., S.J.

Jerome D'Aste, S.J.
Source: Jesuit Archives and Research Center, St. Louis, Missouri, #1037.02.

Document 30

Bitterroot Salish Join Whites Fighting
Nez Perce Hostiles
June 1878

Source: C. S. Nichols, "Stevensville Pioneer Tells Interesting Story of the Chase After Chief Joseph's Renegades," *The Daily Missoulian*, May 28, 1916, ed. section, page 1, col. 1-7.

Editors' note: Nichols' account described how in 1878 prominent Salish leaders joined the army and the Bitterroot whites in chasing a band of hostile Nez Perce out of Montana.

Stevensville Pioneer Tells Interesting Story of the Chase
After Chief Joseph's Renegades

Editor Missoulian: —

I have been much interested in reading, in recent number of The Missoulian, the stories by Frank B. Brown, Frank Keim and W. B. Harlan regarding the raid by the Nez Perce Indians under the leadership of the half-breed, Chief Tabahoe, in the early summer of 1878.

Having been one of the number of the settlers who pursued this band of renegade Indians through the upper Bitter Root valley in June of that year, I want to add my version of the story, as it may cover some points not touched upon by the local historians.

I came to the Bitter Root valley with my father and brothers, from Iowa, and landed at Fort Owen (now Stevensville) July 10, 1865. I have lived in the Bitter Root valley ever since. In June, 1878, my brothers, Cash and Webster, and I were living at the Joe Pardee ranch, on Gird's creek, now a part of the Marcus Daly ranch at Hamilton. At that time Mr. Pardee with eight or ten men was building the first wagon road over Big Hole mountain. Our camp was about halfway between the foot of the mountain and the top — about six miles east of Ross' hole, and about 25 miles east of the forks of the Bitter Root river.

The first news we had of the presence of hostile Indians in the valley was brought us by my Brother Webster, Al Harris and Sam Chaffin. They rode all night to Pardee's camp, arriving there just at daylight. It was early June. They told us that a band of renegade Nez Perces, who had been living in the northern country since the capture of Chief Joseph and his band by General

[Nelson] Miles the fall before, had killed two men in the Flint creek valley and were then headed up the Bitter Root. That they would probably come through the Ross Fork trail and advised us to move down to the Pardee ranch on Gird's creek until they had passed through.

We hitched up our teams and moved camp that morning, but Mr. Pardee rode over to the Big Hole to meet Ed Bass' freight team that was expected any day from Corinne, Utah. We reached the Pardee ranch the second night, but saw no sign of Indians. A day or two afterwards my Brother Webster and I saw a band of horses coming down the ridge into the valley, between Willow creek (now Corvallis) and Gird's creek, but we could not tell whether the horses were being driven or running loose. We suspected, however, that they might be Indians.

That night they camped somewhere in the vicinity of Skalkaho canyon, about eight miles southeast of Hamilton. Early the next morning they raided Jerry Fahey's camp, before he had gotten up. He and one other man, with 16 pack animals and two riding horses were camped at the mouth of Sleeping Child, where it empties into the Bitter Root river. He had outfitted at Stevensville and was en route to Gibbonsville, Idaho. The Indians captured the pack train, but Fahey and his man escaped into the brush.

The Indians proceeded up the valley, arriving at the Lockwood ranch, at the mouth of Rye creek, where Robert Bell, his brother, Myron Lockwood and a discharged soldier from Fort Missoula were eating their supper.

The Indians surrounded the house, Tabahoe coming in at the back door. The soldier grabbed the only gun the white men had, together with 50 cartridges in a flour sack. He placed the muzzle of the gun against Tabahoe' stomach, and told him he would shoot unless he allowed the white men to get away, holding the gun in that position until all but himself had gained safety in the brush. He then took the Indian with him until he thought he was safe, and then plunged into the brush himself. As he did so one of the other Indians shot him through the left arm. The soldier wanted to open fire from the brush, but the Bell brothers persuaded him not to do so. That evening the Indians killed a beef that they had taken and camped about one mile from the ranch near the river. The next morning they took the Elk City trail for Idaho.

When the settlers learned of the raid on Fahey's camp and the Bell brothers' ranch, about 30 of us gathered at the crossing of the Skalkaho to give pursuit. We halted at Sleeping Child creek and organized by electing former Sheriff John Miller captain. Among the number I now recall W. B. Harlan, Mark Slocum, Winfield Moon, Sam Chaffin, Newt Chaffin, Jacob Goff, Gus Nelson, John Sheehan, Jerry Fahey, Rev. Edwin Stanley, a man by the name of Stubblefield, my Brother Webster and myself.

Assembled with us were four Flathead Indians, then living in the valley, our neighbors and friends — Francois La Moose, Narcisse, Louis Vanderberg and Martin Charlot, son of Charlot, the Flathead chief, whose home was across the river, west from Stevensville. Being hurriedly called together, we took only our guns, fishing tackle, salt and about one day's rations. Our commissary department was not very extensive.

About 6 o'clock that evening we met Lieutenant [Thomas S.] Wallace from Fort Missoula with his command of 18 men, and William Turnage, packmaster for the outfit, at the crossing of Vanderhoof creek, where W. B. Harlan's ranch is not [now] situated. They were returning from Ross' Hole, where they had been in search of the Indians. We made them acquainted with the course the Indians had taken, they joining our party and turning back up the river. That night we camped at the mouth of West Fork canyon, the Indians being one day ahead of us.

That night one of the Indians, Francois, came to my Brother Webster and myself, wanting to know if we wanted to "Make Wolf," meaning to go scouting. I asked him who would go with us. He replied, "La Moose, Louis Vanderberg and Martin Charlot," but Lieutenant Wallace would not hear of it unless we took two of his soldiers with us. The Indians would not go if the soldiers went with us, so the idea was abandoned. I believe if we had gone that night the Indians would have been captured, as we came upon their camp about 15 miles up the West Fork the next day.

The idea of the Flathead Indians was to take our horses and follow the Nez Perces until we had located their camp and then as soon as it was light two of us to remain with the horses while the other four should skirt the foothills and get in front of the camp and there hold the hostiles by "pot shooting" until the command could come up.

We followed the Nez Perces until we had crossed the divide into Idaho and were about 12 miles from the south Fork of the Clearwater, perhaps 60 miles from the forks of the Bitter Root river. At dark we made a dry camp on top of a bald mountain and the next morning we had a consultation as to what should be done. A majority of the settlers thought that we had followed the Indians far enough, so we turned back. Lieutenant Wallace, with his soldiers and Fahey and Turnage, kept on after the Indians. They came up with them camped on the Clearwater, but the Indian pickets discovered the approach of the soldiers and gave the war whoop to warn the camp. The Indians took to the timber when Lieutenant Wallace's men opened fire at long range. The only damage done was to kill and wound about 30 head of horses and mules, capturing about 25 more horses. I was told afterwards by an Indian that one of the s....s was shot through the arm. There were 16 bucks and two s....s in the band.

The first night we made camp on our return trip. Gus Nelson was detailed sergeant of the guard. About midnight he went out to relieve the guard and as he passed through the horses, which were picketed near the camp, to see if any were "cast," he was mistaken by the man on guard for an Indian, who shot him through the left arm. It was a terrible wound. Fortunately, Jacob Goff's 15-year-old daughter, when putting up her father's lunch and packing his kit, insisted on putting in an old worn out tablecloth and two pillow slips. When her father asked her "why?" she told him: "They might come in handy for bandages in case any of us were wounded." We took the tablecloth and bandaged up poor Nelson's arm as best we could.

We had camped that night on the West fork of the Bitter Root river, about 16 miles above the forks. Our commissary had completely disappeared, the question confronting us was how to get supper. My Brother Webster and I had brought along with us an extra quantity of salt. We took our fishing tackle and soon had an abundance of trout. Fishing was good in those days. Mr. Stanley, the young minister who had come out to Montana only a year or two before, wanted to know how we were going to cook the trout without any cooking utensils. I told him to wait and he would see; that a man raised on the frontier among the Indians would find some way of cooking it. We did so by building a fire out of dry willow branches and broiling the fish on the coals as you would a beeksteak [sic], except that we had no broiling irons. When we had finished broiling the fish, Stanley remarked that "is a new way of cooking to me. If I stay with you boys long enough I may make a full-fledged Indian fighter."

We afterwards learned that Tabahoe and his band of hostile were captured by the Indian police over in Idaho and sent back to the Indian territory. So ended the last hostile Indian raid in what is now Montana.

C. S. Nichols.

Stevensville, Montana.

Document 31

Chief Michelle Wants Peace with the Whites

July 14, 1878

Source: Peter Ronan, "Indian Matters," *The Helena Independent* (daily), July 21, 1878, page 3, col. 3.

Editors' note: According to Agent Ronan, Pend d'Oreille Chief Michelle refused to join the Sioux in fighting the whites, despite threats from Sitting Bull. Michelle also refused support for Nez Perce refugees traveling home through western Montana.

Indian Matters.
Agent Ronan Interviews Chief Michel.
Sitting Bull Wants the Pen d'Oreilles to Join Him.

Flathead Agency, M.T.,
July 14th, 1879 [i.e., 1878]

B. F. Potts, Governor Montana Territory,
Helena, M. T.:

Sir —

I have to report the following council held with Michel, head chief of the Pen d'Oreilles, Sunday, July 14th, for your information, and any action you may suggest:

Having narrated to Chief Michel the particulars of the murders committed by a band of Nez Perces, who came from the North by way of the north fork of Sun river, murdering as they came along two men at the Dearborn, in Lewis and Clark county; two men at Deep creek, Bear gulch, Deer Lodge county, and four or five miners at the head of Rock creek, in Missoula county; all of which murders were committed in the direct Nez Perces trail from the North to Idaho Territory, known as the Elk city trail. In reply the chief said:

"A few days ago a messenger came to me from Sitting Bull's camp with word from that chief, that if I valued the lives and welfare of my people to gather them together and leave the reservation. If I did not feel like joining him and making war upon the whites — that after he had done his work among the settlers myself and people would come back again and occupy our land without fear of obtrusion."

Agent — "What reply did you send back?"

Michel — "I told the runner to tell his chief that the Pen d'Oreilles were friends of the whites; that years ago, when I was young, the Pen d'Oreilles and the Sioux had met in battle and were enemies. We are now quietly settled down, supporting our families by raising stock and planting crops. Our homes we love. Our lands are beautiful. The crops are ripening, and we will soon be gathering them in. We are not well armed, and have nearly forgotten the modes of war; but a mouse, though small, if trodden upon will turn and bite. Tell your chief if he comes we will give him battle, and die by our homes. This is my answer."

Agent — "What do you think of the murders just committed?"

Michel — "I think that perhaps White Bird — the Nez Perces chief, whose voice is for war — has arranged with Sitting Bull and has sent out small murdering parties to come through Montana to the Lapwai reserve in Idaho, to murder as they go through this country and commit all sorts of crimes in Idaho, and incite the reservation Nez Perces to war, with a promise that Sitting Bull with his warriors will come and help them. This is only my opinion. Perhaps this band of marauders has broken away from White Bird without his consent."

Agent — "Do you not think it best, in order to be prepared, to send scouts on the two trails leading from the North through this reservation?"

Michel — "It is the only way to protect the country. Indians can scout on the trails north of here, and can give you and me information in time to head them off?"

Agent — "Will you send out scouts?"

Michel — "Yes; if they can have arms, ammunition, blankets and provisions and some hope of reward."

Agent — "Providing I can get you these things will you be willing to have white men go with them!"

Michel — "Yes; provided you choose the white men and half-breeds, and that the scouts will be under your and my own control and report to you, when you can easily report to the soldiers when signs are seen. Three lodges of my people are camped on the trail leading in by the Jocko, I will send them word to look out for Nez Perces and bring in news of what route they take. These people are fishing at the lake and are not well armed; they cannot fight, but they can bring us news. If regular scouts go they should be armed, because they cannot otherwise protect themselves if they get into a fight, which they would be apt to do, as the Nez Perces do not feel friendly because we would not join their cause last summer."

Very respectfully,
Peter Ronan,
U.S. Indian Agent.

Document 32

New Farms and Herds on the Reservation

August 5, 1878

Source: "Journey to the West Side," *The Helena Independent* (daily), August 9, 1878, page 2, col. 2-3.

Editors' note: Flathead Reservation Indians made progress in farms and herds in the Jocko and Mission Valleys. The reservation tribes celebrated St. Ignatius day.

Journey to the West Side.
The Peaceful Disposition of the Flatheads.
Butte and its Growing Mining Industries.
                                        Missoula, M.T., August 5, 1878.
To the Editor of the Independent:

Thinking a letter from this part of the country might be acceptable to your readers, I write briefly as possible an account of what I have seen in a few days.

When I left Helena there was much excitement there and along the whole road to this place about the raid the the [sic] Indians (Nez Perces) had made through the country, arising from the murders and robberies they had committed on their route. That is all over now, and Lieut. [Thomas S.] Wallace, of Fort Missoula, has given the murderers such a lesson as will deter others from traveling in their tracks.

After visiting the Jocko Agency and St. Ignatius Mission I am certain there will be no outbreak among the Indians under charge of Agent [Peter] Ronan.

In the course of my journeying I visited Butte, and notwithstanding the strike, which has continued nearly two months, I was astonished at the rapid improvement in the growth of the town since last April. Many new residences and business houses have been built, and new structures are going up all over town. As soon as the strike is over mining will increase rapidly, as a number of new mills are now being constructed ready for working the ores that lay on the dump piles.

From the head of Deer Lodge valley to Frenchtown I have never seen the grain crops look better. The breadth of ground sown to wheat and oats is much larger than ever heretofore, and the yield will surpass that of any previous year.

Along the Bitter Root and Missoula rivers the farmers have mostly finished haying and are in the midst of the wheat harvest. In proportion, the oat yield will exceed that of wheat. I have never seen such uniform growth of high oats, which promise a heavy crop as in this country this year.

Another thing noticeable since I visited the West Side some seven years ago, is the great improvement in the grades of stock cattle and horses. Then Texas cattle and cayuse horses were the rule. Now half-breed Durhams and good Eastern horses are almost the only ones seen.

At. Col. Baker's, sixteen miles southeast from Missoula, I found many people flocking to the new quartz mines lately discovered in the mountains six miles from his station. The lodes are reported as enormous in width, mostly cropping above ground, and many of them traceable for a mile with the eye. The ore is silver and copper combined, but what I saw of it is not of high grade; yet it all comes from or near the surface. It is very likely rich discoveries will be made, as so many are out prospecting.

It happened that Mr. Andy O'Connell and Mrs. LaCroix, of Helena, arrived in Missoula several days since while I had leisure. The next evening Major Peter Ronan, the agent of the Flatheads, came into town from the Jocko Agency. The next afternoon, upon Mr. Ronan's invitation, we hitched up our teams and accompanied him home. I had been to the place several times in the last few years. We were all pleased with the beautiful valley below Missoula, and the prettiest view in the mountains — the Valley of the Jocko. The substantial improvements and large fields of grain at every suitable place for farming excited my surprise.

When I first visited the Jocko Agency in 1870 there was but one small field of a few acres under cultivation. Judge of my surprise, when from the door of Major Ronan's house I could see one continuous wheat field, extending from the head of Mill creek, in the mountains, to Finley creek, every acre of which had been fenced in and cultivated by the Indians. Major Ronan says the Indians cut and put around their fields 52,000 rails last winter. He estimates they will harvest 25,000 bushels of wheat in a few days, besides a quantity of oats, potatoes and other vegetables, sufficient for their own use. Half of their wheat they can sell.

Along the Jocko fourteen or fifteen houses were built by the former agents, but in two or three years past, under Agents [Charles S.] Medary and Ronan, the Indians have constructed twenty or more good substantial and comfortable cabins for themselves, and following their example, and under their advice, have engaged in raising domestic cattle in addition to a large number of horses. Agent Medary introduced fine stock among them, and by the advice of Agent Ronan they have bought many fine cows from the farmers of the Bitter Root valley, and their herds are increasing rapidly. Here, as well as at the Mission, which we all visited, I found a great improvement in the breeding of horses. Instead of the Indian pony, fine American horses can be seen everywhere.

Father [Leopold] Van Gorp and the Sisters at the school welcomed us heartily. The Indians from a hundred miles around were gathering to celebrate St. Ignatius Day — the day of their patron saint — and the several hundred gathered there appeared orderly, although it had been told us before we arrived at Missoula that these Indians were going to join the Nez Perces in their war against the whites.

The Mission valley showed many signs of improvement since my last visit. The old teepes were gone and many new log houses were in their places. I counted nine new ones in the course of construction. The farming and stock raising appeared very flourishing. After all I saw I dismissed all fear of any outbreak among these Indians.

After this pleasant visit, leaving Mrs. LaCroix and her little son Claude to visit Mrs. Ronan in her pleasant home, we left this happy valley and its grand frame of rugged mountains, and returned *via* Frenchtown to Missoula, which is as pretty a village as can be found in the mountains.

We found the command at Fort Missoula all feeling proud of Lieut. Wallace's victory over the Nez Perces.

Helena.

Document 33

Indian Returns Lost Horse

October 17, 1878

Source: "An Honest Indian," *Helena Weekly Herald* (October 17, 1878), page 7 col. 1.

Editors' note: Salish Indians worked hard to get along with their white neighbors.

An Honest Indian.

A year ago, when the Flatheads were *en route* through Helena to their hunting grounds Mr. Silverman bought a pony of them. A week thereafter the pony was missing and could not be found, although strict search was made. Yesterday the Indian appeared at Mr. Silverman's store with the horse, which he had found at their agency upon returning from their winter's buffalo hunt, and turned the property over to its rightful owner. That Indian is a pretty honest sort of a chap.

Document 34

Farms and Economic Progress
on the Reservation
November 8, 1878

Source: "On the Reservation," *The Weekly Missoulian*, November 8, 1878, page 3, col. 2-3.

Editors' note: Another visitor noted agricultural progress and ancient battle sites on the reseervation.

On the Reservation.

Fifteen miles from Missoula, on the road to the Jocko, the traveler comes to the southern border of the reservation set apart by the government for the exclusive use and abiding-place of the confederated tribes known as Kootenais, Pen d'Oreilles and Flatheads. This country has been inhabited by the above-named tribes for ages, and every foot of the ground is replete with history written on the forest trees and furrowed in the hills. It is a beautiful country, and though principally val[u]able for grazing purposes, is also well adapted to agriculture. Once over the divide between the valleys of the Hellgate and Jacko, the appreciative eye is rewarded by a series of grand mountain views. Coming down toward the Agency, from the high grade along Finlay creek, one can see the precipitous peaks of the Mission range, rising abruptly from the plain, with no formal foot-hills to mar their grandeur, their summits clad in fresh white snow, rugged, rock-ribbed and stern.

The U. S. Indian Agency,

twenty-eight miles from Missoula, is composed of a group of building comprising the residences and offices of Agent [Peter] Ronan, head-farmer [Henry A.] Lambert, Dr. [L. H.] Choquette, and the dwelling houses of the various employes at the Agency. Two stores are located here, of which Duncan McDonald and T. J. Demers are the respective proprietors, the latter confiding his interests to the efficient superintendence of Mr. William Barron. The stores are neat, comfortable log structures, and are well stocked with goods suitable to the trade which they are called upon to supply. The Agency is furnished with a good flouring and saw mill, of which Mr. Frank Decker is the overseer; there are also carpenter and blacksmith shops, and competent workmen in charge of the same. The creek is bordered with small farms, and during last season Mr.

Decker informs us that he ground 8,000 bushels of grain for the inhabitants of this region. Various dwellings are scattered about the neighborhood, the group inhabited by Arlee and his family being more especially noticeable. Arlee now occupies the buildings which were once the quarters of the U.S authorities during Major [Daniel] Shannahan's time.

Starting from the Agency, the pleasure-seeker can find many paths for adventure or diversion. One of the most popular is the trail up the Jocko to the lakes from which it takes its rise. Twenty miles above the Agency, over a rough mountain trail, through fallen timber, up the beds of streams, and creeping along the sides of mountains, we came to the first of a series of four beautiful lakes, lying, as it were, on shelves, one above the other. The trail leads high up on the mountain side, and far down below, imbedded deep in the canyon, lies a glassy lake, two and one-half miles long, and varying from two to four hundred yards in width. Looking down into its depths at this season of the year, one sees the green pines and yellow tamaracks reflected from mountains turned upside down, and fleecy clouds floating in the depths below them. Here the artist, the hunter and the disciple of the fishing-rod and line can find ample employment. The depth of this lake is not known, but lines have been sunk from a raft in the centre of the lake to a depth of 600 feet, and "no bottom" found. Fish are unusually plentiful in these lakes, and game of all kinds abounds.

Twenty miles from the Agency lies Saint Ignatius Mission. Leaving the Agency, and proceeding down the Jocko over ten miles of as fine a stretch of hard, level road as ever a horse trod, the way debouches into the hills, and crosses over a low range into the Mission valley. As we gain the summit of the divide, the spires of St. Ignatius appear in sight, and in the background, five miles beyond, lie the snow-capped mountains. In a canyon between two of the peaks is a beautiful cascade, shooting over the rocks in three successive leaps, a distance of 1,500 feet. At this season of the year the mountains are covered with snow, and the cataract is scarcely visible; but in the summer time, when the snows have melted and increased the volume of its water, it is plainly seen from these hills (though twelve miles distant), sparkling in the sunlight, like a narrow stream of silver pouring down the mountain.

Saint Ignatius Mission

was founded by the Jesuits in 1854, the fathers spending many years in a number of rude log buildings, which are still to be seen, though now in a tumble-down condition. They have been supplanted by commodious and handsome buildings — the present church, erected in 1860, being one of the largest in the Territory, accommodating worshippers to the number of 1,000. It is furnished with a handsome Mason & Hamlin organ, and is ornamented with three elegant life-sized statues. The residence for the Fathers is a very roomy one, furnished with sitting-room, library, office, dining room and kitchen, and various ante-rooms for sacred uses. The Mission has also a flouring and saw mill in connection, farming machinery of every description, including reapers, threshers, rakes, mowers, etc., workshops, presided over by the brothers, large barns, a well-cultivated farm, and last, but not least, a very complete little printing office. A girl's boarding school, under under [sic] the superintendence of she [sic] Sisters of Charity, is in progress here, and is well attended. The girls are taught all kinds of domestic employment and useful arts, and evidence of their skill is evinced in the fact that three specimens of their handiwork carried off prizes at our late county fair. The Indians of the Mission valley have raised from six to seven thousand bushels of grain during last year, which was ground at the Mission mill. Their farms are usually small — ten to thirty acres usually satisfying the ambition of the Indian farmer. Fra [Leopold] Van Gorp, Superior of the Mission, very courteously showed us over the buildings, and explained matters in a manner very gratifying to the heart of the newspaper man, and is entitled to a vote of thanks therefor. A boy's boarding-school is soon to be erected, which will partake of the nature of an industrial or trade school, each individual scholar being taught that branch of mechanics for which he shows the most aptitude.

It was the privilege of the writer, upon the return trip, to be accompanied by a gentleman who has spent his life among the hills and mountains of this region. Instead of traveling the main road, we followed the Indian trails, coming through a noted battle ground, on which, some fifty years ago, a large number of Blackfeet and Flathead Indians were engaged. Arlee was then a little child, and Victor, the old chief of the Flatheads, participated in this battle, though but a boy in years and statue. The trees for miles are still marked with evidences of the conflict, which was an obstinate and bloody one, and resulted disastrously to the Flatheads. The places where noted warriors fell are still pointed out, and rock-piles, used for breastworks, are scattered over the whole region. As we traversed the hills over the Lavalle creek trail, other noted skirmish grounds were pointed out, in which noted braves of the past had lost their lives, and when we reflected on the unwritten history which these scenes present to the imaginative mind of the red man, we could not help feeling it was a sacred ground to him of which we had had no previous conception.

A.

Document 35

Agent Ronan Tries to Untangle a Complicated Business Arrangement December 30, 1878

Source: Peter Ronan, *"A Great Many of Us Have Good Farms": Agent Peter Ronan Reports on the Flathead Indian Reservation, Montana, 1877-1887*, ed. Robert J. Bigart (Pablo, Mont.: Salish Kootenai College Press, 2014), pages 89-93.

Editors' note: Ronan interviewed Indians and whites involved in a complicated conflict over a ranch on Horse Plains. His report gave each side of the conflict, but finally suggested that the Montana state courts try to straighten out the disagreement.

Flathead Agency, M.T.
December 30th, 1878

To the
Hon. Commissioner of Indian Affairs
Washington, D.C.
Sir:

I have the honor to communicate the following correspondence, and the result of my investigation, together with suggestions in connection with the affair:

Missoula City, Dec. 9th.

Agent Ronan,
Dear Sir:

I have been informed by several parties that the Indians that roam between the Agency and Horse Plains, have broken open my house, and taken possession of my ranche at Horse Plains, and used and destroyed a lot of vegetables I had put away there, and other plunder that I had left there. I had made arrangements with Duncan McDonald to take the place, and a day or so ago I received a letter from him (Duncan) that he started down to the ranche and only got as far as the crossing of the Pend d'Oreille river, and the Indian known as Louis Cultis-toe told him he would neither let Indian or whiteman go on the Ranche as it belonged to him. About a year ago his mother, old Mrs. Cultis-toe, wanted to build a house there to put her grub or Camas in and I gave her permission to build some distance from my house, and even gave her harness and tools to build with, and now he acts in this way. I hope you will look after this Indian or Indians, and if you cannot do anything I will take the matter in my own hands, and protect my rights and will find plenty friends to help me.

(sgd) James Laughlin.

The foregoing letter did not reach me for some ten days after it was written, owing to the fact that it remained in the coat pocket of the carrier, and in the mean time I received the following from the same party:

Missoula, Dec. 21st, 1878

Agent Ronan,
Dear Sir:

I wrote you a letter some time ago in regard to the Indians that had taken possession of my ranche at Horse Plains, not Knowing whether or not you received it I here write you a few lines as I just have been talking to Mr. Duncan McDonald, and also some others, and I understand the Indians have completely destroyed almost everything on the ranche. When I left Horse Plains I left my ranche in possession of Mr. Tranum, for I was so annoyed by the Indians that I could not stay there in peace, and as Mr. Tranum changed his mind and left there, as I was about to sell or trade the ranche to an Indian by the name of McSims, and in the mean time Louie Cultistoe went to him and told him I owed his mother some wheat, which is a falsehood for an excuse to steal and plunder. When Mr. Tranum went back this Louie Indian had keys and unlocked my door and divided up with other Indians my potatoes and other things, to get those Indians to help him hold my ranche — he is the meanest Indian in that tribe. I have been annoyed and lost more by him than any other Indian. He has camped in my pasture which was well fenced when I forbid him to, and many such instances I could name which others could tell you, I paid three hundred and fifty dollars for the ranche with but few improvements on it, and have worked on it for 6 years, and now for a lazy Indian to take it from me, it is more than I can tolerate, I send this by D. McDonald. If there is not something done I have friends enough to go with me, and I'll

surely protect my rights, as I have plenty witnesses who have
seen what him and his band have done.

(Sgd) James Laughlin

On Friday, December 27th I summoned those Horse Plains Indians to the
Agency, although they live and have what they call their home at Horse Plains,
outside of the reservation and claim "Petal" or "Victor," Chief of the Lower
Kalispels as their Chief, who resides in Washington Territory; and after having
had carefully interpreted to them the charges of James Laughlin as contained
in the foregoing letter, Elize, Loui Cultis-toe's mother, made the following
statement:

> "A number of years ago a whiteman called John came to
> the Horse Plains, where I lived, and fenced in the land that
> I claimed — he did all the work — and when the fence was
> done he took me into the field, made a mark and said one-half
> is yours and one half is mine — he gave me my choice of the
> division — John plowed up a portion of the field, and had no
> seed to sow on his share. I had wheat enough to plant all the
> plowed land. John sowed the wheat and told me I could go
> off with my people whereever they went, and to come back at
> harvest time and help gather the crop, and it would be then
> taken to the mill and made into flour and after the flour was
> brought home I could get half. I went back at harvest time and
> John told me as there was not much wheat it would be better
> to keep it for seed and sow it all in the spring, when he would
> plow up a bigger piece of land and sow it all with our wheat
> and that I would have half the crop. When the second crop
> was raised John advised me to let the division of the wheat
> go until the next season, and said the third yield would give
> us both plenty. I agreed to it, and after the crop was in went
> out to pick and dry berries for winter. I came back to help to
> harvest and divide our produce but did not find John — he
> was gone — but there was a whiteman there with a family.
> This man was Laughlin. I asked him where John was, he told
> me John got a letter and was gone to see his mother. I asked if
> John left any word for me. Laughlin said no. I told Laughlin
> that half the growing crop was mine. He told me I lied. I went
> to a white neighbor named McMiller, who carried the mail last
> winter, and who lives at Horse Plains now, and who knows all
> about my trade with John, and I told him what Laughlin said.
> McMiller told me to keep quiet, not to take anything away,

and if Laughlin did not give me anything to leave it to some good man and he thought Laughlin would do right with me. I never got my wheat. That is all I have to say."

Louie Cultis-toe, son of Elize, said:

"I was out hunting in the summer and when I came back, I found Laughlin had gone away from his place, and heard he moved away from Horse Plains. I found this old man Se-lah, and my mother camped near the house. The doors were open and I went in. There was nothing in the house except some potatoes in a cellar. As the house was open I thought the potatoes would be taken, and my people blamed for it, and I dug a hole away from the house and covered them up and they are there yet. I met Duncan McDonald at McSims and told him I took the potatoes and hid them, and who ever owned them could come to me and I would show him where they were. I had some talk with Duncan who claimed the ranche. I told him that half of it rightfully belonged to my mother, and that half of the crop which was growing when Laughlin came there was hers but she never got anything. Duncan said the ranche was his, and he wanted to send his father-in-law there to live, but the old man did not want to go; he also said he wanted his bother-in-law to go but he would not go. I then told Duncan he need not send anyone there, as I thought I had more right to it than anyone else if Laughlin left it. When I said I owned the house, Duncan said, 'all right; that is all I want to know.' I told Duncan in our talk that I thought I had a better right to it than anybody else, if Laughlin left it, because the first whiteman who lived there cheated my mother out of her wheat. Duncan said, 'how much wheat does your mother claim?' I said, 'you can figure; he owes her for half the crop for three years, and I think that is worth the whole of the field.' — But I will say no more — my mother is old and poor — if I do not protect her who will? I tell the truth; she tells the truth. I leave it to the whiteman to do her Justice. Any body who comes there to live with your knowledge will not be molested by me because I think you will tell the truth about it as we have told you. I am done."

Agent to Se-lah: — "Louis Tranum complains that you took his gun out of Laughlin's house."

Selah: — "I did, and have it safe for him. Tranum lives at Horse Plains, and as the house was open I thought the gun would be stolen. I took it and left it at a whiteman's house and told the whiteman to give it to Tranum."

Upon this evidence I wrote the following letter to Mr. Laughlin:

Flathead Agency, M.T.
December 28th, 1878.

Mr. James Laughlin,
Missoula,
Missoula Co., M.T.
Sir:

Your letter of Dec 9th, after a delay of some ten days came to hand and in the mean-time I received your letter of Dec 21st, and immediately took measures to investigate the charges preferred by you against Loui Cultis-toe, an Indian claiming his home at Horse Plains. The band of Indians who claim Horse Plains and of which Cultis-toe and his mother are members are a fragment of "Petals" or "Victors" tribe of Lower Kalispel Indians who have their head-quarters on the Pend d'Oreille river in Washington Territory and do not claim this Agent or any chief of this reservation as having jurisdiction over them. It is my opinion that as you pay taxes in Missoula County which is a regularly organized county of Montana, and a roaming Indian over whom the Agent can claim no control because he claims no allegiance to the chiefs of this reservation, is amenable to the laws of the Territory, and that you should regularly proceed against him according to the statutes; however, this is but my own opinion. I have laid your Complaint and also the statement of Cultis-toe and his mother before the Hon. Com. of Indian Affairs, and asked instructions as to whom this business properly belongs. In the mean time, if yourself or any agent you may designate will call upon me I will put you in possession of the ranche and see that you will not be molested by Indians until I am properly informed as to the modes of proceedure.

Yours respectfully,
(Sgd) Peter Ronan.
U.S. Ind. Agt.

In connection with all of the forgoing, I would respectfully call the attention of the Hon. Commissioner of Indian Affairs to Communication "C" dated

Office Indian Affairs, Oct. 10th, 1877, and my reply thereto, dated at this
office December 10th, 1877; also to my report in connection with the matter
then brought before me, dated January 2d, 1877 [sic, 1878].

In reviewing the whole matter it will be seen that a few families of white
settlers not over six in number have taken up ranches at Horse Plains, outside
of the western boundaries of the Jocko Reservation; that a fragment of a band
of Indians belonging to "Petals" or "Victors" tribe of Lower Kalispels, who
have their home on the Pend d'Oreilles river, claim a right to some of the land
occupied by the whites — that the conflicting claims engender bad feelings,
which may result some time in the near future, in precipitating a fight which
may result in an Indian war. The settlers look to me for protection against
the Indians — while the Indians naturally resort to me with their complaints
against the whites, and as the settlement is outside of the limits of the reserve
and inside of the boundaries of an organized county, to the revenues of which
the settlers contribute by the annual levy of tax; and, also, as the Indians are a
fragment of a band claiming the Chieftainship of a chief who has his home in
Washington Territory, I have expressed the opinion that their intricate disputes
on questions of land and other annoying disputes properly belong in the
Territorial courts; unless Horse Plains be declared a portion of this reservation,
the settlers indemnified for their improvements, and this band either compelled
to come under the Control of this Agency and acknowledge the authority of
the proper chiefs of the reservation or move off to the home of their own chief
in Washington Territory. All of which I respectfully submit with the hope that
I may be fully and plainly instructed in the matter, so that I can take prompt
and efficient action or give intelligent instructions to the disputants.

Very respectfully,
Your obedient servant,
Peter Ronan
U.S. Ind. Agent

Document 36

Will Sutherlin Tours the Flathead Reservation

April 1879

Source: Will Sutherlin, "Visit to the Flathead Agency," *Rocky Mountain Husbandman* (Diamond City, Mont.), May 1, 1879, page 2, col. 3-4; Will Sutherlin, "Visit to St. Ignatius Mission," *Rocky Mountain Husbandman*, May 8, 1879, page 2, col. 2-3; Will Sutherlin, "St. Ignatius Mission," *Rocky Mountain Husbandman*, May 15, 1879, page 2, col. 2-3.

Editors' note: In these three newspaper articles Sutherlin gave a detailed account of the Flathead Indian Reservation in 1879. He described the Indian farms and livestock, the St. Ignatius Mission, and the Good Friday and Easter celebration and feast.

Visit to the Flathead Agency.

Having accepted an invitation from Mr. Harry Lambert, head farmer of the Flathead agency, to visit the reservation and witness the Good Friday and Easter Sunday celebrations which promised to be of more than usual interest, I had the good fortune to secure a seat with Messrs. Daniel Welch and John Hayes, on the 10th ult., for the trip. The seat was easy, and mounted in an elegant new spring wagon, to which was hitched a splendid team. With the reins in the hands of Jack, who, for short, is usually called "Mulligan," we glided out of Missoula and across that level bench land, viewing some pretty farms and many acres of unclaimed lands. Eleven miles from town we faced toward the north, passing the premises of C. C. O'Kief, an old residenter, known here as "Baron O'Kief." As we sped up the valley toward a gate in the mountains the story of how Mr. O'Kief got the title of "Baron" was listened to with interest, but it will be enough to state that the title still clings to him, and that the castle in which he lived in early days still stands; that his farm of 200 or more acres is well improved, for he still reigns in a manner suited to his making — king of the hills and herds thereon.

Into the gate of the mountains and along the pebbly road we went, but slowly, for it was up hill. Mulligan asked me "what color were my stockings," and I told him they were not stripped. Then he said something about pedestrians, but I told him I had no love for them. Then he said "walking is pleasant and healthy," and I was about to tell him that my health was splendid, when he said, "its fashionable and profitable, too; women do it." "This is too much," said W. "Can't stand the press," and I was too full for utterance. So we all dismounted and walked, though there was none who could do 3,000 quarter miles in 3,000 quarter hours. The top was reached and we entered the reservation. At this point a low level plain called Camas prairie, skirted with pine forests, extending high up the mountains on all sides. The prairie is marshy, produces good hay, and is a noted place of summer resort for Indians who spend the fall season in gathering Camas roots, a sort of potato-like vegetation that grows abundantly here, and which, when cooked, has a palatable taste, answering to some extent as a substitute for bread. It was here that Col. [Charles S.] Medary, when Indian agent, built a hog ranch, the remains of which still stand. His design I suppose was to utilize the reservation by feeding his hogs on the Camas root. Several prairies were passed through, when we descended a long grade cut around the mountain and through a grand pine forest, crossing a gay little stream at the foot. The banks of the stream are noted as having been the scene of many hard fought battles by the contending Indian tribes years ago. The last battle of which there is any record happened in 1830, or about that time, when, it is said, a great brave chief was killed. The only "record" is a circle of round stone lying upon the place, showing where he fell, and two long rows of stone stretched out across the flat representing the lines of battle. A historian distinguished for his long residence in these parts tells an interesting story of the battle and the victory. The only strange thing about it is, that twenty-five years ago those stones lay on top of the ground, and now they are nearly covered in the earth. He can't see why the only record of the event should be so obliterated, and that in the face of eye witnesses, for he has been there often.

A minute's drive took us out on the level land, the beautiful valley of the Jocko, and a ten minutes' drive further, landed us at the Flathead agencey [sic], the home of Major P. Ronan, where we were kindly cared for and remained until the following day. The Jocko valley varies in width from two to six miles and is about 12 miles long. The land is level from the river rising slightly to the mountains which are very high and rise up abruptly without foot-hills. Just back of the agency which is near the head of the valley the scenery is the most charming I have ever beheld. The land is level rising only a little until the mountain is reached, then a skirt of timber covers their base when they rise in majestic splendor, scolloped and fluted, pointed and oval, partly covered with green pines, then craggy, draped in snow so far up that their summits seem like great pillars proping [sic] up the etherial heavens. It was a pleasant view I had from the porch at the valley below, for it is one of the prettiest I have seen for many a day. Not only did I see the winding river, shady forests and grand snow-clad mountains overlooking them, but fine farms, and comfortable homes dotted the plain as far as I cared to look. The farms were not large, few of them not covering more than 80 acres, yet none was less than 30 acres, but they were the property and homes of Indians. The farms are enclosed with spit [sic] rail fences, and the dwellings made of logs, except occasionally at a new location the tepee is used. The land inside the fields was nearly all broken, the seeding season being well nigh through, but busy Indians could be seen making fence, hauling logs, wood and doing other work, just as is done in other parts of the country. The soil is deep, free of stone, and very productive. The Indian farmers raise wheat, oats and vegetables; grow their own pork and beef, and raise horses. Many of them own several hundred head each. The entire estimate of cattle belonging to the Indians on the reservation is 6,000 head; horses, 2,600 to 3,000, and about 500 hogs. The number of acres under fence and farmed is about 2,600. The product raised last year was 10,000 bushels of wheat, 5,000 bushels of oats, and 1,500 bushels of potatoes. The reservation is provided with a threshing machine, which the Indians use, helping each other with that work. There is also a saw mill and flouring mill on the reservation, and the flouring mill has run constantly through the fall, winter and spring, but still has grain on hand. I did not learn the number of Indians farmers, but was informed that the agency blacksmith put 93 plows in repair this spring. I believe these Indians are as prosperous as any people need be. The more they work the more they are encouraged by a return for it, and I am convinced that they can be civilized. They have confidence in Agent Ronan; he teaches them how to work and helps them when they need help. He is their judge, mediator and benefactor, He settles their disputes and they abide by his decisions.

To-morrow we go to the mission, twenty miles distant, Major Ronan, his estimable wife, Hoit-some-high and the Sho-sho-to-ma accompanying us.

Will.

* * * * * * * *

Visit to St. Ignatius Mission.
Notes of the Trip — The Work the Priests are Doing —
Over One Thousand People March in the Procession on Good Friday

To reach the mission we passed down the Jocko valley ten miles, then crossed over a low ridge that divides the Jocko from Mission Creek valley. On this route we passed many Indian farms, but it was a holiday and all was quiet about their homes, except the preparation to go to the Mission, and before we had left the valley great numbers of them had fallen in behind. There were old men and women, dressed in red calicoes and blankets, crowded in wagons, and men, women, boys and misses on horseback. At first they appeared to try to go in regular order, but they soon broke into clusters, and the bucks and lasses of the valley went galloping, prancing and racing over the plain in a manner peculiar to their taste and customs. "Mulligan" directed my attention to the dignified manner they assumed on horse back. Said he, as a score of young men and women darted by at gallop speed: "See how nice those men sit, their legs astride, so erect and perfectly straight with the body!" and the answer was, "the women ditto." Then the conversation run on etiquette, in which we all had our say, and, though no definite conclusion was reached, it was intimated that the Indian maidens practice less mock modesty than the whites, and are deserving of credit for clinging to the customs of their ancestors. Mulligan's talk was the best. Said he: "Riding astride is Western style — it will be adopted in the East — by and by, for old styles often become new. As soon as the walking mania is over you may expect the French ladies or the belles of Long Branch to adopt that style, for after long walking they'll want to rest and ride, and then striped stockings will show to good advantage."

The valley in which St. Ignatius Mission is situated is the largest and most beautiful in western Montana. A chain of lofty peaked, snow-clad mountains extend from the head of Mission creek to and around Flathead lake, 60 miles distant, then break off toward the west fencing the north boundary of the Pend' Oreille river and enclosing within the triangle an area of many thousand miles of low, level lands, most of which are susceptible of cultivation. The mountains are covered with timber at their base, which extends several miles down on the flat, here and there for miles surrounding lovely dales, grassy glades, parks and prairies, the natural orchards of the West, wherein wild plums, strawberries and several other fruits flourish, and mature year after year. The Mission is near the head of the valley on the south bank of Mission creek. On our arrival we were cordially received by Fathers [Joseph] Giorda, Latanzi, Benedine [Joseph Bandini] and [Aloysius] Parodi. The first named has been here many years, and I am indebted to him for much valuable information concerning the establishment and work of this and other missions, which cannot, for want of space, be given here. Father Giorda speaks the Flathead language perfectly. He is engaged in compiling a dictionary of the Flathead language, which is to be used in the schools in Rome for the instruction of missionaries. The book will contain about 700 pages, and 350 copies are being printed. He has a job press and type. Mr. Butler, who is engaged upon the work, thinks he will be a proficient "Ingin" talker by the time the work is completed. The mission buildings now occupied are large, two and one-half stories high, and the church is the second largest in Montana, it being 100 x 40 feet, 20 foot ceiling, pointed roof, with belfry on top. Inside the ceiling is supported by columns all snow white, but are strung with festoons and fringed ornaments. At the left of the main entrance is the choir rostrum with a fine organ, and at the further end the beautiful altar, together with the elegant statues, that stand on each side occupy the whole end of the room. Still it is capable of receiving about 1,100 persons. The other valuable property here consists of a saw mill and flouring mill, blacksmith and carpenter shops, herds of horses, cattle, hogs, farm machinery, fields of some hundreds of acres, in which 18 teams are employed, making it a self-sustaining institution. But it is Good Friday, and the day is fairly spent, and I must leave off further mention of the place until after the celebration, which promises to be the grandest that has ever been witnessed here. The number of Flatheads, Kootenays and Pend' Oreilles (Kalispel) Indians assembled are estimated at 1,350. Some of the Kalispels and many of the Kootenays having come a long way to take part in the event. The usual mass had been well attended through the day, but in the afternoon the church was jammed to its fullest extent, while Father Giorda's sermon was being delivered. After the sermon, which was in the Indian tongue and ferverently [sic] spoken, the devotional exercises of the "Way of the Cross" was begun and gone through with, the Indians rising at each station facing the priest and sang in regular tone:

> "From pain to pain, from woe to woe,
> With loving hearts and footsteps slow,
> To calvary with Christ we go
> See how his precious blood
> At every station pours!
> Was ever grief like this?
> Was ever sin like ours?

The singing was in Indian tongue, but followed the proper tune, and it was rich, rare, quaint and pleasant. At early dark the 14th station was reached and fires had been kindled at the church door and in the front yard. Then some stallwart [sic] chiefs bore from the altar of the church the crucifix, the priests acting as pall bearers, and four little Indian girls dressed in white carrying the nails. As the procession filed down the long aisle and out of the door way, the Indians with lighted torches made of pine knots, stepped into line two abreast moving slowly. It was truly a grand spectacle to witness in the dark still night that procession nearly a half mile long, and it was easy to fancy in those solemn moments that Mary Magdalen and the other Mary were there standing over by the sepulcher or following with saddened hearts, while in the background were standing the scoffing Roman soldiers and deriding Jews. Passing around the cemetry [sic], an enclosure of about four acres some 200 yards from the church, the procession returned silently to the altar and were dismissed in perfect order.

To-morrow we visit the sister's school, see the Easter Sunday celebration, and may have something more to say.

Will.

April 12th.

* * * * * * * *

St. Ignatius Mission.
A Visit to the Sisters' School — Church Service — Easter Sunday Feasts — Indian Speeches — What they Need

Besides the religious instruction given at this mission, it is made a place of general learning, and now has two schools, one for boys and one for girls — young Indians. B. F. Williams, late of Comba's company 7th infantry, is the teacher of the boys. They are learned to read, write and work. The material for an industrial college is on the ground and is to be erected as soon as crops are harvested. The girl's school is conducted by the Sisters of Charity, and is indeed a fine institution of learning. My visit to the school was truly enjoyable, and I am indebted to sisters Mary, Paulmiki, Remi, Jene de Chantal, and Mary of Trinity, for courtesies shown. The school is surrounded by a high, close board fence, enclosing within it about one acre of land. In the yard they have a beautiful garden and orchard. They raise strawberries in great quantities. The apple and plum trees were the largest I have seen, and fruit buds were abundant. The Sisters' home and school is in one building, two and a half stories high, probably 100 x 50 feet. On each floor there is a hall running lengthwise through it. The house is cut up into probably a dozen rooms, all neatly but plainly furnished. The school room is on the second floor. It was recess and the girls were enjoying themselves, but we entered and silence reigned. At the bidding of the sisters some recitations and songs were given by the younger ones. Then they were told to show us their copy-books and our whole party were abashed to acknowledge that young Indian girls of 15 years and less could write so well — better than we, many of them exhibiting penmanship equal to any school in the country. The third story is used for the sleeping apartment, and a cozy place it is. Each scholar has her own apartment and is required to make her own bed clothes and wearing apparel, all of which is kept as clean and tidy as could be desired by the most fastidious. The best room visited was at the south corner, where the sun shone in brightly. It is the sisters' place of worship. The altar is delicate in design, yet so supremely elegant that one could not kneel there at the feet of the images of Mary and Christ without being touched by the thoughts of God's presence. I remember when Sister Mary came Diamondward some years ago to have contributed $ — to the cause, but I never realized until this visit the extent of the good work being done by these noble Sisters of Charity. At early dawn of Easter Sunday, Indians, mostly women, were seen passing to the church where they went to kneel at the altar, before the morning meal. The ten o'clock mass, however was the grandest church-going scene I have witnessed. I went inside and took a seat. There was just room and no space left, for there were Indians on every side of me, filling the church to a perfect jam. Mass was gone through with, the Indians repeating the prayers. Then I listened with good attention to the eloquent divine Father Geordia deliver a sermon in the Indian tongue. Though I could not understand much of it, I enjoyed it, for he is a fluent speaker of the Indian language. The nicest part of the services was the singing of the "gloria," In which the Indians are very proficient. At noon the service was dismissed and the Indians repaired to the yard to partake of the feast which had been in preparation all day, and consisted mainly of fat beeves and potatoes presented them by the priests. Before this meal was served the women seated themselves on the ground in two large circles around the stewing pots and the men clustered about in the rear, except the chiefs, who dined at the priests table, after we were through. While seated awaiting the repast, speeches were made by one or two chiefs. The first speaker was Enyas, a Kootenay chief. He stood up in the centre of the circle and said: "Three years ago he and his tribe were wild men; they feared the white man and were eager to fight them. They saw in their rambles how other Indians were doing and undertook to follow in their footsteps, taking the advice of Father Geordia, through whom they secured seven plows for their men. Seeds were sown, but the Great Spirit must punish them, so he sent the hoppers to prey upon their fields and they were destroyed. Again they had tried, for the priest told them that the mother soil would grow them food, and it did. He hoped the agent and Great Father would give them more plows, that his tribe might do as the seven had done. This was a great day and he was glad so many had come to join in the feast. This time they had a few beeves to feast on, and if they were good Indians, industrious and honest, they would have a greater feast next year. It was plows and seeds he and his men wanted, and he hoped the Great Father would send them instead of blankets. The home of this Indian is 80 miles distant to the north of the mission, where it is said fine crops were grown.

Arlee, chief of the Flathheads [sic] spoke also, giving words of encouragement to the Kootenays and Pen d'Oreilles, and cautioning his men to be good and worthy Indians.

The feast then commenced by the women first serving those in the circles with beef and potatoes. Then the men came forward and helped themselves. While the feast went on Mulligan and I strolled about the yard taking in the situation as best we could. It was a good time get a peep at the "dusky maidens of the forest," and we walked around them, for it was the first feast we had witnessed. Over close to No-ah-ha-ha (the chief of police) sat Eli-mul-ko, the daughter of La Salle, a half-breed. Further on, Mrs. Brown, an unpretending widow, with half a thousand cattle roaming on the free hills, sat dishing up potatoes and beef. It was about handsome "Injuns" that the conversation run, and I fancied that my friend Mulligan was in a "Brown" study, but then the widow was delinquent in that respect. To-shin-ma and In-kihe were the next worthy of admiration. To-shin-ma is, I believe, just sweet sixteen, and a mulatto. She wore a neat fitting calico dress, cut bias and trimmed with red, many beads on her neck and rings on her fingers. Her long wavy hair was partly platted, tied at the end with a red ribbon, and dangled carelessly over the shoulders. She was almost handsome, though I could not see the color of her eyes. My friend said they were "Brown." I would have liked it better if he had said blue, but we finally agreed that Brown would do. Not long ago she completed her education, and it is stated that she reads well and writes a good hand. She was to have married a young Indian, but the match is broken and she now roams at liberty. This may all be true for it is an interpreter's story, and Mulligan believes it. Another member of the circle in the feast, was a s.... 100 years old. She looked healthy, but her face was as black as a negroe's, and her hair nearly as white as snow. It is stated that she tells a thrilling story of meeting Lewis and Clarke. While speaking of old persons it will be in order to state that while at the mission I enjoyed making the acquaintance of Wm. Classens, of Belgian birth, who was born in 1811, and Wm. Pepper, born in Prussia, in 1808. These two gentlemen are the oldest white residents of Montana, they having come here in 1840, since which time they have spent their lives in building missions and laboring to civilize and christianize the aborigines of the West. The last named is a blacksmith and still does the work in the mission shop. He is hale and hearty and never gives a day to idleness. It was he that made the first sledge hammer, which he welded with a small hammer, using frying pans and sheet iron kettles to make it of; and it was with this sledge that the first plow that turned the virgin soil of Montana was made, thirty years or more ago. He built mills, made wagons, mended guns and quaint indeed are the tools and contriviances [sic] used in those old times for making the necessary machinery used at the missions.

                                                                           Will.

Document 37

Justice for an Indian Murdered by White Men

July 18, 1879

Source: "The Murders Near Lincoln," *The New North-West* (Deer Lodge, Mont.), July 18, 1879, page 3, col. 2.

Editors' note: Duncan McDonald, like most tribal members, thought the white justice system should punish white men who murdered Indians as well as Indians who murdered white men.

The Murders Near Lincoln.
Letter from Duncan McDonald on the Subject.

Duncan McDonald writes us as follows on the recent trouble near Lincoln Gulch: "The name of the 'Big Indian' was Moses. He was quiet and reliable and neither quarrelsome nor a thief. Accompanied by two other Indians, Moses went to Lincoln July 6th, to trade for some provisions they needed. They were met in the town by [John] Eagleson and [Richard] Evans. Moses had in his possession at the time a blanket belonging to the men. The blanket was stolen by another Indian who claimed the white men had swindled him. Moses did not recognize a right to the blanket and took it from him by force, intending to return it to the owners. On meeting the whites they requested Moses to accompany them. They were then on the road to Helena. Pierre and Chrissquilla, the Indians who accompanied Moses, wanted to go along with him. To this the whites objected and Moses told his companions to return to camp — that he would go alone. The whites had two large bottles of whisky. After Moses had accompanied them some distance the whites fired on him with a needle gun and shot him through the body. Then they took turns in beating him over the head with the butt of the gun until his head was literally beaten to a jelly. Some Indians who were hunting deer saw the whole occurrence, but not in time to save their comrade's life. They gave the white men chase, however, killed Eagleson and wounded Evans."

— — — — — — —

The above is a condensation of a long letter received from Mr. McDonald, a part of which we think best not to publish. If the statements are to be made at all the courts are the place in which to make them. If the facts are as stated by Mr. McD., whose sincerity we do not doubt, there should be complaint made and the parties brought to trial. The letter concludes: "Michell, the Pen d'Oreille chief, would like to see Mr. Evans arrested and tried. * * * I ask of the people of this country if they ever knew of a white man being hung for the murder of an Indian in Montana? The oath of an Indian is not taken in a court, but that of a white man is taken under all circumstances. We claim protection under the flag of the United States and we also claim our right to a hearing in this case."

Chapter 2

Documents of
Salish, Pend d'Oreille, and Kootenai
History Between 1880 and 1884

Document 38

An Indian Guest Compliments the Cook

ca. 1880

Source: "River Upsets Wagons," in S.O.S. Writers' Club, *Montana's Little Legends* (Hamilton, Mont.: Daily Ravalli Republican, 1963), page 66-67.

Editors' note: This account of the interaction of Gregg family hospitality with Indian courtesy illustrated the way cultural differences could complicate social interactions.

River Upsets Wagons

With the influx of homesteaders to the Bitter Root, came the O. P. Greggs. Like the Chaffins, the Gregg family crossed the plains by covered wagon, stopping for a short time near Bonita. When they had almost reached their new home in the Bitter Root Valley they attempted to ford the river between the village of Grantsdale and the present Charlos Heights, but the channel, deep and swift, upset their wagons and washed away nearly all their worldly goods. After they came to understand the Bitter Root River and her eccentricities they journeyed to Grantsdale for supplies by a more circuitous route, fording where Hamilton was later founded, making it a round trip of approximately thirty-five miles; several times the distance by which "the crow flies."

However, after having established a comfortable home, water was to plague the Gregg family again. A cloudburst in the dark hours of a summer night, swept down a gully behind the house; water rushed in the kitchen door and tore up the woven rag carpet, raising its particular brand of havoc before pouring out the front way, swirling down the steps into the wagon road.

Mr. Gregg awoke and swung bare feet out into nearly knee-deep water to find that his treasured violin and case had wandered out from under the bed and was floating around like a small lost craft. At daybreak, when the family joined forces to shovel out the deep deposits of silt it was noticed that the damage was not confined to the house, for their colony of bee-hives had been swept out into the meadow.

Indians were frequent visitors at the Gregg place. One morning a friendly Indian arrived early and was invited to join the family at breakfast. A plate piled high with biscuits, a standard item on the Greggs' morning menu, was politely passed to the visitor first.

"Goo-ood bread — Goo-ood bread," said the red man in deep throated tones. It is said that Mrs. Gregg was not pleased at his compliment and the family waited quite nonplussed; while she flounced into the kitchen to mix and bake another batch. The guest had accepted the plate and emptied the entire contents — down the front of his calico shirt!

Mr. Gregg was proud of having "worn the blue" in the war between the states and was an ardent supporter of the Civil War Veterans' reunions when yearly encampments were attended by the whole family and most of the descendants. These affairs usually lasted four days with a program made up of speakers, meetings, & music. A barbecued beef headed the bill of fare and the campers were housed in tents. This writer, I am told, went along also, at the ripe old age of three months.

Eight children were born to Oliver and Sabrina Gregg, one of whom, Noah, at this writing, resides in a Hamilton rest home. And not the least of their accomplishments was their helping to rear ten orphans.

The old-old house still stands between Gold Creek and Charlos Heights. Many memories hover near — of a hop-vine-shaded milk-house — of the ice-house where children covered each other with wet, cool sawdust to escape the heat of a summer day — of raiding the screened pantry, where squatted heavy crocks of comb-honey and preserves — of bedding down on the front porch to the music of the crickets and waking to the songs of the coffee grinder in the pre-sunrise hours and of roaming the apple orchard where one could scarcely put a foot to the ground through the carpet of fallen yellow apples.

"Grandpap" Gregg never told the children they must not do "this" or "that," but he had an ally in "Old Billy" a cantankerous ram who liked nothing better than upsetting people. If there was a place they must not go, or a tree they must not climb, he simply stationed "Old Billy" there. Being tethered did not lessen their respect for his malevolent eye and ready horns.

Document 39

Proposal to Settle Chief Joseph on Flathead Reservation August 1880

Source: Peter Ronan, "Eagle-of-the-Light," *The Anaconda Standard*, May 14, 1893, page 9, col. 1-3.

Editors' note: Eagle-of-the-Light's proposal to settle Chief Joseph and the other Nez Perce prisoners from the 1877 war on the Flathead Reservation was never approved, but it does raise some interesting historical possibilities.

Eagle-of-the-Light.

Written for the Standard.

This was the name of a former chief of the Nez Perce Indians who was one of the most influential men of his tribe before the war broke out in Idaho in 1877, led by Chief Joseph, Looking Glass and White Bird. At the last council that was held by the Indians to decide whether they would commence war by massacreing [sic] the settlers, Eagle-of-the-Light pleaded eloquently against it; but his voice was not heeded by the older chiefs and braves in the council, and it was decided to commence the bloody work by murdering the settlers in the vicinity of Walula valley. The brave chief finding his advice was received with derisive scorn by the gathered braves, tore off his insigna of rank as a Nez Perce chief, trampled it under his feet, and strode out from the council lodge. He called his family together, with a few Indians who clung to him and held to his views, and left the Nez Perce country. With 11 lodges of his people he traveled over the mountain trail which leads to Montana, coming down through the Lo-Lo pass to Missoula, and thence pushed forward through O'Keefe canyon to the Flathead agency, where he reported to the United States Indian Agent [Peter] Ronan who was then, as well as at the present time, in charge of the agency.

The red cloud of this terrible Indian war had already broken, and although nearly 16 years have passed, the older citizens of Missoula and of the Bitter Root valley have a vivid recollection of the terror of the days when Joseph and his warriors flushed with victory over the United States soldiers in Idaho, under command of General [O. O.] Howard marched down the Lo Lo, right by the entrenchments of Captain [C. C.] Rawn with one company of the old Seventh infantry from Fort Missoula and 200 citizen volunteers.

As Joseph and his warriors, followed by their women and children, filed past their armed band of citizens and soldiers no word was spoken, no shot was fired. Had there been it would have been a repetition of the Custer massacre. The Indians marched up to Stevensville, the soldiers marched to Fort Missoula and the armed citizens went to their homes. The history of this famous Indian march has been published, together with the battle which followed at Big Hole, where General [John] Gibbon was wounded and many of his brave officers were killed; and the retreat of Chief Joseph across the Missouri river, through the National park, and his final surrender to General [Nelson] Miles. The escape of Chief White Bird and 40 of the bravest warriors across the British line, and all the circumstances, with the placing of Joseph and the remnant of his braves on a reservation in the state of Washington.

During all of those bloody scenes Eagle-of-the-Light remained encamped with his followers at the Flathead agency. When peace was restored he bent all of his energies to securing the release of Chief Joseph and his band from military confinement. The following copy of official documents from Brig. Gen. O. O. Howard will show the effort he made before that officer:

Headquarters Dept. of the Columbia in the Field.

Spokane, Aug. 29, 1880.

To Commanding Officer Fort Missoula, M.T.

Dear Sir:

"Eagle-of-the-Light" comes to me, and pleads for the return of Joseph and his people. I rather think that he hopes to bring them to the Flathead reservation. I told him that that reservation was in General [Alfred] Terry's department and that his petition had better be sent through you. I myself am not prepared to judge of the advisability of granting the petition or not. I think it would be disastrous to the Indians to send them to the vicinity of the Lapwoi reservation, but possibly the remnant might be gathered to the Flatheads, where their former chief "Eagle-of-the-Light" lives, without endangering the peace. But whether this is better than to remain where they are the interior department probably will be better able to determine than any military commander. Many of the murderers of whites are indicted in Idaho. To try them in the courts would appear to the Indians to violate the terms of surrender. I promised "Eagle-of-the-Light" to write this in substance to you. Very respectfully your obedient servant.

O. O. Howard.
Brigadier General Commanding Department.

With letters of similar import from several commanding officers, Eagle-of-the-Light presented himself before Agent Ronan and requested that he should present the matter before the interior department. The chief delivered the following speech on the occasion which is preserved in the archives of the Flathead Indian agent's office:

"You do not understand the Nez Perce Indian language, but Baptist Marings [Marengo] is a good interpreter. I do not want my words to be lost and ask that they may be taken down and sent with your words to the Great Father in Washington. I listened to all of the words that you wrote to the great chief and understand, and in turn I want to be understood. My heart is sad now because I lost all my children, all my brothers, all my women, in the war. It was not my fault that my children and my tribe were killed in war and made prisoners. I was opposed to war, and because I opposed it in the councils of my nation I was compelled to leave my tribe and come here and ask permission of you to live among the Flatheads until peace would come. Now I will speak as clear as the light in the morning, as in the morning the sun is clear after the darkness of night — so will my words be clear. I speak as it were from the earth and from heaven, because both the Indians and the white people are made strong or weak from Him above. I know that all of the Nez Perces that are now prisoners in the south, among whom are some of my children and relations, are very sad because a great many are already dead and the rest are fast dying in a climate they are not used to; so I beg of you, great father of the white people in Washington, to give them back to me. We are now, as it were, in midday — there is the sun in the heavens very bright. It is by the law of that brightness that I ask from you to give me back my people. I am sorry that it is said that they cannot go back to Idaho, but they can live in the good air at the Flathead reservation, while all will die if they are kept in the warm air of the south. I am a chief, as well as you, and when war is over we should agree that brave men and women and children should not die if it can be helped. That is the reason I say again — give me back my children! I speak for Chief Joseph and his fellow prisoners. I was the chief of those Indians before Joseph was, and left my people because I believed in peace. If you cannot let them go to Idaho, I beg that you may let them live in the country of the Flatheads."

Joseph and his people were finally transferred from their prison to the Colville agency in the then territory of Washington, where they now live. Eagle-of-the-Light went back to visit his tribe, and died near Lapwai agency, Idaho. Among the Indian curios forwarded to the Montana state building at the world's fair by Mrs. Ronan is a cap made from the skin of a brown bear head by Eagle-of-the-Light, and worn by that chief at the council where the made the foregoing speech.

P. R.

Document 40

The White Justice System and a Murdered Indian

October 1881 – July 1882

Source: "Murder at Stevensville," *The Weekly Missoulian*, October 21, 1881, page 3, col. 3; *The New North-West* (Deer Lodge, Mont.), November 4, 1881, page 3, col. 5; "Court Proceedings," *The Weekly Missoulian*, November 25, 1881, page 3, col. 3; *The Weekly Missoulian*, December 2, 1881, page 3, col. 2; *The Weekly Missoulian*, December 9, 1881, page 3, col. 2; *The Weekly Missoulian*, July 7, 1882, page 3, col. 1.

Editors' note: The white Montana justice system stumbled to find justice for the murder of Cayuse, a Bitterroot Salish Indian in October 1881. The two white men responsible were arrested and jailed in Missoula. Howard Preece died in custody and James Morris served at least eight months in jail before being found innocent of murder.

Murder at Stevensville.

A serious disturbance took place at Stevensville, in this county, which, it is charged, — as is usually the case in all local disturbances with Indians, — had an illicit whiskey trade at the bottom of it. The results were very disastrous to the native element, and they are naturally and deservedly, we think, indignant thereat. But, inasmuch as the case will come before the courts for adjustment, we have no desire to prejudge the case, and give only such facts as we can learn from hearsay. On Tuesday morning news of the affair was brought to Missoula by Amos Buck and Billy Bay, and from the former we received the following account of the affair: On Sunday evening as the little son of Mr. Morris started to go home on horseback, he was stopped by an Indian, who endeavored to take his horse from him. The boy resisted, and called on Anderson Buker to assist him. The latter then called on Mr. Preece for help, and they succeeded in driving off the Indian, and taking the horse to the stable; but in the melee Preece was struck and quite seriously hurt with a stone thrown by the Indian. On Monday, Preece — who, in company with Jas. Morris, is employed in the blacksmith shop of Messrs. Chatfield & Bass — feeling sore from the effects of the rock practice, threatened several times during the day, to "put a head" on the Indian who had done the damage. During the day he saw an Indian whom he thought was his man, and said to Morris: "If I put a head on the s–n of a b–h, will you stand by me?" Morris said he would. They then repaired across the street to the vicinity of Gates & Co's saloon, and attacked the Indian, Preece using a club. Several Indians engaged in the row, and Morris, seizing a "s... ax," sailed in to "stand by" his friend with such murderous effect that the whites cleaned out the Indians by a large majority, nearly killing one man known as Delaware Jim's boy. The Indians scattered, and the white men shortly afterwards appeared on the street armed and breathing profane defiance to all Indians who dared oppose them — Morris firing a shot over the heads of several who were across the street from him. This excited the native population, and in a few moments two armed Indians, known as Sapiell and Cayuse, came down the street and, taking position behind the old Alex Matte blacksmith shop, opened fire upon the saloon. This was replied to by parties inside the citadel (said to be Morris and Preece) with deadly effect, inasmuch as the Indian known as Cayuse was shot through the breast and killed. After he fell firing ceased, and Sapiell, mounting a horse, took his wounded comrade in front of him and made off to the lodges above town. This affair took place about five o'clock in the evening. The news scattered rapidly among the Indians, and later in the evening a messenger arrived with a message from Chief Charlos, stating that the people of Stevensville need not be alarmed, as no one would be hurt; but that the Indians demanded the delivery to them of the two white men who had assaulted them, and that they would have them. After delivering his message he went into Eddy, Hammond & Co.'s store and sat down by the stove. While there he encountered Morris, who fired on him, the ball striking his forehead and glancing off. The messenger is known as Big Mouth Charley, and is well known among residents of the valley. Much excitement ensued, and for some reason the men were not arrested until the following day. A preliminary examination takes place this (Thursday) afternoon — Frank Woody appearing for the Territory and (very probably) W. J. McCormick defending the prisoners. We are told that the Indian version of the original difficulty is in effect that the disputed horse was traded to Morris for two bottles of whisky, and that the Indian, forgetting the obligation of the whisky contract, endeavored to take the horse back again. Both Morris and Preece had been drinking on the day of the difficulty.

* * * * * * * *

James Morris and Howard Preece, who did the Indian shooting at Stevensville last week, are lodged in the Missoula jail awaiting trial.

— November 4, 1881.

* * * * * * * * *

Court Proceedings.

Ter. vs. Morris and Preece. Cause tried and given to jury. After the jury were out 22 hours, they then reported that they were unable to agree and were discharged. Defendants remanded to the custody of the sheriff.

— November 25, 1881.

* * * * * * * * *

Howard Preece, one of the principals in the late shooting affair in Stevensville, has been having a hard deal of late. The jail is not a pleasant place in which to sojourn, according to report of the last grand jury; but to be sick there makes a man think of his childhood's home. We are told that the court-scenes made a telling effect upon Preece's facile mind, and for some time afterwards he was unable to close his eyes in sleep without, in a dreamy imagination, finding himself upon the prisoner's bench before Judge Galbraith on trial for his life. His nightmares were wearing, and finally ended in a case of typhoid pneumonia. He was removed to the hospital on Monday.

— December 2, 1881.

* * * * * * * * *

Howard Preece died at the Sister's Hospital, Missoula, on Monday morning, at two o'clock. Preece was a young man of but 27 years, a vigorous, healthy blacksmith, but confinement in the jail, coupled with the constant worry of a murder trial, the uncertainty of his fate, and the lack of exercise, so told upon him that he sickened, and, as reported last week, was removed to the hospital. The disease with which he was attack [sic] is pronounced by Dr. Ives intussusception of the bowels: but it is very probable that the worry of mind, the anxiety over the trial, and the violent change of daily habits had more to do with his sudden death than anything else. His vigorous form faded away to almost a skeleton, and his intimate acquaintances would have been puzzled to identify the attenuated corpse, which was buried last Tuesday, with the late stalwart prisoner before the bar of Judge Galbraith. While at the Hospital Preece had a horror of going back to the jail; he told the Superior that he would never live to see another trial through if compelled to go back again. Shortly before his death, he inquired of the attendant whether the jury had gone out.

"Yes," was the reply. "Then, I shall soon know the verdict." Poor fellow; he will worry no more about the verdict. His trial is over.

— December 9, 1881.

* * * * * * * *

The jury in the Morris case acquitted the prisoner last week, but he was held to answer to two further indictments. The verdict of acquittal on the charge of murder seems to give general satisfaction.

— July 7, 1882

Document 41

Trading and Cooperation in the Bitterroot Valley

Autumn 1881

Source: Excerpt from "George Washington Ward," Bitter Root Valley Historical Society, *Bitterroot Trails* (Darby, Mont.: Bitter Root Valley Historical Society, 1982), vol. 1, pages 345-346.

Editors' note: The Ward family traded with their Salish neighbors in the Bitterroot Valley, and also exchanged courtesies. In one humorous case, Mrs. Ward even threatened a Salish warrior with a broom.

George Washington Ward

In July 1881 Mr. [George Washington] Ward came over the mountains into "the most beautiful valley" he had ever seen [the Bitterroot Valley]. It was a case of love at first sight. There Mr. Ward stopped and there he brought his family whom he had left back in Missouri.

G. W. Ward had married Miss Hannah L. Wan in Lawrence County, Missouri, April 14, 1869. They became the parents of six children: Charles William, Ralph, Sidney Myre, Iralee, Dale and Ruth. The Wards, with children Charles William, Sidney Myre and Ruth, made the trip when Ruth was only three weeks old. Ralph and Iralee had died when very young.

The family lived in the wagon until Mr. Ward built a cabin on what is now the Duus Ranch. Shortly after this he went back to Missouri and brought household goods, farm machinery and livestock.

During the three months' absence, Mrs. Ward and the three children lived alone. She was afraid of the Indians and didn't understand that they were friendly. However, the young Indians would take advantage of the small children. They would come to the cabin where there was an open well with a bucket. One Indian would force William who was about ten years old to draw water for his horse. Although Mrs. Ward feared them she got tired of her son's treatment and one day confronted the young Indian with a broom. She took the bucket from William, handed it to the Indian, indicating that he draw his own water. Taking Will by the arm she marched him into the house. She heard the Indians whooping and yelling and thought they were going to break into the house and scalp her. She looked out the window and the Indians were bent over with laughter at the one she had threatened with the broom. The Indians never pulled that trick again.

During the same time an Indian came to the cabin with a quarter of beef. He presented it to Mrs. Ward and with a motion that meant "you give to me." He said in English, "Baby Didies," repeating it several times. She gave him a bundle of cloth diapers and he went on his way. The Indian was Sappiel and he came many times to trade. Mrs. Ward might even find him inside the house lying on the floor on her return from being away.

Another incident involved a young Indian woman who rode up on a horse with her baby on her back. She motioned to Mrs. Ward to hold her horse so she could take the baby from her back to nurse. When Mrs. Ward approached the horse, it shied and jumped away. The Indian woman indicated that Mrs. Ward remove her bonnet and braid her hair which she did and the horse became calm and allowed Ms. Ward to hold the bridle while the Indian woman attended her baby.

On Mr. Ward's return to the valley, as he neared the Gird Creek home, one of the horses named Salem heralded their arrival. Mrs. Ward called out, "Children, your father is home. I hear Salem squealing."

Document 42

Tribal Elder Recalls School and Work

1882-1907

Source: Mildred Chaffin, "Smallpox Epidemic Recalled," *Missoulian*, May 21, 1967, page 11-A.

Editors' note: Mary Finley Niles of St. Ignatius was 90 years old in 1966. She had attended the Sisters' school at St. Ignatius (1882), worked for Duncan McDonald as a waitress (1896), and witnessed the 1901 smallpox epidemic and the buffalo roundup (about 1907). She described her experiences at the Sisters' school and as Duncan McDonald's employee, as well as the 1901 smallpox epidemic.

Smallpox Epidemic Recalled
by Mildred Chaffin

Mrs. Mary Finley Niles of St. Ignatius has seen considerable Montana history in the making.

A sprightly 90 last August, she keeps a tidy house, helps tend her own and sometimes a neighbor's yard and has a delightful sense of humor.

"I'm planning to flood the market," she said last week, pointing to three strawberry plants thriving among her flowers.

She comes from hardy Indian stock. Her mother's father, Eneas Eneas, or To-Cha, was one of the group who went to St. Louis to bring the Blackrobes to the unsettled West.

Mrs. Niles has been told that when her grandfather died some months after returning, his legs were still swollen from the poisoning incurred in the long marches through the prickly pear. One of his companions and one priest were killed by hostile tribes but her grandfather lived to finish the journey and help in the building of St. Mary Mission at Stevensville.

At the age of six, her mother having died, Mrs. Niles was put in the first Sisters of Charity School at St. Ignatius, a dirtroofed log building where she remained until she was 20, graduating from the tenth grade which she considers equal to some college courses of today.

She remembers her school days as a bright part of her life although she was prone to trouble. She once had to kiss the ground from the chapel to the girls school because she didn't know the catechism. Another day when water pipes were first being installed she was sent to paint the inside of the water tower as punishment for (twice) blowing out the plumber's lantern, leaving him to wiggle about under the building in darkness.

"I'll be a good as they are," she related herself. "I'll just stay here!" So she painted until the paint was gone then instituted a one-girl hunger strike.

Her superiors had forgotten about her being sent to the tower and it was two days before someone looked in the window and saw her sleeping on the steps. "The Sisters were so nice to me," she recalled. "They took me into the kitchen and fed me."

Mrs. Niles credits the Sisters of Charity with everything she learned, not only the knowledge of books, but sewing, cooking and housekeeping also.

She knew most of the early-day priests, having been about seven years old when Father [Anthony] Ravalli died. She had a very fine voice and sang in the choir and at special functions, for which she received a gold award of merit with her name engraved.

Mrs. Niles' first job after leaving school was waiting tables at Duncan McDonald's stage station at Ravalli. Mrs. [Louise] McDonald was her godmother and she lived with the family in the huge log house that still stands, converted to a barn near the railroad bridge at the Dixon turnoff. The cook, she remembers was a "nice little Chinese."

"We called him John Smoke and I scared him out of his wits," she laughed, explaining how she brandished a butcher knife and threatened, "Now, I'm going to cut off your queue!"

The fastest travel was by horseback and she broke her own horses to ride, one throwing her against a tree when a girl came out to shake a blanket, causing her to spend eight months in the infirmary with a splinter near her spine.

Her second job was teaching at the Jocko Agency, a branch school operated by the Sisters of Charity and the first school at Arlee.

"There were about 75 girls," she recalled, "And I made all the uniforms. They were all red and grey, in nice wool material."

When the Jocko school was moved to Chemawa, Ore., due to discontinuance of government funds, she didn't go along. She took care of children for a while but finding it rather dull, threatened to marry "the first hobo that comes down the track." However, she married a Frenchman named Wilfred Peche instead and went on living at Jocko Agency. While she was there, the agency suffered an epidemic of infantile paralysis. Her eldest son, Basil, contracted the disease and lay packed in ice for two weeks. But he came through with one affected arm.

She vividly remembers the smallpox epidemic when the stricken were treated at a big tent and teepee camp just west of St. Ignatius. She related that 181 people died and lie buried nearby, under farm fields of today. They had moved from the Jocko Agency and her husband had the task of bringing in people to be vaccinated. Many refused to come, and many homes had to be burned after the occupants fell ill.

"Oh, it was horrible," she commented with a shudder.

"But there were happier days," she said, "when we had big dinners and dances at the Pablo ranch. And the buffalo were all over the hills and our home place north of Arlee. They came to lie down in our cow corrals. They got used to me peeping through the corral poles, sometimes offering a handful of hay."

She witnessed the buffalo roundup, saw herds of the big beasts swimming the river near Dixon, and knew two riders, Felix Cope and Joe Brooks, who were drowned.

"I can't stand buffalo meat!" she declared emphatically.

Her first husband died in 1915. Later, she married Wallace Niles, who died in 1962.

Mrs. Niles lived in Wyoming 39 years before returning to St. Ignatius six years ago. Of her four children two sons remain. One son, Basil Peche, lives with her at St. Ignatius. Frederick Peche, with his family, lives in Wyoming. She has one grandson.

"Yes, I've had a great life," she said, bustling into her kitchen to serve home-made bread and fresh lemon pie.

Document 43

Indian vs. White Justice

June 1882 – January 1883

Source: "Murder on the Jocko," *The Weekly Missoulian*, June 23, 1882, page 3, col. 3; *The Weekly Missoulian*, June 30, 1882, page 3, col. 3; *The Weekly Missoulian*, June 30, 1882, page 2, col. 1; "District Court," *The New North-West* (Deer Lodge, Mont.), December 22, 1882, page 3, col. 4; "The Kuntza – Marengo Murder Trial," *The New North-West*, January 12, 1883, page 3, col. 4.

Editors' note: The legal proceedings to punish Koonsa for murdering Marengo were a classic case illustrating the differences between Indian and white concepts of justice. Many leading Montana white men were incensed at the conclusion of the trial which allowed Koonsa to go free. See the article in a Missoula newspaper on September 19, 1888, about Koonsa's death.

Murder on the Jocko.
One Hundred Dollars Reward Offered for the Capture
of the Murderer by Maj. Ronan.

We are just informed that Frank Marengo, a half-breed, well-known in Missoula, from the fact that he was at one time interpreter at the fort, was fouly murdered by another half-breed by the name of "Koonsa," on Wednesday night, June 21, on the Jocko reservation. The particulars of the affair we glean as follows:

Koonsa, in company with two half-breeds, came to the house of Pete Finley, whose ranch Frank Marengo was working on shares. It appears the party had whisky and commenced drinking. In the carousal a quarrel occurred between Koonsa and one of his companions, when the latter picked up a Henry rifle, which belonged to Pete Finley, and fired at the man he was quarreling with, but missed him; whereupon Frank Marengo begged Koonsa not to shoot. Koonsa raised his gun and fired at Marengo, killing him almost instantly. The only words spoken by the murdered man after the fatal shot were, "Oh, my poor wife!" The party who accompanied Koonsa ran away, and the murderer, with gun in hand, ordered Marengo's wife under penalty of being shot to mount and go with him. This the woman refused to do, stating that she preferred to die with her husband. The cowardly murderer then raised his gun, which was caught by the woman, and in the struggle for possession the weapon fell to the floor and was immediately grasped by the woman. Koonsa then fled into the darkness, and to the mountains. The murderer is supposed to be well mounted, as two of his best horses are missing from his band of some eighteen head.

Koonsa, the murderer, is about twenty-five years old, and has lived from young boyhood until about three years ago among the Blackfeet Indians. A war party of Blackfeet Indians in one of their raids upon the Indians of the Jocko reservation, killed the mother of Koonsa, who was the wife of Bason Finley, and carried off the boy, and as stated above was found among the Blackfeet at the age of some twenty-two years, and brought back to his father by the Pend' Oreille Indians some three years ago.

The wife of Frank Marengo belongs in Bitter Root. She was educated by the Sisters of St. Ignatius mission on the Flathead reservation, and is an intelligent and well conducted young woman. Her name before marriage was Philomine Brooks.

Every effort is being made to capture the murderer, and we are informed that Major [Peter] Ronan, the agent, has offered a reward of one hundred dollars to any person who will bring the murderer in to him.

* * * * * * * *

On Wednesday night last Agent Ronan brought in the half-breed Koonsa, who killed Frank Marengo. He had concealed himself about the reservation for several days, but finding the trails guarded came back to the Agency and surrendered himself to Chief Michel. The Indians held a council over the matter, and after hearing Koonsa's story to the effect that it was "whisky and not himself, that caused the murder — a matter which no one regretted so much as he did, for Marengo was his friend, and he had no quarrel with him" etc., they decided that it would do no good to hang him, and that as a punishment, they would divest him of his property and turn him loose. They made this proposition to Maj. Ronan, and were quite surprised when he took the bull by the horns and told them that the man was his prisoner, and that he was going to take him to Missoula. Michel said he was "chief"; but the Major replied, "Yes, over a few Indians; but this man has committed an offense against the United States government, and I, as its agent, propose to hold him." He then ordered Koonsa into his wagon and drove off to Missoula with him. The man will have an examination before Commissioner Woody, and the probably be sent to Deer Lodge for trial before a United States court.

— June 30, 1882.

* * * * * * * *

— When Agent Ronan took the murderer of Frank Marengo into his hands on Wednesday, Chief Arlee said to him: "This man has committed a murder under the influence of whisky. Why do you not go to Camas Prairie, and get the man who sold him the whisky. Strike at the heart of the disease; not at the victims." It was explained that no proof could be brought as to where the man purchased his liquor, and that positive proof must be given; but the old Indian failed to see the point, and thought the men who sold whisky, knowing its effects, was just as guilty of murder as the drunken assassin, and equally deserving of punishment. Don't know but he was about right.

— June 30, 1882.

* * * * * * * *

District Court.
December Term, 1882.

96 — United States vs. Koonsa, a Pen d'Oreille Indian. For murder. Motion on continuance overruled, and cause on trial. Witnesses, including Arlee, Chief of the Flatheads; Maj. Peter Ronan, Indian Agent; Mrs. Marengo, Little Francois and others were introduced and testified in substance — that about June 22d, Frank Marengo and Koonsa furnished money to Little Francois to buy whiskey, and that he took them about three quarts; that Marengo, Koonsa and two or three others drank at Marengo's place on the Jocko river, in the Flathead reservation, that Francois started to carry a bottle of the whiskey to Peter Finley, when Koonsa commenced throwing stones at him. Koonsa and others went back to Marengo's house, where the prisoner obtained possession of Marengo's rifle. Marengo attempted to get the gun away from him, when Koonsa shot him; that Koonsa was tried for the killing by a council, headed by Michele, chief, and others of the Pend d'Oreille tribe, and sentenced to forfeit ten horses.

The court found that the defendant had been convicted and punished for the crime in accordance with the customs of the tribe, and ordered that he be discharged, and the jurors in attendance discharged for the term.

— December 22, 1882

* * * * * * * *

The Kuntza – Marengo Murder Trial.
Testimony of Arlee Chief of the Flatheads.
The Indian Penalty for Murder —
The White People Held Responsible for What an Indian Does When Drunk.

(Prior to the convening of the recent term of District Court we gave Agent Ronan's account of the murder of Marengo, the half-breed, by Kuntza, a Pen d'Oreille Indian, on the Flathead reservation last summer. When the case came up in court its dismissal was moved on the ground that Kuntza had been already tried and punished by the laws of his tribe for this offense, that the laws of the United States recognized these Indian trials, and that the man could not again be placed in jeopardy for this crime. The court sustained the motion, the case was dismissed and Kuntza discharged. Incidental to this trial, previous to this motion, Arlee, Chief of the Flatheads, gave the following testimony, through Chief Michelle [sic], interpreter, a stenographic report of which was made by W. I. Lippincott, Esq., who kindly furnished us with a verbatim transcript of the same. It explains the Indian penalty for murder, and concludes with a startling proposition concerning responsibility for what an Indian does when drunk, in which there is more truth than poetry. — Ed. N. N-W.)

Arlee's Testimony

My name is Arlee; I am seventy-one years old; the Big Chief at Washington put me on the Flathead Agency and told me to live there; am one of the chiefs of the three tribes of Flathead Indians on the agency. Have been chief for ten years; we punish our people for crimes committed on the reservation by our own laws. The Indian has no written laws for the punishment of Indian criminals; the chiefs keep the laws through the mouth; they are written in the heart; when an Indian kills another Indian, chiefs call all the other Indians together and send for the criminal; then the chiefs talk among themselves, and if the criminal has any horses or other property, the chiefs sitting in council over him will take all and give it to the relatives of the man who was killed. If the man who was killed has a wife or children, the chiefs decree that everything the criminal has shall go to them; then the chief will make his speech, and admonish them, and tell them not to do that thing again.

I know Kuntza; he is a Pen d'Oreille Indian. A long time ago, when Kuntza was a little boy, the Pen d'Oreille, the Piegan, and Blackfeet had a war and the Blackfeet killed Kuntza's parents and captured him. After while we held a big council and made a treaty and Kuntza came back a big boy. I know Marengo, the man Kuntza killed. He was a half-breed. His mother was a full blood. After Kuntza killed Marengo, he came and delivered himself up to Michelle, one of the chiefs. I was in my house. After Kuntza and Michelle hold a talk they came to my house and hold council, and I heard Michelle talk, and I said "this is your law, and my law, and our people's law." When Michelle and Kuntza come to my house, Michelle said: "Now, Arlee, I want to tell you. I don't want Kuntza to go out of this reservation. We have our jail here and our laws, and we will punish him here ourselves," and I told him "all right, we will do that." Then Michelle took all of Kuntza's horses, and gave one to me, kept one himself, and I don't know whether he gave one to the other chief or not, and kept the balance to take care of them. Most of the Indians were away hunting and Michelle took care of the horses until they returned. Then we hold a big council and divide the horses amongst Marengo's relatives, and put Kuntza in jail. Then the Indian Agent came and took him away. We didn't want Kuntza to be taken away; we were afraid of the white people outside. In the little council we held first we decreed that one of Kuntza's horses will go to me, one to Michelle, and all the rest to be divided amongst Marengo's relatives, and when the Indians came back from their hunt we held a big council, with all the men and women present, and ratified the action of the first council and then divided the horses. That is the Indian law now and always has been the law.

When an Indian is drunk and kills another Indian we don't consider that he did anything. The Indian never had whisky before the white man came here, and we blame the white people who gave him the liquor.

Document 44

Indians Insist on Agreement Before
Railroad Construction
July 28, 1882

Source: *The Weekly Missoulian*, July 28, 1882, page 2, col. 1.

Editors' note: The Northern Pacific Railroad was close to the Flathead Reservation, but tribal members refused to allow construction on the reservation until a deal was reached, and the Commissioner of Indian Affairs backed them up.

— In response to the wishes of the railroad company, Major [Peter] Ronan last week called a council of the Indians to consider a proposition to go ahead with the work of grading on the reservation prior to the meeting of the commission to negotiate for the right-of-way. Some three or four hundred Indians were present, and after discussing the matter fully decided not to allow any work to be done until a bargain had been closed with the railroad company. Inasmuch as there has been considerable newspaper talk of pushing through the reserve with the consent of the Indians, if possible, but without it if necessary — it is perhaps as well to state that Maj Ronan showed us a telegram instructing him to "allow no work to be done on the reservation without full and free consent of the Indians. *This is absolute.*" One of the Indians at the recent council is reported as saying, "The railroad has come to within a few yards of our border, and suddenly gets in a hurry. We are in no hurry for the railroad. We can wait till we sell our lands before we let people use them."

Document 45

Traveling Across Flathead in 1882

July 1882

Source: Excerpt from Ernest Ingersoll, "The Last Remnant of Frontier," *The American Magazine*, vol. 6, no. 2 (June 1887), pages 136-143.

Editors' note: Ingersoll crossed the Flathead River on Antoine Revais' ferry and then traveled through the reservation. Most of the inhabitants were attending the St. Ignatius Day celebration at the mission. Ingersoll did note a number of Indian farms, cattle, and horses and the hospitality of most of the few Indians he met.

The Last Remnant of Frontier

Wide crops of hay began to appear here and there, surrounding small log-houses without barns or any out-buildings. These, Pete [Ingersoll's German traveling companion] said, belonged to Indians, and indicated that we had entered the Reservation of the Flatheads, but not a human being of any race showed himself. At last a final sunbaked ridge was surmounted, and before us lay the elusive ferry.

Seeing us, the ferryman came across with his boat. It was a small scow suspended by two pulleys upon a wire-cable stretched high above the water, and operated by the force of the current against which it was set at an angle. As passengers, he brought over two young fellows who were walking across from Montana to the railway-front. These were not the first nor the last we met. Two or three times a day such tramps appeared, each one trudging with a small roll of blankets over his shoulders as his only luggage. In Montana, whence they came, there was plenty of work at large wages for all men who were willing to toil steadily; nothing better could be hoped from the region to which they were going — certainly nothing enough better to pay for this long journey on foot through the blinding heat and dust and over the rugged mountains, where the chances to get anything to eat were few and dreadfully far between. Yet if you had called these men tramps, as certainly they were, they would have been very indignant.

Their idea was that the railroad construction-work was a sort of public enterprise upon which they had a right to prey; or, at any rate, was an employer requiring far less return in work for wages than any private employer would exact. The camps of engineers marking out the route ahead of construction were considered by these tramps as places established for their special benefit — hospices, as it were, for the fastidious gentry who are careful never to *find* the chance of labor for which they are always "looking."

In the fall of 1881 this theory was acted upon so boldly that large, armed parties of tramps used regularly to capture small camps, and at the muzzle of revolvers outnumbering the engineers' force, insist upon full entertainment for several days. They learned where depôts of supplies had been stored against the snow-blockades of winter, and raided them, endangering not only the continuance of the work in hand, but the lives of the engineers, and they openly threatened, in case they were resisted, to burn and destroy the railroad's defenceless [sic] property.

Eventually all the railroad camps were moved to the bank of the river opposite the trail, though involving the expense of laboriously ferrying all supplies. The rage of the cormorants who nearly starved to death as they found camp after camp inaccessible was only amusement to those who witnessed it, because the wide river lay a safeguard between. Then a combination of sheriffs from Idaho and Montana was arranged; some judicious, if not judicial, hangings occurred, and the tramp-nuisance upon this trail was abated.

The men we now saw were not dangerous — they were only miserable, lazy and utterly *cultus*, as the Chinook puts it. Most of them were young — some mere youths. They always traveled in couples and called each other "pardner."

> The worst man living hath some fear, some love,
>
> Holds somewhat dear a little for life's sake,
>
> Keeps fast to some companion.

The ferryman was a thick-set, gray-headed Frenchman, who spoke only broken English. As we slowly traversed the emerald surface of the full-fed stream, sweeping between banks where the weeds and bushes were mirrored in lovely hues, I said to him:

"Why this is almost as large as Clarke's Fork!"

"It *is* Clarke's Fork," he replied.

I did not waste time in disputing, but I knew differently. If you look at the map you will see that out of Pend' d'Oreille lake into the Columbia flows a great river called the Clarke's Fork of the Columbia, after the intrepid explorer who, with Captain [Meriwether] Lewis, ascended it in 1813 [sic]. Into Pend' d'Oreille lake comes from the eastward a great river, which you may consider only the other half of this and one with Clarke's Fork, if you like; but as you ascend it you will meet with difficulties. About one hundred miles above the lake it forks. One of the branches is a big stream (the one I was now crossing), draining Flathead lake on the north. This is called by trappers and Indians the Pend' d'Oreille river, and it is fed by the Flathead river, which flows into Flathead lake from mountains far up in British Columbia. The other branch is the Missoula (or Mesooléh, as the Kalispel language pronounces it), which is itself formed by the junction of the Bitter-root and the Hellgate rivers. Taking the whole of it — Hellgate, Missoula, Pend' d'Oreille and Clarke's Fork — into consideration, this great stream is the most important feeder of the mighty Columbia, and is navigable for steamboats for hundreds of miles.

The ferry-house was a log-building, where the ferryman lived a bachelor's life. Two or three tents in the neighborhood showed campers waiting until morning to cross. Before the door a small fire was heating a kettle and coffeepot. Very hungry and tired, I begged the ferryman to get us supper, or at least a cup of coffee, but he declined in a surly way, alleging that anything of the kind was forbidden because he was on Reservation ground. The statement was nonsense so far as it applied to the present case, but the man was obstinate.

"You mus' go on to Rive's ranch, ten mile from 'ere. Dere you fin' plenty grub and place to sleep."

An old man squatted by the fire, smoking a coal-black pipe. He was a half-breed, very dark, wrinkled like a frozen apple, lean to gauntness, with narrow forehead, small sparkling eyes, hooked nose, and thin, clean-shaven lips and chin, so that he resembled an aged eagle as he perched there on a log of cottonwood. It was Rive himself, of whom I have heard it said that when he was young, and went into public, he always took a boy and broom with him to clean up what remained of the men with whom he happened to quarrel. But we didn't know him at that time, and so did not appreciate the old rascal's sublime irony when he beamingly urged us to go on to his own ranch, understanding perfectly well what awaited us.

However, there was no way but to march ahead, and it was during that late middle darkness between nightfall and moonrise that the long ten miles was completed, and we came to Rive's *rancheria*. It consisted of a score or so of log-houses and stables huddled together and surrounded by redskin teepees, corrals, and small stagings sustaining harness, etc., out of reach of dogs and coyotes. Ahead, along the bottoms of the Pend' d'Oreille river, to which the road closely approached at this point, stretched a long line of well-fenced fields and meadows; but no fence or hedge separated the rough, bare houses from the road, or from the treeless, rocky plain and hills behind.

Plainly this was an Indian settlement. Everything was perfectly still; even the two dogs that came to meet us made no noise about it.

"All asleep," muttered Pete, as though that remark settled the case.

"Then they must be waked up," I rejoined with some asperity.

Very unwillingly and cautiously, therefore, Pete sidled up to the door of the foremost house, which was veiled under hop-vines, followed by the two dogs. Softly he touched his knuckles to the door, and the dogs turned away as though hopeless of any excitement.

"Knock louder, Pete," I shouted.

"They might be on the shoot!" replies he, and retreats to his horse.

Then I go myself and bang the door with my whole fist. It delights the dogs, but nobody responds. It is evident that the hamlet is deserted. What next? Plainly nothing is left us but the hills. The night is still and warm, and the medallion of the full moon rises fresh from the mint through the motionless topmost sprays of the poplars along the creek. We hear the bell denoting where the horses of a freighter, asleep under his wagon, are feeding beyond the thickets, but otherwise everything is profoundly quiet, save for the high-pitched, fine-spun songs of thousands of mosquitoes pirouetting about our ears. Perhaps on top the high ridge we may escape them, so we force our jaded horses up two or three hundred feet, but the mosquitoes are here too, and our only hope of peace lies in the coming of a breeze to blow them away.

Rest must be had at any rate: forty miles in the saddle on a blazing day, with nothing to eat after breakfast but a handful of crackers, is no child's play. Anchoring one horse to a rock, and letting the others loose, we take a saddle-blanket and an overcoat apiece, search out comparatively smooth spots among the rocks and lie down. Already notice of the feast had gone abroad, and from far and near the no-see'ems had gathered to their merry-making. Were ever mosquitoes so hungry! They were open to no reasoning in any language or phraseology, and we tested a great variety with some vehemence. They had no fear whatever — could neither be scared nor brushed away — had "three-o'clock-in-the-morning courage" — stuck in their needle-pointed picks as soon as their feet touched the skin, without pausing for a single second's prospecting; and I cannot recall a more miserable night out of doors than that one proved.

The hill upon which we had camped was the outer ridge of a low range bounding the valley on the south. From its eminence the course of the river could be traced eastward for many miles, by the line of trees which fringed its banks, and which were the only trees in the landscape. Beyond, a gap in the hills disclosed the jagged, blue-back outline of the Mission range of mountains, behind which the sky was afire with the sunrise. The blaze of a few twigs of sage-brush setting off the smutty silhouette of a coffee-pot would have excited far more interest just then, but it occurred to me, as I wearily folded my thin blanket, that the irregular, black sierra might be the rough edge of the shell of the night, through which the half-hatched day was bravely poking his yellow head. This was a momentary fancy — the absorbing idea was *breakfast*, and we decided to seek the teamsters passed the night before, and if possibly buy something to eat from them. Their fire was crackling on the further bank of the creek when we found it, and one man was mixing bread in the mouth of a sack of flour, while another brought in the four horses and began to harness them.

One of the teamsters was an old German, who, in twenty-five years of frontier life as a "freighter," had acquired a most excellent pronunciation, at least in American profanity. His companion was a stalwart half-breed, who announced breakfast by handing to each of us a tin plate and a tin cup, both thickly coated with the grease of former meals. Into the cup was poured half a pint of strong tea — a beverage I detest at home; then he slapped down upon the plate a fat slice of half-fried pork — an abomination to civilized palates anywhere. The bread had been baked before the fire in the frying-pan, was half-done, and golden with saleratus. But we ate and drank, paid two bits, lit our pipes and went on, thanking heaven it was no worse.

Barring the evil remembrance of the saleratus in my mouth, that first five miles across the level valley through the cool of the morning air was very pleasant, and the clever work of the sunrise in dispelling the brooding mists of the purple hills was something good for a man to see.

Then we came to a prosperous-looking house and hoped to buy some grain, but there was nobody at home. We didn't try the house-door, but the dairy was open, where a dozen or so great pans stood full of our milk mantled in thick curdled cream, upon which Pete regaled himself. While we were conducting these investigations, an old Indian, wearing civilized clothing — albeit very ragged — made his appearance, and began to *coo-ee* to the chickens, tossing them handfuls of wheat. He could not speak English, and his Chinook flowed in so thick a stream of Kalispel gutterals that I could make little out of it.

Speech failing, we had recourse to signs, partly those conventional among all Indians, partly extemporized, and soon learned that he was merely a neighbor of the red owner of this ranch, but that oats were to be had if we would go on a few rods to the old fellow's own farm.

His home proved to be two log cabins, a big conical lodge (made of poles, green cowhides and matting) and a root-cellar. All around it were fields of oats, barley and wheat, with a patch of potatoes and kitchen vegetables left to grow pretty much as they pleased. He had no barn, stacking his grain and using his cabins for storehouses as well as winter quarters, his teepee serving as a summer house. The kitchen was at an outdoor fire, where his wrinkled old kloochman was now stewing some dusty dried beef for breakfast.

While the horses were feeding and resting I walked on, taking a cut across the weedy fields till I stumbled upon a big snake, after which I kept to the road. The soil here is light and gravelly, but seems to produce well when water is brought to it by irrigation. All along the river side stood Indian cabins and fields, but the road bore away from there, keeping along the dry benches at the base of the hills, so that I had walked four or five miles before I found a bit of shade at the crossing of the Jocko — a lively stream flowing down from the south-east. Here were encamped more freighters who had come over from the Mission, five miles distant, and were on their way westward. Just ahead a nice-looking little cabin stood near the road, with a woman and several children at the door, and I asked permission to sit in the shadow of the house until my horses came up.

The woman was a young half-blood, two of whose children were regular little brown Indians, while a third had a white skin and blue eyes. Her husband, a Frenchman, was off at Flathead lake looking after cattle.

"What has become of the people in the valley?" I asked; for though houses and farms had been plentiful we had seen nobody at all except the aged Indian who sold us the oats.

"They are all away at church," she explained. "I was going too, but I was too sick. This is not my house. I live ten miles below."

By "the church" I understood the Jesuit mission of St. Ignatius, which for many years has been a center of religious influence among the Indians of all this region, and where there now resides a colony of hard-working priests and nuns — missionaries in the most practical sense of the word, and having almost boundless control over the aborigines of western Montana, who, without exception, are devout Roman Catholics.

"This is the feast day of the patron saint (Ignatius)," she continued. "Yesterday (Sunday) they had high pontifical mass celebrated by the archbishop of Oregon, who is visiting the mission. There are about a thousand Indians over there and a great many French people. When the archbishop came, all the Indians went out to meet him, running their horses, yelling and firing their guns, and so escorted him in with great ceremony. To-day they have a big dinner and horse-races and great sport. I wish I could have gone."

Just then one of the youngsters came out with his fists full of crackers, and I thought it a good opportunity to ask my entertainer if she could not sell me some coffee and crackers. No, she couldn't; the crackers were only a few a gentleman had given to the boy. I was not to be baffled so easily, however. A hungry man's wits become sharp. So I said no more about it, but presently began to give a casual account of my adventures — the failure of supper at the ferry, the hard night on the hill-top, the scanty bad breakfast with the teamsters, and wound up by my mild wonderment where I should see another meal in the blank country ahead. Suddenly she interrupted me with an amazing proposition:

"I can give you a plate of oyster soup if you like."

And half an hour later, on the remotest edge of an Indian reservation in northern Montana, I sat down to oysters stewed in new milk, to good bread and butter, to whole-souled coffee, to preserved peaches and crisp cookies!

The twenty miles remaining of the day's ride were shadeless and horribly exhausting under the shimmering noontide heat, reflected by the circling smooth hills and the gleaming plain; but all along the lowlands lay Indian farms, while the uplands were dotted with cattle and horses. The latter were a constant attraction to my vagrant kiyoos pony, and an equally constant source of annoyance to me.

The night was spent at the Jocko agency, headquarters of the Flathead (Kalispel) Indian nation, and was made a most pleasant and restful one by the hospitality of the agent and his family.

My route the next morning — I should now be able to follow a good wagon-road all the way to Missoula and civilization — ran for a half a dozen miles straight across the unsheltered plain; round, brown, close-shaven hills on one side, and the wooded mountains on the other, broken only by the narrow valley below the agency, where Indian ranches were scattered beautifully among the willow thickets beside the stream, and the bottom-lands were checkered with squares of wheat and oats. How grateful after this arid exposure the arched aisles of the pine-woods through which the road presently wandered, avoiding rocks, creeping cautiously in and out of gullies, circling knolls, and dodging the big trees! There was one long hill surmounting miles and miles of level tree-tops spread beneath the path; but after that the traveler was immersed again in the cool shadows; the needle-strewn earth, the orange trunks and the light-green foliage so filling his eye with yellow that, when glimpses of the clear sky were caught, it seemed a more vivid violet than ever was seen elsewhere by mortal vision.

In an open glade by a stream-bank I came upon a small company of immigrants making a late start. They had three ordinary farm-wagons covered with cotton-sheeting and piled full of miscellaneous furniture. There were two brown-skinned old women and three young ones, none of them blooming to any extent, while children of all sizes, ages and degrees of hungriness swarmed about the camp-fire. They had come from Missouri in the wagons, and were going to Oregon, spending a whole summer on the trip. Missouri lost some ague victims and Oregon gained some — that's about all this two thousand miles of migration would amount to.

Presently I became aware that I had passed out of Indian territory, but coming upon the long embankment of the new railway grade which had stopped at the boundary line. There were no signs of mankind about, and the fresh, evenly piled earth looked as though it might be the upheaved track of some huge sort of a mole that had passed that way the night before. Half a mile farther the real origin was manifested by the hasty log-cabins, the bark shanties and canvas tents, the wagons, scrapers and log-chopping of the grade-makers.

Document 46

Tribal Chiefs Bargain for
Railroad Right of Way Land
August 31 — September 2, 1882

Source: U.S. President, "Message from the President of the United States, Transmitting a Letter from the Secretary of the Interior Respecting the Ratification of an Agreement with the Confederated Tribes of Flathead, Kootenay, and Upper Pend d'Oreilles Indians, for the Sale of a Portion of Their Reservation in Montana Territory," Senate Executive Document No. 44 (1883), 47th Congress, 2d Session, serial 2076, pages 8-18.

Editors' note: The transcript of the 1882 negotiations for the Northern Pacific Railroad right of way through the Flathead Reservation was a remarkable document of the astute and capable tribal leadership in the late nineteenth century. The tribal leaders held discussions before the actual council, so they could decide on strategy and present a united front to Joseph McCammon, the government negotiator. Their first choice was to have the railroad avoid the reservation entirely. When this object proved unattainable, they asked McCammon to extend the reservation north to the Canadian line. They pointed out that many of the government promises in the 1855 Hellgate Treaty had not been fulfilled and most of the annuities had not been received. McCammon's condescension was palpable, but he did agree to support the tribes' appeal for a northern extension of the reservation. This question became moot in 1883 when Senator G. G. Vest visited the reservation, because tribal leaders feared that the whites would manipulate any changes in the reservation boundaries against the interests of the Indians and withdrew the request. Two hundred nineteen tribal members signed the agreement in 1882. At the negotiations, McCammon argued that the railroad was only getting the use of the land, not full ownership, however the agreement stated the land was selling all their interest in the right of way land. McCammon promised free rides for Indians on the railroad, but there was no mention of this in the agreement. The written agreement was vague, but the government did finally pay for the land in a cash per capita payment rather than annuities.

Council held by Hon. Joseph K. McCammon, Assistant Attorney-General, appointed by the Secretary of the Interior to negotiate an agreement with the Indians

on the Flathead Reservation for right of way for the Northern Pacific Railroad
through the reservation.

August 31, 1882 — 3 p.m.

Present: Arlee, Adolphe, Eneas, and Michelle, with headmen and Indians of the Flathead, Pend d'Oreilles, and Kootenais tribes.

Agent [Peter] Ronan said: Mr. McCammon is here from Washington, representing the United States Government, to meet the Indians in council; and it is desired to have them listen attentively. He is here with the voice of the Great Father, and brings his words to the Indians. I have no further words of introduction.

Commissioner McCammon. My friends of the Flathead, Pend d'Oreilles, Kootenais, and other tribes living on the Jocko Reservation: I have been sent by the Great Father at Washington a great many miles to see you and talk with you. He knows how well you have treated the white people these many years; that you have been peaceful and happy, and have taken care of yourselves; that you have always been his friends and the friends of his people. Knowing these things he does not wish to take from you your lands. He knows, however, that a railroad is to be built on the borders of your reservation. Twenty-seven years ago you and your fathers made a treaty with the whites. That treaty which you and the others made provided for a country here in which you and your fathers should live. In that treaty you and your fathers agreed "if necessary for the public convenience roads may be run through the said reservation." By another treaty, made the same year at the treaty grounds, near the mouth of the Judith River, in Nebraska, which treaty was signed by the Flathead Nation and other Indians, it was provided that "for the purpose of establishing traveling thoroughfares through the country, and better to enable the President to execute the provisions of this treaty, the aforesaid nations and tribes do hereby consent and agree that the United States may, within the countries respectively occupied and claimed by them, construct roads of every description, establish lines of telegraph," &c. The Great Father and the Great council in 1864 gave the Northern Pacific Railroad Company the right to build a railroad through this country. The railroad company now say to the Great Father, "We want to build a railroad through the Jocko Reservation a few miles." The Great Father says, "The Indians on the Jocko Reservation gave me consent, years ago, to have roads of every description built through their land." He understands that a wagon road has been built and used for some time. That is one kind of road. Another kind of road is a railroad. It is a better and quicker way of traveling. It is a kind of road that other Indians all over the country have allowed to be built. But the Great Father says that he thinks the Indians should be paid for the little land that will be used by the railroad. He says he thinks the railroad will be good for the Indians as well as for the whites. The building of the road may bring white men on the reservation in order to grade the road, lay ties, &c., but when the road is built, no white men will remain except at stations and there only so many as are necessary. I will now show you a map of your reservation (shows map). The railroad is to come up here from the Missoula, entering the reservation by the Jocko River, and then going along the Jocko and Pend d'Oreille Rivers to the west line of the reservation. Now, as all the lands on the reservation belong to the Indians the United States wants to pay, and thinks it right to pay, for 100 feet of road on each side of the track, for a distance of 53.26 miles on this narrow line; and also for five squares of ground alongside, to be used as stations, being about 130 acres in addition, fully described on the map. These stations are where cars will stop to take on passengers, Indians and others, and Indian wheat and grain, if you want it carried off to sell; and where goods will be sent or received. This will cover a very small part of the reservation — like a spider web or fly track across the reservation (illustrating). Your reservation contains about 3,000,000 acres; the railroad will occupy 1,500 acres, just about as much as an ordinary wagon road. Now the Great Father asks me to inquire of these Indians what will be a fair price for this small tract. He says you ought to be paid a fair, reasonable price, just as much as he would pay a white man, no more and no less. Where the railroad runs through the farms of Indians, those Indians will be paid for their fences, farms, houses, and crops, if interfered with, the money to be paid to each Indian, or to the agent to be used for them. I am appointed to find out how much this will damage each Indian farm. This refers only to houses, fences, crops, &c., that belong to individual Indians.

Michelle. You don't know how much individual Indians will get, do you?

Commissioner. No; that we will determine hereafter. I went last year to Fort Hall Reservation. The Indians there allowed a road to be built, and no white men have come on the reservation because of the road. That is on the same plan as this. Hundreds of miles of road are built through the Indian Territory, and yet white men are kept out, except the agents of the railroads. The Northern Pacific Railroad has stopped at the line of your reservation, and wishing well to the Indians, does not want to interfere with them, except by some arrangement so that the Indians may be paid. So the Great Father sends me to ask you what you want to be paid for this land which the railroad company needs. I want you to consider this matter and ask questions. I don't want any one to misunderstand. I want to be just to the Indians. I want to protect their rights. I want them to talk. I am ready to hear from Arlee, Michelle, Adolphe, Eneas, or the headmen who know what they want to say.

Eneas. I presume you will not ask us to answer now. There are some men here who have wild ideas, and we want to adjourn and talk the matter over.

Michelle. We don't want to detain you for a lot of humbug. Of course you and the Great Father claim that we ought to be paid for the land taken; we are not to be cheated; we are to be treated just the same as whites.

Commissioner. The Crows last year sold land to this company just the same as you are asked to do. Whatever time you wish will be granted.

Arlee. I am going to talk not about what you are talking about. The Great Chief don't pity me. I am crowded on both sides. White men go up and down the reservation with cattle. I lose cattle in plenty. I want you to get the whites off the land at the head of Flathead Lake. I am old. I will soon die. There are a lot of young ones. I would like to have them live happy. But they will always be in trouble with the white men if they remain so near us. It may be true that the railroad would help the Indians, but I would like to get the whites off the Flathead Lake.

Commissioner. Cattle are driven through the reservation because the treaty provided for it. White men who steal are bad men. There are bad white men and bad Indians. White men punish bad white men when they can find them. Fewer cattle will go through the reservation after the building of the railroad, for then many cattle will go through on cars. I will report your wishes to the Great Father. The Great Father did not know them.

Arlee. The country we gave to the government is very valuable. Lots of white men have made independent fortunes in my country. Since twenty-seven years ago, when my forefathers made the treaty and gave you the country east and south of this, you have been digging gold there; that country is very valuable. You must not think there are so few here. Lots of others think of coming over here and living on this reservation. Be sure to tell the Great Father my wishes.

Michelle. I and Eneas think as does Arlee.

Commissioner. Tell him I (not the Great Father) think if they want that country up north they should have it. I will tell the Great Father. They got the price they asked for their land; they sold it to the white man. Gold was not yet discovered there. They yet have fine lands, noble rivers, and majestic mountains.

Ronan. In my talks I feel as if I knew what Arlee wished to say. On the north side of the Flathead reservation there is a narrow tract of United States land. Arlee fears that strip will be settled by whites, and Arlee feels if the Great Father will let the Indians have that then they will not be surrounded by whites.

September 1, 1882 — 1.40 p.m.

Commissioner McCammon. My friends, I am glad to see you to-day, and hope your hearts are good towards the Great Father. I will be pleased to hear what the chiefs have to say. If there is anything they don't understand in the talk of yesterday I will try to make it clear. I am ready to hear from them now.

Eneas. I am the chief and you see me now. I have not [sic] doubt you are sent to see us by the Great Father. I am the chief and this is my country. I am not joking in telling you I would like to get the Flathead Lake country back. There are things that the government promised me in that treaty that I have never seen. The government promised me everything we needed. The government told me it would send a blacksmith, and build school-houses, and furnish teachers at the agencies to instruct Indians, and a head farmer, and build houses for us. The government wished us to be like white men, and these were to instruct us. It promised me a tinner, a wagon-maker, a plow-maker, a hospital, and a doctor to look after the sick; and that is the reason we signed the treaty. I was glad to think we were to have these things. We had a big country, and under those conditions we signed the treaty. Seven years after that we learned that the line of the reservation ran across the middle of Flathead Lake. We didn't know that when we signed the treaty. That is the reason we want that country back. Besides, we did not get one-half of the annuities that belonged to us. It was divided among yourselves. You told us that after a while we would be intelligent and rich and like white men. We are poor now. We try to have whites to assist us, and they won't because we are Indians. That is the reason we want to have the whites kept out of that Flathead Lake country.

Commissioner. I am glad to hear Eneas. I know what a good man he is. Major Ronan has told me what wrong has been done years ago; he can now trust Major Ronan; what he gets he gives the Indians. One reason why the Great Father forgot the Flatheads is that they have been so far from Washington; but now when the railroad is built they will be within four or five days from Washington; and the Great Father and his people will see and pity the Indians. That is one thing the Great Father means when he says the Indians will be benefited by the railroad. I will tell the Great Father about Eneas's desires, and do all I can to carry out his wishes.

Arlee. What is the reason you are not able to treat with the Indians about that country? You have full power.

Commissioner. Arlee is mistaken; I have not power to treat about everything. As I said yesterday, the Great Father did not know what your wishes were about that strip of land. He only knew about the railroad, and he told me to agree to pay for the land to be used by the railroad. The land is not taken by the railroad, but is taken by the Great Father, who lets the railroad use it. Possibly you will understand my power by an example. You are a chief of your tribe; you send one of your young men to fish, but he goes off to visit his friends miles away; you are waiting for your fish all the time; the young man had no right to visit his friends until he got his fish. So I have no right to do more than the Great Father told me, but must return to him. Do you understand?

Arlee. I understand.

Commissioner. That is my position.

Arlee. Is it true the Great Father don't know of the men north of the Flathead Lake?

Commissioner. The country there belongs to the Great Father, so whites have a right to go there; but I will tell the Great Father all you say. It is all written down.

Arlee. We will now quit talking about the head of Flathead Lake.

Commissioner. Now, I will be glad to hear about the money to be paid for the use of the land for the railroad.

Eneas. You know what I said, that the government did not give half it agreed about annuities; and I think I don't wish the road to pass through this reservation. The Great Father is a good man, and when the Great Father tells me a thing I do it. I wish the Great Father to do me a favor and consult my wishes, and not let the road go through this reservation. There is a good way down the Missouri [i.e., Missoula] to Horse Prairie. You are a great people, and when you want to do a thing you can do it. What makes you think the railroad can't go down there? This reservation is a small country, and yet you want five depots upon it. These are the best spots on the reservation. What is the reason I should be encouraged when you take the best part of my country? My country was like a flower and I gave you its best part. What I gave I don't look for back, and I never have asked for it back. The Great Father gave it to us for three tribes, Flathead, Upper Pend d'Oreilles, and Kootenais. What are we going to do when you build the road? We have no place to go. That is why it is my wish that you should go down the Missoula River. I am not telling you that you are mean, but this is a small country, and we are hanging on to it like a child on to a piece of candy.

Commissioner. The line selected by the railroad company was selected ten years ago, because it was the best route, and because down the Missoula River would not be a good route. The men who selected it then and continued to prefer it are able men, and know the best route; and they say this is the only route that is good. The Great Father believes these men, and he sent me to represent him, not them, in this council. He thinks it is the best route, and the Indians won't be injured, the amount of land to be taken is so small. The Great

Father has respect for the wishes of the Indians, but he thinks he knows what is best for them, and feeling that way he wants to know what money they want for the land. The Great Father will take care that bad white men do not sell whisky to Indians. He thinks he can do that better with a railroad through your reservation than with one down the Missoula. He wants it here. He says, "You have told me I can build roads through your reservation"; but he also says you shall be paid, he having pity on you. The Indians should remember that they got no pay for the wagon road built through their reservation, but he thinks they should be paid for the land used by the railroad. The amount of land that will be taken by the government is very small. Only a few pieces of land owned and improved by Indians will be taken. There is plenty of good land in this and other valleys and reservations, and all that have to move will be paid; they will have the money to pay them for moving, or to do what they please with. I am now talking about improvements. The land belongs to all the Indians, but the improvements to individuals. All the Indians will be paid by the Great Council at Washington for all the land taken, when an appropriation is made, and this money will be used for the benefit of all the Indians; but the money for the fences, houses, and other improvements will be paid to the individual Indians whose improvements are taken. The Great Father has this matter much at heart.

Eneas. Who established the lines of this reservation? It was the Great Father that got these lines established. Why does he want to break the lines? If we had no lines I would say no word. Lines are just like a fence. He told us so. No white man is allowed to live and work on the reservation. You know it is so in the treaty. That is the reason I say you had better go the other way. Why do you wish us to go away? It is a small country; it is valuable to us; we support ourselves by it; there is no end to these lands supporting us; they will do it for generations. If you say you will give us money for our lands, I doubt if we get it, because we didn't before.

Commissioner. Eneas and the rest do not understand what I said yesterday. The two treaties signed by your chiefs provide for roads of all kinds through your reservation. The Great Father is not asking for leave to build roads through your reservation; that was given twenty-seven years ago. The Great Father is not treated with great respect when I am told you will not get the money. The matter will be submitted to the Great Council, and the Indians will get the money; and whatever has been done in the past about these matters, you can rely upon the good faith of those who now have control of the government. I do not understand why this opposition comes, when the Indians gave their faith years ago to the Great Father that this road might be built. I am sorry to hear what has been said. I come here as an honest man to talk to honest men, and I want you to consider well the words of the Great Father.

(An Indian in the audience says, "Railroads are not mentioned.")

The commissioner read from the treaties of July and October, 1855, about roads, and continued: You can read it in the paper Arlee has. As I have told you, railroads run through nearly all the reservations in the country. There are a few they do not run through; but where they go Indians see less of whites than they did before, because the whites traveled by railroads. This very railroad runs through the Crow Reservation on the Yellowstone. A railroad runs through the country of the Shoshones in Idaho, and this same railroad through the Umatilla Reservation. None of these Indians object to it. They are wise Indians; they have received their money. The Crows and the Bannocks and the Shoshones have received theirs. The Great Father expends the money for the benefit of those Indians. The Great Father will be sorry when he hears that Indians do not believe in his good faith. Shall I go back and say to the Great Father that these Indians do not believe he is treating them right? He has but one object, and that is your good; and if I go back without your having named a price for the lands, he will say they are not the good Indians and faithful friends I thought.

Michelle. I am going to speak to Indians and no word to white men. I told the agent it was useless for us to oppose giving the white men this strip of land. We don't know the plans of the white man; there is no use of us thinking. Just now he has something to compel. You spoke yesterday of the land at the head of Flathead Lake. I agree with you. That is my wish. You were here yesterday. No word he mentioned was bad. I think it was all good. When you get a gentle horse if you beat him he is bound to get mean; and you are to blame when you beat a dumb brute. He spoke to us gentlemanly; he used no hard words; and we ought to be glad. We are all Americans. The British line is north, and beyond that are the British Indians. If the President thinks it best for a railroad to run through this land, I am quite willing. It is true this country has been reserved for us. When [James] Garfield came here he told us this was our country; our agent and another big chief from Washington told us the same. Our agent is acting friendly with us. I do not think this gentleman has said a wrong word to us yesterday or to-day. He only wants a little strip of land; he might take it without asking, but he is going to ask us first, and then leave it to the chiefs. It is a thing that is bound to go through anyhow; and so you must not blame your chiefs.

Commissioner. The whole country is not taken from you; just a little narrow strip is used for railroads; you can use it, except the narrow strip for a track and depot grounds. I remember last year, the Great Father, General Garfield, sent me to the Bannocks and Shoshones on this business. You all knew that great and good man, and he knew you and loved the Indians. I have heard that he thought much of you. What he said to me last year about the Shoshones and Bannocks, the Great Father said of you this year. Consider well his words and be men. I want to ask Arlee and Michelle if the wagon road has taken the country from them? If not, then a railroad will not. It is only a road with rail ties and locomotives to go through.

Arlee. We don't think anything bad, but we don't want the railroad to go through the reservation here, because these white men are bad people. At Camas Prairie they sell whisky; they go there and get whisky, and our boys bother us about whisky. This is why we don't want the railroad to go through our reservation, because when the white men come in to work there will be trouble; that is all.

Commissioner. About the man who sold liquor, we had him arrested and taken to jail. The same thing will be done by your agent; when he finds white men selling liquor he will arrest them. While the road is being built white men will have to come and build it; but after it is built there will be no white men to sell liquor. On the Crow and Shoshone reservation no liquor was sold to Indians while the road was being built. It won't be as bad as Arlee thinks; I hope not bad at all for the Indians. No liquor will be sold on the reservation at the depots.

Arlee. It was our old people that were good; we had good chiefs; I don't know how many years it is since the white people came, and we have never had fights between us and the whites; nor have we ever killed you at all; and that is why I want to remain in my country quiet and undisturbed. I hear every few days that other tribes of Indians are fighting with the whites; then you win their country. You did not win my country from me at all; the big chief made our lines and told us to stay here all the time, and a few years ago Garfield sent me here to stay. But you don't mind what he said at all. Garfield said, "Take it easy, don't be uneasy." It was nine years ago that Garfield said "Don't think we will thrust you from that country; that land belongs to you." Last winter I was at home lying down, when they told me men were surveying the place. Some said it did not amount to anything, but I said it would cut our reservation in two; and now to-day I see you here trying to get our land from us for the railroad. But I do not want any railroad here, for this is my country.

Commissioner. This is your country; there is no doubt about that. The Great Father did not send me to ask for your country; he sent me to say he was going to build a railroad across your country, and he wanted to pay you for it. All this country is still yours and will remain yours. He wants you to feel good and remember his kindness. There is no intention to take the country away from you. A railroad is like the wagon road. The wagon road did not take your country from you and the railroad won't. How long has the wagon road been here? Your fathers were good men; they knew the treaty allowed a wagon road, and the same treaty will allow a railroad. The railroad will help you more than the wagon road. It will keep white people out of your reservation. You can ship grain and all other goods by it. I want you to let me go to Washington and tell the Great Father you believe in his word. I will tell him what faithful children you are, how kind, and full of peace and happiness you are. I will tell him of the great sight I saw yesterday; how well you treated me because he sent me. My heart was glad, and I said the Indians will listen to what the Great Father has to say and obey his words. I will again ask you if you can name what money you want for this right of way. If you cannot, I will name a sum for you. When the railroad is built, the Great Father will probably come out himself to see his country and you. It is too far from the railroad now.

Adolphe. It is true that you only want a small strip of my country; it is true that there will be no white men in our country. All will be glad if you only take a small strip of our country. Look at my hand (uplifted); this is what they do in Washington. I lift my hand; the President does the same thing. It is true that what you say is in the treaty in regards to roads. In the treaty at Hell Gate in 1855 the Indians said the white men could have railroads through here. Governor [Isaac] Stevens said to Victor, "You are the head chief of three tribes here, and of the whites here too"; and they said we will talk about this land here by and by; and we are having that talk now. Some time ago I did not know about talking, nor what it was to sign my name; now I know. If the whites are good I am good. When there is blood on my hands, they are not wet with white people's blood. If what you have told me to-day is true, I will be glad. In this country you see no blood; other countries are stained with blood. The line of my country extends from earth up to heaven.

Commissioner. I want to talk again about this road going through your reservation. I want to explain to you that the Great Father sells land near and adjoining your reservation for $2.50 per acre. The railroad sells its land for $2.50 per acre near your reservation. It has land down towards the Missoula. I wish to be liberal. The Great Father told me to propose a fair price, and I think that $10 per acre is a fair price for the 1,500 acres. That is four times as much as the Great Father gets for his land. This would make altogether for the land $15,000. The Crows got only about five thousand, and the Shoshones seven thousand, or nearly eight. In addition, each Indians will be paid for his fences and barns where this railroad interferes with him. The $15,000 will for the benefit of the whole tribe.

Arlee. I object to depots.

Commissioner. Arlee never having seen railroads, don't know the amount of land required. Here is a glass with a few drops of water in it (illustrating). The whole tumbler represents the reservation, the water the amount of land wanted for the rail- railroad [sic]. The railroad wanted six stations; the Great Father said five would be enough. They wanted these for water for the engines. The railroad wanted a strip 400 feet wide; the Great Father said, "No 200"; the railroad wanted larger and more stations; the Great Father said, "No, five stations, and these must be small ones." The Great Father was thinking of the wishes and the interest of the Indians. . . . .The railroad down below is not done. The Indian don't know, but the Great Father knows and the engineers know how much is required. The railroad don't want the Indian lands, nor does the Great Father, but he cares for your interests.

(After a delay.)

Commissioner. Have you anything to say?

Arlee. I want to know about the depots; what are they?

Commissioner. Every railroad in this country has stations once in 10 miles for water, at the side of the track. If the railroad at Spokane has not stations every 10 miles it is because it is not yet finished. I have here the law of the great council, and it says the right of way through the lands of the United States is given for 100 feet each side, and station for depots, &c., every 10 miles of its road. Let any young Indian read it if you want to hear it.

Arlee. It is so.

Commissioner. These stations are to accommodate you. We are not trifling with you. Arlee ought to be satisfied.

Arlee. I want $1,000,000 for it.

Commissioner. The whole reservation would not be worth that.

Arlee. I thought you were here to help us.

Commissioner. I am. I represent the Great Father, as well as the Indians. I offer for the land four times what the government sells its land near here for — $2.50 per acre. And $10 would be eight times what the government usually sells its land for. Michelle, Eneas, and Arlee, are you ready to come to agreement with the government.

Eneas. There is one thing I don't understand. How big are these stations?

Commissioner. Eight hundred yards long and ninety yards wide, for small ones; and all others about four times as large, right along the road (shows a sketch and also a map). I hope Eneas' mind is happy and that he understands.

Eneas. I understand it now.

Commissioner. I will read to Michelle the agreement drawn by direction of the Great Father.

Michelle. When, I heard you the first time I was glad; but now when I hear what you offer, I do not feel so well, because now you say that all the reservation is not worth $1,000,000. Now I do not agree with you.

Commissioner. I am sorry if Michelle misunderstands me. I do not mean that the land is not worth $1,000,000 to the Indians, but that the same kind of land would bring no more among the whites. I only referred to that, as they all refused four times what was the selling price of such land among the whites.

Michelle. When a railroad runs through the railroad company will get the money back in one day. They will run through my ranch and take my timber to build it with. I would not take $15,000. I do not mean we will make trouble; I only say we will not take $15,000. If you want to go through, go; but we won't take $15,000. I don't speak now, any more, because you offer only $15,000.

Commissioner. Michelle should understand that what I offer is four times as much as the government sells the same kind of land for to white men. Don't let him say that $1,000,000 is a fair price; I say I offer what is reasonable. I do not represent the railroad, nor have I anything to do with the railroad; I represent the Great Father.

Arlee. We have said.

Commissioner. We will not talk any more about the million dollars; the Great Father will not allow us to talk of that.

Arlee. All right; then go by the Missoula. If the railroad don't want to give the money, let it go by Frenchtown.

Commissioner. The Great Father says the railroad is to go here. The railroad, according to the agreement, does not pay the money to the Indians, the United States pays it.

Arlee. Why do you want to pass here? You have to make a big bend to come here; why not go by the Missoula? The treaty only talked about a trail, not about a railroad.

Commissioner. Why, Governor Stevens was here to survey this country for a line of railroad. There is no attempt to take the country from you. You know that we are not proposing to take the country from you at all, and yet you speak as if we were.

Arlee. Governor Stevens said in twenty years another treaty would end this.

Commissioner. Arlee is mistaken. Of course this treaty is in force. Governor Stevens may have said that he or others would come back in twenty years, but not that the treaty would expire in that time. Do you want me to return to the Great Father and tell him that the good Indians, whom he always thought his friends, refused to sell a little land for ten dollars per acre, when not even the bad Indians of the country have asked that for their lands?

Michelle. How would it be if you had a good horse and I offered you a price that you did not think was right; if I took the horse wouldn't you complain? When we made the treaty we did not say railroads could pass through our country, only common roads.

Commissioner. They said roads of every description. Suppose I were to give Michelle a loaf of bread every day, and then were to ask him to return me a very small slice, would he not be a very bad Indian if he did not give me the slice when I needed it? Especially if I had paid him the money for it? So the Great Father says, "You can have this country, but I want a small slice or strip for a road," and afterwards offers to pay for it.

Michelle. If you wanted a small piece of bread, I would say, "Here is a piece." If you say it is too small, I would say, "Take what you want."

Commissioner. Michelle does not understand; he never saw a million dollars; he don't know what it is. It is nearly seventy times $15,000. The Great Father could not afford to pay $10 an acre for the Indian lands in the United States. He could not afford to pay the price now offered you, and would not have offered this if these Indians had not always been friends and good. We are not trying to make a hard bargain; we want to be liberal to the Indians. That is all. Do you want me to go home and tell the Great Father, or do you want me stay till to-morrow?

Michelle. Do as you wish.

Commissioner. What do you wish?

Michelle. I do not understand. You know it is not done; the agreement is not made.

Commissioner. Then I will stay. Ask them to meet me earlier to-morrow.

September 2 — 1.30 p.m.

Commissioner McCammon. My friends, I am glad to see you; I hope you did not think I had unkind thoughts yesterday. I had none but kind thoughts in my mind. I desire to hear from you or to answer any questions you wish to ask. I talked long yesterday, but I wanted to make everything as plain as possible. I did not want any one to misunderstand what I said. I am sincerely your friend. I have had much to do with Indians, and I believe they all consider me their friend. The Great Father wishes to make a present to good Indians, and although the Indians had agreed, in the treaties of 1855, to let roads be built through this reservation without pay, he thought none the less they should be paid. The Great Father had the right to build the road without pay, but he thinks you should be paid; he thought you ought to receive some money from him as a present. I would like to hear from any of the chiefs what is in your minds this morning.

Arlee. I don't wish to change our calculations. When we heard that you were coming we made up our minds what to say to you. Yes, we are all good Indians, and we have a nice country, and I don't wish the Great Father should bother us by a big railroad through the reservation. When we heard of your coming we made up our minds what to say to you, and I said it to you yesterday. You seem to like your money, and we like our country; it is like our parents. I have the same feeling I had yesterday, and I am not the only one. I told you about the money, what we ask; and you said it was an exorbitant price. We do not wish to change our ideas; we told you yesterday about our wishes.

Commissioner. In the treaty of 1855, made by Governor Stevens, the Indian tribes now represented here sold to the Great Father the country which was then claimed by them. That country was great; it extended from the British line to Big Hole River, and was very broad east and west. The Indians were then satisfied with the treaty, and have never been dissatisfied since. The money paid to your tribes was the sum of $120,000. That was only about one-ninth of what you now claim for a little strip of country through your reservation. You ask about nine times more for this little strip than what you received for all that vast amount of land. So you see you are mistaken as to the value of this little strip of country. I want you to think of this; that the $15,000 I offered yesterday is very much more per acre than the money you received under the treaty of 1855. As I have been fair and reasonable, I have a right to ask that you should be, and that you should trust me. I am afraid some bad white men have been misleading you about the price. No man is your friend who tells you that you should receive $1,000,000 from the government.

Arlee. We are not any way dissatisfied or hostile towards you or the government. We only want a fair bargain; fair play on both sides. My forefathers, our chiefs, the head chiefs of the tribe, were like men with veils over their heads; they could not see at all; they were like blind men; and when Governor Stevens arrived and he began talking about this part of the country, they had no idea of their country; they were stupid. They signed the treaty. This reservation was offered by the man who made the treaty, and we are holding on to it. Our forefathers are all dead, and we are the chiefs nowadays, and are hanging on it.

Commissioner. You are quite right in holding on to your reservation. As you friend, I say hold on to it; it is your land. I would be willing to give you the land you want up north; but the little line that the railroad wants won't interfere with your land; it will give the Great Father a better chance to protect you. There are many white men in the East who look after your interest more than you do yourselves; they would not allow a wrong to be done to you; they would, I know, approve of what I have told you. If I have not told you what the little strip is worth, I would not dare to go back among those people. You can ask any of your friends here and they will tell you that those white people know more about your wants than you do yourselves. Their hearts are always good towards you. These friends will watch me, and if I have not a good heart towards you they would blame me; but I know you think I have a good heart for you.

Arlee. Now won't you try to raise it a little more?

Commissioner. I will consider for a moment. (After a pause.) I will tell the Great Father I gave you $16,000. I will tell him that you are good Indians, as he knows, and I thought you were entitled to $16,000.

Adolphe. How many years will this $16,000 last? (They consult.)

Arlee. We want the money. The reason we did not get the money before was because we took it in annuities. We prefer the cash.

Commissioner. The Great Father knows more about you than they did years ago; and whatever wrong was done you then, will not be repeated now. This very railroad will bring the Great Father nearer to you. The money will be expended for the benefit of the Indians in the manner the Great Father thinks best. If he thinks, after hearing from you, that it is better to let you have the money, he will pay the money. You must depend on his judgment as to how the money will be paid. The Great Father will never forget you. He gives you money from year to year; he has many whites and many Indians to look after, and he gives you what he can. Something has been said about your timber; no timber will be cut from your lands, except on the right of way through. Your forests will remain, except as they cut trees out in building a road. They may have to cut so the trees won't fall on the road; that is all the trees that will be cut.

Arlee. Yes, that is so. The timber is my property, and we demand some money for my property. There is timber cut on the reservation. I am sure you don't know; it is off the road entirely; it is on the creek near Pig Pen. I went up there and saw it.

Commissioner. The white men had no right to cut it, and they will be very careful not to repeat it.

Arlee. Yes, this council don't amount to much, because cunning white men cut it on the sly.

Commissioner. But the railroad cannot afford to allow white men to cut timber on your land.

Arlee. I am sure I saw it with my own eyes.

Commissioner. It may have been a mistake. The railroad people have been very careful in not coming on the reservation.

Arlee. It is tie timber.

Commissioner. Arlee should remember that there may have been a mistake as to the line, and if within the reservation they did not cut the timber intentionally. We will have that line surveyed, and see if timber has been cut inside of the reservation.

Arlee. It came to my mind and I wanted it explained.

Commissioner. I introduced the matter of timber to you because I do not wish any misunderstanding about it.

Arlee. Yes, that is right.

Commissioner. Arlee and the rest are wise to protect their people.

Arlee. I am glad for one thing to-day. I am happy about that strip of country north. Do you think we will get it back?

Commissioner. I hope so.

Arlee. I am your friend. I hold your hand a long time.

Michelle. Now, my friend, I am glad about this strip of country north. We want that strip of country. I don't wish to be bothered by men on the other side. I want a road clear to the line where the other Kootenais are. If we get it we want to get the few settlers away who are there. We have lost many cattle in the reservation by men going up and down and driving them away; and these Indians are glad when when [sic] you said you would increase the land. The railroad line goes right through my land; I am not uneasy about it; I am glad I am going to get money for it.

Commissioner. I will report to the Great Father what you say about the strip of country north.

Michelle. It won't take long, and you have got a telegraph.

Commissioner. The Great Father; is not now in Washington, and it will take longer than you think. I shall have to go back and explain to him by word of mouth, the same as I do to you here.

Michelle. I had five head of horses on the road lately, and the whites stole them. I am afoot now. I am very happy to-day. At first you said you would increase our land, but now you say you will report to the Great Father. I don't quite understand.

Commissioner. I said I was willing, but it is the Great Father's land, and if he thinks best he will give it to you. As to the strip north, the Great Father did not know what was in your minds, but when he does he will do what is best for you.

Michele. The way we understood it in 1855 was that the land north belonged to us, but the man who ran the line got lazy and did not go north far enough.

Commissioner. I now ask the interpreter to read the agreement to the Indians.

Michelle. I don't consider this a *bona fide* bargain; it is borrowing this strip of land.

Commissioner. It is the use of it.

Michelle. I don't want you, after you get away, to let the white people suppose you have bought the reservation, and let the white people squat on it. That is the way I think. It is like the railroad borrowing the strip of land.

Commissioner. It is just buying the use of the strip of land.

Michelle. When I buy a horse I pay for it. You told us the country was ours. I considered the matter, and let you have it for public travel on the road. You have told me there won't be any white men on the reservation; that is the way I consider the matter.

Commissioner. Michelle is quite right; he understands it. The railroad will only use the little strip, just like the wagon road. Michelle and the rest understand it perfectly. I suppose this by their approving what Michelle says.

Michelle. If you fulfill your promise I will be enjoying the reservation. Now, I understand you to say that when we go visiting we can jump on the railroad wagons and ride without paying expenses. I don't wish to pay a cent when I visit your country. Tell that to the Great Father.

Commissioner: Michelle is right; the Indians always ride without paying whenever they want to visit their friends or the white people; but the white people will not be allowed to go on the reservation. I will come every year or two, as often as I can, to see him, so he will see that my promises have been kept.

Michelle. I wish that you would come once in a while, so that I can complain of not being treated right by the white men. You say you are our friend and will come. I will be glad to see you. I want you to know my heart. I despise liquor, cards, a liar, and a thief. I don't want to see such people here. Tell that to the Great Father. A lot of Indians of this tribe are below; if they want to come here they can do so; and if other tribes want to stop here we will let them stop if they behave.

Commissioner. I promise for the Great Father and myself to help put gamblers and liquor sellers off the reservation, and all other bad men; and also to let such Indians as you want come on here and live. You must let the Great Father know when you want these Indians to come here.

Michelle. And I trust that the commanding officer over at the camp at Cold Springs will fix the bad white men and Indians. I am taken care of by white men, and my own Indian agent tells me Major [Wm. H.] Jordan will get after the bad whites and Indians. Of course if any of my Indians should spill blood, you can do with them as you please; I have nothing to say about it. Also I have nothing to say if you put in jail my drunken Indians. You need not ask my permission. Do the best you can to keep peace and the white men from our country. Try and keep the white men from selling whisky to my Indians. We are uneasy about whisky matters, for fear of getting into hostilities and losing our lands. I am glad to hear that the man on Camas Prairie is arrested, and I hope you will punish him severely. You saw how it was the day you came here.

Commissioner. Major Jordan, your agent, and the United States marshal will see that men who sell liquor to Indians are punished. They hate whisky; that is, they hate to have it sold to Indians, and they will do all in their power to prevent your young men from getting into trouble. You see what your agent did the other day in having that man on Camas Prairie put in prison. It is bad for Indians to drink whisky, but worse to sell it to them.

Michelle. My agent told me when that big gang of men came here from below, "I will be the man to watch and keep them from selling whisky to the Indians." I wish white men to come no nearer than Horse Prairie with liquor. My agent says we will be bothered while the road is being built, and I understand what he tells me. I wish you would do the best you can to keep bad men from doing damage. I suppose we will be bothered while the new road is being built, and I want Major Jordan to be ready any day to take my part. I will let the agent know first, and he will say to Major Jordan — and this big chief is listening.

Commissioner. Michelle understands it perfectly, and the rest.

Arlee. I don't want white men to bring stock here any more. There will be lots of people here when the railroad is finished. The officers can clear off white men.

Commissioner. While the road is being built some stock will be used by the white men. When an agent wants the commanding officer at Fort Missoula, he sends for him. I want you to understand that while the road is being built much stock will be here. If your agent wants troops he will send for them to protect you.

Afternoon Session, 3 p.m.

Commissioner. My friends, I am about through with our talk. From my heart I say you have done well. When you see me another year I hope you will say you have done well. You will not regret one thing that has been done. You have done the best that could be done for yourselves and for the white man. I will go down the river and put a value on the individual improvements on the ranches used by the railroads. I want you to ask Arlee, Adolphe, Eneas, Big Sam, Pattie, and all the rest, to come and sign this paper to-day, or go to the agency, so that all of their names will be on this paper. Then this will be the last time I will see my good friends of these tribes. To-morrow I will leave, and will go and see the Great Father, and will tell him all your wishes, particularly about your wanting that strip of land to the north. The Great Father wants to do the best for all his people, and he will listen to me and do what he thinks best about that and all other things. I am through.

Michelle. You told us you were going to have a fair understanding. You told us that you would be glad to have the amount of land increased. I was glad when you mentioned that; I jumped up from my chair and shook hands with you, and then you said it was not in your power, but you would mention it to the Great Father. It was that that made me let go of the million dollars. I don't quite understand why you say now you have no authority to treat for that strip, but will mention it to the Great Father. I would like to have a copy of the treaty, and have men who can read explain it to me.

Commissioner. Michelle is right; the land is not to be sold to the railroad company. He shall have a copy of the agreement. Michelle is mistaken if he thought I told him I had authority to treat now for the strip of land at the head of the lake. I said all along, yesterday and to-day, that I could only report to the Great Father what they wished, and he will likely send some one out here to see them about this land. I don't want to have Michelle make a mistake.

Arlee. I don't consider we are mistaken; that is the reason we jumped up and shook hands.

Commissioner. I explained it to Arlee, as I had done before. You must trust the Great Father, and trust that I will tell him. Now, I would like to go with the agent and see the farms. I would like to have you ask the agent whether I said I would treat about that north land to-day. I didn't understand Michelle's remark to be that he would sign this agreement on account of that strip of land. I said I would give you $16,000. I said we would stop talking about the north land.

Arlee. You were talking about that to Michelle. That money is a small sum. Donald says so. So far as I am concerned I agree with you. You said that personally you would be glad to have them have the land.

Commissioner. I told them from the first I had no authority to treat regarding that north land. I illustrated it to him yesterday when I spoke about his sending a man for fish.

Michelle. If we could get the strip of country north, we would not ask anything for the right of way.

Commissioner. I repeat what I before said, that I have no right to give the strip of land north; but I said I would tell the Great Father. Suppose Michelle, Arlee, and Eneas wanted to sell the reservation, and came to me for that purpose, you would say, "They have not consulted our people and have no right to sell our reservation." Unless they consult their people they could not bind them. That is what I said. I could not bind the Great Father until I told him about it. Your chiefs can do nothing without consulting their people. I can do nothing except by the orders of the Great Father. He has given me no orders about this strip.

Arlee. I knew you would not give that million of dollars. My people don't want the railroad through here, and that's why I asked a million dollars.

Commissioner. All I said is written down, and you can have a copy of what I said. I have told you the Great Father said the road was to be built, not for the benefit of the white man only, but also for the Indian.

Arlee. I don't know how the road would benefit the Indians.

Commissioner. That is because Arlee never saw a railroad. The Indians will be nearer the Great Father, and he will be better able to protect you. I told you also that if you followed the Great Father's wishes in this matter, he would do what was best for you and might give it to you.

Arlee. Yes, the only benefit I see is if you give us that strip of land north, when I die it will benefit my children. The papers you have do not say that we have sold the country.

Michelle. A great many have clear ideas; others are stupid, and cannot understand it; so we want a copy.

Commissioner. The white men think I have been very kind to the Indians, and have tried to explain everything as plainly as possible. The agent and commanding officer will say so. Agent Ronan and I will have to leave now. I want the men to sign the agreement.

Michelle. I am not bothering my head about the railroad going through my field. I know that is right. If we can get back that country north we don't care about the railroad going through; it may go through free. Don't have hard feelings toward us for saying this. We are all one. My skin is dark. We are one nation. The international line is far north, but we are under one flag. You treat me as one of your people, and I want to do the same. The agent told me himself that he had instructions to see that the Indians get their rights.

Commissioner. I will promise to use my influence to get that strip of land for you, and I want you in return to get signatures for this agreement. I feel kind to all the chiefs and to the rest of you. We all belong to one nation. We were all born in the United States.

Michelle. This reservation is only large enough for three depots.

Commissioner. The depots will be as small as possible. You will see what the railroad does. If you find reason to complain, your objections must be made to the Great Father. Everything possible will be done to make the Indians contented and happy. There will be only five stations, and if the Indians are good and sober, the railroad will probably employ them.

Michelle. That is all I have to say.

Adolphe. I am one of the Flatheads. I am going to speak to you. This and Bitter Root is my country. You told us once we should respect the Great Father, and I think you should respect what I have said; for this reason I have great faith in the Great Father and you, and therefore talk of this strip of land. I guess we will be happy on this reservation. Look at the blood the white man has spilled. Where is the blood we have spilled? Just for this I respect and honor the Great Father and you, for I know he is a good-hearted man. Our God is a good kind God. Our chiefs have been directed from above to treat your people well.

The council then adjourned.

Document 47

Indians Good Negotiators

September 7, 1882

Source: "The Flathead Right-of-way Treaty," *The Helena Daily Herald*, September 7, 1882, page 2, col. 2.

Editors' note: This editorial from a Helena newspaper provides an interesting comment on the negotiating skills of Flathead Reservation chiefs.

The Flathead Right-of-way Treaty.

The return of the commissioners from the Flathead Reservation discloses the terms of the treaty entered into for the right of way for the Northern Pacific. We understand that at first the modest demand was made for a million dollars, about the same as for running a road through the better portions of New York city. But Indian generosity is made manifest by the liberal discount from the asking price in accepting finally the $16,000 offered. If true, as stated by the *Missoulian*, that it takes only 1,212 acres, that is, for the width of 200 feet across the 55 miles of reservation, this is paying at the rate of more than $13 per acre. And if it is further true, as reported, that not 50 of the whole of this 1,212 acres could be regarded as arable, it would be paying at the rate of $100 per acre for arable land, and about $10 per acre for the rest, which we presume to be much like most of the upland and foot-hill surface of Montana.

We have figured it out, that supposing the Flathead reservation is an average chip of the Montana block, the whole Territory is worth at this appraisal $1,215,385,600, without counting improvements, personal property or mines. At this rate Montana is worth nearly enough to settle the national debt, without considering the rest of the country. Again, the land grant to the Northern Pacific is roughly estimated at 47,000,000 acres, and if the whole could be marketed at the rate paid the Flatheads, it would return the handsome little sum of $611,000,000, or enough to build twenty thousand miles of railroad at the cost of $30,000 per mile. We presume the company would sell at some less. And these are the poor, simple savages who have no idea of the values of property and are swindled by all who deal with them, and the great United States has to be invoked to give its consent to the little trades that these simple-minded wards may feel inclined to make! Why, the shrewdest of our real estate dealers can't hold a candle to these savages as land traders, and it is fortunate for the inhabitants of our rising cities that the Flathead reservation is as far away as it is.

But we are glad, nevertheless, that the treaty has been made; glad for the Indians, for they are pretty fair, as Indians run; glad for the company, because it can go on with its work without any further obstacle or delay; glad for the Territory and all its people and interests, because there seems now no remaining doubt of the completion of the road next season, in good time and shape.

Document 48

A Visit to Chief Arlee's Home

1882

Source: Lucy S. White, "Garfield!: An Incident," *The Christian Union* (New York), vol. 32, no. 21 (November 19, 1885), pages 10-11.

Editors' note: Warrington provided an interesting description of his 1882 interactions with Chief Arlee and Arlee's home in the Jocko Valley.

Garfield!
An Incident.
by Lucy S. White.

We had just dined at Colonel Warrington's. The Colonel and his wife give dinner-parties which are delightful to every sense, and favored indeed may their chosen guests consider themselves. The dinner is always just what a dinner should be, the house is home-like, the grounds are spacious and beautiful, and in both house and grounds the guests are made to feel at home. But in all the place there is, perhaps, no spot so thoroughly charming as the Colonel's own little "den." That is a cozy little room, with its hard floor, half covered with soft rugs, the great open fireplace, where, on shining andirons, a cheery fire hospitably crackles when the weather affords the slightest excuse for it; with the Colonel's open desk, giving many a hint of his busy life, the wide-armed easy chair, and, here, there, and everywhere, the curios, beautiful or quaint or rare, which serve as milestones to mark his many wanderings.

It was in this delightful room that we had all gathered after dinner. The Colonel was showing us the various knickknacks which lay scattered around, and telling us, as only he could, the story of each. For many years after the war he had lived at the South. There was some cotton — a miniature bale — from his own plantation; there was a complete suit of Ku-klux disguise, arrayed in which a Southern gentleman had *not* killed the Colonel — an omission resulting from no lack of will. There were Ku-klux warnings, in the shape of coffins, daggers, and various pleasing and ingenious devices.

"Did I get all these?" said the Colonel. "Oh, yes, and lots more. I burned a good many. They were too profane and horrible in every way to have in the house; I was afraid they might breed leprosy, you know. Yes, as you say, these are bad enough, but they are nothing to some I've had."

There was an iron, a fiendish-looking instrument — a huge ring, with long spikes projecting out on each side. Its weight was many pounds.

"I took this off a slave's neck myself during the war," said the Colonel. "Put on for punishment. Do you see its capabilities for torture? He could hold his head in only just such a position; he couldn't lie down at all; the weight galled his shoulders. And they meant it should stay well, too — it was *riveted on*. I had to take him to a blacksmith and have the iron cut with a cold chisel. Poor fellow, how glad he was! Gentlemen," added the Colonel sternly, turning to the group around the fireplace, "you sometimes speak wonderingly of how bitter I am against slavery. Yes, I *hate* it, and when you see all that I have seen, you will hate it as bitterly as I do."

The Colonel has been West, too. There were peace-pipes and wampums, photographs and fossils, buffalo horns and tarantula nests, and to each belonged an anecdote.

"Who is this handsome gentleman?" asked a lady, laughingly, as she took up a large photograph of an Indian in full glory of paint and feathers.

"That is Ah Lee," answered the Colonel; "and he is a man I like to call my friend, too. He is to me a standing refutation and rebuke of the monstrous doctrine, 'There is no good Indian but a dead one.' His name savors of the Chinese, doesn't it? But he is a full-blooded Indian, chief of the Flathead tribe, in Montana Territory. He's a real good old fellow, and rich, too, as Indians go. I guess he is worth some fifteen or twenty thousand dollars, gathered in trading cattle and such ways. I was out that way in '82, you know. Our party was exploring things generally out there, and by and by we came to where this old chief lived with his people. We had an interpreter, and through him I talked a good deal with Ah Lee. We got pretty well acquainted, and he asked me if I would like to see his house. Of course I was glad to do so. I found he had quite a large yard fenced in, and in it was his *tepee*, or Indian wigwam, and also a log cabin, built somewhat more after white man's fashion. The well-to-do Indians always have such a house, though for living purposes they generally prefer the *tepee*. Well, I went into this house and looked around. There wasn't much to see — a rusty stove, with an old tin coffee-pot on it, a deal table, a chair, a pile of blankets down in one corner, for a bed; that was all. I was just about to go out when the chief touched my arm, and pointed anxiously, as if fearful that I would not notice it, to a print tacked up on the wall over the pile of blankets. He made signs that I must go up and look at it. I did so. It was an illustration cut out of a "Harper's Bazar," and it represented the deathbed of President [James] Garfield. The old chief stood by my side, and looked long and earnestly and very tenderly upon the picture. Then he turned to me, and, pointing to the picture, said simply, 'Garfield!' It was the only English word he knew.

"I cried like a child; I couldn't help it. There was this man, away out in the wilds of Montana, a poor, ignorant Indian, and the only attempt at art or beauty of any kind in his bare little hut was this old print, this death scene which moved him just as it had moved the world. The only English word he could say was 'Garfield.' The brave General had no sincerer mourner or more eloquent eulogy — just 'Garfield!' Friends I call that fame."

The Colonel's voice broke, and we all were silent.

Chief Arlee
Source: Peter Ronan, *Historical Sketch of the Flathead-Indians from the Year 1813 to 1890* (Helena, Mont.: Journal Publishing Co., 1890), p. 78

Document 49

Salish Indians and Piegan Horse Thieves

January 25, 1883

Source: "Capture of a Piegan Indian and Stolen Horses — An Indian Court Martial," *Rocky Mountain Husbandman* (White Sulphur Springs, Mont.), January 25, 1883, page 6, col. 1-2.

Editors' note: The incident recounted here showed the complications confronting the Salish Indians as they tried to keep the peace with the whites. They feared that some white men might accuse them of theft when they were only trying to return white owned horses stolen by the Piegan Indians.

Capture of a Piegan Indian and Stolen Horses
— An Indian Court Martial.

A short time since while a posse of Flathead Indians were camped near a farm house down the Musselshell, they spied a strange Indian some distance away and sent a party of warriors in pursuit. The party made chase, and after some time finally captured the stranger, who proved to be a Piegan. He was mounted on a good horse and well armed with breech-loading and ammunition. On bringing him into camp they learned that he had associates in the neighborhood. A party then went in pursuit, and after an exciting chase, pursing two Indians for several hours, they returned to camp, bringing in 16 head of horses. A glance at the horses showed that they were the property of white people and had been stolen by the Piegans. Being convinced of this the Flatheads were afraid to keep the horses in their possession lest their owners might come in pursuit, and they would be unable to prove their innocence of theft. What to do with the Piegan captive in their possession was also a vexed question. They held several councils of war. First they determined to shoot him, but in that decision they were divided, a portion of the Indians fearing that the Piegan tribe might retaliate in the same manner. At the second council it was decided to release the Indian, giving him a chance to escape under fire of their rifles. A third council and it was agreed to deliver him and the captured horses to Messrs. Cameron & Fowler, wool-growers in that section, but the latter refused to take them, another council was held.

The final decision was to take the Indian's gun, ammunition and clothing from him and set him free. This was done, and the Indian without a particle of clothing when last seen was making quick steps toward the Snowy mountains. There were some good horses in the lot, and they all bore evidences of having been used by white persons. After giving Messrs. Cameron & Fowler a description of the horses they moved off with them. There were four fine black animals in the lot that appeared to have been matched teams. Two of them were branded with the letter L. A day or two afterwards the Flatheads were visited by two suspicious whites, who claimed the band of horses, and drove them off, going in an easterly direction. It is believed that these white men were thieves and took this means of getting possession of the stock, since the direction they went was away from all settlements.

Document 50

Chief Arlee Complains of Alcohol

January 26, 1883

Source: *The Weekly Missoulian*, January 26, 1883, page 3, col. 2.

Editors' note: Chief Arlee supported efforts to keep alcohol from Indian customers, but the white justice system failed to buttress his efforts.

A few days ago a step son of Chief Arlee, Flathead reserve, imbibed too much bug juice, and donning his war paint, went to the agency, bent on the destruction of Arlee. He was prevented from doing any injury; but it set the old man to thinking, and he set up a job on the whisky-sellers. He called two trusty men to his aid, gave them a dollar and told them to go and buy some whisky, drink of it, and bring the bottle to him. They went to a cabin saloon kept by a man Kibble and a woman named Belle Ross (Calamity Jane), stepped to the bar and called for drinks, which were set out to them with a glass of water alongside. They drank and paid their bill, sat around awhile, smoked a little, and then took another drink, exhausting half a dollar in this social way — the drinks being set up each time by the woman. They then asked for a bottle in exchange for their half dollar. The man refused on the ground that it was not money enough, and then went out of doors. They then asked the woman for the liquor, and she poured out a half bottle, and gathered in the four-bit piece. With this, they returned to Arlee and reported progress. He then sent them into town to make a complaint, and Under Sheriff Leamer went out and arrested the pair. Their trial took place on Wednesday and Thursday, when they crawled through some sort of loop-hole in the law, and shortly afterwards were ingloriously drunk.

Document 51

Death of Bitterroot Nez Perce Indian Leader

June 1, 1883

Source: *The Weekly Missoulian*, June 1, 1883, page 3, col. 4-5.

Editors' note: Parishe was widely known both for this wealth in horses and his leadership in the Bitterroot Indian community.

The Indian feast given in honor of the dead Nez Perce chief, Parishe, took place on the creek just above town on Saturday afternoon. A large number of both sexes went from town as spectators. Parishe, like the most of his tribe, was noted for accumulating wealth, and was a large tax-payer for years in Bitter Root. Something over three thousand head of cayuse horses bear his brand in the hills, and he is said to have eight thousand dollars in money hidden away in his cabin. A barrel of coffee and three large beeves were served in his memory. The ceremony lasted about half an hour, and consisted in giving away the dead warrior's hunting accoutrements to some one of his near friends; also eighty head of horses. One young buck, a Nez Perce warrior, celebrated the event by coming out in a full war-path rig, something after the dime novel fashion. A wide band encircled his forehead. It was ornamented with feathers and beads, with two horns fastened in front to add to his already hidious [sic] appearance. Judging from the way some of the Flatheads partook of the bread and roast beef, they would enjoy having a Nez Perce chief die once a month.

Zeb.

Document 52

Newspaperman Visits the Flathead Reservation

August 5, 1883

Source: Paul Dana, "Among the Kallispell," *The Sun* (New York, N.Y.), August 5, 1883, page 4, c. 5-6.

Editors' note: Dana's description includes much information about the economic development on the reservation and St. Ignatius Mission. Unfortunately, much of his history was second hand and mangled. Especially problematic was his description of the naming of the Jocko Valley for Jocko Finley. The author's name was given when part of the travelogue was reprinted in Paul Dana, "Among the Kalispel," *The Northwest* (New York, N.Y.), vol. 1, no. 10 (October 1883), page 2. The dispatch was dated as July 25, 1883, but the text refers to the St. Ignatius celebration of July 29, 1883, in the past tense.

Among the Kallispell.
Observations of a Traveller Through the Country of the Flatheads, Spokanes, and Nez Perces — Progress of Christianity and Civilization in the Northern Rockies.

Flathead Lake, M. T., July 25. — About seventy miles from the northern boundary of the United States, in the Territory of Montana, between the western slope of the Rockies and the more westerly chain of mountains known as the Cœur d'Alene, and, as you travel further south, as the Bitter Root, lies the reservation which has been assigned to the tribe of Indians called the Flatheads; and probably no tribe have adapted themselves more to the manners of civilization at the expense of their former customs and habits than these. Why they are called Flatheads, no one in their part of the country seems to know. They do not flatten their children's heads, nor is there any trace or tradition among them of such a custom having been practised [sic] formerly; and their Indian name is Selish, it is probable that the name of Flathead was given to them, as often happened in this country, through the unaccountable freak of some traveller [sic].

The reservation covers about one and a half million acres, and the tribe number about 1,500 souls. The agency for the reservation is near its southern line, and is known as the Jocko Agency because it lies on the Jocko River.

Nobody seemed to know why a river in Montana came to be named the Jocko any more than why the Indians living on it were called Flatheads; but we learned at last that the person responsible for such a title was Jim Finn. He established himself on its banks before the year 1840, and the stream became to be known as Jim's Fork. Then the Jesuit Father [Pierre] de Smet settled in the neighborhood, and, following his own language, he called it Jacques' Fork, which finally was contracted into Jocko.

The Northern Pacific Railroad passes through the reservation, and runs for eight or ten miles through a mountainous pass, where at one place the track rides upon a trestle nearly 250 feet high, before it comes into a country bearing evidence of the inhabitation of the Flatheads. The Indian lands, like the greater portion of this part of Montana, consist of detached mountain ranges, all covered with evergreens, separated by rich and long valleys, level and rolling, or basin-shaped, as it happens, on which no trees grow except on the banks of the streams which come from the mountains and flow off into some of the larger rivers. The first valley encountered is the valley of the Jocko, and after that river has travelled for about thirty miles through one of the most picturesque mountain gorges in the West, the valley becomes a plain of five or six miles in width and twenty in length. At one end of this plain is situated the house of the agent, Major [Peter] Ronan and around that are the first Indian farms. They raise wheat, oats, corn, grass, and vegetables; and over the greater part of the prairie are scattered their droves of horses and cattle. As you come down from one of the mountain passes and see the farming land shut in by rail fences, the hay fields look like any in the country of white men. The grass is now being cut by mowing machines and the hay is raked by horse rakes; but on nearer approach the man sitting on the mowing machine or on the horse rake is found to be an Indian, as are all the other laborers pitching or loading hay.

Irrigation is necessary here only to a slight extent, although the crops would be improved if it were practised [sic]. The vegetable that flourishes best seems to be the potato, though peas and cabbages and onions and celery are grown.

Where we camped, at the upper end of the reservation, on the Flathead Lake, a lake of such broad and noble scenery as perhaps belongs to no other, an Indian brought in from his farm close by a large pail of strawberries, which were not very big but of most excellent flavor, and about a gallon of delicious cream. His cattle were short-horns of first-rate quality. Instead of their live stock being confined to horses as formerly, the Indians now pay considerable attention to the breeding of cattle. They had good stock to start with and herds of as fine cattle are seen on their prairies as on any ranges in Montana. Each individual cattle owner has his own brand for his stock, and none of it is held in common by the tribe; and this is also the case with their other agricultural enterprises.

The Flathead dwellings are about evenly divided between wigwams and log huts. The wigwams are no longer made of the bark of trees, but of good duck woven especially for the purpose, shaped like an enormous cloak, and wrapped around the old lodge poles. But even these are evidently soon to go out of use. Many new huts are building close to where wigwams are standing, and on several of the huts lately finished could be seen the old discarded lodge poles leaning against the side of the house, where they will probably stay until taken down to be used in making a rail fence or to be split up for firewood. The huts are made of pine logs of some six inches to a foot in thickness, with their sides hewn flat, and the ends neatly dovetailed into each other. Small poles are used for the roof, and these are covered with clay, which bakes hard and smooth and makes an excellent roofing. Such a house has a neat and comfortable air.

Of course, in such an enormous tract of land inhabited by so few people, only a very small portion can be cultivated, but it is none the less true that the Flathead tribe owe their support almost entirely to agriculture. They depend very little on hunting, and yet, though they all live by the soil, they cannot be said to be all cultivators. Nothing is held in common by the tribe, but when one really industrious man is found, the old customs are sufficiently observed to allow his relatives to live on the proceeds of his labors. This is often a heavy burden, but it is not usually shirked. This cannot last long, however, and before long these Indians will show the same proportion of active men among them as are found in other communities.

One of the most potent causes in producing such a state of affairs among the Flatheads has been, no doubt, the presence and influence of the Jesuit Mission of St. Ignatius. This is situated in the next valley north of the Jocko; and I learned from Father Bandolini [Joseph Bandini], who came from Italy twelve years ago to live among the Indians of this country, much that was interesting about the Jesuit labors among this tribe and those in the neighboring regions.

At the mission is a school for boys and another for girls, under the care of some Sisters of Mercy, who joined the Fathers a few years ago. At these schools the children, in addition to learning to read, write, and cipher, receive an industrial education sufficient to fit them to become practical farmers. They learn a little carpentering and the log huts that they have built show evidence of considerable skill. Then they learn the care of farm machinery and how to manage crops and to cultivate a garden. Crime among them is very rare. Father Bandolini said that during his sojourn here he had known of only two homicides. One was in self-defence [sic] and the other was committed under the influence of liquor. Stealing is almost unknown, except in one particular, and that has been of such long-established custom that the Fathers have not yet been able to stop it entirely.

The Flatheads live on the western slope of the Rocky Mountains, and right across on the eastern side is the country of the Piegans. From time immemorial these two tribes, without often engaging in actual warfare, have been chiefly interested in stealing each other's horses. Parties from either tribe would suddenly come through one of the many mountain passes and run off with a band of horses belonging to the other; and before long those horses or their equivalents would be back with the Indians who had been first plundered. No Indian's horses nor any white man's horses are safe in an Indian country; but probably no set of animals every changed owners so often as have the horses that have travelled back and forth over the mountains between the Flatheads and the Piegans. But now this practice is almost abolished. Seven years ago a treaty was made between the tribes that they would let their horses stay where they belonged. Some of the younger members have not been able to resist altogether the temptation to do a little of the old raiding; but before long the Flathead colts will grow up to be Flathead horses without ever having crossed the Rockies; and so also with the stock of the Piegans.

The Flatheads are one of about fifteen kindred tribes that the Jesuits knew under the collective name of *Kallispell*. This included the Spokanes, the Cœur d'Alenes, the Pend d'Oreilles, the Nez Percés, the Octonagons, the Iroquois, the Kootenays, and others. In 1839, the Iroquois, who had been visited by some Jesuits from Canada, sent down to the nearest Bishop, who was then in St. Louis to ask that more missionaries should be sent among them. This expedition was obliged to enter the country of several tribes with whom they were at war, and the Iroquois messengers were killed before reaching their destination. A similar attempt to send to St. Louis was made again the following year, and a third in 1841, each with the same result; but in 1842, the Iroquois succeeded in getting through to St. Louis, and Father [Pierre] de Smet was sent north and labored among the Bitter Root tribes until, in 1854, he established the mission among the Flatheads. Those have come more completely under the influence of the mission than any other tribe. All the Flatheads are Catholics; but even among the tribes that were more difficult to deal with at first, Father Bandolini says that there is a decided change. At the time of the trouble with the Nez Percés, the few of the tribe who had professed Christianity did not follow the others into the war; and since then many more of this and other tribes have become Christians and evinced a disposition to take up agriculture and to become more peaceful.

On Sunday the 29th, there was a celebration of the feast of St. Ignatius at the Jocko Mission, and throughout this week's journey we have constantly met small bands of Indians going to the festival. They have been of all tribes, and some of them come from a distance of two hundred miles. The finest looking men have been the Nez Percés. For this name of Nez Percé there also seems to be no explanation. Their noses are not pierced, and it is not known the custom ever was practised [sic] among them. Yet the name of Nez Percé seems to have driven out all others, and I could not find that even among themselves they are called by any name of a true Indian nature. At the celebration of the feast at the mission, in addition to the religious ceremonies, there are always races for horses and for men, the contests for both varying from one hundred yards to five miles.

But probably the most vital cause for the Indians beginning to pay attention to agriculture is the almost complete extinction of the buffalo. When these animals were plenty there were two great huntings every year, one in the spring and one in the fall, and Father Bandolini says that the excitement among the Indians as the time approached to leave for the hunt, became so great that everything else seemed forgotten, and even the Fathers were completely ignored.

But when the annual wandering of the buffalo stopped, and other sorts of game became comparatively scarce, the problem of self-support became more difficult, and the necessity for some other methods than those that were formerly sufficient was more pressing. Then, again, the increased difficulty of supporting a large family is gradually stamping out polygamy and bringing these Indians more closely to the ordinary ways of civilized life.

P. D.

Document 53

Senator G. G. Vest Negotiates with Charlo
for Bitterroot Valley
September 1883

Source: Excerpt from G. G. Vest, "Charlot: Chief of the Flathead Indians: A True Story," *The Washington Post*, July 26, 1903, page A11.

Editors' note: This is the most detailed account available of Senator G. G. Vest's dealings with Chief Charlo, when Vest tried in 1883 to convince Charlo to move to the Jocko reservation. Modern readers will not agree with many of Vest's comments on government policy and Indian culture, but he did describe his dealings with Charlo and the reservation chiefs. Unfortunately we do not have Charlo's side of the story.

Charlot: Chief of the Flathead Indians: A True Story.
by G. G. Vest, ex-United States Senator from Missouri.

The following narrative, which is absolutely true, furnishes a striking illustration of the manner in which Indian lands have been acquired by the whites. It is not pretended that such means have been used in all instances, but the indifference which has been exhibited to the commission of a great outrage upon an unoffending and friendly chief, even after the facts were made known, is not complimentary to a great and just people, as we proclaim ourselves to be.

On March 2, 1883, the United States Senate adopted a resolution providing for the appointment of a special committee to visit a number of Indian tribes in the West, and, among others, the Flatheads of Montana, and to make report as to their condition, and the troubles which existed between them and the white settlers in what is known as the Bitter Root Valley. Three members of the national House of Representatives were invited to join with the Senate committee in the proposed work. I was made a member of the special committee from the Senate, and, on September 6, 1883, the Hon. Martin Maginnis, Territorial Delegate, and the Hon. Schuyler Crosby, governor of the Territory of Montana, and myself left Helena, Mont., for the Flathead reservation on the Northern Pacific Railroad. When we arrived at Arlee, a station on the railroad in the reservation, the scene which presented itself was picturesque and interesting. Some 500 Chinamen, lately engaged in the construction of the railroad, were encamped near the station, and their callow countenances exhibited unmistakable evidence of apprehension as the Indians extended us a welcome in one of their characteristic dances, accompanied by a good deal of noise and much reckless riding on their ponies around the Chinese camp. The pigtails of the Chinese seemed to be very attractive to the young braves, and they amused themselves as they dashed by the Chinamen, in attempts to seize the long plaits of hair dangling down the back of every Chinaman, each warrior doubtless thinking how valuable would be such a scalp-lock to the string of scalps worn by him as evidence of his prowess in war. Surrounded by this wild but hospitable escort, we proceeded to the agency, and upon the following day met the Indians in council, the tribes on the reservation being represented by Michelle, head chief of the Pend d'Oreilles, Arlee, second chief of the Flatheads, and Eneas, head chief of the Kootenays.

The Flathead reservation, through which the Northern Pacific Railroad runs from east to west, contains 1,400,000 acres of land, nearly all of good quality, and much of it very fine. The Indians upon the reservation, and belonging to the three tribes above named, numbered about 1,400, the Pend d'Oreilles and Flatheads each outnumbering the Kootenays. They were making rapid advances in agriculture, mechanical pursuits, and education of their children, and, altogether were in better condition that [than] any tribe we visited. Many of them had farms in good cultivation, well fenced, and their pastures were covered by herds of cattle and horses.

The common impression caused by the name of the tribe that they practiced the hideous custom of flattening the heads of their children is entirely erroneous. The Indians themselves are unable to account for the name the tribe bears, as, according to their own account, they have never tortured their children in any such fashion. On the contrary, they are well formed, rather slender, but very active and athletic, their heads being round in shape and their features quite agreeable. It is their proud boast that they have always been the friends of the white man and this is absolutely true.

Their present advanced condition as to religion and civilization is due to the teaching of the Jesuits, who came to the Flatheads in the Bitter Root Valley in 1841 and established the St. Mary Mission at the head of that valley.

In 1836 some of the Iroquois Indians from Canada visited the Bitter Root Valley Flatheads and told them of the Christian religion, which the Jesuits had taught to the Iroquois. Four of the young Flathead braves volunteered to make a journey to St. Louis for the purpose of asking the "black robes," as they called the Jesuits, to come and teach the Flatheads the Christian religion. These four dauntless young men who volunteered the dangerous journey of thousands of miles over mountain, plain, and river and through tribes of hostile and bloodthirsty enemies were never heard of after they commenced their journey.

In 1837 three Flatheads, one Nez Perce, and one Iroquois Indian made the same attempt to reach St. Louis for the same purpose, but were murdered by the Sioux, the hereditary enemies of the Flatheads.

In 1839 two young Iroquois announced to the Flatheads that they were willing to attempt the journey to St. Louis, notwithstanding the tragic fate of their predecessors. These two envoys reached St. Louis, and in the spring of 1841 Father [Pierre] De Smet, an intrepid and self-sacrificing Jesuit, returned with them to the Flathead camp on the headwaters of Snake River in Montana. These persistent efforts by savages, utterly ignorant of the Christian faith, to become acquainted with its teachings is without parallel in the missionary annals of the world. The result can be seen by the traveler on the Northern Pacific Railroad as "the iron horse with the heart of fire," as the Indians call the locomotive, swiftly conveys him across the Flathead reservation through herds of cattle and horses and cultivated fields, on which are comfortable dwellings and all the evidences of advanced civilization.

Michelle.

The Flatheads and Pend d'Oreilles speak the same language, and Michelle, the head chief of the latter tribe, was the spokesman at the council which was held at the agency on the day after our arrival. He was a large, fleshy Indian, with pleasant features, and impressed me as sincere and truthful. Michelle was his treaty name, given him by the whites, but he had also an Indian name (as is the case with all the chiefs of any distinction), which had been borrowed from the Chinooks on the Pacific Coast.

[Here Vest related the story of Chief Michelle giving his Indian name to Agent Peter Ronan's new baby, six months after Ronan took charge of the agency in 1877, and Michelle's later assumption of the Indian name of the recently deceased chief of the Lower Pend d'Oreilles. See Mary Ronan's account above.]

St. Ignatius' Mission.

As my principal object in having a talk with the Indians on the Jocko reservation, through which the Northern Pacific Railroad runs, was to ascertain if they were willing to receive Charlot, their hereditary chief, who, with 360 of the tribe, was then in the Bitter Root Valley, having refused to go with the majority of his people to the Jocko reservation, I asked Michelle if they were willing to take Charlot as their head chief instead of Arlee, the second chief, who was then acting as head chief over that portion of the tribe which had left the Bitter Root Valley, and come over to the Jocko reservation. He replied that they would be very glad to have Charlot again as their chief, and after discussing some other matters of minor importance, Maj. Maginnis and myself went over to the St. Ignatius' Mission, some four miles distant, and spent two days there examining into the statements made by Michelle and Arlee that the "black robes" were compelling the Indians to work the mission fields as payment for the tuition of their children. The first mission established by the Jesuits in the Flathead country was at the head of the Bitter Root Valley, called St. Mary's, near where the village of Stephensville is now located. This mission was abandoned in 1850 on account of its exposure to the attacks of the Blackfeet, and in 1855 the mission of St. Ignatius at the foot of the Mission Mountains, was established, it being the most central and eligible locality on that reservation. It is interesting to notice the history of this mission, as it demonstrates the fact that self-support and habits of industry furnish the only solution of the Indian and negro problems. The mission when first established was devoted to the education of Indian girls alone, but this proved to be a miserable failure. The young women were taught by nuns, brought from Montreal, to cook, wash, and sew, and to speak the English language. When graduated, they returned to their respective homes and became the objects of ridicule and derision by the older Indians, who were utterly opposed to everything but the Indian life to which they had been accustomed, and finding themselves unsupported and the constant objects of attack, being told they had white hearts, and were renegades, these girls relapsed in a barbarism more degraded than that from which the Jesuits had sought to rescue them. Finding this to the be the case, Father De Smet and his colleagues built a dormitory one hundred yards distant from the female dormitory and established a dual system of education for both sexes. Five Jesuit fathers and brothers had charge of the male school and dormitory, while five nuns had charge of the female school and dormitory. The Indian boys were taught the English language and how to read and write while they were also taught to herd cattle, plow, and cultivate the fields of wheat, and neither male nor female pupils were permitted to return to the tepees, but were compelled to remain at the mission, their parents not being allowed to see them except on each Saturday, and then only in the presence of the fathers and brothers or nuns. This change in the system of education worked admirably, and when the pupils were graduated, they intermarried, when the Jesuits fenced in a small tract of land and built the newly married couple a comfortable house and furnished them with a small herd of cattle and a few ponies, so that the husband and wife became a nucleus of civilization and Christianity where they located.

I found among the Jesuit brothers a very accomplished young Frenchman, from Paris, who had spent a large fortune in dissipation and then became a brother of the Company of Jesus by which he was ordered to work among the North American Indians. He was an excellent musician, and was engaged during my first visit to the mission in teaching the young Indian boys to play upon wind instruments, and when I visited the mission again two years afterward I was met at Revalli, a station on the Northern Pacific, five miles from St. Ignatius, by a brass band composed entirely of young Indians, who played "Dixie," "Yankee Doodle," and "The Star Spangled Banner" as they escorted me to the mission. I found the charges made by Michelle and Arlee to be entirely groundless, and so reported to the full Senate committee on my return to Washington.

I was so much impressed with what I saw at St. Ignatius that at the next session of Congress I was fortunate enough to secure an appropriation of $10,000 for the establishment of an industrial school at the mission, and on my return two years subsequently, I found that the Indian boys had been taught to do carpenter's work, make their own clothes, including hats, boots and shoes, and had erected a grist and saw mill, which they were managing themselves, and had also built an addition of twenty rooms to the male dormitory, all the work being done by the pupils. I mention this to show that the condition of the younger Indian is not hopeless, but that he can be taught to consider labor not disgraceful, but honorable, and that self-support is the first step toward self-respect. Booker Washington is engaged in the same great work for the negro at Tuskegee, Ala., and he should be encouraged by every intelligent and patriotic citizen.

Charlot.

From Saint Ignatius' Mission Maj. Maginnis and myself went back by rail to Missoula, and from that place we proceeded to Bitter Root Valley to Stephensville, named after the first Territorial governor of Montana, and near which is located at Saint Mary's Mission.

The Bitter Root Valley is the most beautiful I have ever seen. On either side of the Bitter Root River, which flows through it, is a forest of large red pine trees, the lowest branches of which are from ten to fifteen feet from the ground, there being no brush or undergrowth, while the solemn silence is unbroken except by the plaintive notes of a pine bird or the leap of a trout in pursuit of some fugitive insect. These immense trees, colored so wonderfully by nature, and the stillness of the great forest impressed one like a vast cathedral from which is excluded the rush and roar of the outside world with its sordid greed and ignoble strife for place and power.

On the next morning after reaching Stephensville we visited Saint Mary's Mission and ascertained that Charlot and five of his men would meet us in about two hours, the Jesuit fathers having sent out runners and notified them of our coming. We found at the mission Father [Anthony] Revalli, who had been brought from Europe in 1842 by Father De Smet, and who had been with the Flatheads more than fifty years. He had been partially paralyzed five years before our visit, and was stretched upon his rough couch in a narrow cell without other furniture than a chair and table, a large wooden crucifix with the image of our Saviour upon it being placed directly above his bed. This remarkable man was a skillful physician and surgeon, an accomplished artist with both brush and chisel, and a mechanic capable of doing all sorts of work in metals and wood. Father De Smet had brought with him from Belgium two fifteen-inch mill stones which were intended to be worked by hand-power, but Father Revalli utilized water, and the first saw and grist mill in the Indian country was set in motion, the machinery being constructed out of old wagon tires and the saw made out of a pit-saw by filing the teeth to the proper shape.

Father De Smet having obtained seed by a journey to Fort Colville, on the Columbia River, in what is now the state of Washington, after his return from Europe in 1842, the Jesuits planted in Bitter Root Valley the following spring the first grain and potatoes ever cultivated in Montana. The grist mill and saw mill constructed under the direction of Father Revalli enabled them to grind sufficient flour for the immediate wants of the mission and the Indians living in the vicinity.

Father Revalli's arrival was a great blessing to the Flathead Indians, for he not only relieved them of disease and suffering by his medical skill, but enabled them to take the first steps on the road to civilized life. Even after being paralyzed and unable to leave his bed, he continued to prescribe and perform surgical operations, and, when able to travel, never refused to go any distance for the purpose of giving his medical skill to the sick or administering the last rites of his church to the dying. He had been wounded by the Blackfeet in one of their raids, and, after being scalped, was left by them under the supposition that he was dead, but his life was saved by a s...., whose child had previously been rescued from death by the operation of a tracheotomy performed by Father Revalli, the simple skill of the Indian being unable to combat with the deadly croup with which the little sufferer was afflicted. [Editors' note: Other sources indicate Ravalli was paralyzed by several strokes and do not mention any wounds or scalping by the Blackfeet.] He had found time amid all his arduous and dangerous duties to prepare a work on the Indian sign language, the manuscript of which was destroyed by the Blackfeet. When I spoke to him of his self-sacrifice in behalf of the Indians, he said earnestly that he had not been actuated alone by his love for the Indian, but by his love of Christ.

Two hours after reaching the mission, Charlot, with four of his tribe arrived, and, with an equal number of white men, both sides being unarmed, we entered upon an interview which was at times dramatic and even stormy. Charlot is an Indian of fine appearance and impressed me as a brave and honest man. That he had been badly treated is unquestionable, and the history of the negotiations which culminated in the division of his tribe, part of them under Arlee, the second chief, being then on the Jocko reservation and part still in the Bitter Root Valley with Charlot, was, to say the least, most remarkable. I told Charlot that we had come from the Great Father in Washington to ascertain what was the real condition of affairs among the Flatheads, and why he and a number of his tribe had refused to join the majority who had voluntarily gone to the Jocko reservation. He replied through the interpreter that he had been shamefully treated, and that he had no confidence in the promises of any white man; that, although the hereditary chief of the Flatheads, his place had been taken by Arlee, a renegade Nez Perce, who was receiving money and cattle from the United States to which he, Charlot, was rightfully entitled. He declared that he did not want anything from the government except the privilege of living and dying in the Bitter Root Valley, where his ancestors had been buried; that he would not go to the Jocko reservation; that, if the Great Father insisted upon his leaving the Bitter Root Valley, he would do so but would not promise to join those of his tribe who had gone with Arlee.

After exhausting all argument and persuasion, I produced a printed copy of the report made by the Commissioner of Indian Affairs in 1872, which contained the treaty made between Gen. James A. Garfield (afterward President of the United States), as special commissioner for the Interior Department and the Flatheads, by which it was agreed that the Flatheads should leave the Bitter Root Valley and remove to the Jocko reservation on the Northern Pacific Railroad, some forty miles distant.

In 1855 a treaty was made between the United States, represented by Gov. Stephens, and Victor, chief of the Flatheads and father of Charlot, known as the Hell Gate treaty. By this treaty a very large territory, extending from near the forty-second parallel to the British line, and with an average breadth of nearly two degrees of latitude, was ceded to the government; and on yielding it Victor insisted on holding the Bitter Root Valley, above the Lo-Lo Fork, as a special reservation for the Flatheads proper.

By the ninth and eleventh articles of the treaty the President was empowered to determine whether the Flatheads should remain in the Bitter Root Valley or go to the Jocko reservation, and he was required to have the Bitter Root Valley surveyed and examined in order to determine this question.

Up to the time of Gen. Garfield's visit in 1872, seventeen years afterward, no survey was made, as the Indians claim; nor were any schoolmasters, blacksmiths, carpenters, or farmers se[n]t to the tribe, as provided for in the treaty.

In the meantime the Bitter Root Valley, by far the most beautiful and productive in Montana, was being filled up by the whites, and on November

14, 1871, the President issued an order declaring that the Indians should be removed to the Jocko reservation, and on June 5, 1872, Congress passed a bill appropriating $50,000 to pay the expense of their removal and to pay the Indians for the loss of their improvements in the Bitter Root Valley.

This order the Indians refused to obey, and serious apprehensions of trouble between them and the white settlers caused the appointment of Gen. Garfield by the Secretary of the Interior as a special commissioner to visit the Flatheads, and secure, if possible, their peaceable removal to the Jocko reservation.

Gen. Garfield states in his report that he found the Indians opposed to leaving the Bitter Root Valley, for the reason that the government had for seventeen years failed to carry out the treaty of 1855, and that no steps had been taken toward surveying and examining the Bitter Root Valley, as provided in that treaty.

It will be noticed that while the Garfield treaty states that the President had caused a survey to be made of the Bitter Root Valley, there had, in fact, been no such survey.

This treaty was signed by Gen. Garfield as special commissioner and had affixed to it the names of Charlot as chief, Arlee, second chief, and Adolf, third chief of the Flatheads. It was witnessed by William H. Clagett, D. G. Swaim, Judge Advocate of the United States army; W. F. Sanders, afterwards United States Senator from Montana; J. A. Viall, superintendent Indian affairs for Montana, and B. F. Potts, governor of the Territory of Montana. I told Charlot that he had violated his agreement as shown by the treaty, and that he must remove with the remnant of his band to the Jocko reservation, where the government would build him and his people houses, give him lands, together with cattle and horses, as had been promised in the Hell Gate treaty. I also told him that he and his followers having refused to take the patents of land in the Bitter Root Valley, which fifty-one had selected, they had no title to any lands in the valley and would be removed to the Jocko reservation unless they voluntarily went there. I pointed out to him what folly it was to resist the United States and that there could be but one result if he persisted in his present course.

I said to him that his young men were loafing around saloons in Stephensville gambling and drinking, and that sooner or later there must be serious trouble between his band and the white settlers. I informed him further that the government did not want to use force, but that I had an order in my pocket to have soldiers brought from Fort Missoula and that he and his fifty or sixty warriors could be tried [tied?] and carried over to the fort like so many bags of grain. The chief, although ragged, dirty, and half starved, drew himself up with great dignity, and said:

"You may carry me to Fort Missoula dead, but you will never carry me there alive. I heard before," he declared, "that your great father had printed a book showing my name to the treaty, but I never signed nor told anybody else to sign it for me. As to carrying me to the fort like a bag of grain, you did not talk that way when your people were going to California and came through my country sick and hungry. I had many warriors then and could have killed them all, but we nursed and fed them and did all we could to make them happy. Nearly all my warriors are dead, and I have only women and children. You have your foot on my head now," he said, as he threw on the floor a fragment of an old woolen hat and put his foot upon it, "but then I had my foot on your head. There is not a drop of white blood on the hands of my people, and when Joseph, the Nez Perce, my kinsman, marched through my country on his way to Canada, I refused to take his hand because it had white blood on it, and told him that if he hurt a single one of the whites in Bitter Root Valley I would attack him with my warriors at once. There," he said, pointing to an old blind Indian in the room, "is a man who drew his revolver and defended the wife of the blacksmith at Stephensville from the Nez Perces at the risk of his life. He," said Charlot, pointing to the cell of Father Revalli, which joined the room in which we were, "was there, and knows that I refused to sign the Garfield treaty. I have no faith in what you say now, for the government has broken all the promises made by your great father in 1855."

I watched the chief very closely when he was speaking, and came to the conclusion that he told the truth. Turning to my companions, I said that we would take a recess for an hour, and I then took the Indians up to the little village tavern and requested the landlord give them the best dinner he could furnish, as they were actually famished for want of food.

As soon as I could do so, without attracting attention, I went back to the mission, and, going into Father Revalli's cell, told him what Charlot had said in regard to the Garfield treaty, and asked him if he was there and knew the facts. He said very earnestly: "I do not want to have anything to do with this matter. I am an old man and have only a short time to live. I do not want any collision with the government nor with the white men in this valley, who seem determined to drive Charlot and his friends out of it. I have heard of this publication by the Indian commissioner, but have never said anything in regard to its truth or falsity. I hope you will not ask me to make any statement now."

I said to him: "Father Revalli, you have devoted your life to the cause of humanity and justice. Charlot and his men cannot remain in this valley. As you know, there will be an armed collision between them and the whites, who are resolved to have their lands. I can call on the commandant at Fort Missoula for troops, but I am unwilling to do so, for such action could only result in the virtual extermination of this remnant of a once great tribe, of which Charlot is the hereditary chief. The United States has not complied with its agreement as to the survey of the Bitter Root Valley. Twenty-eight years have elapsed and the President has ordered the Flatheads to leave the Bitter Root Valley and go over to the Jocko reservation. If Charlot did not sign that treaty, he has been grossly outraged, and I do not blame him for feeling as he does. It seems to me your duty to tell the whole truth and prevent bloodshed, which must occur unless matters are changed."

Father Revalli was silent for some minutes, and then said: "I hoped to avoid any statement, but you are right. I will soon join my Master," pointing to the crucifix above him. "I was there, and I know that Charlot refused to sign the treaty, while Arlee and Adolf, second and third chiefs, did so. Charlot is a brave, honest man, while Arlee is a shrewd, bold, and cunning Indian, and always takes good care of himself."

After the Indians were brought back from the village in much better humor, and we had again assembled at the mission, I asked Charlot how he would like to go to Washington and talk with the Great Father, bringing with him the agent and interpreter. After consulting together for some time he replied that he would be very glad to go, as he wanted to ask the Great Father for permission to remain in the Bitter Root Valley, but he did not commit himself to anything further. On the next day we returned to Fort Missoula and then visited the Blackfeet, Crow and Piegan agency, near Fort Shaw, and the agency at Fort Assinniboine, journeying before reaching the Canadian line though what is known as the buffalo plains, the most desolate and depressing region imaginable. Besides the crows, which cawed harshly over our heads, and a single wolf, we did not see a living thing in going 150 miles. This is the country where countless buffalo once roamed, and where the Flatheads and Blackfeet fought sanguinary battles every year. The only evidence of the buffalo having existed here is found in the old trails and wallows of these animals. From Fort Assinniboine we crossed into Canada, and at Green River entered a train on the Canadian Pacific Railway, reaching St. Paul in three days.

On the day after I arrived in Washington City I called upon the Secretary of the Interior and asked him to have a search made for the original Garfield treaty with the Flatheads in 1872, and, after some hours, the document was found, with the signatures of Gen. Garfield as special commissioner, and those of Arlee and Adolf, second and third chiefs of the Flatheads, but there was no signature by Charlot. The names of the witnesses, which have already been given in this narrative, were affixed to the treaty, but it was manifest that the signature of Charlot had been forged to the instrument as published by the

Commissioner of Indian Affairs. The Secretary agreed with me that a great outrage had been perpetrated upon Charlot, and readily consented to permit him, with a few of his tribe, to visit Washington in the hope that he could be persuaded to resume his place as hereditary chief of the United Flatheads on the Jocko reservation.

In the latter party of January, 1884, Maj. [Peter] Ronan, agent for the confederated tribes of Indians living upon the Jocko reservation, under instructions from the Commissioner of Indian affairs, came to Washington with the following Bitter Root Flathead Indians:

Head Chief Charlot, Slem-Hak-Kah ("Little claw of a grizzly bear"); Antoine Moise, Callup-Squal-She ("Crain with a ring around his neck"); Louis [Vanderburg], Licoot-Sim-Hay ("Grizzly bear far away"); John Hill, Ta-Hetchet ("Hand shot off"); Abel, or Tom Adams, Swam-Ach-Ham ("Red arm"), and the official interpreter, Michel Ravais, whose Indian name was Chim-Coo-Swee ("The man who walks alone").

They were kindly treated by the [P]resident, the Secretary of the Interior, and the Commissioner of Indian Affairs, and every argument used to induce Charlot to move from the Bitter Root Valley to the Jocko reservation. His only answer was that he had come to see the Great Father in order to obtain his consent to his remaining in the valley where he was born and wished to be buried. He declared that under no circumstances would he go to the Jocko reservation. At this time Charlot was almost totally blind, and I finally suggested to Maj. Ronan, the agent, that if we could restore or improve his sight it would certainly do much to gain his consent to reuniting the tribe on the Jocko reservation and his resumption of authority as hereditary chief. Maj. Ronan had told me that Charlot, was much depressed by his loss of eyesight, as he was a great hunter and could no longer see how to shoot game in the mountains.

In a letter to J. A. Viall, superintendent of Indian affairs, Montana, bearing the same date with the contract, and to be found on page 115 of the report of the Commissioner of Indian Affairs for 1872, Gen. Garfield says:

"In carrying out the terms of the contract made with the chiefs of the Flatheads for removing that tribe to this reservation (Jocko), I have concluded, after full consultation with you, to proceed with the work in the same manner as though Charlot, first chief, had signed the contract. I do this in the belief that when he sees the work actually going forward he will conclude to come here with the other chiefs and then keep the tribe unbroken."

It is unfortunate that Gen. Garfield came to this conclusion, and it is still more unfortunate that the published agreement, as shown by the report of the Commissioner of Indian Affairs, has the signature of Charlot affixed to it,

while as before stated, the original agreement on file in the Department of the
Interior does not show the signature of Charlot, but confirms his statement
that he did not sign it. The result of this false publication was to imbitter
Charlot, and render him suspicious and distrustful of the government and
its agents. Many interested parties believed, or pretended to believe, that the
agreement as published was correct, and that Charlot really signed it, and they
repeated the statement until he and his band became exasperated at what they
considered an attempt to rob them of their land by falsehood and fraud.

The great cause of Charlot's bitterness, however, was the fact that Arlee,
second chief, was recognized as the head of the tribe by the government, and
had received all its bounty. This was such an insult as no chief could forgive, and
it must be remembered that Charlot was the son of Victor, and the hereditary
chief of his tribe. Looking at all the circumstances, the removal of part of his
tribe without his consent, the ignoring his rights as head chief, and setting him
aside for Arlee, the publication of his name to an agreement which he refused
to sign, I could not blame him for distrust and resentment.

When and by whom the publication of the Garfield treaty with Charlot's
signature affixed was placed in the report of the Commissioner of Indian
Affairs in 1872 will never be known, but it must have been done in the Interior
Department after the treaty and report of Gen. Garfield were made to the
officials in Washington. The original treaty shows that Charlot never signed it,
and it is evident that interested parties caused the treaty with Charlot's name
affixed to be published by the Commissioner of Indian Affairs, who, at the
time, was the Hon. Francis A. Walker, afterward Superintendent of the Census
of 1880. No one who knows the high character of Gen. Walker could believe
that he was privy to any such fraud, but it must have been done without his
knowledge by a miscreant who wished to make the people of Montana believe
that Charlot had deliberately violated his treaty obligations and that the whites
were fully justified in forcing him to leave the Bitter Root Valley.

Maj. Ronan, after I mentioned to him the good results which might come
from restoring or improving Charlot's eyesight, talked with the chief on the
subject and reported to me the next day that Charlot was willing to have
an operation performed, as both of his eyes had been attacked by cataract. I
consulted with the Secretary of the Interior, and he authorized me to employ
the best oculist in Washington, and agreed to pay the expenses of the operation
out of the contingency fund. I sent for Dr. Marmion, who stood very high
as an oculist, and requested him to examine Charlot's eyes and determine
whether they could be successfully treated, but I urged upon him the necessity
of being absolutely certain before he performed any operation, as I knew any
bad result would cause the adherents of Charlot in the Bitter Root Valley to

believe that he had been brought to Washington for the sinister purpose of making him totally blind. Dr. Marmion reported that the cataracts could be removed, and the operation was successfully performed. But even after this Charlot still persisted in his refusal to leave the Bitter Root Valley and go to the Jocko reservation. All offers by the Secretary of the Interior of pecuniary reward could not shake Charlot's resolution to remain in the Bitter Root Valley. An offer to build him a house, to fence in and plow a sufficient quantity of land for a farm, to give him cattle and horses, seed and agricultural implements, and to do likewise for each head of a family belonging to his band, and to give him a yearly pension of $500, and to recognize him as hereditary chief had no effect.

After remaining in Washington a month Charlot and his companions returned to the Bitter Root Valley, nothing having been accomplished toward inducing him to make his home on the Jocko reservation.

Since writing the above I was much surprised on the 2d instant (April, 1903), by a visit, at my residence in Washington, of Charlot and several of his tribe, who had come here on business with the Interior Department. He is now about eighty years old, but his general health is good, and, although his eyesight is not fully restored, he informed me that with a fast horse and a good gun he thought that he could yet kill a buffalo. He said that twelve years ago he had gone to the Jocko reservation, and was now the first or hereditary chief of the Flatheads, but that the promises made to him in 1884, that if he would remove to the Jocko reservation, he should have land, and a good house, with some cattle, and a yearly pension of $500 have never been fulfilled.

Father Revalli, Arlee, Michelle, and Maj. Ronan have passed away, and it will not be long before Charlot will be placed in that windowless chamber of the grave, but he will not sleep with his ancestors in the beautiful Bitter Root Valley.

Senator G. G. Vest
Source: U.S. Senate Historical Office, Washington, D.C.

Senator G. G. Vest Negotiates with Flathead Reservation Chiefs September 5, 1883

Source: G. G. Vest and Martin Maginnis, "Report of the Subcommittee of the Special Committee of the United States Senate, Appointed to Visit the Indian Tribes in Northern Montana," part of Senate Report No. 283 (1884), 48th Congress, 1st Session, serial 2174, pages xxv-xxvii.

Editors' note: The transcript of these negotiations was especially important because it showed how tribal leaders met ahead of time and presented a united front when dealing with representatives from Washington, D.C.

Flathead Agency, Montana, *September* 5, 1883.

The Commission, having first had submitted to it a copy of a letter from Agent [Peter] Ronan to the Hon. Commissioner of Indian Affairs (a copy of which is hereto attached), more especially referring to Flathead Indians still resident in Bitter Root Valley, but also touching upon the desire of the Indians of this reservation to have their northern border extended to the British line, the better to enable them to welcome an immigration of friendly Indians, who, having been crowded out of their own homes, are anxious to settle here, held a council with the confederated tribes of Pend d'Oreilles, Kootenais and Flatheads, during which the following remarks, questions and answers were made:

Senator [G. G.] Vest, addressing the Indians, said: I desire, in the first place, to have you understand that this Commission is not sent to make a bargain for your lands; that the great white council from which we came does not want to take your lands away, or to do anything else which you do not wish done. We are sent here to find out your condition, and to learn what you want. Something was said during Mr. [Joseph] McCammon's visits about extending your reservation farther north, and we now desire to have your views on this subject. Your agent sent a writing to Washington making such a statement, and we now want to know whether you wish to exchange some land here for some farther north, or wish to keep the reservation as it is. Again, we understand that you have been somewhat troubled as to the payment of the money promised you for the railroad right of way; that you have had some apprehension that the money would not be given you. The reason of its nonpayment up to this time is that before the matter was quite settled the great white council finished its business for the year; such matters require to be attended to by it, and before the money was paid it adjourned. Since then the payment has been made, and the money will be paid over as soon as the council meets again; so you need have no uneasiness on that point. We also wish to talk with you about the Indians in the Bitter Root Valley. Do you wish them to come here? We are going over there, but do not wish to talk there until we get your opinions here. These are some of the matters about which we came to speak to you, and if you wish to counsel concerning them among yourselves, we can get your views by and by.

Michelle, chief of the Pend d'Oreilles, replied: It will not require much time to give you the answers to your questions, as we Indians have held a council together for the last two days; we have arrived at mutual conclusions, and what I am going to say is in the hearts of all the Indians. We never expect to move the lines of our reservation. Our children have been born here, and we like our country. The Great Father promised that we should always have it, and we depend on that promise. As to the Flatheads now living at Bitter Root, they are our people and our friends, and we will be glad if they come to live with us. These are our opinions on these two questions, and all that is necessary to be said.

Senator Vest. The replies on these points are plain. I understand them. Now let me know if you are satisfied as to the payment of the railroad money?

Michelle. Yes, we are satisfied. Before we were not. We have been looking for it. We did not know when it would come, but now, you having told us, makes us content.

Senator Vest. There is one other subject of which we desire to talk, and we wish an answer when you have had time to think it over. It is as to your each taking up 160 acres of land. We don't propose to decide this question at present, but only ask to have your views upon it, so as to be able to report them to the great council.

Michelle. It is with this as with the other questions. We don't require time to consult. That we have already done. We don't want to take up 160 acres each and sell the rest of our land. We want to keep the whole reservation, for there are plenty of Indians who wish to come and live with us, and we have told them they will be welcome.

Senator Vest. Don't you think it would be better to have more money and cattle and less land?

Michelle. If I had good and plenty of land and a few cattle and a little money I would be glad. The reverse would not please me, because my children are cultivating the land more and more and so get money.

Senator Vest. How are the Indians satisfied with the schools?

Michelle. Well when the treaty was first made we were told we would have a school-house, and I thought it would here at the agency, but it was placed at the mission.

Senator Vest. Do Indians like to send their children there?

Michelle. I don't know exactly, but I think the desire is stronger on the part of the fathers to get the children than on the part of the Indians to send them. When Governor [Isaac] Stevens made the treaty he said that no money would be required on account of the school, but now some of the people require to pay some money.

Senator Vest. The great council gives money for the school. This year it gives $8,000.

Michelle. I have heard so. That's why the fathers want all the children they can get.

Senator Vest. How much does any Indian have to pay for tuition?

Michelle. The Indians don't pay money, but work for their children. When we made the first treaty we were promised a school-house — where, we were not told, but some of the Indians would like it at the agency.

Senator Vest. Is the school-house not situated at about a central point?

Michelle. Yes; right in the center.

Governor [Schuyler] Crosby. We understand the children are happy. Is that so?

Michelle. Yes; because their fathers send the children to learn, and therefore they will be happy if they are taught to read and write.

Governor Crosby. The question was, are the children happy and contented?

Michelle. I don't know personally, having no children young enough to be at school.

Senator Vest. Well, you must have heard how they feel?

Michelle. No; I don't know; I never want to find out; the parents are satisfied.

Senator Vest. We wish now to hear anything that any other Indian may wish to say. Is there any of them desirous of expressing their views?

Michelle. What I have spoken is the voice and heart of all my children.

Baptise Shtil-Tah (a sub-chief of Pend d'Oreilles). What Michelle has said is what we all say.

(This was followed by unanimous "ughs" of approval from the Indians.)

Michelle. I already mentioned that we have for two days held a council, and that I came here to tell you the views we all hold; but now you wish to be told of other matters, and I wish to tell you of something I don't like. Liquor comes on the reservation — how, we don't know, but seeing you here to-day, I ask you to help me to stop that; to tell white people not to give any liquor at all to my people. Besides this my people gamble; the whites sell cards, and with them my people gamble off goods and horses, and the women and children are often to be found crying about their horses which have thus been lost by their relatives.

Senator Vest. We have already made many laws to stop these things, but we cannot even stop them among ourselves. We occasionally catch and punish the guilty parties. We have done the best we can, but bad white men will sometimes manage to break the law and evade punishment.

Michelle. I think white people are strong enough and smart enough to do what they please. Why don't they stop it?

Senator Vest. White men were never strong enough or smart enough to put a stop to gambling and drinking.

Major [Martin] Maginnis. How would you like to sell your ponies and buy cattle?

Michelle. That is what we are always doing, and that is the reason so many Indians here have cattle.

Agent [Peter] Ronan. In the course of my official duties I was directed to locate the northern boundary of this reservation, and, on proceeding to make an examination in connection therewith, found certain monuments and posts placed and marked in order to designate such boundary by Surveyor Thomas, sent for that purpose from the surveyor-general's office at Helena, in this Territory. Now, the Territory claims the line as surveyed by Thomas to be the correct boundary, while the Indians claim a line some four or five miles farther north, running through Medicine Lodge. The strip of land in dispute is generally unfit for settlement, there being only a small portion of it, sufficient perhaps for one or two occupants, suitable for pasture. This quantity, may not be inadequate to cause trouble, as the Indians have already removed one settler therefrom, and I desire Eneas (the chief of the Kootenais), whose home is in that vicinity, to express his views on that subject to the Commission.

Eneas (chief of the Kootenais). We don't know anything about the surveyor's line, or the authority under which he acted, but we do know the line as to which we made the treaty, and it is a well-defined natural boundary, marked by a ridge of hills.

Senator Vest. No one had a right to run any line unless sent from Washington and until such is done the boundary as described by Governor Stevens must be regarded as the proper one.

Michelle. There is only one thing more I have to mention. It is about the railroad. I like to see the cars, but they kill some cattle and horses, and this is done sometimes through carelessness. I wish to have good engineers employed so as to avoid this.

Governor Crosby. When any stock is killed have the owners immediately report to your agent, giving him all the particulars, and you will find there will be no trouble in obtaining a settlement.

Senator Vest. Before leaving let me say that we are very glad to see you doing so well. We will tell our people how well you are getting along.

Governor Crosby. Of the Indians of this reservation I have heard very good accounts, and throughout the Territory, in which he is very well known, your agent, Major Ronan, bears an excellent character. And I wish to impress upon you that, while so many dishonest people are dealing with Indians you ought to appreciate such a man and do as he tells you. I also wish to say to you that, as you have told the great chief here from Washington that you wish to retain your reservation, which is large, you ought to remain on your lands and not interfere with the lands of white men, who are prevented from intruding upon your reserve. Had those bad Indians, who came here and created some disturbance some days ago, been unable to cross white men's lands and so prevented from coming you and others would have escaped considerable annoyance.

With these remarks and an interchange of expressions of good will the council was dissolved.

Document 55

Charlo Refuses to Leave Bitterroot Valley

September 1883

Source: "Chief Charlos," *The Helena Independent* (daily), September 13, 1883, page 5, col. 2.

Editors' note: In 1883 a delegation from Washington, D.C., came to western Montana and Charlos again refused to move to the Flathead Reservation in Jocko.

Chief Charlos.
A Spirited Debate between Senator Vest and the Flathead Chief.

The Indian Commission — Senator [G. G.] Vest and Delegate [Martin] Maginnis — returned to Helena yesterday from their council with the Flathead Indians. They state that the Indians at Flathead Agency are unwilling to sell their reservation, and refuse to move to another. The Indians said they were well satisfied with their present condition. They have no grievances, are highly pleased with the agent, Major Rowan [Peter Ronan], and all that they desire in addition is that whisky may be kept away from the young men. The Pen 'dOreille and Kootenari [sic] chiefs expressed substantially the same opinions.

The St. Ignatius Mission schools, which are upon the reservation, were also visited by the commission. About fifty Indian girls and the same number of boys are being educated there and show a remarkable proficiency in their studies. The schools are excellently conducted by the Sisters of Charity and the priests. Senator Vest expressed a high opinion of the teachers and pupils.

A council was held at St. Mary's Mission on Monday with Charlos, the Flathead Chief. The council was held in the church there, which was built some forty-three years ago by Father [Pierre] DeSmet. Besides the Commission and Charlos, there were present several of the latter's head man and an interpreter. Charlos, it should be understood is the hereditary Flathead Chief, who with a few hundred followers has held himself aloof from the rest of the tribe and has steadfastly refused to go upon the reservation. They have cultivated some land, but have been growing poorer year by year, and their valley is thickly settled with whites. Trouble with them had been feared, and on this account the reservation Indians and the settlers want them removed to the reservation.

In the council there was quite a dramatic scene. Senator Vest and Major Maginnis sat on one side of the council room, and Charlos sat facing them. Vest, through the interpreter, explained the object of the commission. During the explanation Charlos, who is a noted brave and has a massive face of wonderful strength and firmness, gazed at the speaker steadily and after a moment's pause, replied:

"We are only a few. We are poor and weak. You would not talk to us this way on the plains when we were many and strong."

"We do not come here to threaten you," replied Senator Vest. "We come as friends to act fairly and honestly with the Indians. We know you are the white man's friend, and we came here to see how you and your people could be benefitted. Your brothers want you and your people to go upon the reservation and to cultivate the lands and become prosperous."

"My hands and those of my people are free from the white man's blood," said Charlos. "When the Nez Perces came here we protected the whites. Why does the white man take his heart from us now?"

At this juncture an old gray headed Indian, one of whose eyes was blind, stood up, and in a bent attitude, with his hands stretched out toward the Senator, said, in an excited manner:

"I am old, and nearly blind; but when the Nez Perces were here I was told they were going to abuse a white woman, and I got my revolver, placed myself in front of her, and told them they would have to kill me before they injured the white woman. My white friends will tell you this is true."

Senator Vest again assured the Indians that he knew they were good Indians, and that the Great Father wished to deal fairly with them.

"We do not wish to leave these lands," said Charlos. "You place your foot upon our necks and press our faces into the dust. But I will never go to the reservation. I will go to the plains."

"Joseph, the Nez Perce chief, and his band attempted to go to the plains," replied Vest. "Look where he is now! There are no more plains. The white men are as thick as leaves from ocean to ocean. Either get a patent to your lands here or go upon the reservation where you can raise plenty to eat."

The Indians refused to take out patents, saying they would not pay taxes upon land.

Charlos then made quite a speech about early treaties, and finally took his hat off, threw it upon the floor, and, gazing steadily at Vest, who returned the look with interest, shouted:

"You may take Charlos to the reservation, but there will be no breath in his nostrils! Charlos will be dead! He will never go there alive!"

Senator Vest stood up and answered the tawny chieftain in language as emphatic as his own that he must obey the white man's laws as implicitly as did the white man. If he did not, he must go where the Government chose to send him.

Before the council broke up Charlos agreed to go the Washington with Agent Ronan and talk the matter over with the Great Father.

Senator Vest said to Charlos that himself and Maj. Maginnis had come there as their friends, and that they left as their friends.

Document 56

Traveling Though the Flathead Reservation in 1883
September 27 – October 2, 1883

Source: Alex. Staveley Hill, *From Home to Home: Autumn Wanderings in the North-West, in the Years 1881, 1882, 1883, 1884* (New York: O. Judd Co., 1885), pages 367-380.

Editors' note: "L" was the Earl of Lathom, one of Staveley Hill's traveling companions. The photographs Staveley Hill refers to in the text have not been reproduced here. Staveley Hill mentions crossing the Flathead River on Baptiste Eneas' ferry and tribal members fishing in the river at the foot of Flathead Lake. His account of Duncan McDonald's actions during the Villard expedition's stay on Flathead, added some interesting details to the story. He spent a night at Ravalli waiting for the next train, but did not rent a room at McDonald's hotel. He camped for the night next to a Nez Perce stick game.

Thursday, 27th. [September 1883] — Up at 6.30. Thermometer 21° F. Off at 9.30. Rode along a slough on the right hand to get a shot at the ducks, but could not get near them, though they were very plentiful. I shot one snipe and L. [the Earl of Lathom] a duck, but in the absence of "Boxer" we could not retrieve them. After five miles, passing through some settlements, we came to the Great Flathead Lake, but there was so much haze and smoke that we could not see the opposite bank, and this we regretted the more, as I believe it to be one of the most magnificent views in this western country, a statement entirely borne out by the report to me by our men after their return. We went on for about eighteen miles through a wood, approaching and leaving the lakes at intervals; about ten miles further we met a wagon, the driver of which told us that we should save two miles by taking an Indian trail on arriving at a pine about a mile further on. The driver must have been making slow progress, as I arrived by the side of the pine in about five minutes, and from there had the longest and dullest ride of the whole route, at the end of which we came down a very steep pitch and camped among some black pine a little above the lake at 5.30. On our way down we passed a curious rock standing by itself in the wood; this had clearly been consulted by the Indians as a medicine stone, as was apparent from the bits of plate and sticks and other trifles that had been stuck about it, and the great amount of foot tracks round it. I walked down to the lake to have a wash. I put up a couple of fool hens, as the spruce partridge is called, but had not my gun. Tea at 6.30. Our provisions were getting low, so we were reduced to bacon and a small tin of soup, but had a comfortable night.

Friday, 28th. — Up at 5.10. Thermometer 28° F. Took my gun and washing things down to the lake and had a bathe, though I found it uncommonly cold dressing, as there was a little bit of a breeze. Saw no birds and got back to breakfast at 6.30. I took the accompanying photograph of a Scotch pine, which I measured with my clinometer, and found to be 126 feet high: it was 13 feet in girth. We started at 8.45, and leaving the wagon trail, I cantered on between the hills. It was a very bleak piece of country, and reminded me very much of the "Valley of Desolation," near Lynton, in Devonshire. I hunted through the scrub along the bottom of the hills, but found no game, and riding on five miles came to Dayton Creek, where there were plenty of geese, and at a distance of 200 yards from the bank there was a pretty island. Still very hazy, and no view to be seen of the opposite shore of the lake. We had lunch at 12.45, having ridden twelve miles, and I managed during lunch time to get two teal. For the last four miles the prairie was all burned. On our getting to the ferry we found that our men, who had been ahead of us while we were looking after some chicken, had just gone across the river, which runs down from the lake and which here takes the name of the next lake which it falls into, and is called Pend d'Oreille River. It is here about a quarter of a mile wide, and for the greater part of its width is shallow at this time of the year, with about fifty yards of deep rapid water, which has to be swum; our men, however, had crossed in the ferry-boat, a luxury not generally availed of by the Indians, which is not surprising, as we found that the fare for carrying across eight horses and four men, necessitating only two journeys across, was six dollars. The ferry-boat was a good conveyance, and on landing I saw that the ferryman's daughter, a half-breed girl, Miss Baptiste [Eneas], had plenty of freshly caught trout, so, as we had no time to fish that evening, after we had made camp, I went up to the hut to buy some. She wanted fifty cents for four trout weighing about one pound each. I grumbled at the price, but the young lady assured me, pointing below the waist, "I stand, so deep, cold water, catch them." So I said no more, but took the fish and paid my money, and very good they turned out to be.

There was another girl in the cabin, who had come over with her mother to enjoy some fishing with their friends. She was the daughter of old [Angus] McDonald, at a place twenty-three miles off, for which we were bound after leaving the ferry. Having made a supper on the trout, which were excellent, and on our teal, we enjoyed our quiet camp by the side of the beach which fringed the river, and after many pipes we turned in to bed. It was a warm night, the warmest we had had since we left Standoff.

Saturday, 29th. — Thermometer 29° F. We made up our minds to give our horses a rest, and to fish and see the falls. After breakfast L. and I walked down the river. Very fine, but a series of rapids rather than falls, with a total descent from the lake down to the first pool of about sixty feet. L. got a little sport shooting, and in the afternoon I went down to the pool, about two miles off. It was a curious walk, the trail leading along a high bank, continued round the bluffs. I had gone by myself, having arranged for Charlie to follow me. I fished in the pool below the rapids, both with fly and grasshopper, but got nothing. I took the accompanying photograph of the pool, looking down the river below it. There must be some very beautiful scenery below the pool. The pool itself is about half a mile wide, and from its far corner the river again descends; below this there must be rapids and some very fine pools; this part, however, as far as I know, has not been visited. On Charlie coming up to me we scrambled out to a rock in the middle of the stream, near the place from which I had taken the photograph of the pool. Straddling the legs of my camera on the rock I took the accompanying photograph of the falls.

The water was tumbling, as will be seen, around me on all sides, and the noise and rush of it all round the rock was very impressive. After some more equally unsuccessful attempts to lay hold of fish, we worked our way back up stream, and found that L. had caught some good trout with a fly above the falls. As to-day was Michaelmas Day, I had been particularly anxious to have a regular constitutional dish, but, as no goose had been shot, we were obliged to keep the feast of St. Michael on trout and bacon, and rice and apples. From a hole in the bank near our tent two skunks emerged during the night, and wandered about the camp, seeking what they could steal, but we, having been warned by the owl a few nights ago, had put our grub safe out of their reach, and out of the reach of the magpies — "meat-birds," as they are called in the North-West — who are always on the prowl. During the night I caught sight of one of the skunks coming up to the tent, and, clapping my hands, I chivied him off. In the morning we missed a bag with some biscuits, and after hunting about we found that skunks had dragged it to the mouth of their hole, but could not get it in, and had not seen their way to get at its contents, so we retrieved it unharmed. The two elderly ladies, Mrs. Batiste [Eneas] and Mrs. [Angus] McDonald, rode past us on their cayeuses to fish in the river, and there they sat perched on the top of them in the middle of the stream fishing with grasshoppers, and they kept the poor brutes standing up to their bellies in the cold water for three hours. They came back with good bags full of trout.

The two daughters had been fishing out of the boat a little nearer the lake with grasshoppers, and seemed to have been almost as successful as their mothers.

Sunday, 30th. — Woke up, after a warm night, with the thermometer at 35° F. As our horses were getting very footsore, and Dan's horse had a bad back, we hired a wagon of Batiste [Eneas] at a dollar per day, the men to take it with our horses, and to bring back 40 lbs. of freight for him. We had a long and interesting talk with Batiste of the early days of this country. I learned from him that the word "Selish," the name of the place at which we had camped, is the Indian name for "Flat Head." Mrs. McDonald passed us, to have an early fish, as we were hitching up. We left at ten o'clock, L. and I riding as usual, and Charlie with a passenger in the wagon. It was a nice firm turf to ride over, with occasional breaks of trees, but all very dry in this very rainless district. After twelve miles we stopped at the Muddy Creek to lunch. It is a very good stream, the mud being at the bottom and not in the water; it winds through some good prairie land, very well adapted for farms. From there three miles brought us to Crow Creek, and riding on through very similar country for twenty-two miles, we reached McDonald's at three in the afternoon, and passing his house, we camped within about a quarter of a mile of Hudson Bay Creek. All this country was considered to have been within the Hudson Bay Territory, and the settlers there still look upon themselves as Hudson Bay men. We found, as before, that the fish had all gone from the creek, and that Mrs. McDonald and her daughter had done quite right in leaving this, their home, to go up and catch, with their neighbours, some of the fish that were passing down from the lake. A more likely-looking stream for fish it would be difficult to find, and the fishing-poles lying about showed that much work had been done there. After tea McDonald came and sat by our camp fire. He is an old Hudson Bay man, who had come over from Scotland in the year 1838, had been in London, and liked to hear of it, and in return gave us many tales of the old time and old-timers; of his journeys up the Columbia River, through the Rockies, between Mount Brown and Mount Hooker, and from that point down the Athabasca, and so on to Churchill, on the Hudson Bay, and back, doing the round trip between April and December. This had been his regular work in the Hudson Bay Company's service for many years. He had come out in 1838, and had married his Flat Head wife, by whom he had several children. He was a remarkably fine-looking old fellow, about 70, with a touch of the military about him; a good tall figure, bronzed face, and grey hair. He was above all things taken with my Norfolk jacket, and said, "I should like to see you at the Horse Guards in your helmet and cuirasse." I informed him that was not my dress, and that a horse-hair wig and silk gown was the dress in which he would be more likely to find me; but he had an idea that tall men like L.

and myself must be soldiers. He sent us down some beef, which was excellent. A heavy rain came on during the night, and it was very wet in the morning, and everything on the low ground on which we had pitched our tent was very soppy. It cleared a little before starting, and then settled into a drizzle.

Monday, October 1st. — A ride over prairie, with an occasional farm, for about five miles, brought us to the Jesuit Mission of St. Ignatius. It was quite a neat little village, with a nice church, and a comfortable little priest's house, and a house for the Sisters. They are building an academy, and are planting fruit trees. The Mission is on the Flat Head Reserve, and is now under the charge of Father van Gorff [Leopold Van Gorp]. I believe that they receive some payment from the United States Government, and most certainly they deserve it, as they are doing really good work. It is the only Indian place I have seen in these wild countries which seems really flourishing and successful. The stream has been turned to work a saw-mill and to irrigate some land. We looked into the church; on all the chairs and desks and benches, was the Catechism of Religion in the Flat Head, called by the French "Pend d'Oreille," and in the native "Kalli-Spelm." The letter "i" signifies the root "camus," "kull" meaning "eater," and "spelm" is translated "plain"; it is also said to signify peoples or tribes, and thus Kulli-Spelm means either, the plain of the root-eaters, or the root-eating tribes. McDonald told me that the number of edible roots which the Indians have is very considerable. Camus is a root of a plant like an onion, with green leaves, and a flower like a lily. They boil it and dry it and prepare it with great care. Kous is a sweet root, and sklocum a much-prized vegetable, with a taste like peppermint. After leaving St. Ignatius, we passed first through some land, which will make magnificent farm or garden land, when watered from the ditch which the Fathers are training round it. After that the trail wound down among some hills, where we lamented more than ever the smoke which obscured the view. In about four miles from the Mission we reached Ravalli, on the Northern Pacific Railway, and our pleasant ride was at an end.

Ravalli is named after a Jesuit missionary priest, and here we found a store and restaurant kept by Duncan McDonald, son of our friend of the night previous. Ryan, the passenger whom we had brought with us from Batiste's ferry, invited us to dine with him, an invitation which rather to our loss we accepted. They had told us that the train would not come in till six, but just after dinner, and before we could get our traps, it ran in, and we found ourselves fixtures by the banks of the Jocko, the stream which runs down past Ravalli, till the next afternoon. We made the best of it, and camped by the line, near the tepes [sic] of some Nezperces, and then went for a walk up the line towards the east. We found many signs in the empty boxes of provisions and empty champagne cases of the enormous Villard picnic that had spent some hours here a few days before. The three trains that had conveyed the guests to the Pacific had stopped here with their burden of German, Yankee, and English notabilities. During their stop, an excursion had been made to the Butte Macdonald, to enable some of the excursionists to see a bear's winter cave. Our informant gave us many amusing accounts of the party.

"They seemed to think they were roughing it," said he; "but they had got as much to eat and drink as they could put away, and more than was good for them; they had good beds to sleep in. They were the most helpless set of men I ever saw: they could not ride, and they were too fat to walk."

I hope, however, that none of this description had any application to any of our English friends who may read this book.

"What were they talking about?" said we. "Well, they were mostly standing about together and talking about London. There was one very jolly-looking old chap with grey whiskers, who did not say much himself, but was always laughing at the others."

The great practical joke, however, seemed to have been, that young Duncan taking the party up to the bear's cave, going on ahead himself, wrapped himself in a buffalo, and when the party arrived at the hole of the cave, in a breathless condition, he gave a growling grunt, at which the visitors took to their heels (as well they might), remembering (to use a North-West phrase) "that they had not left anything behind them."

After we had gone to bed we found ourselves disturbed by the noise in an Indian tent; they were playing their favorite gambling game. The game is of a most simple character, and is played by two rows of men sitting opposite one another, to one of whom is handed, on behalf of his side, two small pieces of wood — one marked by being bound round or stained in the middle of a different colour, and the other left plain. The player who receives the two sticks on behalf of his side takes one in each hand, and throwing up his arms and, ejaculating, shows them, and putting his hands behind his back, changes them quickly from one hand to the other; the whole of his side shouting and crying and singing, so as to distract if possible the attention of their opponents, and prevent the eye watching the movements of the player. At last, when his hands are still and held behind his back, the bets are made, small bundles of sticks or "chips" indicating the amount that is wagered by the one side against the other, the side on which the player sits backing him, the opposite side laying against him. A certain number of these sticks counts for a blanket, so many more for a cayeuse, which has been named by the party wagering. When the bets have been arranged, the man with the pieces of wood produces his hands from behind him, and if the parties wagering against him have been successful in naming the hand in which the marked stick is, the stakes are handed over to them. This game began about ten o'clock at night, and having been kept awake by the yells and shouting until nearly midnight, I got up and went out to look through the tent at the scene that was going on; but I soon returned to bed, and the game and shouting continued till late on into morning. Some of the Indians were pretty well cleaned out, and we noticed next morning one Indian who was pointed out as having lost everything that he possessed; — a more wretched-looking played-out gambler I don't think I ever saw, as he stood by a bush with no blanket and very little clothes, looking thoroughly chapfallen, twiddling his fingers, whittling a bit of stick and utterly miserable. I succeeded in getting the accompanying photograph of the tents, and then turned my camera round to take an Indian and s.... who had wandered up to have a look at my operations. There was still the same belief that I was a "Boston man," and was after no good; a look at the photograph will show how completely the buck rolled his face up in his blanket to prevent his likeness being taken; the little s...., however, by his side, with a woman's curiosity, could not help looking over her blanket and laughing. These Nezperces are a very fine set of men, but are entirely given to gambling and horse-stealing, and are, I believe, as worthless a set of fellows as is to be found in the North-West. About noon we prepared for our departure by train, sitting down by the side of the line, and at 1.45 it rolled in, and we got all our goods on board, saying good-b'w'y' to our friends Dan and Charlie, not forgetting a kindly pat for the animals that had carried us so well, and with a wave of the hand steamed away up the slope of the mountains.

We soon began to ascend, and rose 1100 feet in the short piece to the Agency, going up the zigzags. The wood was not unlike much that we had driven through in the Rockies. About the summit and on the descent we crossed several cañons on high tressels, one being as high as 225 feet, very well and solidly built of wood. On our way down we seemed in several places to be almost doubling back, and reached a good grassy plain sloping to the south. We arrived at Missoula, a dull-looking town at the very end of a valley, having descended 700 feet. Thence we went up the Missoula valley, the water for the first time being muddy in colour. Many Chinamen's camps along the road; the men not very strong in physique, but looking clean, and every tent having a stove. The day was closing in as we left Missoula about 5.15, and it was late in the evening when we arrived at Helena, the mining capital of Montana, and being met by some friends, soon found ourselves in a tolerably comfortable hotel.

Document 57

Hints of a Crow-Salish Skirmish
in the Yellowstone
November 12, 1883

Source: "An Indian Fight," *The Daily Enterprise* (Livingston, Mont.), November 12, 1883, page 1, col. 4-5.

Editors' note: This note in a Livingston newspaper was only a hint of a great, but unrecorded, war story of Salish Indians stealing Crow horses.

An Indian Fight.

This year of grace, 1883, was destined not to pass without a slight — very slight — revival of the spirit that a decade ago made the Yellowstone region one of the most dangerous sections of Indian country in the northwest. The cause of this little exhibition of aboriginal valor was that fruitful, though unromantic, source of modern Indian troubles — horse-stealing. Last week a party of Flatheads, or as the Crows call them, Nez Perces, came across the country from the western part of the territory, made a raid upon the pony herd near the Crow agency and ran off about fifty head in one night. As soon as the loss was discovered a small band of Crows started in pursuit, following the trail of the thieves as hastily as possible. On Saturday morning they came up with the Flatheads and their prize in the Shields river valley about twenty-five miles from Livingston, and made a dash to recover the stock. Only three Flatheads were in sight, but they defended their booty vigorously until two of their number were killed, when the other fled precipitately. The Crows did not escape entirely unscathed. One of them received a bullet through the fleshy part of his legs above the knees, and though able to ride his pony was evidently badly hurt. Saturday afternoon the whole party arrived in Livingston in search of Major [George] Pease's "tepee," and through his influence received transportation for their wounded man by railroad to the agency. They numbered eight in all under Plentycoos, one of the leading of the younger chiefs. They spoke of the enemy as Nez Perces, though it appears that they were Flatheads most probably of Charlos' band, who are roving Indians, and make frequent excursions to this part of Montana.

Document 58

Salish Customers Patronize Helena Merchants

January 17, 1884

Source: "When the Flatheads Come to Town," *The Sun* (New York), January 27, 1884, page 6, col. 5.

Editors' note: This article had some important observations of the economic value of Salish sales of buffalo robes, and their astuteness as customers. The writer described friction between Indians and Chinese in Helena, but he did not make clear which tribe he was referring to relative to the Indian-Chinese marriage. The article also included some of the writer's prejudices towards Salish culture.

When the Flatheads Come to Town
Their Love for Gaudy Dry Goods — Fate of a S.... who Wedded Hop Lee.

Helena, M.T., Jan. 17. — Regularly every spring some roving band of Flathead Indians, on their way north for the annual hunt, visit the different towns of the Territory, stopping in each place several days to sell robes and skins, the product of the previous season's shooting. As the buffalo-hides readily sell for from $4 to $10 each, and the market is never over supplied, each Flathead realizes a handsome sum for his season's work. But in display only is he ambitious to be considered wealthy. Immediately upon supplying himself with ammunition, the buck enters a dry goods store to spend the remainder of his money for red-striped calico and yellow-barred blankets for himself and s....

"They never boggle over prices," said the proprietor of a Main Street store, "but count their money, and if they have enough to buy the articles wanted, make the purchase there and then. If you treat the Indian fairly, and don't cheat him you'll enjoy his whole tribe's custom whenever they come to town."

The s....s are not to be trifled with. They do not hesitate to defend themselves when called upon, without asking for the assistance of the bucks; but even here, where they are so well known, very few persons ever imagined that a s.... dared assume the aggressive toward her liege lord, until a recent occurrence proved that such a thing was possible. As a small band of Flatheads was riding up the principal street, one of the s....s became incensed at some remark her buck made, and urging her cayuse alongside of his, she beat him unmercifully across the head and face with the butt end of her whip. He tried to catch her arm, but failing sprang to the ground and retreated down the street at a rapid walk. He was next seen an hour afterward. The light of proud manhood had vanished from his eye, and his face was so bruised and swollen that one could scarcely recognize him.

About a dozen Chinamen were coming down the street in a body yesterday, when a small party of these Indians was in town, and as they were passing by an auction store in front of which two bucks were standing one of the bucks grabbed a Chinaman by the queue, and, drawing his scalping knife, circled it around the Celestial's head in a threatening manner, uttering the characteristic "Ugh!" His expression was so ferocious that John Chinaman, thinking his last hour had come, gave vent to several ear-splitting shrieks, and would have fainted had not some white men standing near compelled the Indian to release him at that stage. The other Chinamen had deserted him at the first alarm, and quickly pattered up the street to Chinatown. Presently word was passed to the bucks to fly for their lives, a piece of advice they promptly followed by mounting their cayuses and heading for camp when they beheld several hundred Chinese coming down the street. Judging by their fierce countenances and violent language no doubt the aggrieved Chinaman's friends meant to have terrible vengeance, yet there are persons in town who insist that the laundrymen were agreeably disappointed to find the bucks flown.

Hop Lee is a laundryman in Junction City. A tribe of Indians was encamped across the river, and, as usual, visited the town. Hop became enamored of a female of the party, and offered to share his rice and laundry back room with her, a proposal she at once accepted. Hop sent $5 to a St. Paul firm to get a wedding present for the bride, and received in return an elegant silk dress, with a train about five feet long. Arrayed in her new garments, Mrs. Hop crossed the river to exhibit herself to her people. After the first murmur of astonishment at her appearance the warriors held a brief consultation, and agreed to alter the dress so as to conform strictly with their idea of the proper thing for a s.... to wear. They set to work with their knives, and carefully cut away that portion of the dress below her knees, distributing the waste among themselves. When the s.... returned to her husband he turned her out of the house, and she returned to her people to receive the sympathy due a heart-broken bride.

Document 59

Reservation Police and Missoula Authorities

January 18, 1884

Source: *The Weekly Missoulian*, January 18, 1884, page 3, col. 3.

Editors' note: Friction between Indian police and off reservation authorities gave protection to a couple fleeing accusations of adultery. Note the willingness of white Missoulians to employ Indian workers.

Indian police from the Flathead reserve came over last week in search of an eloping couple, and found them industriously cutting wood for Andrew Logan of Missoula. In accordance with their notions of right and wrong they immediately set to work to flog the offending sister, who, after receiving considerable punishment, took refuge in her employer's house, and for the time eluded her captors. The half dozen policemen then turned their attention to the man in the case, and after a struggle succeeded in tying him securely, and endeavored to carry him off. Although he did not do very valorous work in defense of his lady love, he proved a good-sized elephant on the hands of "the perlice," for he rolled and squirmed about so that it was all the half dozen of them could do to carry him. Meantime, in response to call for interference, Marshall Myers put in an appearance, and, after cutting the thongs of the loving brave, informed the police that they could not infringe on the rights of the town of Missoula with such aboriginal impunity. The disgusted police folded their robes about them and marched off for the Agency, leaving the adulterous couple to saw wood, at their leisure. We presume Missoula will hereafter prove a veritable free-love paradise for wood-sawing Indians and their industrious paramours. We understand that Joseph and Rosalie, whose little romance is partially told above, have moved into town, and decided to stay within our sacred precincts. "The course of true love," etc.

Document 60

Agent Ronan and the Salish Indian Delegation to Washington, D.C. January 23 – February 10, 1884

Source: Peter Ronan, *"A Great Many of Us Have Good Farms": Agent Peter Ronan Reports on the Flathead Indian Reservation, Montana, 1877-1887*, ed. Robert J. Bigart (Pablo, Mont.: Salish Kootenai College Press, 2014), pages 246-251.

Editors' note: Ronan's letters to his wife during his 1884 trip to Washington, D.C., with a delegation of Bitterroot Salish Indians, gave a detailed account of the whirl of events on the trip. Charlo still refused to remove from the Bitterroot to the Jocko Valley, but, while in Washington, a surgical operaton restored his eyesight. The deletions in the letters were included in the original version in Peter Ronan's daughters' masters thesis in 1932: Margaret Ronan, "Memoirs of a Frontiers Woman: Mary C. Ronan," unpublished masters thesis, State University of Montana, Missoula, 1932, pages 355-362.

Willard Hotel,
O. G. Staples, Proprietor,
Late of Thousand Island House
Washington, D.C., Jan. 23, 1884.

My Darling Wife:

At eleven o'clock last night we arrived in Washington. Commissioner [Hiram] Price had a man waiting for us at the depot; and [Martin] Maginnis, Hugh McQuaid and Al Hamilton were also there to meet us. The Indians were provided for at the Tremont House and I was taken to Willard's Hotel, where Major and Mrs. Maginnis have always had rooms since Maginnis resided here as delegate.

Of course I was tired after the long journey, but this morning I was up with the lark, and after a nice bath and shave felt fresh as a daisy. After breakfast in company with Maginnis, I reported to Commissioner Price, who received me very cordially and informed me that the President and Secretary [Henry] Teller were both out of town and would be gone for several days, and to show the Indians the sights and enjoy myself as well as I could as no business would be done until their return. I was then introduced to the Indian office clerks

Bitterroot Salish Indian delegation to Washington, D.C., 1884:
back row, left to right, John Hill, Indian Agent Peter Ronan, and Michel
Revais; *middle row,* Antoine Moiese, Chief Charlo, and Louis Vanderburg;
front row, Thomas Abel Adams. Photograph by John K. Hillers.
Source: Montana Historical Society, Photograph Archives,
Helena, Mont., 954-526.

and visited Mr. [Joseph K.] McCammon, who really exhibited both friendship and pleasure at our meeting, and inquired very particularly about you and the children.

From Mr. McCammon's Maginnis and myself went to the Senate Chamber and met Senator [G. G.] Vest, who received me in the most cordial manner. Tomorrow Maginnis, myself and other guests are invited to dinner at the Senator's residence. The dinner is to be given in honor of the Indian Delegation and Charlot and all the Indians are to be present.

Today I took the Indians to call upon Father Brouilett [J. B. A. Brouillet], but we could not see him, as he was not expected to live through the night. On Friday we are to be escorted through the halls of Congress and all the public buildings. Saturday's program is not yet laid out; but the program for Sunday is, which is no less a treat, than to have seats reserved for us in the church for Mass and to listen to a sermon from Monsignor Capel, who is now in Washington. I anticipate my greatest pleasure on Sunday is listening to the great Catholic prelate.

I took Michel and Charlot to a doctor today, who says there is a chance, and only a chance, of restoring Michel's sight. Charlot he says will, in the course of a year, be as blind as Michel if an operation is not performed on his eyes. After the return of the President and the Secretary, when their business is settled, I will see what can be done for them.

Major and Mrs. Maginnis. . . are out to a party tonight, given by a congressman whose name I forget just now. I had an invitation but I concluded rather to retire to my room and scratch off a few lines to sweetest love — my darling wife, and my dear little children. . . .

Before I close I must tell you what Senator Vest said about my standing in the Indian Department, for I know it will please you. He said, in a conversation with Commissioner Price, that gentleman told him that there were only three Indian Agents in the Service, that were up to the standard of what he considered fit men for their positions and that I was one of the three and stood at the head of the class. . . .

* * * * * *

Willard Hotel, January 27, 1884.

. . . . This being Sunday morning I arose early to write first to you, and then to prepare myself and the Indians for Mass at the Jesuit Church of Saint Aloysius. . . . I am just beginning to get uneasy and restless to hear from you. . . .

President [Chester A.] Arthur and Secretary Teller returned from New York last night, and I expect my Indians and their affairs will be brought before them on Monday. In the meantime I have been enjoying myself immensely.

Just now (I suppose for lack of other beasts) Agent Ronan and his Indians are the lions of Washington. I am actually over-run with invitations for myself and the other animals. Senator Vest, on account of the rush on me, postponed his entertainment until yesterday, when we spent a delightful day with the Senator, his family and invited guests, among them were Major Maginnis and other acquaintances of mine. I attended a garden party, a hop at Willard's, a masquerade, and Senator Vest's dinner party since I wrote you, and my memorandum book is filled with engagements up to Saturday next, when we dine with Captain Mullen [John Mullan], who has taken the place of General Ewing at the head of the Catholic Indian Bureau. . . .

* * * * * *

Willard's Hotel, January 29, 1884.

. . . . In company with Major Maginnis and Senator Vest I had an interview today with Secretary Teller, and tomorrow I will bring Charlot and the Indians before him to talk business. With filling engagements and visiting with the Indians my time is constantly occupied. This evening I took them to Ford's Opera House to witness a grand performance by a troupe of "sure enough Negroes," and the Indians enjoyed it very much. They are all well and Charlot is in the best of spirits. Tomorrow night I must take them to the "Council Fire," residence of a Dr. and Mrs. [T. A.] Bland, where we are to have a reception. I know this will be an infliction — but as I am on the rounds with the Indians I cannot afford to act discourteous with anyone. . . .

* * * * * *

February 3, 1884.

. . . . I feel as gay as a young colt. . . .

Darling, you ought to have seen your dude of a husband yesterday at Mrs. [Mary Arthur] McElroy's reception at the President's house. He was compelled by force of circumstances to order two suits of clothes; one an evening dress suit — "claw hammers" coat, white kids, white satin necktie, a beaver hat, etc., etc. The other is an afternoon calling suit — a four button cut-away coat with everything else to match, and if you think I have had an idle moment since I arrived here you are mistaken. Every night I have to make a list of engagements for the next day and evening.

Yesterday I took the Indians to the Smithsonian Institute where we were all photographed in groups and singly. I say "we" because an order was issued from the Secretary's office for me to have my photograph taken with the group. I have been informed that I will be supplied with a dozen copies of each of the pictures. After that was over I had an interview with the Secretary, then an interview with the Commissioner of Pensions, and then made my call with Major and Mrs. Maginnis at the President's, and in the evening took dinner with Captain John Mullen and his interesting Catholic family in their magnificent mansion. So you see how yesterday was. The day before I had a similar round and wound up with a dinner party at Mr. McCammon's, where I met a young Frenchman who is a great grandson of Lafayette. He conversed in French with Michel and was delighted with the Indians at the McCammon's table, who ordered fish for dinner because it was Friday.

On Monday we are to have a final talk with the Secretary and make a call on the President. I do not know how Charlot's business will turn out. He has had most tempting offers to remove to the Jocko, but he still clings to his wish to remain in the Bitter Root. However it will terminate, the visit will result in great good to the Indians and most beneficially to me, as I have been thrown among and formed a personal acquaintance with all the officials in the Indian Department, who, from the mightiest to the lowest, have treated me in such a marked and courteous manner, that I have excited the curiosity of Inspectors Benedict and Howard who are both here settling their accounts. . . .

Besides other engagements on Monday, I am going calling with Mrs. Maginnis, in a carriage which has been placed at my disposal by the Indian Office. Oh! they do things up here in shape, and a government official is "some pumpkins," but I am afraid you will think I am drifting into the same groove with the Virginian who held a position here, and was so elated over his honors that he wrote to his friends that he was "a bigger man than old Grant.". . .

I feel happy because I stand so well with my superiors and because my present position, humble as it is, seems to me to have opened up a bright and prosperous career, and will enable me to educate and bring up our little darlings and fit them for a life of usefulness and morality. . . .

. . . . Our expenses here will fit us something like forty dollars a day, but as they are all paid here by the Government, and as it seems to be the disposition of the Department to give me plenty of time, and to go to the trouble to inform me that as far as I am concerned time is not pressing! . . .

I had a letter from my sister Theresa enclosing a letter of introduction to Congressman [Patrick] Collins of Boston, who is the brightest man in Congress.

* * * * * *

February 5, 1884.

. . . . I will have to remain East some three weeks longer to have operation[s] performed on Michel's and Charlot's eyes. . . . I have only time to write a few lines this morning, as I am very busy today. At eight tonight Maginnis and I will attend the President's reception, accompanied by the Indians.

* * * * * *

February 6, 1884.

. . . . It is strange that it takes a letter three days longer to reach here than a traveler. . . . I assure you that I have either written or sent you marked newspaper notices of my movements every day since my arrival here.

I attended the President's reception last night and was required to bring the Indians along. Our position was opposite the President and Mrs. [Mary Arthur] McElroy and the ladies of the Cabinet, who assisted in receiving. We were placed there by wish of the President so that we could hear each name pronounced as introduced and view the callers as they passed. The night was oppressively hot, and after an hour's gazing upon the most gorgeously dressed and beautiful women, and fine looking gentlemen, that I ever saw congregated together, I made my exit followed by the Indians, who received a perfect ovation.

Charlot is the hero of the day, and although there are four other Indian Delegations now in the city, he and his people receive most exclusive attention from the government officials and citizens. Most of this has been brought about through the courtesies shown them by Maginnis, McCammon, Captain John Mullen, Major Blacke, Captain Clarke, and a host of others, who have been in Montana, and have social influence and standing in Washington.

The operation which was to have taken place on the eyes of Charlot and Michel has been postponed until tomorrow, on account of lack of accommodation in the hotel and they will be transferred to Providence Hospital tomorrow, where they will be operated upon. Chloroform will be administered, and Charlot has particularly requested that I be present. In a day or two after the operation I will go to Boston and leave the Indians here. I will stop there a few days with my mother and then return here. It will probably be three weeks from date before I can leave for home. . . . This city, with all its charms and gaities [sic] of society possesses no nook or corner in my heart and I long for my quiet home. . . . Tell Michel's wife that he will soon be home and I trust with his eyesight restored, at all events he will not lack for skill and money.

* * * * * *

February 8, 1884.

. . . . Yesterday the operation was made on Michel's eyes and also on Charlot's, and of course I had to be with them. Today with the other Indians I attended the funeral of Father Brouilett at the Church of St. Matthew and witnessed one of the grandest pageants of the church. I will not attempt to describe it, as it will be published. After service myself and the Indians in a carriage attended the funeral to the cemetery. . . . Our carriage was placed next to the hearse. I will send you the full account as soon as it is published.

Now that the operation has been made the Indians will be kept in a dark room for about two weeks and then we will return home. . . . I attended a brilliant party tonight at Willard's, and tomorrow I will attend Mrs. McElroy's reception.

* * * * * *

February 10, 1884.

. . . . I must tell you what I have done since my last. Saturday morning I visited Michel and Charlot, who are in a darkened room. Charlot will be entirely restored to sight, but there is only a hope that vision will be restored to Michel in one eye, sufficient to go around without being led. I then visited the Indian office and then went out with Mrs. Maginnis to make some little purchases . . . for you and the children, which will be forwarded . . . tomorrow. I then attended Mrs. McElroy's reception, and in the evening went to the theatre with Major Maginnis. Today I attended mass with the Indians at St. Matthew's church and listened to the finest music and finest sermon you can imagine. . . . After luncheon I was invited to drive around the city with Mr. and Mrs. Maginnis. After dinner I retired to my room and here I am for the night.

Document 61

Charlo Impressed by Trip, But Will Not Move

March 14, 1884

Source: "Returned from Washington," *The Weekly Missoulian*, March 14, 1884, page 2, col. 1-2.

Editors' note: Charlot and the Salish delegation to Washington, D.C., were impressed by what they saw in the East, but Charlot would still not agree to leave the Bitter Root Valley. He did appreciate the surgical operation that gave him his sight back.

Returned from Washington.

Major Peter Ronan returned from Washington City last Friday, bringing with him the Flathead chiefs whom he had taken there for conference on the question of removal from the Bitter Root valley to the reservation. The party consisted of Major Ronan, agent; Michelle [Revais], the interpreter, his Indian name being Gin-coo-swee, meaning "The man who walks alone" (apparently a piece of satire, as he is blind and has to have some one lead him); Charlot, or Sklem-chre-ke, or The Little Claw of a Grizzly Bear; Louis [Vanderburg], or Bee-coot-sum-ke, or the Grizzly Bear Far Away; Antoine [Moiese], or Kalp-squal-she, or The Crane with a Ring around His Neck; Abel, or Chwam-kon, or Red Arm; John [Hill], or De-etcht, or The Wounded Hand. The Indians were about as fine looking specimens of their race as could be scared up and were the most reliable men of the tribe in the Bitter Root that could be found.

The conference was ineffectual in bringing about the removal of the Indians to the reservation but the indirect results will probably be good. Every possible inducement was offered to gain the consent of the Indians to removal, but Charlot said he did not come there to beg, but for his rights only. He owned the soil where he lived and he wanted to stay there. "The Bitter Root valley is my home, my land. I own it. The blood of my ancestors is mixed with its dust and I feel as though I were resting on my mother's bosom. I am like a tree whose roots are imbedded in the soil and nothing but a hurricane can tear me out."

Secretary [Henry] Teller said the Government had no right to use force to remove the Indians. They had as much right to their homes as white men. Major Ronan, however, was instructed to offer special inducements to families to remove to the reservation and it is hoped by this means all will be gradually moved away from the Bitter Root. The party visited the President in Washington, accompanied by Delegate [Martin] Maginnis. The latter made a neat little speech of introduction, reciting the kindness of Charlot to the whites during the Nez Perce war and mentioning the fact that the grandfather of Charlot received and aided Lewis and Clarke, the first white men the Indians of this section had seen. The President replied, and, extending his hand to Charlot, said: "For the kindness of you and your tribe to the people of my race I thank you from the bottom of my heart."

The Indians named the President "The Man with the Big Heart." Mr. [Joseph K.] McCammon they called "The Handsome Man." Secretary Teller they called "The Man who Turned Around," he having turned in his office chair rather quickly as they entered his office. Dinners were given to the party by Senator [G. G.] Vest, Mr. McCammon and Capt. John Mullan. In Washington they saw Mr. Shohn [Gustavus Sohon], an interpreter who had in early days come to prepare them for the Stevens treaty. He was recognized immediately by Charlot who called him by his Indian name signifying "Camas Prairie," and the two conversed together in the Indian tongue. Shohn is engaged in the manufacture of ladies shoes in Washington.

During the trip Major Ronan left the Indians in charge of friends at Washington and went to visit his mother in Boston, whom he had not seen for twenty years. He spent three weeks very pleasantly with friends and relatives, and on his return to Washington was told he had the finest and best behaved delegation of Indians that had ever visited the Capital.

Charlot, who was nearly blind when he reached Washington, has been completely restored to sight by the operation performed on his eyes and feels very grateful for what has been done, saying he is a man once more. The cause of his blindness was contraction of the pupil. One of Michele's eyes was operated on, the physicians saying that the nerve of the other eye was completely dead. Michele was first placed under the influence of ether. While inhaling the ethr [sic] he was rather obstreperous, yelling war songs and fighting. Charlot took more kindly to the anasthetic [sic], he delivered a speech to the Salish, reciting their battles and other great deeds, which was interpreted by Michele for the benefit of the physicians. When Charlot found that he could see he gave a whoop and was quite delighted.

Major Ronan says Charlot was much more talkative on the trip then he usually is. In Chicago he was struck with the great number of people and was puzzled to know how the Great Father could provide supplies for so many people. (It is the custom among the Indians to look to their chief to provide the necessaries of life.) Going through Ohio Charlot thought the people must be richer toward the rising sun, because they were better dressed, where shaved, and looked better generally, and expressed the opinion that the Great Father sent all the scrubs west to grab up Indian lands.

Document 62

Two Salish Indians Murdered Near Bozeman

April 16, 1884

Source: "Murder of Two Indians," *The Bozeman Weekly Chronicle*, April 16, 1884, page 3, col. 3.

Editors' note: The 1884 murder of two Salish Indians near Bozeman generated considerable comment and even a $300 reward offer, but was apparently never solved. Incidents such as this emphasized how ineffective the nineteenth century Montana justice system was in protecting peaceful Salish Indians.

Murder of Two Indians.
Found Lying on the Prairie About ten Miles from Town Yesterday.

Alex. Profitt while coming from his ranch on the Gallatin discovered the bodies of two Indians lying near the roadside, at a point about ten miles from Bozeman near the old Bridger crossing of Middle creek. He brought the word to Bozeman and coroner Didawick summoned a jury and repaired to the spot and made an examination, and buried them. They proved to be a Flathead and a half-breed named Frank Enos, son of old Enos.

That Flathead came to his death by a gunshot wound in the right ear, with about a 38-calibre pistol or rifle, the side of the face all powder burnt.

The half-breed was shot in the right ear, the ball coming out in the left ear. He had a purse containing $1.55 in silver; also shot in the back of the head, the ball coming out at the forehead. Both were killed with the same kind of a pistol or rifle. At the side of the head of the half-breed lay a paper reading as follows:

Stillwater, M.T., March 27, 1884.

To whom it may Concern:

The bearer, Frank Enos and his companions — Flathead Indians — are on their way to the Jocko agency from a visit to the Crow Indians. Any courtesies extended will be gratefully appreciated by them.

[Signed.] J. H. Norton.

These Indians it will be remembered had been arrested for horse-stealing and had been discharged and were on their way home with about thirty head of ponies. No clue has yet been found to lead to the discovery of the perpetrators of this foul deed.

The coroner's jury returned the following verdict:

Territory of Montana.

County of Gallatin.

An inquisition holden on the plains about two miles west of Middle creek, on the old Bridger road, and from thence adjourned to Bozeman on the 13th and 14th day of April 1884, before me Jacob Didawick, coroner of said county, upon the bodies of a half-breed Indian, known as Frank Enos, and a Flathead Indian, known as Peaille, there lying dead, by the jurors whose names are hereunto subscribed, do say, that on or about the 5th or 6th day of April, 1884, the said persons came to their death by pistol or gun shot wounds feloniously, wilfully and maliciously fired, by the hands of some person or persons unknown to this jury. In testimony whereof the said jurors have hereunto set their hands this 14th day of April, A.D., 1884.

Geo. Ash. Foreman.

Geo. W. Doll.

Alex. Profitt.

Ed. L. Fridley.

Sol. Carman.

George C. Howard.

Document 63
Photographic Tour of the
Flathead Reservation
Photographs by F. Jay Haynes
1884

Source: F. Jay Haynes Collection, Photogaphic Archives, Montana Historical Society, Helena, Mont.

Editors' note: In 1884, F. Jay Haynes toured the Flathead Indian Reservation and compiled a portfolio of reservation scenes. His work included many scenic views as well as shots of St. Ignatius Mission, the Flathead Indian Agency, and Indian farms. Fortunately Haynes' photograph collection has been preserved in the Photographic Archives of the Montana Historical Society in Helena and provides us with a unique visual tour of the Flathead Indian Reservation during Peter Ronan's term as agent.

During the 1880s, F. Jay Haynes was the official photographer for the Northern Pacific Railroad Company and the Yellowstone National Park Company. Based in Fargo, North Dakota, he traveled the railroad and surrounding area in a specially designed studio railroad car to take promotional photographs for the Northern Pacific publicity department. The railroad used Haynes photographs to attract passengers and, especially, settlers to the towns, mines, and agricultural areas around the Northern Pacific Railroad line.

Haynes made his living selling copies of his photographs to the public, and he left a legacy of many of the earliest views of the Pacific Northwest. In 1884, photographic equipment and supplies were bulky and fragile. Haynes had to haul his camera, photographic plates, and supplies across the reservation by stage or wagon. The resulting record of life on the Flathead Indian Reservation in 1884 provides us with unique and valuable historical evidence.

Haynes photographs of scenic features on the reservation are not reproduced here. The editors have selected views of reservation landmarks and life. All photographs in this section were taken by F. Jay Haynes and are reproduced courtesy of the Montana Historical Society Photograph Archives, Helena, Montana.

References: Freeman Tilden, *Following the Frontier with F. Jay Haynes: Pioneer Photographer of the Old West* (New York: Alfred A. Knopf, 1964); Montana Historical Society, *F. Jay Haynes, Photographer* (Helena, Montana Historical Society Press, 1981).

Flathead Indian Agency, Jocko, Montana.
(MHS H-1271)

Major Peter Ronan and family. Indian agent's residence, Jocko, Montana.
(MHS H-1333)

Mt. Ronan, Mission Range. Peter Ronan standing at left. (MHS H-2011)

Above: Flathead Agency sawmill with Indian crew. (MHS H-1334)
Below: Flathead Reservation Indian farm (MHS H-1341).

A band of Flathead Indian ponies. (MHS H-1340)

Jocko Valley, Flathead Reservation. (MHS H-2009)

Above: Indian farmer, Flathead Reservation. (MHS H-1335).
Below: Flathead Indian chief and family. (MHS H-1337).

Above: St. Ignatius chapel, exterior. (MHS H-1346).
Below: St. Ignatius chapel, interior. (MHS H-1347).

Above: St. Ignatius boys school. (MHS H-1348).
Below: St. Ignatius girls school. (MHS H-1349).

Flathead Indian band, St. Ignatius Mission. (MHS H-1350).

Above: Trader's residence (Alex L. DeMers). (MHS H-1352).
Below: Trader's store, St. Ignatius Mission. (MHS H-1351).

Mission Valley, Flathead Reservation. (MHS H-1345)

Above: Flathead Lake, looking north. (MHS H-1360).
Below: Trader's store, Foot of Flathead Lake. (MHS H-1365).

Chapter 3

Documents of
Salish, Pend d'Oreille, and Kootenai
History Between 1885 and 1889

Document 64

Disagreements Over the Number of Land Patents Available in Bitterroot February 12, 1885

Source: Peter Ronan, *"A Great Many of Us Have Good Farms": Agent Peter Ronan Reports on the Flathead Indian Reservation, Montana, 1877-1887*, ed. Robert J. Bigart (Pablo, Mont.: Salish Kootenai College Press, 2014), pages 303-306.

Editors' note: Charlo was not pleased when he returned to the Bitterroot Valley and found out that there were only half as many land patents available as he had been told in Washington, D.C. Charlo also continued to worry about the efforts of Missoula County to tax the Bitterroot Salish Indians.

United States Indian Service,
Flathead Agency,
February 12th, 1885.

Hon. Commissioner of Indian Affairs
Washington, D.C.
Sir,

I herewith have the honor of enclosing a petition sent to me by Charlos, Chief of Flathead Indians, now residing in the Bitter Root Valley. It will be seen that Charlos still retains the idea that he was promised one hundred and four patents for lands, instead of the number surveyed for his Indians, fifty one, which I Still hold. In a letter addressed to you bearing date March 12th, 1884, I had the honor of alluding to this matter as follows:

"At one of the meetings at the office of the Hon. Secretary of the Interior, I stated that it was my opinion that the fifty one patents in my possession, were all that has been issued, but information was then offered that there had been issued one hundred and three or four, and that if they were not all in my possession, some would be found in one of the Departments at Washington. The Indians naturally returned with the impression that this information was correct, and it will require considerable tact to eradicate the idea."

Again in my special report in regard to a Council held with Charlos and his band of Bitter Root Flatheads, bearing date March 27th, 1884, that Chief stated in the Council that he "had been told that there were 103 or 104 land patents issued, while I stated there were only 51, and that if he had sufficient money he would return to Washington, and ask the Hon. Secretary if his words were to be depended upon, I informed him that it was a private and unofficial gentleman (Captain John Mullin [Mullan]) who had made the statement, and that the necessary data, not being immediately at hand, neither the Hon. Secretary nor myself were then in a position to contradict it, but that I had advised that the matter be examined into, and that as a result, I had a letter with the Hon. Secretary's own signature, which was equivalent to his own spoken words, and that therein I was notified that 51 was the correct number. I then produced the letter which was read by a few of the tribe capable of So doing, having in addition my remarks sustained by the rest of the delegation which visited Washington."

The letter above alluded to bears date at the Office of the Secretary of the Interior March 1st, 1884.

In regard to the wishes of Charlos, as stated in his petition I will offer a few suggestions.

1st. As the Indians desire to accept the patents in my possession, a proper map of the Bitter Root Land District should be furnished, so as to be able to properly show the boundaries of the same, and if the original patentee is dead the next of Kin, or in case no heir survives, then the patent be transferred to any Indian, being the head of a family, whom a majority of the Indians of Charlos Band may select, with the consent of the Department or Agent whichever may be deemed most advisable.

2nd. Charlos is correct in stating that under the Garfield Agreement several Indians removed to this reservation, abandoning their right to the Bitter Root patents and have made permanent homes here, and the lands that have been granted to them in the Bitter Root Valley is [sic] now unoccupied and will still continue to be owned by them, they holding said land under patents containing a clause preventing them from alienation. It would in my opinion be well to transfer such lands to any Indian of Charlos' band who might select to live upon and cultivate the same.

3rd. In connection with Circular #133, dated Washington July 28th, 1884, published for the information and guidance of Indian Agents in relation to the appropriation of $1000.00 "to enable Indians to make selection of homesteads and the necessary proofs at the proper land office" without payment of fees or commissions on account of entries or proofs, I respectfully submit, that in as much as the Register and Receiver of the Land Office are located at Helena, 150 miles distant from the Bitter Root Valley, and the Indians desirous of entering homesteads as provided in said act of Congress are poor and unable to defray the expenses of such a long journey, it would be a matter not only of justice in aiding them to take advantage of its beneficent provisions, but of economy (as the Indians would look to the Government to defray such travelling expenses for the reasons stated) that such entries and proofs be made either before some attorney authorized by the Land Office to perform such duties at Stevensville, in the Bitter Root Valley, or before the Clerk of the U.S. Court at Missoula, and a sum sufficient to defray the actual expense thereof be placed to my credit in order to accomplish the same, and upon presentation of the proper vouchers the expenditure of said sum be allowed.

4th. While at the office of the Hon. Secretary of the Interior, last winter, in conference with Charlos Band, complaint was made by the Indians to the Hon. Secretary that each year they were annoyed by the County Commissioners, and other officers of Missoula County, who claimed that the Indians of the Bitter Root Valley were amenable to taxation, and that said tax would be levied and payment of same enforced. The Hon. Secretary stated emphatically to the Indians that they would not be forced to pay taxes, and I trust this matter will be carefully looked into that I may be advised how to proceed should the county officers attempt to force payment of taxes from Indians living in Bitter Root Valley.

In conclusion I would state thirteen families of Charlos' Band have already removed to the Agency in compliance with arrangements made by me, under instructions from the Hon. Secretary of the Interior, and that houses are now under course of construction for them, and I expect to have them comfortably settled and cultivating the soil of the Reservation this season, and that more families will continue to follow until a large majority, if not all of the tribe will finally settle here. But I would suggest that the petition of Charlos be acted upon so that the Indians will have nothing to complain of in the future, in regard to their rights to the lands of the Bitter Root Valley. It is my humble opinion that this course will have a tendency to show the Indians that they can place reliance upon the promises and good will of the Indian Department and its servants, and when their rights in the Bitter Root are secured, they will be prepared to dispose of the same as the Department may direct and remove to the Reservation.

Very respectfully
Your obt. svt.
Peter Ronan
U.S. Indian Agent.

Enclosure in handwriting of Jerome D'Aste, S.J.:

Stevensville, Feb. 7th, 85

Major P. Ronan
U.S. Indian Agent
Major

Last winter I and some of my Indians came back from Washington to Bitter-Root valley with our hearts gladdened thinking we had secured for our families and tribe a home, in this valley, having been promised by the Government one hundred Patents. But we have been Sadly disappointed when, after coming home we heard from you that only fifty one Patents were offered to our people. Waiting in vain for the fulfillment of the Government's promise, I refused until now to receive the Patents already issued for some of my people. I felt bad in thinking, that by receiving those Patents I would exclude a good many of my people from having land in this valley, and that for the only reason that they were not here to give their names as willing to remain here, at the time of Garfield's treaty, and thus secure a farm. But now that I see that not only we are refused what we have been promised, but that white people are trying to take from my people even the few farms we are in possession of in this land of our forefathers, I beg of you to protect us in our rights. Knowing that you have taken so much interest in the welfare of the Indians under your charge, I hope that you will be willing to make the Government acquainted with our needs and wishes.

1. I with my people came to the conclusion to accept the Patents issued so many years ago for some of us. But the lands so patented having been surveyed when most of the Indians were off on the Buffalo hunt, only a few Know where the lines of their respective farms are. Hence I ask that the Government appoint some trusty man to find out for us the lines of such lands, not leaving the whites to take advantage of our ignorance.

2. In the second place we ask, that since we see very little hope of getting the other Patents promised in Washington, last year, at least, the Patents issued for those Flat-Heads, who agreeably to Garfield's treaty, moved to the Jocko, be turned to some of our people who got no land, because they were not here to represent their lands at that time.

3. In the third place I ask that some of our people who for several years are farming on lands which were not surveyed for them, be by the Government protected against those greedy whites, who having come here only lately are trying to jump these lands, though the Indians are living and have improvements on them. There is a case in particular, on eight-mile creek, where a white man, P. Lafountain, pretends by force to take the land from an Indian who has been farming several years and has a house on it. I would ask that the Government

would send some trusty man to inquire into the matter, and if found that the Indians have the first right to those lands, that said lands be surveyed for the Indians and Patents issued to them.

4. In the fourth place, since I have been promised, in Washington that we would be exempted from paying taxes, we ask that the Government should look in this matter and see that we be not bothered by County Officers, as they began to do with some of our people.

Thanking you for the help you obtained for our people by getting them wagons, plows, harnesses and provisions, and hoping that you be willing and able to assist us in our present needs, I am with all my people in whose name I send this petition.

Yours Respectfully
Charlos Chief of the
Flat-Head Indians
His signature +

Document 65

Indian Police Arrest Indians and White Man for Assault
March 14, 1885

Source: "How It is Done Nowadays," *The New North-West* (Deer Lodge, Mont.), March 20, 1885, page 3, col. 4.

Editors' note: In 1885 the tribal police forces on the Flathead Reservation controlled by the traditional chiefs were replaced by a government paid force under the direction of the Flathead Agent. Note that the white man accused of abusing an Indian woman was also arrested as well as the Indians involved in the assault on the railroad men.

How It is Done Nowadays.
Chasing Indians on a Locomotive.
Agent Ronan's Steam Round-up and the Occasion of it.
Correpondence New North-West.

Flathead Agency, March 14. —

On the night of Tuesday, March 10, your correspondent was partaking of the hospitalities of Major and Mrs. Peter Ronan, (the Agent and his pleasant spouse), at Flathead Agency, and while

Enjoying a Pleasant Conversation

(as also a pleasant cigar) with the host, before a blazing fire in the open fireplace of his cozy quarters, prior to retiring for the night, a horseman rode up to the door, inquiring for the Agent. At this the Major approached the door, when a letter was delivered to him. After glancing at it he begged to be excused for a few moments, as business called him out. I heard him

Give Hasty Orders,

and in a few moments Indian messengers were flying from his door in various directions, mounted on horseback. The Agent returned and resumed the conversation (and cigar) and quietly informed me that he was gathering his Indian police force, and as soon as collected would obey a call to suppress some

Indian Troubles.

He then handed me a letter for perusal, which read as follows:

Major Ronan: A large number of Indians are drunk two miles east of Victor, and have placed obstructions on the

Northern Pacific track. The section man who undertook to remove them was knocked down and driven away at the point of guns. Assistant General Manager Buckley requests that you organize a force and go there to-night and arrest them. The Roadmaster is at Arlee station, and will go with you. Please answer by bearer if you can do so, and I will arrange to have an engine at Arlee to take you down and back.

I. B. Cable,
Supt. N.P.R.R.

Upon reading the above, I asked permission to accompany the expedition, which was cheerfully accorded.

Several Indians, well armed and mounted on fleet ponies, reported for duty at midnight. The Major and myself were driven to Arlee in a carriage, the Indians following on horseback. Upon arriving there

An Engine and Tender

was placed at our service and we all piled on the tender. We steamed out from the station in a cold and drizzling rain and soon arrived at Ravalli, a station some six miles from St. Ignatius Mission, whither the Agent had dispatched a messenger. Here the engineer was directed to await reinforcements. After a halt of about fifteen minutes a mounted posse of seven Indian policeman rode up, reported, dismounted and joined us on the tender. Major Ronan then explained that the messenger he had the precaution to send from the Agency to the police at the Mission to join him, had faithfully carried out his instructions; but I was astonished to learn that he had ridden twenty miles to the mission, gathered the posse and was at Ravalli to meet us before daylight with his men.

From Ravalli We Went Flying

over the track, and in the early dawn arrived at Horse Plains. Here we found the section-boss who was maltreated by the Indians the evening before. He was taken in the car to which we coupled on, and again went flying back to Victor station. Here the section man recognized an Indian as

One of His Assailants,

and he was arrested. We then steamed on for a few miles and halted at another camp. Here we arrested three more Indians who were pointed out by the section man, took them out of the encampment and placed them under arrest in the car. Major Ronan was here informed that the

Whole Cause of the Trouble

grew out of the finding of a twenty-gallon barrel of whisky by the Indians in the Pen d'Oreille river, which was lost by the upsetting of a freighter's wagon some three years ago in a tributary of the river. The barrel was washed out of sight, and there remained until found, the night previous to the disturbance by the Indians. Learning that the whisky was "cached" at an Indian camp on the opposite side of the river, a skiff was procured, a detail of three Indian police crossed the river and found the barrel, which contained about fifteen gallons, and by order of the Agent the same was

Emptied Upon the Ground.

At this juncture an Indian woman made complaint against a railroad employe for abuse in her husband's absence. A description of the man was given and the engineer was directed to run back to Horse Plains, where the offender was found and placed under arrest, much to the delight and satisfaction of the Indian police. The object of our mission having been attained, we started up the road, halting at Ravalli station, where the Indian prisoners were taken off by the Indian police, by direction of Major Ronan, and escorted to the jail at the mission. The engine then proceeded to Arlee, where we arrived at 3 o'clock p.m., after a ride of

One Hundred and Eighty Miles.

Upon alighting from the engine Major Ronan was handed the following telegram from Missoula:

> *P. Ronan*: — We congratulate you on the success of your trip and thank you for the very prompt manner in which you have dealt with the offenders.
>
> I. B. Cable.
Supt. N.P.R.R.

The following was also received from Secretary Lamar:

> Washington, D.C., March 12, 1885.
>
> *Agent Ronan*: — Complaint made here that your Indians are placing obstructions on railroad and endangering lives of passengers. You must attend to this immediately. If your police force is not sufficient, call on the military.
>
> L. Q. C. Lamar.
Secretary of the Interior.

Happily there was no occasion to call upon the military, and the Secretary of the Interior was so informed by the Agent by telegraph.

The Indian Police

at the Flathead Agency have recently been organized by Agent Ronan, and are a fine body of men, always ready and prepared to execute any order emanating from the Agent.

As will be seen by the following (the original of which I was permitted to copy) the police force of the Flathead Agency are an authorized and organized body:

Office of Indian Affairs,
Washington, March 5, 1885.

Peter Ronan, U.S. Indian Agent, Flathead Agency, Montana:

Sir: — In reply to your letter of the 12th ult., enclosing a code of rules for the government of the Court of Indian Offenses for your Agency, I have to say that the honorable Secretary of the Interior, under date of the 2d instant, approved the same, and hereafter your Court will be governed by said rules.

In your letter of the 14th of February you nominated Baptist Joseph and Louisor [Louison] as Judges, and on the 25th of the same month their commissions were forwarded, duly approved.

Very respectfully,
H. Price, Commissioner.

Document 66

Duncan McDonald Visits Portland

May 1885

Source: *The Northwest* (St. Paul, Minn.), vol. 3, no. 5 (May 1885), page 10, col. 1.

Editors' note: This account of Duncan McDonald's reaction to his first visit to a big city emphasized his ties to the reservation. The writer also readily displays his personal prejudices and bigotry.

Apropos of the fraternizing of half-breeds and Indians in the Riel revolt — a half breed is always an Indian at heart. I never knew an exception to this rule. It is the same as with the mulatto and the negro. In Montana I meet every summer a remarkably intelligent half-breed, son of a Scotch father and a Nez Perce mother. He is pretty well educated for a frontiersman, and keeps a little store on his reservation. When the railroad was finished he went down to Portland and for the first time in his life saw a city. After his return I drove up to his [s]tore one day for a smoke and chat. "Well, Donald," I said, "What did you think of the city?" "I saw the ships, and the streets and the big, fine houses," he replied, "but I did not care a copper for them all. I would rather get on my pony any day and go to the mountains to hunt than to see the biggest city in the world."

Document 67

Flathead Reservation Farms, Stock, and Schools

May 26, 1885

Source: Excerpt from William F. Wheeler, "A Journey to the West Side," *Montana Live Stock Journal* (Helena, Mont.), vol. 2, no. 2 (June 1885), pages 4-5.

Editors' note: Wheeler described the progress in farming and stock raising being made by tribal members on the Flathead Reservation in 1885. He mentioned that tribal farmers took their surplus production to Missoula to sell.

A Journey to the West Side.
From our Special Correspondent.

Helena, M.T., May 26, 1885.

. . . . .

I cannot close this letter without describing something of what I saw in the journey from Missoula to Flathead Lake. Two hours on the cars of the N.P.R.R. landed me at Arlee, a station five miles distant from the Jocko Indian Agency. Having telegraphed ahead, Major [Peter] Ronan being absent, his amiable lady sent a conveyance for me, and I spent a busy, pleasant day in the Jocko valley.

The improvements at the agency and all over the country, in the past five years were very noticeable. Comfortable houses and small, well fenced and cultivated fields extend for fifty miles from the head of the Jocko and Mission valleys, on all the small streams, and along the foot of the sheltering mountains to the shores of the beautiful Flathead Lake. At no point on the road were we out of the sight of houses. Since the destruction of the buffaloes in Montana the Indians remain at home, and under the painstaking care of Agent Ronan, and the kindly advice of the Catholic fathers and sisters at St. Ignatius Mission, backed up by their ever faithful example, they have settled down in good earnest to make homes for themselves. They dress like white people, they cut logs for lumber and haul them to the mill at the Agency, where they are sawed by the government without charge; they build their own houses, split rails and make their own fences, build corrals for their stock, milk the cows and make butter for themselves, harvest their grain and market it. Almost every farm has a few pigs, and all have more or less cattle and horses, the surplus of which they take to Missoula and sell.

During the whole distance from the Agency to the Lake, herds of cattle and horses were in sight. The Indians have learned the value of cattle as well as of horses, and make the best kind of stockmen. So fast have their herds increased in a few years that they have, in grand council assembled, issued orders directing that each and every white man heretofore pasturing stock on their reservation, remove the same by the first day of July next, under the penalty of having enough seized and sold to pay all back dues for rent, and costs that may accrue in consequence.

They have enough fine pastures now for both summer and winter ranges for their own stock, but feel and know that they cannot lease them out to other stock owners, or they will soon be in the same situation as the stockraisers of the Bitter Root valley — they will have to raise hay to feed their stock during the winter.

To one who has never visited the enchanted valleys of Missoula county, a journey through the Bitter Root, the Jocko and Mission valleys and to Flathead Lake, will be a surprise and a delight. Lofty mountains rise far above them on all sides; the purest brooks course across them at short intervals, from the mountains to the main streams, and they all abound in delicious trout; the loftiest pines, firs and cedars, this side of Puget Sound, frequently border the streams and extent [sic] far down into the valleys, and fill every canyon and make green the high mountain sides, furnishing forever an unfailing supply of lumber and fuel, while on every cultivated farm can be found apple, pear, plum and cherry orchards, producing their fruits in abundance.

St. Ignatius Mission has grown into a pretty village. The fine new three story college of the fathers and the roomy and handsome new front to the Sister's school, loom up, and in style, finish and accommodations, equal the best class of similar buildings in the best towns of Montana.

Eighty-four girls and eighty-two boys, children of the Flathead, Pen d'Oreille, Kootenais and Blackfeet tribes, meet here, and being without much, if any, knowledge of the fierce and unrelenting wars waged by their fathers not a generation ago, they mingle as of one family, and study, and play, and work together, without a sign of enmity. This is indeed a triumph of a Christian attempt at the civilizing of a savage race. The glorious part of it is, that the result is now an assured success, and the patient labor of devoted men and women is every day receiving its well merited reward.

The U.S. Government last year sent a number of children of both sexes from the Blackfeet and other tribes to be instructed here. I believe the plan of instruction in general is similar to that adopted by the Government at

Hampton, Virginia, and Carlisle, Pennsylvania, in educating young Indians from the West.

At St. Ignatius the children are all instructed for a part of the day in the simple branches of a common English education. About the same time is spent in manual labor.

The girls are taught everything relating to house-keeping, hand-sewing, making and repairing their own and the boys' clothes, cooking, milking the cows, making butter and cheese, and everything to fit them to become good wives and mothers after leaving the school.

The fathers are erecting a number of shops in which the boys will be taught every ordinary trade necessary for a working community. They will all be taught farming, and how to take care of stock, for they will all have farms on their reservations. Some will learn blacksmithing, wagon making, carpentering, painting, harness making, shoemaking and other useful trades, so that after leaving school and being once settled in their own homes, they will be an independent and self-supporting community. All the children seem to take great interest in their work, which is a good sign for their future success.

When hearing the children recite their lessons, and going through the great buildings erected for their use, and seeing the workmen building the shops in which they are to labor and learn trades, I could not help think that here, and now, the fathers had in practical operations a great university for Montana. It seems to me that only good can come out of their self-sacrificing labors, and that all our churches and people may take example from what has been done at St. Ignatius.

From here I had business at the foot of Flathead Lake. A five hours drive over a smooth prairie road, through a country where valley and mountain, river and lake, made it all beautiful, brought me to the hospitable house of our former fellow-townsman, Harry Lambert, where I remained two days. Mr. L. keeps a nice little store, and also a hotel for the accommodation of the public, and is doing well.

It would take a finer pen than mine to describe the charms and beauties of Flathead Lake. The fishing now, and the splendid opportunity of hunting grouse, ducks and geese, after Aug. 15, and deer in the mountains, is unsurpassed at any other place in Montana.

A stage line started to carry the mail last week, between St. Ignatius Mission and Salish, at the head of the lake, and I was the first passenger. The lake can be reached in twenty hours from Helena or Butte, by leaving the N.P.R.R. at Ravalli, and writing in advance to the stage agent at St. Ignatius for a conveyance.

I have no doubt but many tourists and pleasure seekers will make this new resort a visit the present year.

W. F. W.

Peter Ronan, Flathead Indian Agent, 1877-1893,
Source: Montana Historical Society, Photograph Archives, Helena,
MMM 900-004.

Document 68

Agent Ronan's 1885 Annual Report

August 1885

Source: Peter Ronan, *"A Great Many of Us Have Good Farms": Agent Peter Ronan Reports on the Flathead Indian Reservation, Montana, 1877-1887*, ed. Robert J. Bigart (Pablo, Mont.: Salish Kootenai College Press, 2014), pages 316-321.

Editors' note: This annual report includes considerable information about the situation of the Flathead Reservation Indians in 1885. Most important, however, was Ronan's list of some of the prominent Indian farmers. The list included a number of full blood Indians and suggests that while most Indians did not have large farms, almost all seem to have had some crops.

Flathead Agency, Montana Territory, *August*, 1885.

Sir: In compliance with instructions from your office, I have the honor herewith of submitting my ninth annual report from the Flathead Indian Agency, which is situated at the head of the Jocko Valley, on the line of the Northern Pacific Railroad, and within ten miles of the southern boundary of the reservation, adjoining the county of Missoula, in the Territory of Montana. The reserve has never been surveyed, but is supposed to have an acreage of 1,300,000, and is described as follows:

> Commencing at the source of the main branch of the Jocko River; thence along the divide separating the waters flowing into the Bitter Root River from those flowing into the Jocko to a point on Clarke's Fork between the Camas and Horse Prairies; thence northerly to and along the divide bounding on the west the Flathead River to a point due west from the point half-way in latitude between the northern and southern extremities of the Flathead Lake; thence on a due east course to the divide whence the Crow, the Prune, the So-ni-el-em, and the Jocko Rivers take their rise; and thence southerly along said divide to the place of beginning.

There are different classes of Indians on this reservation, composed as it is of three different tribes, the Flatheads, the Pen d'Oreilles, and the Kootenais. Some have made great strides towards civilization; others not so much, but have made a good beginning; and still a few others who are loath to change the wild freedom born of their savage nature. A large majority have advanced greatly in all the arts of peace in matters of religion, education, agriculture, mechanism, as also in commercial pursuits. A great majority are also owners of herds of cattle and horses, and take as good care of them and have as much pride in the ownership as the average white farmer or stockman. They use their own brands and marks, have their regular "round ups" and the property of individuals is respected and protected. The attention of those Indians is turned to stock-raising, agriculture, education, and religion, and every inducement should be held out to them to continue in such pursuits. They are attached to their homes, and are beginning to learn that by pursuing a peaceful and industrious life they can surround themselves with plenty and are able to support themselves without resorting to the hunt except for recreation and sport, as in the case of our own race.

In order to give an illustration of the advancement of the tribes of this reservation, I will here cite the names of some of the prominent Indian farmers, with an estimate of their grain crops, which are now being harvested. In addition to the grain crop each farmer raised a small patch of vegetables, such as potatoes, turnips, cabbage, carrots, parsnips, onions, &c., sufficient, perhaps, for family use.

Name	Under fence. Acres.	Wheat and oats produced. Bushels.	Name	Under fence. Acres.	Wheat and oats produced. Bushels.
Jocko Valley			Adolph Finlay	160	800
Arlee, chief of Flatheads	160	800	Espanol	160	800
Antoine, Kicking Horse	100	200	Mary Finlay (widow)	50	200
Lassah	100	150	Alex Matte	160	200
Big Sam	100	200	Mat. Coture	160	*
Louison	100	300	Joe Coture	160	800
Tawa	50	150	Octare Rivais	160	*
Alex See	50	100	Joe Tuion Finlay	100	500
Eneas Lorette	50	200	Courtois Finlay	60	300
Partee	50	100	Pierre	100	400
Alexander Morrijeau	160	1,200	Joe Barnaby	20	200
Joe Finlay	100	400	Antoine Moise	10	100
Charley Plant	160	1,500	Louise (widow)	10	50
Alex Poirrier	160	800	Samwell	10	100
Isadore Laderoute	160	1,600	Thomas	10	100
Frank Finlay	160	300	Adophe	10	100
Louis Valle	160	500	Antoine	10	100

Name	Under fence. Acres.	Wheat and oats produced. Bushels.	Name	Under fence. Acres.	Wheat and oats produced. Bushels.
Eneas	10	100	Red Mountain	50	60
Michelle	10	100	Isaac Chel-Kau-See	50	60
Aneas	10	100	Philip Stel-sa-Kau	60	80
Antoine Partico	10	100	Michelle, Chief of the Pend		
Timothy	10	100	d'Oreilles	160	250
Joseph Coolmanie	10	100	Artemus Tallman	100	250
			Ooyste Finlay	160	500
Mission Valley			Grand Joe	100	250
Joseph	160	450	Joseph Finlay	160	500
Charloanie	100	500	Abraham Finlay	200	1,200
Partee	100	300	Dupee	200	1,000
Lowman (son of Joseph)	200	400	Joseph Aslin	160	800
Vetal	100	300	Lorette Pablo	160	800
Petell Halks	50	150	Jim Michel	100	400
Joseph (Qui-Quil-Cha)	100	200	Philip Iandra	60	100
Felix	160	400	Michelle Pablo and Charles Allard		
John Solee	160	150		300	†
Deaf Louis	160	300	Slone	200	*
Francois	50	100	Peter Finlay	100	100
Pierre Eneas	50	60	Baptiste Eneas	100	400
John	100	150	Polson	100	200
Adolph	50	80	David Finlay	100	*
Michael Colville	160	800			
Eneas Pierre	50	60	**Pend d'Oreille River, Mouth of Jocko**		
Nicholas	160	400	Paul and Samwell	200	500
Frank Camille	100	500	Pe-Arlee	300	300
Dandy Jim	160	500	Little Salmon	50	60
Koosack Matte	100	300	Peter Matte	100	500
Joe Guardapuis	100	400	Kaimee	100	250
Alex, the Snake	160	700	Baptiste Eneas	200	200
Pierrish (See-You)	100	250	Spokan Jim	60	100
Big John	100	400	Pierre Paul	50	150
Louie La Rose	180	600	Adrian	50	300
Clatch-Kee-Lasa	50	100	Sin-Cla Stanislaus (blind)	50	100
Angus McDonald	300	‡	Pierre Qui-ma (blind)	50	100
Charley Moolman	160	300	Marceal	100	150
Pierre Moolman	160	150	Benwa Nenema	60	50
Louie Moolman	160	300	Antoine Rivais	300	200
Alexander Bonaparte	100	200	Isaac	100	200

Name	Under fence. Acres.	Wheat and oats produced. Bushels.	Name	Under fence. Acres.	Wheat and oats produced. Bushels.
McSeem	160	250	Louie Pierre	50	100
Dominick Rattlesnake	50	50	Michelle Yolt-em-mee	100	250
Big Lee	60	150	Big Semo Sinta	100	400
Petall	50	50	Chita-masca	100	300
Charles Skieshen	50	60	Gregoire Che-took-tah	50	100
Eustah	60	40	Nichola	150	300
George Chumkanee	50	60	Joseph Eu-cootle-stoo	100	300
Big Head, Chi-ka-kee	100	150	Joseph Morrijeau	50	100
Norbert Seepa	200	100			

Camas Prairie			* No crop.		
Joseph Who-lem-too	100	100	† For pasture for their cattle.		
Benway & Son	150	300	‡ For hay only, 380 tons produced.		

Dayton Creek. — Eneas, chief of the Kootenais, 200 acres fenced for use of tribe, about 1,000 bushels of wheat raised in common, besides potatoes, turnips, cabbage, onions, carrots, parsnips, peas, &c.

There are several other small garden patches in different portions of the reservation under cultivation, and not a few other Indians have located their farms with a view of fencing in the same, the coming winter.

Charlos' Band of Bitter Root Flatheads.

The visit of Charlos, the hereditary chief of the Flathead Nation, to Washington, accompanied by myself and a party of his Indians, resulted in a failure to induce that chief to abandon the Bitter Root Valley, and remove with his tribe to the Flathead Reservation on the Jocko. In compliance with verbal instructions from the honorable Secretary of the Interior, a full report of which I furnished the Indian Office under date of March 27, 1884, I made certain propositions to individual families to remove from the Bitter Root and settle at the Flathead Reservation, and the result was that twenty-one heads of families concluded to remove, and to them, following the views of the honorable Secretary of the Interior, as expressed to the Indians in Washington, I promised to each (1) a choice of 160 acres of unoccupied land on the reservation; (2) the erection of a suitable house; (3) assistance in fencing and breaking up ten acres of land for each family; (4) the following gifts: two cows, a wagon, set of harness, a plow, with other agricultural implements, seed for the first year, and provisions until the first crop was harvested.

Taking into consideration the very kindly and just expressions made use of in connection with the deserts of these Indians by the President and honorable Secretary, I could have made but an unfavorable impression by offering less. I would add that even after the first year they will depend somewhat on the generosity of the Government to uphold their hands in striving for a civilized independence and a sustained well-doing. My action met with the approval of the Government, and I have been enabled to carry out every promise made to the Indians. Ten families reported at the agency, and for them I erected ten houses, fenced in their fields as agreed upon, and to-day they are harvesting their crops. Three other families followed after I sent in estimates for the first ten, and to them I assigned land, but could not fence or build, although I provided them with fields, which I plowed inside of Government and other inclosures, where they raised crops this year. These additional three families have been provided with cows, as well as the original ten for whom houses were erected. Two more families soon followed the thirteen mentioned, and this week I have been notified by three other families that, they will remove here at once. I have no hesitation in saying that if the same policy is carried out in the future as in the past year, it will be only a brief matter of time until Charlos band, with exception of that chief and a few of his relatives, will be settled on the reservation.

Fears were entertained that by the issue of agricultural implements, provisions, and seed, which were supplied by the Government last year for Charlos band remaining in the Bitter Root Valley, it would be an inducement and an incentive to them to refuse to remove to the reservation. On the contrary, it has encouraged and given these poor people faith in the promises and fostering care of the Government should they leave their homes and remove to the reserve.

The Police Force.

For several years a volunteer force of Indian police used their best energies to keep peace and good behavior among the tribes, but the building of the Northern Pacific Railroad through the reservation changed the condition of affairs, and caused so much lawlessness along the line that I deemed it best to disband the old force and organize a paid force under immediate control of the agent.

The Indians now have their own judges, three in number, a code of rules governing the court of Indian offenses, and the laws are enforced by imprisonment, hard labor and fines. The administration of the laws in all respects are borne out with good judgment and dignity. I would recommend, however, that the judges of the court be paid as well as the police, as upon them principally rests all the good that police can perform upon the reservation, and they should be encouraged. Since the organization of the paid force of police and the adoption of the rules governing Indian offenses, we have had scarcely any trouble upon the reserve, and I trust good encouragement in the way of equipments, food, and clothing, in addition to pay, will be granted them.

Pay of Indians for "Right of Way" Through and "Timber Cut" on Reservation.

Early in the month of January I commenced and concluded the payment per capita to the Indians of the reserve for the right of way of the Northern Pacific Railroad and for timber cut on the reservation for construction purposes, involving the sum of $21,458. The payment was entirely satisfactory to the Indians, as I took especial pains to see that no person entitled to payment was left off the list. The task was a great one, as the Indians are scattered all over the reservation, living in their farm-houses, hamlets, and lodges, and in such an inclement season, and considering the vast extent of the reservation, I feel especially elated that no complaint has yet reached me of a man, woman, or child having been forgotten or overlooked in the payment.

Sanitary.

The health of the Indians was very good during the past year, with exception of the Kootenais. A malignant disease broke out among them early in spring, which carried many of them to the grave. The sickness first visits the patient by severe pains in the body and stomach, followed by an eruption resembling chicken-pox. Where advice of the agency physician was followed the disease as a general thing yielded to his remedies; but the Indians of this unfortunate tribe are isolated by a distance of 70 miles from the agency, and in reaching them the Flathead Lake must be crossed by an Indian ferry-boat. It will thus be seen that medical attention from the agency physician could not have been of the most desirable character. Owing to the long distance from the agency to the settlement of the Kootenais Indians the agent cannot give the desired attention to their relief and advancement, but it is to be hoped that in the near future the agency may be removed to a more central portion of the reservation, as has been so repeatedly advocated from this office.

Irrigating Ditch.

The irrigation ditch authorized in letters dated, respectively, October 11 and December 8, 1884, and which was made the subject of a special report in a communication from this office dated November 21, 1884, has been excavated and nearly completed for a distance of over 5 miles, including a large amount of blasting and an estimated expenditure of 60,000 feet of lumber for fluming. With the additional amount asked for in my estimate, forwarded on the 7th instant, I am confident I can thoroughly complete the ditch, which would prove a credit anywhere, and it would be hard to estimate the advantages that can be derived from it.

Education.

Special attention is given to the subject of education, and among these people will be found separate industrial schools for boys and girls and a church that would be a credit to any community. The[s]e schools have 171 scholars, of both sexes — an increase of 71 over last year — and the Government pays $150 annually for the board, tuition, and clothing of each scholar to the number of 150.

On the 2d day of August, of this year, the annual exhibition of these schools was given, and attended largely by citizens of Montana, who take interest in the advancement of such institutions. From the report of the editor of the Missoulian, published in that paper, I extract the appendix marked A, which will convey the news of a non-interested party concerning the schools of this reservation.

[The enclosed newspaper clipping was not published with Ronan's report.]

I have the honor to inclose herewith the statistics called for, and remain,

Very respectfully, your obedient servant,

Peter Ronan,
United States Indian Agent.

The Commissioner of Indian Affairs.

Document 69

White Pilgrim Makes Friends with Salish Indian

Summer 1885

Source: Excerpt from Frank B. Linderman, *Montana Adventure: The Recollections of Frank B. Linderman,* ed. H. G. Merriam, by permission of the University of Nebraska Press, Lincoln, copyright 1968 by the Board of Regents of the University of Nebraska, pages 6-9.

Editors' note: Writer Frank Linderman left a detailed account of meeting and making friends with Red-horn a Salish Indian, in the summer of 1885. Linderman was living in a cabin near Big Fork in the Upper Flathead Valley. Most Indian-white social interactions in the 1880s were friendly and peaceful. Some footnotes from the original publication have been omitted.

My excursions from the cabin had not been distant, and yet they had been sufficient to make me wonder and worry a little. I did not know if the Indians in that remote section were friendly to white men. There was nobody to tell me, and during all this time I had not seen an Indian. Then one morning before sunup when I was rekindling my fire to cook some venison I heard a horse whinny. The sound was friendly enough, and yet I felt a little jumpy, *especially* when I saw twenty-five head of cayuses feeding between my cabin and the skirting timber across the prairie. I knew that they were Indian horses, and the sight of them made me feel as lonely as a hole in a hillside. I forgot my breakfast to watch the horses, and to look carefully for a camp which I confidently expected would be somewhere on the edge of timber about the prairie.

I had a large bowie knife, which I then fondly believed was the proper thing for a hunter to carry, a glittering mistake with "a sure defense" etched on its blade. The knife was sticking in a log near my fire. I hastily slipped it into its scabbard on my belt, put on my powder horn and bullet pouch, and picked up my antiquated Kentucky to have a look farther down the prairie. A strip of jack pines grew on a succession of little knolls that extended through its middle, and I hobbled from knoll to knoll without seeing an Indian or a camp. Reaching the last timbered knoll, I sat down near a good-sized jack pine tree, not far from the grazing horses. The sun was just coming up. The whole setting was so startlingly beautiful that I nearly forgot Indians. The snow-capped peaks began to take on color. The frost crystals on the thick stools of bunch grass were sparkling like millions of diamonds, when suddenly the horses stirred like wild things. I saw them all lift their heads, prick their ears in one direction, toward the Big Fork. The light, crisp breeze was coming from that direction. I crept behind my tree, watching the skirting timber with the horses, until an Indian with a rifle across in front of him rode into the prairie on a pinto horse. The loose horses now began to move about restlessly, at last trotting away up the prairie back of my cabin, where the Indian, by riding hard, turned them toward the Big Fork, the whole outfit going lickety-split. "It will soon be over," I thought, when suddenly the Indian reined his horse to a short stop. I saw him look up and down the prairie, nosing the wind like a wolf. Then he rode straight to my little cabin, which was well hidden by jack pines. He had smelled the smoke from my fire.

What ought I to do now? I wondered. My overcoat and the axe were in the cabin. Everything else that I owned was with me. "Let him have 'em," I thought, watching for the Indian to ride away with my property. But he didn't appear. The horses, not being followed, stopped to graze again. I sat down by my tree to wait. An hour passed, or I thought the time that long, before I finally began to hobble toward my cabin without knowing exactly why. Anyway, I saw the Indian before he saw me; and I stopped, fascinated. He was seated on the log beside my smouldering fire, calmly filling his black stone pipe out of a long, slender buckskin sack. His blanket, a white Hudson's Bay, was tucked tightly about his lean hips, his rifle leaning against the log beside him. I thought him a middle-aged man. While I watched, he bent forward, raking a glowing stick out of my fire, lit the pipe, and then settled back with such an air of peace and contentment that I fairly ached to shake hands with him, if he'd let me.

My first step forward was upon a tiny patch of frosted snow among the trees. His ears caught the sound of the cracking snow crust. Without the least startle or show of surprise his head turned slowly until he saw me. Then he stood up with extended hand. "How! How!" he said so pleasantly that I answered, "Very well, sir, how are you?" giving his hand a good shake. What a fine face he had, that red man! We tried hard to talk together, but with little success. However, we smoked together, *my* tobacco in *his* pipe. I remembered long afterward that he had wished to impress me with the fact that he was a Flathead and not a Kootenai, telling me this in the sign language over and over again. But of course the sign language was Greek to me then. There was good reason for his wanting me to know that he was not a Kootenai. The Kootenais were unfriendly to white men. We had trouble with them later on.

My Indian visitor instinctively knew that I was a rank pilgrim. His smile said as plainly as words that he thought me a babe in the woods. However, he was exceedingly polite, and tried to treat me as he would a grown man. This made a deep impression on me. From that day I frequently fibbed about my age. I did this so consistently and for so long a time that I finally forgot the true number of my years. It was only when I saw my mother again more than twenty years afterward that I learned exactly the date of my birth. I remember that when I attempted to argue with her, my mother said with a grim smile, "I was present when you were born, my son, and therefore I ought to know."

For many years after our meeting I knew my first Indian intimately. His name was Red-horn, a renowned Flathead warrior who had counted several "coups" and had taken more scalps than any other living member of his tribe. It was Red-horn who gave me my first glimpse of what men in the old Northwest called the "moccasin telegraph." I cannot prove that old-time Indians transmitted messages through thin air over long distances, and yet I have more than once believed that only by some secret means could Indian news travel as it seemed to. Several years after my first meeting with Red-horn I was camped alone in an Indian lodge at the foot of Swan lake. Red-horn and his woman and two young sons reached this camping ground at about sunset. Knowing my lodge by sight, Red-horn came at once to visit me. He stayed until late in the night. The next morning he came again, sitting exactly where he had sat the night before, talking signs and pidgin English as he had before, till suddenly he stopped short, lifted his eyes to the smoke-hole, and sat motionless, as though listening. His attitude, so suddenly assumed and so tense, caused me, now a hunter like himself, to strain my ears to catch the sounds that disturbed him. But heard nothing unnatural. When I again looked at Red-horn's face his eyes met my own.

"My friend killed. Bad work," he said in signs.

"When?" I asked, wonderingly.

"Now," he signed positively.

"What name?" I asked in the sign language. He told me, but I have forgotten it.

"Where?" I asked. He pointed south.

Fortunately I happened to know the day of the week and the month, which was out of the ordinary. I had no watch, but by the sun I thought the time of day to be about nine o'clock in the forenoon. Later in the year when I visited the lower country I learned that Red-horn's friend *had* been murdered on that day, and approximately at that hour. I have experienced other seeming exhibitions of the efficiency of the "moccasin telegraph," but I will leave them and get on with my story.

Document 70

Conflict at Arlee Railroad Station

December 1885

Source: Peter Ronan, *"A Great Many of Us Have Good Farms": Agent Peter Ronan Reports on the Flathead Indian Reservation, Montana, 1877-1887*, ed. Robert J. Bigart (Pablo, Mont.: Salish Kootenai College Press, 2014), pages 343-346.

Editors' note: This December 1885 incident at Arlee was a good example of Agent Peter Ronan relying on the chiefs to maintain law and order. Ronan called Chief Arlee to the scene to help mediate the situation. During the course of events, the Missoula County Sheriff and his deputies were disarmed by tribal leaders to avoid trouble. Ronan feared the U.S. Army would come on the reservation and aggravate the tension. He made his arguments to the tribal members that the injured Indian, Big Jim, should be turned over to Missoula County authorities. After much debate, a tribal council finally agreed to surrender Big Jim to the Missoula County Sheriff. The dead man was Baptist Kakashee's son. The incident was widely covered in the newspapers. The conflict was even reported in *The New-York Times*. Big Jim was quickly released for lack of evidence. The two white men involved — V. H. Coombs and P. Bader — were freed on grounds they acted in self-defense. Big Jim died of exposure near Ravalli in January 1890.

United States Indian Service,
Flathead Agency,
December 17, 1885.

Hon. Commissioner of Indian Affairs
Washington, D.C.
Sir,

Owing largely to the abandonment by the Railroad employes of the station at Arlee, as also telegrams for troops, a rumor was spread of Indian troubles at this Agency; as no trouble or even an apprehension of such, has agitated the Agency or its people, I have the honor to address you and report all the circumstances which caused the said employes to leave their posts, and the unnecessary calls upon the military authorities.

A couple of drunken Indians arrived at Arlee, from without the confines of the Reservation, on the east bound train and made some demand for goods upon the clerk at the traders store, to these demands the clerk (Mr Coombes) would not accede, and they then forcibly attempted to obtain the same, which attempt was resisted; the clerk seeing danger called upon Mr Bader, the Postmaster, who came armed with a shotgun loaded with bird shot and the clerk likewise armed himself with a revolver, then suddenly one of the Indians drew a bull-dog revolver, aimed at the clerk, when the Postmaster seized him by the wrist of the armed hand; then the Indian with his left drew a large Knife, and while attempting to make a desperate plunge, the Clerk shot him dead, the confederate raised his gun and fired at the Postmaster, but missed his aim, when he in return emptied his shot gun wounding him in the thigh; (the Indian escaped to the brush was subsequently found and arrested) the Postmaster and clerk fearing for their lives telegraphed to Missoula for an armed posse and sent a messenger to me.

Upon arriving upon the scene, the Sheriff and posse having also arrived from Missoula; the clerk was immediately placed in arrest and taken to Missoula leaving a deputy and assistant to arrest the wounded Indian and the Postmaster, in order to bring them to Missoula for preliminary examination; in the meantime I notified Chief Arlee and several of the headmen to come at once to the scene of the tragedy, and after their arrival it was then and there agreed upon to take the wounded Indian as well as the white man to Missoula; everything being so arranged and agreed upon befor the arrival of the east bound train, and having full faith in the agreement, I returned to Agency as everything was quiet at the depot and no signs nor apprehension of either danger or trouble; soon after my departure a party of mounted Indians, accompanied by the father and relatives of the dead man arrived at the depot, and informed the Sheriff "that he could take the white man who did the shooting to Missoula, but they would hold the Indian, and try him according to Indian laws and usages," to this the Sheriff objected when himself and deputies were immediately disarmed by the Indians, the wounded Indian was then placed upon a horse behind another Indian who galloped off with him, the Indians then returned their arms to the Sheriff and deputies and directed them to return to Missoula upon the train; the railroad employes including the Agent, I presume fearing danger, leaped upon the train and the Postmaster who was then under arrest also departed, leaving the depot tenantless and the Agency without mail or telegraphic facilities.

Knowing that intense excitement would be created at the next station, I immediately despatched a messenger to that point (Evaro) conveying the following telegrams to the Commanding Officer, Fort Missoula, Robert Lane, Sheriff Missoula County, and F. W. Gilbert, Supt. N.P.R.R. Missoula M.T. viz:

Commanding Officer
Fort Missoula, M.T.

The Indians prevented the Sheriff from Arresting an Indian prisoner, there is no excitement here among the Indians, neither do I fear any trouble from any Indian source in fact, I apprehend neither trouble or danger. The fact of the R.R. employes leaving the station will no doubt create excitement. I hope to be able to turn the prisoner over to the civil authorities myself. Answer.

(Sgd) Peter Ronan
U.S. Ind. Agent.

* * * * * * *

Robert Lane
Sheriff Missoula M.T.

I think there will be no trouble, Indians excited on account of Coombes leaving before having a talk, let the matter rest until you hear from me. I am of opinion that I can turn the prisoner over to you myself when the excitement is over. Answer.

Peter Ronan
U.S. Ind. Agent.

* * * * * * *

F. W. Gilbert
Supt. N.P.R.R.
Missoula, M.T.

The excitement occasioned by the death of the Indian at Arlee has subsided. I apprehend no trouble, am convinced there is no cause for alarm.

Peter Ronan
U.S. Ind. Agent

The Indians conveyed the wounded man to a house near the Agency, his wounds were attended and there he is at present. I immediately called a Council of all Indians and explained to them clearly and intelligently the trouble that was liable to arise from their hasty action in rescuing the prisoner from the officers of the law; that unless they agreed to turn the prisoner over to the civil authorities for an examination, trouble would surely follow and probably a large posse of armed men, if not the military, would soon appear, demand and force the surrender of the prisoner and all connected with his rescue. The

Indians deliberated for over ten hours, and after heated discussions, finally acquiesced in all my suggestions.

Having heard that the military authorities had been called upon by some party or parties the dispatch quoted before reached Missoula in time not to introduce them upon this reservation, as they were armed and equipped and had already boarded the train at Missoula.

Intense excitement, I have no doubt, prevailed in Missoula and the surrounding country owing to my inability to hold communication, but as soon as the dispatches heretofore cited were received the excitement was allayed.

The dead Indian has been buried, the wounded Indian is here subject to any order from the civil authorities; everything in and about the Agency and reservation is quiet, peaceable and orderly, and even during the excitement at the depot nor [sic] an echo, could be heard at any other point, except when the Council met here for deliberation over the delivery of the Indians to the civil authorities, wherein stormy speeches were delivered, but by the calm, cool and deliberate reasonings and arguments of older and more experienced and enlightened headsmen, the latter eventually prevailed.

Very Respectfully
Your obt svt.
Peter Ronan
U.S. Indian Agent.

Document 71

Chief Arlee Seeks Pardon for Indian Inmates

March 19, 1886

Source: "Indians Pardoned," *The Helena Daily Herald*, March 19, 1886, page 3, col. 3.

Editors' note: This newspaper article illustrated the interconnection between white man's law and tribal petitions for clemency. Arlee again expressed his argument that crimes committed by tribal members while drunk, should be blamed on those white men who sold them the whisky. See also article about Benway's or Bendois' re-arrest on October 7, 1887.

Indians Pardoned.
Three Imprisoned Flatheads Liberated from the Pen.

The east bound train this morning brought into Helena unusual and distinguished visitors in the persons of Arlee, chief of the Flathead nation, and Anton and Michelle, two chiefs of the same tribe of subordinate station. They were accompanied by Alex. Matte, an English speaking half-breed, who is the blacksmith at the Flathead agency. The visitors were driven to the Grand Central Hotel on their arrival, where they were seen and interviewed by a Herald reporter.

Chief Arlee, though bending under the weight of 80 years, undertook this journey in company with two of his honored braves to intercede with Montana's Executive for the pardon of three young men who were sent to the penitentiary six months ago for an assault committed upon residents of Missoula county last year. The aged chief brought a formidable petition with him to back his suit, which no doubt determined the Executive in his act of clemency. The petition sets forth that the act which caused the arrest and imprisonment of the young braves was committed while they were in a state of intoxication, produced by the white man's whisky, and was not the outcome of malice. It therefore suggested the three Indians as fit subjects for pardon and prayed the Governor to exercise his clemency in their behalf. The petition was signed by the District Attorney who prosecuted them, the attorney who defended them, the U.S. Indian agent for the Flatheads, and several prominent citizens of Missoula besides those first mentioned.

In an audience with Acting Governor Webb this morning the old chief presented his petition and urged his suit for the liberation of his erring children. The Executive gave the case his full consideration, and, after consultation with the U.S. Marshal and others familiar with question, decided to extend a full pardon to the imprisoned Flatheads. Accordingly, in a letter addressed to Chief Arlee, he informed the old man that the three Indians were fully pardoned and at liberty to leave the penitentiary and rejoin their people. The Indian convicts, whose names are Benway, Michelle and Bazil, were undergoing sentences of one, one and a half and two years respectively.

Upon receipt of the good tiding old Arlee expressed his gratitude to the beneficent Governor, and, with joy in his heart over the successful accomplishment of the object of his visit to Helena, will leave with his retinue on the evening train to rejoin his subjects and convey to them the glad news of the liberation from durance vile of their hitherto unfortunate countrymen.

Document 72

Chiefs Meet with the Northwest Indian Commission April 21-29, 1887

Source: Excerpts from Jno. V. Wright, Henry W. Andrews, and Jared W. Daniels, "Report of Northwest Indian Commission," in "Reduction of Indian Reservations," House Executive Document No. 63 (1888), 50th Congress, 1st Session, serial 2557, pages 43-46, 69-74.

Editors' note: In the agreement signed at this meeting, the Salish, Upper Pend d'Oreille, and Kootenai Indians of the Flathead Reservation accepted the removal of the Lower Pend d'Oreille and Spokane Indians to the reservation from Idaho and Washington. Two sections of land on the reservation were to be "set apart" for the Jesuit fathers and the Sisters at the St. Ignatius Mission for "as long as they are used for said [educational] purposes and no longer." The last article of the agreement provided for a new saw and grist mill and blacksmith shop for the northern part of the reservation. Unfortunately, the agreement was never approved or funded by the U.S. Congress. The commission received a very impressive welcome at St. Ignatius Mission. In the transcript look beyond the condescension of the white negotiators at the concerns voiced by the chiefs. Chief Arlee was particularly upset about the government paid judges and policemen taking over the law and order powers of the traditional chiefs.

Report of Northwest Indian Commission.
Flathead or Jocko Reservation.

Having concluded our work with the Calespels, we left Sand Point, Idaho, on the 21st day of April [1887], and arrived at Arlee, a station on the Northern Pacific Railroad, on the night of that day. We found in waiting for us Mr. Thomas E. Adams, the clerk of the Flathead Agency, with a conveyance, and we proceeded immediately to the house of Maj. Peter Ronan, the agent for this agency.

On the morning of the following day Chief Arlee, of the Flathead tribe, paid us a friendly visit. The agency is situated near the south border of the reservation.

The Saint Ignatius Mission, 20 miles from the agency, was deemed, from its more central position, the best place for the Indian council.

It required time to give the different tribes notice of time and place of meeting, as some of them resided upwards of 90 miles from the agency.

The following Tuesday (April 26) was therefore agreed upon as the day of meeting, and messengers were dispatched to notify the various tribes.

Before leaving Sand Point we sent a dispatch to Agent Ronan, notifying him of our coming and of the day we had named for the council.

On Tuesday we were conveyed in private conveyances by Agent Ronan to the Mission, being accompanied by Clerk Adams, Dr. [John] Dade, agent physician, and the Government interpreter.

This gave us an opportunity to see a large part of the reservation, more especially that part occupied by the Flatheads, who mainly reside on this part of the reservation. The Pend d'Oreilles reside near the Mission, and the Kootenais still farther off near Lake Pend d'Oreille.

Saint Ignatius Mission is located in about the center of the Indian population of this reservation.

The Commissioners were driven through the Jocko Valley and along the foot-hills skirting the valley, which is traversed by fine irrigating ditches constructed for the use of the Bitter Root Flatheads of Charlos's band, who are now settled by Agent Ronan, and who occupy cozy houses, surrounded by well-fenced fields, which the Indians were engaged in planting and seeding.

An account of the trip by an eye-witness says: "Turning off from the line of the Northern Pacific Railroad at Ravalla Station, and while driving across the divide leading to the Mission, the party were met by a large band of armed Indians, headed by the Indian police, dressed in their bright uniforms. Upon meeting the Commissioners the Indians ranged themselves upon each side of the carriages and fired a salute, giving a wild whoop of welcome, regardless of the plunging and rearing of the excited horses attached to the carriages in which the gentlemen of the Commission were driven. Arranging themselves on each side of the carriages, alternately firing their guns and ringing out their fierce whoops, the carriages dashed over the hills, followed and preceded by the wild escort."

On arriving at the Mission the party were welcomed by loud strains of music, pealing out from twenty-three brass instruments, drums, fifes, and clarionets, the soul-inspiring notes of the Star-Spangled Banner, rendered in excellent style by as many Indian boys from the veranda of the college.

In the evening, while discussing their cigars, the Indian band, composed of boys whose ages range from 11 to 18 years, gathered under the windows and gave a serenade. After rendering several airs, such as Hail to the Chief, Bonnie Blue Flag, etc., Judge [Jno. V.] Wright stepped to the door and made the following remarks: "My young Indian friends, in behalf of my associates of the

Northwest Indian Commission and other gentlemen present, I return thanks for the beautiful serenade we have just listened to with delight and astonishment. Your performance is indeed astonishing, and furnishes an evidence of the talent which the Great Creator has given you to acquire and master music with your other educational accomplishments. As the thrilling strains echo and vibrate this night under our windows, beneath the shadows of the grand old Rocky Mountains, it furnishes a good contrast to a few years ago, when these gorges, glens, and lonely valleys echoed only to the howl of the prowling wolf and other wild animals or the terror-striking war-whoops of your ancestors. What a deep and lasting debt of gratitude you owe to the pains-taking patience of the good Father and the kind protection of a liberal Government, who have made it possible for you to advance from savage barbarism to education and civilizing pursuits, and also to the mastery of music, the inspiring strains of which touch and thrill the hearts of your visitors of another race.

"Again, I thank you and bid you goodnight. May you all live to manhood and to old age, a pride to your race and a source of gratification and joy to the fathers of St. Ignatius Mission, to whose attention, teaching, and devotion you owe your present elevation and refinement of character and morals."

The Commission, by invitation, visited the various workshops and mills connected with the industrial system of the mission schools.

These consisted of a saw and grist mill, printing office, tin shop, shoe shop, museum, saddle and harness shop, carpenter shop, and blacksmith shop. Specimens of industry were exhibited which demonstrated the capacity and skill of the boys. Everything is conducted in an orderly and systematic manner. On the farms the boys are also taught and practiced in all the details of the cultivation of the soil.

We were entertained by recitations in the various studies at the boys' school. An Indian boy, aged fourteen years, read an address to the Commission as follows:

"Honorable Gentlemen of the Indian Commission:

"Allow me to thank you for your kind visit to St. Ignatius Mission, and to welcome you in the name of my companions to our school. We look upon you as the chosen representatives of our Great Father in Washington, who so kindly cares for the children of the Indians and spares no expense to educate us in the same manner in which white boys are educated. In honoring you we mean to honor our Great Father, and to show him our gratitude for the great benefits which we are receiving from his fatherly kindness.

"We have learned from our father superior how kindly you have spoken to all the Indians west of us, and especially how pleased you have shown yourselves to be with the progress of the Indian children of the Cœur d'Alene school.

"We hope that you will be pleased with us also. It will encourage us in our efforts to learn, and it will also be a source of gratification to our teachers. However, we are but poor and timid Indian children, not quite at home in the ways and manners of white boys, and we hope you will kindly overlook our shortcomings."

To this the chairman replied as follows:

"My Young Friends: Every friend of the Indian and every generous human heart would rejoice to see what we have seen since we came on this reservation. The degree of progress which is manifested here gives promise of a bright future for you and your race. In the name of the Commission I thank you for the address of welcome you have made us, and I can say without flattery that you compare well and favorably with other schools we have visited in our various travels. You are greatly favored indeed. I can assure you that I never attended a school, and I doubt if any white man present ever attended one, with better school facilities than this. Some of you no doubt dislike to be at school. This should not be so. All whom you see here had to go through the same process through which you are going. Continue on in the way you are now traveling and your course will be onward and upward. The great Government whose flag floats over your building is your friend. No pains will be spared to advance you. We promise you all the encouragement and aid in our power, and we will look forward to the day with pleasure when the Indians of the Jocko reserve will be an educated, industrious, and independent people."

After being shown through the girls' school, which was perfect in all its arrangements, and hearing the various classes recite, we were satisfied that nothing was wanting. A little Indian girl read to us the following address:

"Honored Sirs: We are rejoiced to see you in our midst and bid you a cordial welcome. We must sincerely thank you for the honor that you bestow upon us to-day by your presence and the interest you thus manifest in our regard. We are confident, honored sirs, that you wish to promote the welfare of the Indians. It is this and your great condescension in deigning to visit us that gave us the courage to present ourselves before you and show you the little we know. We are but little children of the mountains aiming to become one day useful and industrious. We can not be learned, but we wish to be good, to please those who take an interest in the cause of our education and to repay them for their kindness to us."

To which Judge Wright replied:

"We are well pleased with what we have seen and heard. You have most excellent advantages provided for you here and you show that you appreciate them. You should continue to do so. If you do your advancement is assured. Respect, love, and obey these good sisters who have devoted their talents to your service and you will grow up wise and virtuous women, an honor to your families, to your school, and to your race.

"We thank you for your kindness of welcome, and will be happy to do all we can to advance your prosperity and happiness."

We give these particulars more for the purpose of laying before you the actual situation of the Indians and the rapid progress they are making than for any other purpose. Each tribe of Indians should be dealt with according to its actual condition, and these we found so different that we have endeavored in this report to accompany a history of our negotiations with such facts and circumstances as may throw light on their present state and condition.

The council met in the evening of the 26th. The three tribes, Flatheads, Pend d'Oreilles, and Kootenais were fully represented. The large school room was filled to overflowing, and many women and children occupied seats on the stoops and verandas outside the council room and grouped around in the boys' playground.

All classes were represented, from the oldest to the youngest, from the well-clad, thrifty looking farmers in business suits to the wild followers of the chase, some in gaudy blankets with broad, beaded belts, others in gaily-trimmed buckskins with beaded leggings. It was, however, noticeable that the civilized dress largely predominated, both with males and females. Some had their dwellings around the mission and the agency, while others had come long distances to meet the Commission.

The dwellers around the Pend d'Oreille River and around Flathead Lake, the tillers of the soil from Hot Springs and Camas Prairie, the Indian cattle-kings from Crow Creek and the Muddy, lonely wigwams in narrow gorges, far-away glens by sparkling water-falls, and wild, remote spots outside of civilized intercourse had been notified of the coming of the Commission.

The object of the visit was made known and the duties and power of the Commission clearly stated. There was but little difficulty in obtaining the consent of the confederated tribes to the removal of the Calespels and such portion of the Spokanes as might desire it to their reservation. They also consented that any other non-reservation Indians might be removed to their reservation on such terms as might be agreed upon by the United States. This was done on account of reliable information received by the Commission as to a small band of Kootenais whom it appeared had received but little attention from the Government or its agents.

Our information with regard to these Indians was derived from Rev. Louis Jacquot, of De Smet Mission, Cœur d'Alerne [sic] Reservation. The Cœur d'Alernes in their agreement with us also gave their consent to the removal to their reservation of all non-reservation Indians in that part of the country.

These Kootenai Indians live in northern Idaho, along and near the international line. They are called Lower Kootenais, or Flat Bows. A part of them are in the United States and a part in Canada (British Columbia). Those in the United States number about 200. Up to this time they have had no treaty relations with the Government and have received no aid. No agent has ever visited them officially. Their country is being slowly taken up by whites, and they are now confined along the bank of the Kootenay River. They are very destitute, having nothing to rely upon for a support but fish, berries, and game. The land on which they live, beginning at Bonner's Ferry, is one vast swamp, unfit for cultivation. At times it appears as one vast lake. He said they were very poor and miserable, and that they expressed their surprise and sorrow that no attention was paid them. The statement of the priest touching the condition of these poor people excited the sympathetic interest of the Commissioners, and it was determined to call the attention of the Department to it.

We have heretofore given an account of the schools and other facilities afforded the Indians on this reservation by those in charge of the Fathers and Sisters of St. Ignatius Mission. The Indians highly appreciate these advantages and manifested the most intense anxiety that they should be fostered and continued.

It was the earnest request of the Indians themselves that article II [providing two sections of land for the fathers and sisters for school use] was incorporated into the agreement. In addition to these, after a careful inspection of the buildings for schools and church purposes, the various mills, shops, barns, agricultural implements and products, together with the farms themselves, all of which has caused an expenditure of from seventy-five thousand to one hundred thousand dollars by the society in charge, we felt that it was nothing but absolute justice that this provision should be made. The Jocko Reservation of itself is a most desirable place for Indians, and, with St. Ignatius Mission and its appliances for educating and civilizing the Indians, it appears to be perfect. Without the advantages afforded by this mission in the past and in the present, it is certain that these Indians would be far from that promising condition in which they are now found.

The land covered by the agreement is already occupied with the various improvements of the society, with an occasional Indian settlement, which latter are fully protected by the last clause in the article.

The prospect of an early removal of other tribes to this reservation and the consequent necessity for houses, fences, and, together with the fact that a large portion of the tribes now on the reservation live at a great distance from the agency where the mill is located, and the earnest desire expressed by the Indians for the erection of another saw-mill, accounts for article 3. Our own observation and knowledge, together with the statement of the agent, satisfied us of the necessity for this provision.

A large number of bridges have to be kept up on this reservation in order to facilitate travel from one portion of it to another, and this was also a consideration making this provision necessary.

The Commissioners beg leave to express their obligations to Rev. Leopold Van Goop {Gorp], S.J., and his assistants at St. Ignatius Mission, for courtesies and valuable assistance. We are also under great obligations to Agent Ronan and his clerk, Thomas E. Adams, of the Flathead Agency, for their kindness and valuable services to us; Major Ronan, whose long experience as United States Indian agent, and his constant vigilance over the interests of the Government and welfare of the Indians in strict obedience to his instructions from the Commissioner of Indian Affairs, offered us every facility in his power. Having concluded negotiations at the Jocko Reservation, we took passage on the Northern Pacific Railroad for Duluth, Minn., the nearest point on the Northern Pacific to reach the Lake Superior band of Chippewa Indians, at Boise Forte and Grand Portage Reservation.

* * * * * * * *

Council with Flatheads, etc., Flathead Reservation, Mont.

The Commissioners met the various bands of Kootenais, Pend d'Oreilles, and Flathead Indians at St. Ignatius Mission on Tuesday, the 26th day of April, 1887.

There were present the Commissioners, John V. Wright, J. W. Daniels, and Henry W. Andrews, the chiefs and head-men of the various tribes, and many other Indians.

The council was opened with prayer by Father Van Gorp, of the Mission.

Judge Wright, then spoke as follows:

"My friends, as Commissioners of the United States, we shake hands with the Flatheads, with the Pend d'Oreilles, and the Kootonais. We thank you for assembling so promptly on our call, and we thank you for the imposing and friendly greeting which you have us on yesterday. We have traveled over much of your beautiful reservation, and it has filled us with delight and admiration. Nowhere can there be seen a more beautiful reservation. Your vast and fertile plains, watered with clear and health-giving streams, skirted with grand mountains, impresses us with the belief that you are indeed blessed beyond most Indians. But what has pleased us more is to find you living in comfortable houses, surrounded by good farms, and all striving to make a support and bring yourselves and your families to independence. We visited your schools on yesterday; and there we saw your children well clothed and well provided for, and exhibiting such progress in learning that it makes our hearts glad, and gave us assurance that in a few years your children will be intelligent, moral, and self-supporting. It was our earnest desire to visit you at an earlier day, but business of great importance with other Indians in different States and Territories detained us so that we could not come until this time.

"You have a large reservation, and although you have many Indians on it, there is much more land than you and your children will use for many years to come. It is doubtless known to you that the white people have been coming this way for many years, and that they much desire to have your reservation opened to white settlement. It is not right that great bodies of land should be permitted to remain unoccupied and uncultivated. It is a part of the policy of the Government of the United States to reduce Indian reservations to proper size when they are out of all proportion to the number of Indians living on them. In order to avoid this trouble the Government desires, where it can be done, to settle Indian reservations with Indians, and open to settlement abandoned reservations. We have not come to open your reservation to white settlement. It is not a part of our instructions to do this, but it is a part of our business to get your consent to the settlement of some other Indians on this, your reservation.

"The Spokane Indians who reside around Spokane Falls, in the Territory of Washington, are poor, and otherwise in a bad condition. They are in the midst of the white people, and are exposed to many troubles. Many of them have no homes and no land. A part of our business was to induce them to remove from that place, and take homes on the Colville, Cœur d'Alene, or this reservation. We have recently come from Spokane Falls, stopping with the Calespels at Sand Point, in Idaho.

"A few of the Spokanes expressed a desire to remove to this Reservation, but the most of them prefer to go to the Cœur d'Alene Reservation. The Cœur d'Alenes, in the councils we held with them, gave their consent, and agreed, that not only the Spokanes but Calespels and other Indians might come and live on their reservation. The Calespels desire to come here, but before removing them it is our duty to get the consent of the tribes on this reservation. The Calespels or Pend d'Oreilles are you know are of the same blood of the Pend d'Oreilles here. They are very poor and have very poor lands. They are wild and have no advantages, no schools, no churches, no agent, and indeed nothing but the poor living they make by hunting and fishing. The Great Father has pity on them and he thinks you should also pity them and allow them to come and live with you. In the agreement which we made with the Spokanes and Calespels, we provided for giving them homes and houses, farming implements and provisions to give them a start. What we want is that you shall give a cheerful consent to this arrangement. It will do them great good and it will also do you good. It is plain that if your reservation were settled up with Indians the white people would quit asking for it, and even if they continued to ask they could not get it, as the Government is your friend and will spare no pains to protect you and advance you in your pathway to civilization.

"There is another thing I wish to say to you. Some of your chiefs have told us that you are much in need of a saw and grist mill on this side of the mountain, which lies between here and the agency. We know it is a long way from many of you to the mill, too far to be of service to you. We therefore propose, if you so desire, to agree that a saw and grist mill shall be built and a miller and blacksmith furnished so as to accommodate those who live on this side.

"Some of you have also told us that you desire to make provision for your schools and the farms and buildings attached to them. This we will also do if you desire it. If you wish that the fathers who have built the houses and opened the farms may continue to use them for these purposes, we will put in the agreement according to your wishes if they are reasonable. I have now explained as well as I can the nature of our business, and we would be glad to hear what you have to say about it."

The three leading chiefs, Arlee, of the Flatheads, Michael, of the Pend d'Oreilles, and Aeneas, of the Kootenais, after a moment's consultation, replied.

Chief Arlee said:

"The land belongs to me. I am Arlee, chief of all the Flatheads. We are glad to see you here. We expected you last fall but you did not come. We heard that you passed by on your way west. You have now returned and we are glad. We have much to talk about to you, about our country and the railroads, and about our judges. We wish to talk about many things. I was in Washington. I shook hands with the Great Father. I will tell you all. We will meet again to-morrow. What you have said is all good. We are glad you have come."

Chief Michael said:

"We heard you were coming many months ago, and then we heard you had gone by us and we were afraid you were not coming. We are glad to meet the Great Father's Commissioners. You come as friends. We have heard what you say and we understand all. My people will all agree to what you say. We wish to do what our Great Father wants. We will throw no brush in his way. We have pity on the Calespels. They are my kinsmen. We say yes; let them come. We say the same to the Spokanes. We are willing to give them homes on our lands. We wish the land lent to the fathers. They have led us on the good path. They teach our children and make them good. We will not sell our land, but we will lend it to the fathers for schools and churches."

Chief Aeneas expressed similar views for his people.

Judge Wright. Shall we proceed now?

The Chiefs. No; we will council together to-night and meet you again to-morrow.

The council then adjourned.

Friday, *April* 29.

Council met as per agreement; prayer by Father Van Gorp.

Judge Wright. We have prepared an agreement in accordance with what was said on yesterday, which will now be read to you and fully explained.

Commissioner Andrews here read the agreement, at which the closest attention was given as requested by the Commissioners, and each article plainly and fully interpreted to the Indians.

Chief Arlee. We don't wish the land sold to the fathers.

Chief Michael. We did not understand yesterday that the land was to be sold to the fathers.

Judge Wright. The agreement does not say that the land is sold. You only agree that the land and houses may be used by the fathers as long as they use it for school and church purposes, and no longer.

Chief Michael. Now we understand you, we are all willing to lend our land to the fathers.

Chief Arlee. We are willing to lend the land; this is all right. We are satisfied with it. I now have something to say. I want to make some complaints. My people do some hunting; there is game on our reservation and my people hunt and kill deer and other game; we want ammunition. Why is it that our Great Father will not allow us to buy powder, shot, and cartridges? We are peaceable, and we will do no harm; we will do only good; we will not shoot the Indian nor the white man; we want to know why our Great Gather [sic] will not let us have cartridges. Is it that he is afraid we will kill his people?

Another thing. The white men make cards and they make whisky. They gamble with the cards and drink the whisky. If whisky and cards are bad, why don't the white people quit making them? They tell us they are bad. Why do they make them and use them? If these things are good and not bad, why will not the white man allow the Indians to have them? I wish you to tell me this. I want to say more. I wish to say another thing about the railroad. When the Great Father sent a commission to ask my people to allow the railroad to be built on my land, he told them if they would allow the railroad to pass through he would let me people ride free without paying money for it. Now he has got the railroad and he won't let us ride. The cars run over my cattle and my horses and they will not pay me for them. I want the pay. Where is the money? We can not get it. They run the cars over my people and kill them. I want the railroad taken off my land. I want it moved away over the land of the whites, I don't want it on my lands. I tell my people not to hurt the road, nor to tear it up. You need not be afraid, we will not trouble the road. I want it taken off my land.

I do not want white men to come on my land and cut the trees and dig up the minerals. We do not wish them to do this. We want them kept off. Some of them bring their cattle on my land and eat up the grass. We don't want this. We want the grass for our own cattle. We want our reservation marked all around so that white men will not come on it. We do not want the judges and the policeman. They do not act right. They do wrong. We want the head-men of the judges to decide the cases. We don't want all three to decide. The head-man ought to decide. How is it when one judge is one way and two the other? I want you to answer this question. We don't want any judges or policemen. We want the chiefs to rule the people. Is it right for the judges to have sick men whipped? And women? They have whipped sick men and they had a woman whipped who was pregnant. She told them she was in that way, but still they had her whipped. And she had an abortion. Do you think that was right? When the judges decide a case does anybody else have anything to do about it? Can there be any appeal? They say they have made laws. We don't want their laws. Let the chiefs make the laws for the people. This is the way Indians do. What do the whites do with a man who commits murder? Do they hang him? Tell me what they do and what we should do. I want to know.

Judge Wright. When we get through signing the agreement I will endeavor to explain all these things to you as fully as I can. They are all important questions and I am glad you have spoken of them. We are very glad you have so readily consented to the agreement. You have shown your respect for the Government. And you have shown your good sense. It will be pleasing to the Great Father to hear of the way you have acted and how well you are doing. It is gratifying indeed, that of all the Indians here there is not a single one who opposes the agreement. A large majority of you are here, and no doubt the balance will all agree as you have done.

Chief Michael. We all understand the agreement; all of my people will sign it. I am Chief of the Pend d'Oreilles.

Chief Aeneas. All of my people are not here. What I do all will do and agree to. I am a friend to the white man. I am a friend of the Great Father. I live a long way from here. My people live a long way. We are poor. We have no mill near us. I think it is 90 miles from where I live to the agency. We have no saw-mill to give us lumber; we have no carpenter, no blacksmith, and no farmer to show us how to work. I want you to ask the Great Father to give us these things so we can support ourselves and our children. This is all I have to say.

Judge Wright. The Calespels have agreed to come to this reservation, and I understand they intend to settle not very far from where the Kootenais are. We have agreed to build a saw and grist mill for them, and you (Aeneas) and your people can get your wheat ground there, and also get lumber with which to build houses. In the agreement we are making here to-day we also provide for the building of a mill on this side, and you can also have the benefit of that, as the agent no doubt will put it where it will accommodate the largest numbers and the most needy.

Chief Aeneas. That will be all right.

After the agreement was signed **Judge Wright** spoke as follows:

"My friends, the business for the transaction of which this council was called has been completed. You have done well. You have shown your good sense. Your respect for and confidence in the Government, as well as your kind feelings toward your less fortunate brothers, the Spokanes and the Calespels. All this we will carry back to the Great Father, and we know he will be well pleased with you and your actions this day. You will never by sorry for what you have done. You will always be glad." Addressing Chief Arlee Judge Wright said: "I will now endeavor to explain to you the things which seem to trouble your mind. You complain that your people are not allowed to buy cartridges. I will tell you why this is so. The Great Father knows that you and your people do not use your guns to shoot white men or to shoot one another. This is not the way with all Indians. Some tribes want guns and ammunition to use in wars against one another and to hurt the whites. It was because of these that the law was passed which forbids selling ammunition to Indians. There are many Indians in the United States besides you. The laws must be made general — must be made for all — as it is not always in the power of the Government to find out where there should be an exception made.

"You seem also to be dissatisfied about the railroad which runs through your land. You say that in order to induce you to give the right of way through your reservation you were promised free passages on the road. This is so. I have read the speeches which were made to you when the right of way was asked, and you were told that you should have free rides on the road. For some reason, I do not know what, it was not so written in the agreement which was made with you. It may have been that it was forgotten. I do not know how it was done.

"For a long time your people were allowed to ride free. At the last session of Congress a law was passed forbidding the granting of free passes. It did not say that free passes should not be issued to Indians, but the railroads said they thought it included Indians, I did not think so. We think when the railroad managers come to look into the question, and when they find that you were promised free rides, they will in good faith stand up to the promises made at the time. Your agent, Major Ronan, tells us that he has already received a letter from the company telling him you will be permitted to ride free on the reservation. We think the Government will see that you have your rights. You also complain that the railroad trains kill your cattle, and that you get no pay for it. In all countries where railroads are this sometimes happens. It can not be provided against. We understand from the agent that you have been paid, and I am sure you will be paid in all proper cases.

"It sometimes requires time and delay. This is the way with the white people also. Because of these things you ask that the railroad be removed from your land. This can not be done. The railroad is of great importance to you, as it is to all the country. By it you get cheap and safe travel, and it brings you things you need and could not get here without great cost. You ought to be glad you have a railroad, and not sorry; not interfere with it, but do all in your power to render it safe and certain. Other Indians where we have been, who had no railroads, have asked for them, and want them to run through their country. This should be the way with you. As to your timber, mines, and grass I have to say that no white man has any right to come on your reservation and carry off your timber or dig for minerals without first getting lawful permission. The Government will protect your reservations in this regard. It has protected other Indians, and it will do the same for you. You need have no fears about this. Neither are white men allowed to drive their cattle or other stock on your reservation to eat your grass.

"If this occurs report it to Major Ronan and he will see to it. Your reservation is so large that it can not be fenced in on all sides so as to keep stock off, and if white men's cattle stray on to your lands and are not driven on you should not hurt or injure them. If they are driven on report it to your agent and he will attend to it for you. As to your judges and policemen, you should be glad that you have them. It is a good thing. White people have judges and police officers all over their country. They are not given to hurt you, but to protect you against outsiders and against bad men among you. They are for the protection of the weak against the strong. There must be some power to decide when men can not agree, and somebody to see that the decisions are carried out. As you advance you will more clearly see the advantages of having good judges and good policemen. You should all respect and obey them. If necessary you should aid them. If they do wrong it can be corrected, but you can not get along without them. Among the whites all are made to obey them, even the

Great Father and all other high officials. If the great chief of the whites obeys the laws the chiefs of the Indians should also. A good chief will make his people obey the judges and submit to the law. It is a bad chief who does otherwise. The Freat [sic] Father will not respect a chief who gives his people bad advice or sets them a bad example.

"You have three judges. We are told that they are good and sensible men. We know them, and we say that they are good men; all of them. When they try a case they should all talk together and try to do exactly right. If two think one way and one another way, the two must govern. This is the way with the white people. No man is perfect, and all men, however good, may make mistakes; but when the judges decide, that is the end of it all and all should stand by their word. The Great Father has given you these judges and laws to protect the poor and weak, for he feels as much for the poorest and weakest Indian as he does for the greatest chief among you. The use of whisky and cards is an evil to both the white people and the Indians. Good men among the whites advise their people not to get drunk and gamble. Indians should not do it. It is the cause of most of your troubles. Wise men among you know this, and he is a bad chief who advises his people to drink and gamble. The Great Father will not respect or favor such a chief. As to white men coming on to your reservation to live, I say that if your women will quite marrying white men you will have nothing to complain of on this account. Every one having Indian blood in his veins has equal rights on the reservation as long as he behaves himself, but men who do not obey the laws and regulations will not be allowed to remain; they will be sent away. This is the law. Some of the whites impose [oppose] whipping as a punishment for crime. All do not. You should not whip a sick man or a woman. This is wrong. It is unusual and cruel. I learn that you are mistaken about a pregnant woman having been whipped, and I am glad to hear it was not so. I think you should treat your women better than you do. You make them do much hard work that you ought to do yourselves. It is enough for a wife to take care of the children and the housework, and attend to the garden, and things like that. The hard work you ought to do yourselves. Among the whites the women are respected and protected, and we hope to see the day when you will do the same. Wherever we have been we have seen the women too much imposed upon. We would be glad to see this different.

"Among the whites, when a man murders another the law says he shall be hung. A man may kill another in order to save his own life, and if one man provokes another so as to put him in a great passion and in that passion he kills the other the punishment is less; but all who kill are punished, unless done in self-defense.

"But let me say to you that if you will all behave yourselves, and when you have troubles submit them to your judges and obey them, you will not have these troubles to talk about. If you will not do right you must be made to do, and punishments will follow. The good Indians have no reason to fear laws, judges, or policemen. It is only the bad who have these things to dread. This reservation is not for the Flatheads alone. It is for all of you and those who are to come in it. You should all be friends and have the same heart. This will make your strong. If you become divided, you will be weak. A big bunch of sticks all bound together by one cord is not easily broken; but take one stick at a time and all can soon be broken. This is the way with you. You have a good agent. The Great Father looks on him as one of the best in the service. That is the reason he has been agent so long. He tries to do right by the Great Father and right by you. Major Ronan does everything he can for you and he gives your people everything the Government sends here to you. He will not cheat you nor tell you a lie. We have seen what he has done for you, and what he is doing now. It is your duty and for your interest to respect and obey him in all things. He knows better than you what is best to be done for you and what is not best.

"If Major Ronan were to do an intentional wrong he would be sent away before many sun's rise.

"And now I have answered all your questions, and I hope you are satisfied with my answers. Soon we go away from you and I may not see you again, but it would give me great pleasure once more to visit your rich and beautiful reservation and find you all living on good farms, in good houses, well furnished, your lands well fenced, and your hills covered with stock. All these you can have if you will but do your duty and take advantage of the opportunities offered you."

Commissioner Andrews then addressed the council:

"My friends, as we are about to part, after having discharged the duty imposed upon us, and I trust to your entire satisfaction and to the satisfaction of the Great Father at Washington who sent us to your beautiful reserve — perhaps never again to meet — you to return to your homes and we to visit the Indians of a far distant State, I take the liberty of addressing a few words to you.

"There is no question before the Great Council at Washington in which the good men and women of the country take one-half the interest that they do in the Indian question, and that interest is not lessened as the years go by; but as the rights of the Indians are more fully understood, the people are demanding that the Great Council shall respect those rights and give to the Indians a part, at least, of what is their just due from the Government. In this connection I can assure you that the Indians of the Great Northwest, of which you, the old and brave confederated bands of Flathead, Pend d'Oreille, and Kootenai

Indians of the Jocko Reserve form such a large part, are not neglected by the Great Father and his Council, but in all their talks your rights and condition are duly considered, all your known wants supplied, and your future welfare and happiness closely studied.

"I know of no tribes of Indians in the United States, or elsewhere, who have so many things to be thankful for as the Indians of the Jocko Reservation, in the Territory of Montana. You are blessed with the finest climate to be found in America. You have on your reservation the grandest prairies of the Great Northwest; you have the purest streams of living water that man has ever seen; you have the most magnificent ranges of mountains in the world; you have one of the very best men in the service of the Government as your agent, Major Ronan, known as well in Washington as he is in Montana, as the great friend of your race, and I only repeat what I have heard many honest members of your tribes say since we came among you, and I have no doubt every Indian on the Jocko Reservation joins in the wish, 'we want him always.'

"You also have to guide you to the happy hunting-ground of the great hereafter good and noble fathers of your church, who voluntarily left their homes and loved ones in far distant lands to spend the remainder of their lives in promoting your present and future welfare. They have also established here at Saint Ignatius Mission schools for the education and civilization of your children, which are not excelled by any schools for the education of white children anywhere in the United States.

"Where, then, I ask, is there a people more blessed than you? With all the comforts of civilized life, with good health and such happy surroundings, with such brave and manly men as Arlee, of the Flatheads; Michael, of the Pend d'Oreilles; and Aeneas, of the Kootenais, as your chiefs, what more can you ask to make your lives one continuous scene of happiness. Then, my friends, place your hands upon the plow, raise up the wheat, the corn, the oats, and the potatoes, and your hearts will be glad. But do not, I pray you, raise up the whisky bottle to your lips, for it will make your hearts sad. Whisky is your curse, as it is the curse of the white man; it has brought down to early graves more brave, strong, and noble sons of the forest by far than the bullet ever did; it destroys the Indian's manhood while living, and takes from him all the happiness God intended he should enjoy. You had better by far be bitten by rattlesnakes and die of their poison than to drink the whisky sold in this northwestern country and die from its poison.

"We are now about to take our leave of you, and should the Great Council at Washington approve the agreement which we have this day made with you, you nor your children will, I trust, never have cause to regret that the Great Father sent us to you."

Document 73

Crimes on the Reservation

May 25, 1887

Source: "Notes from Flathead Reservation," *Missoula County Times*, May 25, 1887, page 3, c. 4.

Editors' note: This newspaper correspondent emphasized the problem of crime on the reservation in 1887.

Notes from Flathead Reservation.

The Arlee correspondent of the Helena *Independent* writes:

A few days ago two deputy sheriffs went over on the Flathead reservation to arrest a young Indian for horse stealing. The fellow had stolen a horse from another Indian and sold it to a white man. The real owner replevined the horse, thus exposing the theft. The two deputies found their Indian but they did not arrest him. He concluded not to be arrested.

A stepson of Chief Arlee was found dead this week. He had got full of whisky and been thrown from his horse, resulting in fatal injuries.

A woman of the Flathead tribe not long ago died from the effects of being raped. Her assailant was a very bad Indian, who at one time was tried in the district court for murder, but released on the ground that he had had an Indian trial and that he should not twice be placed in jeopardy for the same crime. The murder was a cold blooded one, but his technical exoneration was according to treaty rights, as he had been tried according to Indian customs. He has not yet been arrested for his latest crime.

Document 74

Duncan McDonald Relates A Story
of Wild Horse Island
June 15, 1887

Source: "Wild Horse Island," *Missoula County Times*, June 15, 1887, page 3, col. 5.

Editors' note: This story of Wild Horse Island in Flathead Lake was compiled from several sources, including Duncan McDonald. There was no way to tell how much the story was changed by the *Missoula County Times* writer.

"Wild Horse Island."
A Scrap of Missoula County's Romantic Indian History.

One of the largest bodies of land in Flathead lake is known as Wild Horse Island, and in connection with it is a singular Indian legend.

According to this legend — and we have as authority Duncan McDonald and others as thoroughly posted — it was about one hundred years ago when an Indian led a large and beautiful black mare across the ice and left her on this island. In the following spring the mare gave birth to a horse colt, and in few years from these two as a beginning the horses began to multiply on this island. Having a natural aversion to water and ice, the horses remained upon the island through successive seasons, until there was a large band of them. They were all black and were a large and powerful species.

About fifty years ago a party of Blackfoot Indians who were at war with a neighboring tribe came down the Flathead river and followed the trail around the lake. They saw these horses on the island, and their own animals being inferior and fatigued, they determined to capture as many of the black horses as they desired for their own purposes. Accordingly rafts were constructed and a party of the Blackfeet rowed over to the island. They then found that the horses were wild as deer, but after a long chase most of the horses were driven into the lake. Some of the Indians got near enough to grab them by the tail and were thus towed across to main land.

But most of the wild horses made good their escape. They fled into the hills, and for years after they lived and multiplied in the vicinity of the lake. One of their favorite spots was at the arm of the lake.

These powerful, handsome black horses are remembered by some of our old settlers. Less than twenty years ago the last of them was killed. They were a nuisance to the earliest settlers, as domestic horses got in with them, and all such the wild stallions kept with their bands.

Document 75

Bendois, Accused Indian Horse Thief, Captured

October 7, 1887

Source: "They Captured Him," *The New North-West* (Deer Lodge, Mont.), October 7, 1887, page 3, col. 4.

Editors' note: Much of the news making it out to the white public about the tribes in the 1880s dealt with law and order. See also article about Bendois' pardon on March 19, 1886. The horse Bendois was accused of stealing was owned by a mixed blood tribal member.

They Captured Him.
"Bendois," an Indian Horse Thief, Arrested.

On Tuesday Sheriff Heffernin and Deputy Baucus, of Missoula, came up to Deer Lodge and stated to Sheriff Coleman they would like to have assistance in capturing an Indian horse thief in camp down the river. His name is "Bendois," and he has already been in the penitentiary for stealing horses, under a three years' sentence, but was pardoned out last winter by Governor Hauser on representations made by Chief Arlee. It seems his old propensity got the better of him again and he recently stole two horses from a half-breed named Finley, at the Jocko Agency. The officers followed him up and recovered the horses he had sold near Bear Mouth. They then "located" him at a camp about six miles below Garrison, where there were eighteen other "bucks," and as the Missoula officers have had some trouble in making arrests of these fellows in Missoula county, they thought it wise not to give them any the best of it here. Sheriff Coleman, Deputy Hatton, and Frank and James Conley, of the Prison Guards, joined them, and they proceeded in a wagon down to their camp. One of the Indian party had been met on the road and he was left under guard at Geerdt's, so the camp would not be apprised of their coming — as it was not. They rode into them and spied their man. He knew the officers, also Frank Conley, and gave himself up without any resistance whatever — which was just as well for him, as the officers went prepared for trouble. The Missoula officers took him to that county and the Deer Lodge officers returned home. Parties who saw the other Indians after the arrest say they appeared very much excited, but whether in sympathy with Bendois or glad he had been captured, could not be told. The party were to be in Deer Lodge yesterday, *en route* to Butte.

Document 76

Accused Indian Murderer Killed on Flathead Reservation September 19, 1888

Source: "Death of Koonsa," *The Weekly Missoulian*, September 19, 1888, page 3, col. 3.

Editors' note: See the newspaper articles between June 1882 and January 1883 for a full account of the trial of Koonsa in the United States Court. By the late 1880s, the Montana newspapers mainly paid attention to reservation affairs that involved law and order.

Death of Koonsa.
The Career of a Wild and Wooly Indian Desperado.

A Flathead Agency correspondent gives the following account of the killing of Koonsa, the notorious desperado, together with a short sketch of his life:

The killing of an Indian or half-breed, by the name of Koonsa, by a Kallispel Indian, on the Flathead reservation, occurred on Wednesday of last week. A quarrel arose between the two Indians while gambling, near the mouth of the Jocko, when Koonsa who had terrified all the reservation Indians for the past ten years, made a break for his opponent, but was shot through the heart by him and died almost instantly. Some six years ago Koonsa created quite a sensation in this portion of the country by the deliberate murder of Fsank [Frank] Maringo, a half-breed Indian, who resided near the Flathead agency, with his wife. Maringo was well known at the time of his murder, having been interpreter at Fort Missoula during Joseph's Nez Perce war. It appeared that Koonsa was infatuated with the wife of Maringo, and having shot her husband, with gun in hand, ordered Maringo's wife, under penalty of being shot, to mount and go with him. This the woman refused to do, stating that she preferred to die with her husband. The cowardly murderer then raised his gun, which was caught by the woman, and in the struggle for possession the weapon fell to the floor and was immediately grasped by the woman. Koonsa then fled into the darkness, and to the mountains. He returned in a day or two from the mountains, and well mounted and heavily armed, kept aloof and defied arrest. Major [Peter] Ronan finally succeeded in his capture by a posse of Indians. He was taken to Chief Arlee's house, and without consulting

Agent Ronan, Koonsa was given a trial under tribal laws and was sentenced by the Indians to a short term in the reservation jail and to pay a fine of ten head of horses, to be given to the widow and child of Maringo. Ronan felt that a redhanded murderer should be more severely dealt with, and demanded the prisoner, at the same time ordering a team to be hitched up, into which he ordered Koonsa, and placed a pair of handcuffs on the murderer. With a driver he went to Missoula and delivered Koonsa up to the authorities of Missoula county. Several months afterwards a trial was given Koonsa in Deer Lodge, Judge Galbraith presiding. The case was thrown out of court on the ruling under the United States laws that Koonsa, having been tried by the Indian laws and placed in jeopardy and judgment passed, he could not again be held answerable. Koonsa was then turned loose and has been, ever since, a terrible desperado on the reservation, drinking, gambling, fighting, boasting of having killed another man in addition to Maringo. The crime of murder has on more than one occasion been committed by Indians since the acquittal of Koonsa by the United States court. The murderer of Frank Maringo has paid the penalty of his crime at the hands of an Indian in a dispute over other matters, but should he have had a fair trial in the courts of justice years ago, he would certainly have hung, and thus spared the Indians of the reserve and the settlers at the head of Flathead Lake from the terror of a red-handed Indian desperado.

Document 77

Inspection Report of Flathead Agency

October 20, 1888

Source: Excerpt from E. D. Bannister to Secretary of the Interior, October 20, 1888, U.S. Department of the Interior, "Reports of Inspection of the Field Jurisdictions of the Office of Indian Affairs, 1873-1900," National Archives Microfilm Publication M1070, roll 11, Flathead Agency, 5261/88.

Editors' note: This inspection report includes details about farmers and ranchers on the reservation in 1888, and law and order. The sections on government owned animals and buildings have not been reproduced here. The mixed bloods and white men married to Indian wives had the largest farms and ranches, but in 1888 many full blood Indians seem to have had smaller farms. Law and order problems dominated the news from the reservation in the late 1880s.

Helena M.T. Oct 20, 1888

The Hon.
The Secretary of the Interior
Sir —

I have the honor to make this report of the affairs of Flathead Agency M.T.

The Indians belonging to this Agency are Charlo's band of Bitterroot Flatheads numbering one hundred and eighty nine, residing off the reservation in Bitterroot valley, and the confederated tribes of Flatheads, Pen d'Oreillés & Kootenais numbering eighteen hundred and twenty nine living on the reservation. There are four hundred and forty two children of School age on the reserve, and forty two in Charlos band. While many Indians and most of the halfbreeds are making good progress in farming and in husbanding cattle and horses, there is a large number of full bloods who have no visible means of support and who lead a lawless, indolent life — their principal occupation being gambling and trafficing in, and drinking, whiskey. There are one hundred and eighty farms on the reservation, worked by about two hundred and thirty families half breeds and s....men included. There was about seven thousand acres cultivated the past season in grain, potatoes and garden vegetables and about three thousand acres in hay. The yield of all crops was good and will exceed the yield of last year, when the yield was forty three thousand bushels, of wheat and forty seven thousand bushels oats.

Among the larger farmers are:

Full blood Indians.

Chief Machel — 60 acres fenced 50 acres cultivated
Chief Patte — 80 acres fenced 30 acres cultivated
Chief Joseph — 200 acres fenced 50 acres cultivated
Louie Chqanta — 80 acres fenced 20 acres cultivated
Louie Sax — 80 acres fenced 18 acres cultivated
Samuel — 140 acres fenced 75 acres cultivated
Francis — 100 acres fenced 60 acres cultivated
Piente — 60 acres fenced 40 acres cultivated
Felix — 400 acres fenced 50 acres cultivated
Sabine — 80 acres fenced 30 acres cultivated
Louis Nchluso — 100 acres fenced 25 acres cultivated
Antoine Jim — 50 acres fenced 20 acres cultivated
Adalaide (widow) — 60 acres fenced 30 acres cultivated

Half Breeds

Charles Allard — 1000 acres fenced 100 acres cultivated
Mechel Pablo — 1200 acres fenced 180 acres cultivated
Abram Finley — 420 acres fenced 95 acres cultivated
James Mechel — 240 acres fenced 65 acres cultivated
Albert Sloan — 200 acres cultivated 50 acres cultivated
Peter Finley — 160 acres fenced 45 acres cultivated
Oust Finley — 160 acres fenced 70 acres cultivated
Robt Irvine — 160 acres fenced 80 acres cultivated

S.... Men

B Dupuy — 640 acres fenced 95 acres cultivated
L. Xavier — 700 acres fenced 110 acres cultivated
D Polson — 320 acres fenced 80 acres cultivated
A McDonald — 640 acres fenced 65 acres cultivated
Jos Blodgett works Chief Arlee's farm 180 acres
Jos Couture 640 acres fenced 100 acres cultivated

Live Stock on reserve are

16000 head of Cattle
7000 head of Horses and Ponies
1500 head of Hogs
8000 Domestic Fowls
35 Head of Buffalo owned by Mechel Pablo
a majority of the Cattle are owned by half breeds and s.... men.

There are five hundred and twenty houses — Indian, Halfbreed and S....
men's — on the reserve, and there being only about two hundred and thirty
families farming, it is reasonable to assume that not to exceed one half of the
Indians living on the reservation are farming.

During the past three years forty seven families, one hundred and sixty
five Indians — (Charlos band,) have removed from Bitterroot valley to the
reservation and others have signified their intention to remove to the reservation
the coming spring. All of these Indians should be removed to the reserve as
they never will do any good while permitted to live in the Bitterroot valley.

Several families of Calispels — included in the treaty of April 21, 1887,
have removed to the reservation — five families worked at farming the past
season (on shares). Chief Victor with several families is now camped at Sand
Point waiting to hear from Washington relative to the Treaty, and anxious to
remove to the reservation. The delay in ratifying this Treaty is very unfortunate
to both the Government and the Indians.

The want of "Administration of Justice" is sorely felt by all progressive and
law-abiding Indians, and whites, living on this reservation, the "court of Indian
offences" being incompetent to cope with crime, and not willing to enforce the
regulations, within their jurisdiction.

Murder and theft are committed with almost brazen effrontery and the
traffic in Whiskey is conducted by Indians, and dissolute white men living
on the border of the reserve, in a bold and reckless manner, and the Agent is
absolutely powerless, under the circumstances, to preserve order or have the
law enforced. Pial, a Calispel Indian, murdered Koonsa, a Kootenai, at the
mouth of the Jocko river, about four weeks ago. Pial with Pierre Paul, Louie &
Benoit, full bloods, left the mouth of Jocko the following morning for Bonners
Ferry and has not been apprehended. Pierre Paul & Louie, full bloods, and
Laurent Finley, half breed, were implicated in the Killing of a white man at the
mouth of Jocko last fall, and Benoit was implicated in Killing a white man at
mouth of Jocko in the spring of 1887.

About three weeks ago the body of a Chinaman was found about three
quarters of a mile from the Agency — he had been beaten to death with rocks
— he was seen two days previous — about eight oclock in the evening —
walking toward the Agency.

Calispel Indians at Sand Point have murdered fifteen or twenty Chinamen
— Big Piel boasts of having Killed several.

Two Kootenais belonging to Eneas band were lynched by white settlers near
Demersville March 24, 1888, for murdering three white men (prospectors).
Louie, belonging to same band, was implicated in the murder, but escaped

to Bonners Ferry and has not been arrested. Eneas made no fuss about the
lynching of the two Indians as they had boasted of the Killing.

Among other desperate characters belonging to Eneas band of Kootenais
are — Jocko, Oostah, La Cass, Fox, and Louie, a Flathead, soninlaw [sic] to
Eneas, on September 28th last, Jocko went into the house of W H Gregg, at
Demersville, and drove Mrs Gregg out of the house at the point of a revolver.
He and other Indians have driven other white settlers from their houses and
plundered their houses.

On December 31st, last, Mr J. E. Clifford & wife of Demersville came
across the country through Dayton Creek country. Eneas and about thirty of
his Indians had a demijohn of whiskey sitting on a chair in Eneas house, and
all were drunk and drinking.

Indians get whiskey at French Town near Missoula — at Horse Plains on
N.P. Ry just outside west line of reserve — at Thompsons Falls, west of Horse
Plains, and at several other places, among which is Missoula where full blood
Indians buy and drink whiskey right at the bar, in Saloons.

Unless a stop is put to this whiskey traffic, and drinking, serious trouble
will surely result therefrom, and the protection of white settlers residing in
the surrounding country, and of the progressive and law-abiding Indians on
the reserve, demand that the crimes committed during the past three years be
thoroughly investigated by the Department of Justice, and that all criminals be
punished to the fullest extent of the law.

The prime reason why Agent Ronan is powerless in the premises is: The
decisions of the Courts has been such as to encourage the Indians in lawlessness,
as I learn: Judge Galbreath discharged Koonsa for Killing Marengo — for the
reason that Koonsa had been tried by Chief Arlee — who had settled the case
by Koonsa giving Marengo's family some ponies.

One Smith — white man — sold Red Arm — full blood, a bottle of
Whiskey at Missoula. John Higgins, Under sheriff of Missoula County; loaned
Red Arm the money and saw Smith give him the bottle of whiskey. He also
took the whiskey away from Red Arm in Smiths presence. The whiskey was
produced in Court and the facts proven, but Judge DeWolfe discharged Smith
because of the conspiracy of Higgins.

Laurent Finley, half breed, drew a Knife on Agent Ronan at Arlee Station
in the spring of 1887. he was arrested and taken to Military prison at Missoula,
but was released in three weeks.

In my opinion the situation necessitates the appointment of a good brave
man as deputy U.S. Marshall at Horse Plains, also the same Kind of a man
at Missoula, and the stationing of two (2) companies of Cavalry at, or near,
Demersville, and one company at the Agency for the purpose of enforcing

law and order and to enable Agent Ronan to establish and maintain proper discipline on the reservation. The reasons for the necessity of troops at or near Demersville are: Tobacco Plains and Bonners Ferry are a rendezvous for the murderers thieves and renegades belonging to the different tribes of Indians living in this section of the country. Tobacco Plains is eighty miles north from Demersville near the British line. Bonners Ferry is thirty three miles north from Kootenai Station N.P. Ry and about thirty miles south from the British Line. Dayton Creek — where Eneas band of Kootenais are located (on reserve) is about thirty five miles south from Demersville, Kootenai Pass, through which Indians must pass in going to and from Eneas Camp, Bonners Ferry and Tobacco Plains, is only ten miles north from Demersville. The trail to Eneas band being within a mile of Demersville. Troops stationed as I have suggested, at or near Demersville, could guard and protect the country specified until such time as the Department may remove all Indians from Tobacco Plains and Bonners Ferry, and place them on some reservation, which I earnestly recommend for your consideration. There are about two hundred Kootenais, besides the lawless Calispels, Colvilles & Kootenais heretofore cited, living between Bonners Ferry and the British line, and just across the line are about one hundred and seventy five "King George" Kootenais, same tribe. These Indians commit depredations on the one side, then cross over to the other side, and vice versa, to escape the law. The same circumstances obtain at Tobacco Plains, where there are Indians living on either side of the line. I am of the opinion that a permanent Military Post should be established near Demersville to prevent Indians from crossing and recrossing the boundary line at will, also for the protection of the white settlers in that section of the country, and to assist Agent Ronan in maintaining order and in Keeping his Indians on the reservation. . . . .

Respectfully submitted
E. D. Bannister
Inspector

Document 78

Case of Insanity on the Reservation

October 27, 1888

Source: "A Crazy Indian," *Missoula Gazette* (weekly), October 27, 1888, page 4, col. 3.

Editors' note: In 1888 insanity was considered a law and order problem on the reservation.

A Crazy Indian.
One of the Government Wards Brought Down from Arlee.

For some time past an Indian boy about 19 years of age has been terrifying passengers on the Northern Pacific trains who occasionally stepped off the cars at Arlee for a brief view of the country from the station platform, by snatching off their hats, gathering them in his arms for a "rough and tumble" and other such amusements as would naturally lead the unsophisticated to believe that they were indeed in the "wild west" and were confronted by a typical savage.

However, the boy has been considered harmless until quite recently, when his increasing strength and growth has demonstrated the danger of his peculiarities and made his confinement necessary. Accordingly Major [Peter] Ronan brought him down from the agency yesterday, and to-day before Judge Anderson he was adjudged a lunatic by a Jury consisting Dr. [L. H.] Choquette, Abbot Hodge and Tom. McGrade and will be taken to the insane asylum for safe keeping.

The unfortunate's name is Francis Matt, a son of Baptist Matt, formerly a resident in the Bitter Root country, and was demented by an injury to his head when a small child. Henry Matt, his cousin, accompanied Major Ronan and is invaluable in controlling the wild man.

Document 79

Chief Arlee Complains About Indian Court and Police
January – May 1889

Source: "Arlee Objects," *The Weekly Missoulian*, January 9, 1889, page 3, col. 3; "Frightful Atrocities," *The Weekly Missoulian*, May 1, 1889, page 3, col. 3; Peter Ronan, *Justice to Be Accorded to the Indians: Agent Peter Ronan Reports on the Flathead Indian Reservation, Montana, 1888-1893*, ed. Robert J. Bigart (Pablo, Mont.: Salish Kootenai College Press, 2014), pages 34-35.

Editors' note: Chief Arlee and some of his followers bitterly objected to the government sponsored Indian police and courts on the reservation. Agent Peter Ronan attributed Arlee's complaints to his jealousy about the loss of law and order powers previously held by the traditional chiefs.

Arlee Objects.
Whipping by the Wholesale on the Flathead Reservation.

Chief Arlee came in to the *Missoulian* Monday so as to have made public certain reforms which he proposes to inaugurate on the reservation. He is intent on abolishing some barbaric customs that have been in vogue there for a long time. According to his statement, the Indians, both men and women, are whipped in a merciless manner for various offences. Recently, it is claimed, men and women have been beaten cruelly and out of all reason. When charged with offences, they are brought in by the Indian police, and alleged justice meted out in accordance with the present Indian rules.

Chief Arlee proposes to have the Indian prison moved from the Mission up to the Agency. He proposes to have all Indians charged with offences tried as at present, but punished with fines and imprisonment, just as white people are off the reservation. He also proposes to have the same rules and regulations apply to whites when on the reservation.

This is the reform he has started in to accomplish, and it looks reasonable and just.

* * * * * * * *

Frightful Atrocities.

The old and venerable Chief Arlee came in to see the *Missoulian* yesterday in company with others from the reservation to complain about the methods of punishment employed on the reservation. He made serious complaint about these things some months ago, but it seems the same inhuman forms of punishment are still in vogue as authorized by the prevailing forms of punishment. The chief's right hand man informs us that only last week an Indian who had broke jail was hung up by his hands and kept there for forty-eight hours. An Indian woman who is supposed to have deserted her husband was given 120 lashes and is now lying in a precarious condition and her recovery is extremely doubtful. Chief Arlee wants all offenders to be justly punished, but not in this inhuman and barbaric custom of 400 years ago. He wants them punished just as white people are punished; no more and no less. It seems as though someone should look into these things and put a stop to such cruel and uncalled for atrocities.

* * * * * * * *

United States Indian Service,
Flathead Agency, M. T.,
May 1st, 1889.

The Hon. Commissioner of Indian Affairs
Washington, D.C.
Sir:

It is my pleasant duty to report from this Agency, that during the month of April, the Indians have been very busy planting their crops and have, already, got in a very much larger acreage of wheat and oats, potatoes and all Kinds of garden seeds, than ever before. Extensive meadows of timothy have also been seeded. The orchards already planted by the Indians show vigorous thrift, and some of the trees are in blossom, greatly to their delight, as they expect to gather this season their first apples, plums, cherries, etc.

Snow fell very lightly in the mountains last winter which will cause low water and a scarcity for irrigation. The irrigation ditch is being put in the best possible condition to catch the water flow, and, I trust, with spring rains the crops will not suffer. Very few of the Indians are away from the reservation, and they constitute an element of young loafers, gamblers and drunkards, who cannot be restrained outside of prison walls. This is the class, who, backed by Arlee, Chief of Flatheads, make all the annoyance and disturbance on this reservation. Arlee has always bitterly opposed the Court of Indian Offences, the Judges and the Indian police, because he imagines it takes away from him full swing of arbitrary power. The vicious and the law-breakers are his only adherents now, and they are doing all in their power to break up the force of police, who do the best they can to suppress the vice of illegal cohabitation, drunkeness and gambling.

Soon as crops are planted attention will be turned to the whitewashing of fences and buildings at the Agency, and also the painting of roofs. The new matching and planing machine has arrived and soon as time will permit, will be put into place and in full running order.

I have the honor herewith to forward sanitary report and report of funds and indebtedness for the month of April, also report of Farmer and have the honor to be

Your obedient servant,
Peter Ronan
U.S. Indian Agent.

Document 80

Grand Joe Refuses to Disclose Whiskey Source

February 16, 1889

Source: "Grand Joe Will Not Tell," *The Helena Independent*, February 16, 1889, page 3, col. 1.

Editors' note: Questions of law and order and jurisdiction on the reservation were important even in 1889.

Grand Joe Will Not Tell
Whisky for the Flatheads.
An Indian Who Stood Punishment Rather Than Tell Where He
Obtains His Supply of Rum.

Arlee, M.T., Feb. 12. — [Special Correspondence of the Independent] — The Indian police at the Flathead reservation got a pointer the other night that a member of the tribe went to Missoula for a supply of whiskey, and when the west bound train arrived at Arlee the Indian police arrested the suspected man, who proved to be Grand Joe, who had a gallon jug of whiskey with him. Joe was taken by the police to Chief Arlee's house and interrogated as to where he purchased the fire water, but the Indian refused to inform upon the man who sold him the whiskey, preferring to go to the Indian jail and serving out a term in prison, or to receive from fifty to one hundred lashes rather than testify against the whiskey vender. The Indian police have taken the matter in hand and are determined not to rest until they find evidence to prosecute dealers who sell whiskey to their people.

Grand Joe took a change of venue from the Indian judges and appealed his case to Agent [Peter] Ronan. In presence of a full council of Indians, Grand Joe confessed to having brought whiskey upon the reservation, and also stated that he got the liquor from a middle man — a white man who makes a business of the traffic. This individual takes the money with which to purchase the whisky from the Indian and is paid one dollar as commission for each gallon he purchases. He shows the Indian a hiding place, and when the whisky is procured it is deposited in the cache, where the Indian finds it and rides off. In this way the Indians procure all they want of the vilest stuff. Instead of imprisonment or the lash Joe asked that he might be fined a mare and a colt for breaking the law. This fine was imposed upon him by the Indian judges as requested. The mare and colt will be sold by the Indian judges and the proceeds applied to charitable purposes among the Indians.

In a private letter from Washington Major Ronan is informed that Hon. J. K. Toole's bill for the sale of Bitter Root Indian lands passed the house on the 6th of February, and the bill is so particularly favorable to the Indians that the writer thinks there is no question about its passing the senate. This news will be hailed with pleasure by the citizens of Bitter Root valley and the residents of Missoula county. The Indians will be glad of the opportunity to sell their patented land in the Bitter Root valley and to remove to the Jocko or Flathead reservation.

In regard to the recent order from the United States Indian agent at the Crow agency, requiring United States Marshall Kelly to remove therefrom certain white men married to s....s, Maj. Ronan, of the Flathead Indian agency stated that in 1886, in answer to a letter from him, addressed to the Indian office in Washington, he received substantially the following reply: "In regard to your communication, dated April 13, 1886, with reference to white men married to women of Indian blood, in which you inquire if an Indian woman who marries a white man loses her tribal rights by that action, and if it is proper for the agent to oppose the man in taking up a farm or living upon the reservation. In reply I have to state that by marriage with a white man an Indian woman does not forfeit her tribal rights. The husband acquires no rights in the tribe. It has been usual to allow such men to reside with their families on the reservation, so long as they conduct themselves properly, and their presence is not objectionable to the Indians. If they are unfit persons to reside in the Indian country, or their conduct or example in any way is injurious to the Indians, they should be removed from the reservation. If they are men of good character and their conduct such as to set a good example to Indians, I see no objection to their remaining on the reservation and cultivating farms for the support of their families, it being understood that all the interests in such farms and improvements are vested in the wife — and that no more land must be taken by any one person than his wife is entitled to as a member of the tribe. All white men living with Indian women should be required to be legally married, and upon refusal should be immediately expelled from the reservation."

Document 81

Accused Indian Murderer Arrested

May 1889

Source: "A Red Desperado," *The Helena Independent* (daily), May 14, 1889, page 1, col. 7; "Finley Caught," *Great Falls Tribune*, May 23, 1889, page 1, col. 3; "Finley Leaves," *Great Falls Tribune* (semi-weekly), May 29, 1889, page 1, col. 5.

Editors' note: The pursuit and arrest of Larra Finley, accused Indian murderer, emphasized law and order problems on the reservation in the late 1880s. For a biographical sketch of Lawrence Finley's career see Peter Ronan, *"A Great Many of Us Have Good Farms": Agent Peter Ronan Reports on the Flathead Indian Reservation, Montana, 1877-1887*, ed. Robert J. Bigart (Pablo, Mont.: Salish Kootenai College Press, 2014), pages 400-401. For Chief Arlee's and Finley's complaints about imprisonment conditions on the reservation see the articles above of interviews by *The Weekly Missoulian*.

A Red Desperado.
Missoula Authorities on the Trail of a Half-Breed Murderer
from the Flathead Reserve.
Some of the Crimes of Larra Finlay, Who Once Threatened
Major Ronan's Life.
Imprisoned Several Times, But Each Time Released for Want of Evidence
— The Cause of Arlee's Complaint.

Missoula, May 13. — [Special to the Independent] — On Friday, the 9th inst., the following was wired to the sheriff of this county, and also to the sheriff of Choteau county:

> Arlee, May 9th. — Arrest Larra Finlay, a half-breed murderer from this reservation. Will probably now be found with Peter Finlay, who is now on his way to Sun River and Fort Benton, over the trail by Haystack Butte with a band of horses. Peter Finlay is all right, but get Larra. His upper lip is split. He talks English.
>
> Ronan, U.S. Indian Agent.

Baptist Piere Finlay and his wife Sophie came to the agency and made the following statement to Maj. [Peter] Ronan:

Several days ago I started with my wife to go to Tobacco plains, from the Jocko reservation. On my way up from the head of the lake I met two Indians with their wives coming from Tobacco plains. They asked myself and wife to turn back with them, which we did. We camped near Demarsville, and a short distance from Egan, on Friday, the 3d of May. It rained all day Saturday, and we remained in our lodge. In the evening Larra Finlay, a mixed-breed, accompanied by a Kootenai Indian, called Jock, came into the lodge and brought two bottles of whisky, and all commenced drinking. Tom, one of, the Indians who camped with us, was outside of the lodge. When he came in Larra commenced to talk to him, when Jocko put his hand on Larra's mouth, and told him to shut up — that he, Jocko, would do the talking. Then all got to their feet and I took hold of Jocko to prevent a fight. I threw Jocko down, when Larra jumped outside of the lodge and picked up a club with which he hit Jocko on the head while I had him down. The stick broke. I said, "don't hit him again — you will kill him," and let go of Jocko to prevent Larra from repeating the blow, but he struck Jocko twice with a piece of stick he held in his hand, and killed him."

Larry Finley is a noted outlaw. In 1887 he committed a rape upon an Indian woman, and from his brutal treatment she died. He was arrested by the Indian police and put in jail at the reservation. From there he escaped, and meeting Major Ronan, who was on his way to Flathead lake, with his family, he followed him into the station at Arlee, and demanded if he, the agent, was looking for him. Ronan made an evasive reply until he was enabled to grab a gun, when he leveled it upon Larra and made him throw up his hands. Larra was then securely tied with a rope and Ronan got on a freight train and delivered him up to Col. Horace Jewett of the Third infantry then in command at Fort Missoula. Ronan reported his action to the Indian office and was ordered to turn Larra over to the civil authorities for trial. Under date of September 26, 1887, Agent Ronan wrote to the authorities in Washington as follows: "I would respectfully report that I ordered the release of Larra Finlay from confinement at Fort Missoula. The woman he abused has since died, and as I can not obtain evidence upon which he would probably be convicted I had the prisoner released. I arrested and conveyed the outlaw to Fort Missoula for safe keeping, because after he escaped from the Indian jail he made a personal attack upon me and threatened to take my life for having insisted upon his arrest by the Indian police for committing rape upon an Indian woman, and from the effects of his brutal treatment asted [sic] above the woman has since died."

Having been released from the military jail, Larra came back to the reservation, a terror to all respectable Indians. From the reserve he went to Chewela, in Washington territory, stole two horses and eloped with the wife of an Indian of that place. He returned to the reservation, when he was arrested by the Indian police and compelled to give up horses in place of the ones he stole in Washington territory. In the mean time the festering body of a murdered white man was found on the Jocko river, and Larra was suspected of the crime. In order to prevent his escape until evidence could be procured against him he was put in jail and his hands were tied in the absence of a guard. This is the villain whom Arlee recently complained of being brutally treated by the police, and took to Missoula to make the complaint a half-breed who was in jail last winter for killing a Kootenai Indian, but released by the Indians on the plea of self-defense. Having been released he brought a supply of whisky to the reserve, and for that offense was jailed by the Indian police, escaped and accompanied Arlee to Missoula to make sensational and lying complaints against the cruelty of the Indian police, particularly in the case of the murderer Sam [Larry] Finlay, who got away from the Indian jail only to commit the crime of another murder, and for which he is now being hunted down.

* * * * * * * *

Finley Caught.
Al Sloane Captures the Alleged Murderer.
An Exciting Chase that Seems Like a Dime Novel Adventure —
How Sloan Managed to Carry off Finley.

Considerable surprise was caused among the sheriff and his officials when word came yesterday that James [Larra] Finley had been arrested for murder. It appears that acting on some intimation Sheriff Downing received, his deputy, Joe Hamilton, proceeded to Sun River and there met Finley and Al Sloane. The latter had tracked the alleged murderer for some time.

The crime with which Finley is charged was committed about a month ago. Finley, two Indians and a "tin-horn" gambler were together on the Flathead agency when a quarrel arose, followed by a fight. In the encounter it is alleged that Finley killed an Indian and fled. Major Ronan promptly issued a circular to sheriffs and Al Sloane set out in quest of Finley. Sloane knows all about Indian habits. This aided him in tracking Finley, whom he found in the country north of Sun River. Sloane, who is a powerful man of determined look, took steps to secure his prisoner and accompanied him to town where he was safely "jailed" while Sloane spent the evening in observing the fine streets and the attractions at the Park theatre.

The story of the pursuit and capture of Finley reads like a romance.

At the instance of Major Ronan, Sloane set out in quest of Finley. He provided himself with horses and hired some half-breeds to go with him. He crossed the range and pushed forward to the Piegan agency, enduring much hardship on the way and incurring considerable expense for the half-breeds knew that he needed them and they became costly companions. At length Sloane got a clue to the whereabouts of the fugitive. He kept on the trail until the other day he found himself near an Indian camp. On going nearer he saw about 30 Indians, assembled. Among them was one whom his sharp eyes saw was Finley, although he was disguised in Indian clothes. Sloane resolved to lose no time. Accompanied by two half-breeds, he dashed boldly into the crowd and seized Finley. The Indians were amazed and were about to defend Finley when Sloane hustled him to a horse, compelling him to mount and then rode off. Sloane hired two more trusty half-breeds, placed them in charge of Finley, and then set out for this city. Resolving to keep clear of Indians he made a long circuit and came here by way of St. Peter's Mission. Here he informed Sheriff Downing of his success and asked him to go back with him and arrest Finley. The sheriff sent his efficient deputy, Joe Hamilton, who returned last evening with his prisoner.

Laurent Finley is about 30 years old and is stout enough to weigh 170 pounds. He comes from Joco and is a half-breed of light complexion. It is alleged that he was concerned in the murder of two prospectors in June last year.

Sloane lives on the reservation and owns a band of horses.

A telegram announcing Finley's arrest has been sent to Missoula.

* * * * * * * *

Finley Leaves.
He Goes with Major Ronan to the Scene of His Misdeeds.
More Light on Finley's Bad Career.
He Tried to Kill Major Ronan, but He Got the Drop on Him — Recent Murder.

Major Ronan left for Helena and Missoula today with Larra Finley, the half-breed who is charged with murder. When Major Ronan saw him in jail yesterday Finley said that he killed the Indian in self-defense.

It appears from Major Ronan's knowledge of Finley that he is a noted outlaw. In 1887 he committed rape upon an Indian woman, and from his brutal treatment she died. He was arrested by the Indian police and put in jail at the reservation. From there he escaped, and meeting Major Ronan, who was on his way to Flathead lake, with his family, he followed him into the station at Arlee and demanded if he, the agent, was looking for him. Major Ronan made him an evasive reply until he was enabled to grab a gun, when he leveled it upon Larra and made him throw up his hands. Larra was then securely tied with a rope and Major Ronan got on a freight train and delivered him up to Col. Horace Jewett of the Third infantry then in command of Fort Missoula. Major Ronan reported his action to the Indian office and was ordered to turn Lara over to civil authorities for trial.

The woman died before the trial and Finley went scot free. He went back to the reservation, a terror to all respectable Indians. From the reserve he went to Chewela, in Washington territory, stole two horses and eloped with the wife of an Indian at that place. He returned to the reservation, when he was arrested by the Indian police and compelled to give up horses in place of the ones he stole in Washington territory. In the meantime, the festering body of a murdered white man was found on Joco river, and Finley was suspected of the crime. In order to prevent his escape until evidence could be procured against him, he was put in jail and his hands were tied in the absence of a guard. This is the villain whom Arlee recently complained of being brutally treated by the police.

Finley's Recent Crime.

Finleys are as plenty as strawberries in Missoula. One Baptist Finley gave Major Ronan on May 9 the following account of the crime with which Larra Finley is now charged: "Several days ago I started with my wife to go to Tobacco plains, from the Jocko reservation. We camped near Demarsville. It rained all day Saturday, and we remained in our lodge. In the evening Larra Finley, a mixed breed, accompanied by a Kootenai Indian, called Jock, came into the lodge and brought two bottles of whisky, and all commenced drinking. Tom, one of the two Indians who camped with us, was outside of the lodge. When he came in Larra commenced to talk to him, when Jocko put his hand on Larra's mouth and told him to shut up — that he (Jocko) would do the talking. Then all got to their feet and I took hold of Jocko to prevent a fight. I threw Jocko down, when Larra jumped outside of the lodge and picked up a cub with which he hit Jocko over the head while I had him down. The stick broke, I said, 'don't hit him again — you will kill him,' and let go of Jocko to prevent Larra from repeating the blow, but he struck Jocko twice with the piece of wood he had in his hand and killed him."

Major Ronan spoke highly of the aid and courtesy he received from Sheriff Downing and his efficient deputy, Joe Hamilton. He also found Saul Yates accommodating.

Document 82

Council with Chief Eneas Relative to Whiskey Trade in Flathead June 8, 1889

Source: "Flathead Council," *The Helena Journal* (daily), June 19, 1889, page 1, col. 7; Peter Ronan, *Justice to Be Accorded to the Indians: Agent Peter Ronan Reports on the Flathead Indian Reservation, 1888-1893*, ed. Robert J. Bigart (Pablo, Mont., Salish Kootenai College Press, 2014), pages 42-45.

Editors' note: Two accounts of the June 8, 1889, council with Agent Ronan, Special Agent of the Department of Justice H. M. Marchant, Chief Eneas, and Chief Michelle emphasized Eneas' efforts to maintain peace with the white settlers in the Upper Flathead Valley. One was a newspaper account and the other was Ronan's report to the Commissioner of Indian Affairs. There was considerable overlap between the sources, but each has some new information. In 1888 a mob of white men had lynched two Kootenai Indians accused of murder and then surrounded the Kootenai camp at Dayton and threatened Eneas. Eneas kept calm and defused the situation so it did not lead to more bloodshed. As he said in this council, he worked hard to keep his young men out of trouble, but local whites sold them whiskey.

Flathead Council.
Major Ronan and Chief Eneas Have a High Old Time.

Ferry, Foot of Flathead Lake, Missoula County, June 14. — [Special correspondence of the Journal.] — One day last week your correspondent, accompanied by a friend, mounted on good horses, dashed along the verdant, flower-strewn Mission valley, with its buttresses of grassy hills, looking very beautiful in the clear morning sunlight. The huge bulk and craggy summits of the Mission mountains seemed loftier and more imposing than ever before, so distinct were all their gorges and precipices, their snow fields and fine forests and lofty peaks, snow-capped and broken — like the ocean lashed by a furious storm. Our journey lay through a lovely valley, in an atmosphere wonderfully perfumed by the myriads of wild flowers that made the prairie a variegated carpet of many colors. Arriving at the foot of the Flathead Lake, which lay gleaming like a sapphire in the bosom of the mountains, we found the encampment of

Major [Peter] Ronan, United States Indian agent for the confederated tribes of Flatheads, Kootenai and Pend d'Oreilles. The agent had two commodious tents and was accompanied by his three little sons. Captain Henry N. Marchant, special agent of the department of justice, Washington, D.C., H. A. Lambert, of the agency, Michel Revais, the agent's official interpreter, also a cook and teamster. An invitation was as cordially accepted as given, to join the camp, and in a jiffy the saddles were stripped from our animals by a bright looking Indian boy and nicely placed with our belongings beneath the shady boughs of a cottonwood tree. Here we passed the night after a supper of delicious lake trout, bacon, coffee, dried venison, yeast powder biscuit, etc.

Major Ronan had called an Indian council and a runner was sent to the Kootenai camp, which was far across the lake at a distant part of the reservation, to call the Indians together. On the morning of the 8th Chief Eneas, of the Kootenai tribe, and a number of his tribe were ferried across the Pend d'Oreille river, just where it takes its rise from the Flathead lake, and joined us in camp. At the ferry house of old Baptist Eneas, a council room was improvised with a table to write upon and chairs and benches for the agent and his party, while the Indians squatted around on the floor and outside of the door where they could overhear the talk. Your correspondent was invited to a seat at the table where he took notes of a portion of the proceedings. After the usual handshaking and greetings were over, Major Ronan addressed his interpreter:

"Tell Chief Eneas I agreed to meet him and his head men here two weeks ago, but one of his men was killed at the head of the lake, and I followed and captured the murderer at Great Falls, on the Missouri river, and that is the reason I did not get here on time. Now tell Eneas that I have very little to say, only what I am here for, and what Captain Marchant is here for. Tell him that for the last two years the drunkenness has been much worse than at any time since I came here, twelve years ago; also the debauchery of women by the young men of the tribes. It is my opinion that the beginning of all Indian trouble is whisky. When whisky comes on the reserve then commences all other crimes. I have asked from Washington the great father's assistance to put a stop to this whisky selling to Indians. The great father spoke to the judge or chief justice to send some one here to put a stop to it, and he has sent this gentleman, Captain Henry M. Marchant, special agent from the department of justice at Washington, to assist me in this effort to suppress the sale of whisky to the Indians. Now tell Eneas that something over a year ago two of his people were hung by a mob at the head of the lake; that though the Indians may have been guilty, no mob had a right to hang them. That is what the law is for, to punish crime; that is why taxes are paid; that is why we have judges, courts, sheriffs and jails; why we have law. In the eyes of the law a crowd of men who take a man and hang him are looked upon as criminals. It is the duty of Eneas or any of his men present, if they know the names of any of the men who did this hanging, to give their names to Captain Marchant. It is also the duty of Chief Eneas and his men, and also of the Pend d'Oreille chief, Michel, who is present, and his men, if they know, to give the names of any white men who are or have been guilty of selling whisky to Indians. If any present have bought whisky it is their duty to give names, times and place to Captain Marchant.

Now I have only to add that there is a big steer out in the corral, and some sugar, coffee, flour, etc., at my camp, and to send men after them and others to butcher the beef, and while the women are preparing the feast, Captain Marchant, through my interpreter, will talk with Eneas and Michel, and he and Mr. Lambert will take what evidence they may have to present.

Captain Marchant then spoke to interpreter as follows:

"Say to Eneas that the agent, Major Ronan, has fully explained to them my mission here. I came from Washington to put a stop to selling whisky by white men to Indians, and that I need their assistance, and without it it will be almost impossible for me to do it; but if they will give me their aid I will do my utmost to stop it. I am here for their good and if they will put confidence in me I will help them. Important business calls the major back to the agency. I shall go to the head of the lake and make investigation as to who is selling whisky to Indians, and other matters connected with the good of the Indians. Say to Eneas that I want to ask him a few questions now."

Chief Eneas here indicated his wish to speak.

"Before answering you I desire to say a few words: Michel, tell the agent when the great father first sent him to us he was much younger man than he is to-day. His children have grown up around him on our reservation, and I see one of his boys with him who was born in our country. I was also young and strong, I looked like a chief, I felt like a chief. In my youth our nation was at war with a great many tribes, and the last of our enemies that we made peace with were the Blackfeet. I was the war chief of my tribe and was called Big Knife. To-day we are at peace with all of our enemies. The Blackfeet are our friends, and some of their children are at school with our children at the mission. Until within a few years, there were few white people near our reservation. Now they surround us on all sides, thick almost as the leaves of the forest. When you came here there was only one white family living at Horse Plains; no white people at all at Thompson Falls; no miners in the Cœur d'Alenes, and where the big city of Spokane Falls now stands, I remember of but two white families living there. At the head of the Flathead lake, where you are now going, there was but one or two white men and no white families. Missoula had a small settlement of whites, but now it is a great big town — full of white people. In the days I speak of my young men could get but very little whisky, and none knew the taste of it but those who hung around your settlements. It is different to-day, they have acquired the habit and love the influence of whisky, and in spite of your laws, can procure all they can pay for. In the old times I would take my whip in my hand and chastise any of my Indians that broke the law either by getting drunk, or committing adultery, or any other crime, and they feared me and my authority the same as your children fear your authority and chastisement as a father when they do wrong. I could control my people then. Take the whip from my hand and I have no control. We have no good jail like the white people, no other mode of punishment in our camp, and the wild and dissolute young men laugh at talk when it is not followed by punishment. The heart of a white man must be very small if he cannot see the necessity of authority by a chief in an Indian camp; and when I lose the use of the whip I lose all power to control my people. I hope the chief who has come here from Washington will help us. I am now ready to answer his questions."

Captain Marchant requested the reporter to withdraw at this juncture of the proceedings and he gracefully complied with the request.

Joseph.

* * * * * * * *

United States Indian Service,
Flathead Agency,
June 12, 1889.

Hon. Commissioner of Indian Affairs
Washington, D.C.
Sir:

In compliance with the request of Captain Henry M. Marchant, Special Agent of the Department of Justice, I accompanied that gentleman to the Foot of Flathead Lake, on this reservation, where I called an Indian Council, for the purpose of obtaining Indian evidence against whisky trading whitemen, who make a business of selling whisky to Indians. Also to inquire into and get evidence against a mob of white men who took the law into their own hands and hung two Kootenai Indians of this reservation, and who after the hanging, with arms in their hands, surrounded the camp of Chief Eaneas, on this reservation, for the purpose of intimidation etc.

On the 8th of June the Indian Council met, and I herewith have the honor to submit a synopsis of the proceedings:

After the usual hand shaking and greeting were over Agent Ronan addressed his interpreter:

Tell Chief Eneas I agreed to meet him and his head men here two weeks ago, but one of his men was killed at the Head of the Lake, and I followed and captured the murderer at Great Falls, on the Missouri river, and that is the reason I did not get here on time.

Now tell Eneas that I have very little to say — only what I am here for and what Captain Marchant is here for. Tell him that for the last two years the drunkeness has been much worse then at any time since I came here — twelve years ago; also the debauchery of women by the young men of the tribes. It is my opinion that the beginning of all Indian trouble is whisky. When whisky comes on the reserve then commences all other crimes. I have asked from Washington the Great Fathers assistance to put a stop to this whisky selling to Indians. The Great Father ordered the Judge or Chief Justice to send some one here to put a stop to it, and he has sent this gentleman, Captain Henry M. Marchant, Special Agent from the Department of Justice, at Washington, to assist me in this effort to suppress the sale of whisky to the Indians.

Now tell Eneas, that something over a year ago two of his people were hung by a mob at the Head of the Lake; that though the Indians may have been guilty, no mob had a right to hang them. That is what the law is for — to punish crime; that is why taxes are paid — why we have Judges, Courts, Sheriffs and jails — why we have law! In the eyes of the law a croud [sic] of men who take a man and hang him are looked upon as criminals. It is the duty of Eneas or any of his men present, if they know the names of any of the men who did this hanging to give their names to Captain Marchant. It is also the duty of Chief Eneas and his men, and also of the Pend 'd Oreille Chief Michel, who is present, and his men, if they know, to give the names of any white men who are or have been guilty of selling whisky to Indians. If any present have bought whisky, it is their duty to give names, time and place to Captain Marchant.

Now I have only to add that there is a big steer in the corrall, and some sugar, coffee, flour etc., at my camp, and to send men after them and others to butcher the beef, and while the women are preparing the feast, Captain Marchant, through my interpreter will talk with Eaneas and Michel, and he and Mr. [Henry] Lambert will take what evidence they may have to present.

Captain Marchant to the Interpreter:

Say to Eneas that the Agent, Major Ronan has fully explained to them my mission here. I came from Washington to put a stop to selling whisky to Indians by whitemen, and that I need their assistance, and without it it will be almost impossible for me to do it; but if they will give me their aid I will do my utmost to stop it. I am here for their good and if they will put confidence in me I will help them. Important business calls the Major back to the Agency. I shall go to the Head of the Lake and make investigation as to who is selling whisky to Indians, and other matters connected with the good of the Indians. Say to Eneas that I want to ask him a few questions now.

Chief Eneas: Before answering you I desire to say a few words:

Michel [Revais, the interpreter], tell the Agent when the Great Father first sent him to us, he was a much younger man than he is to-day. His children have grown up around him on our reservation and I see one of his boys with him who was born in our country.

I was also young and strong — I looked like a Chief — I felt like a Chief. In my youth our Nation was at war with a great many tribes, and the last of our enemies that we made peace with were the Blackfeet. I was the War Chief of my tribe and was called Big Knife. To-day we are at peace with all of our enemies. The Blackfeet are our friends, and some of their children are at school with our children at the Mission. Until within a few years, there were few white people near our reservation. Now they surround us on all sides, thick almost as the leaves of the forest. When you came here there was only one white family living at Horse Plains. No white people at all at Thompson Falls; no miners in the Coer'd Alenes; and where the big city of Spokane Falls now stands I remember of but two white families living there. At the Head of the Flathead Lake where you are now going there was but one or two white men and no white families. Missoula had a small settlement of whites, but now it is a great big town — full of white people. In the days I speak of my young men could get but very little whisky — none knew the taste of it but those who hung around your settlement. It is different to-day! They have acquired the habit and love the influence of whisky, and in spite of your laws can procure all they can pay for. In old times I would take my whip in my hand and chastise any of my Indians that broke the law either by getting drunk or committing audultry [sic] or any other crime, and they feared me and my authority the same as your children fear your authority and chastisement as a father when they do wrong. I could controll my children then — I call all my tribe my children. Take the whip from my hand I have no controll. We have no good jails like the white people — no other mode of punishment in our camp, and the wild and desolute young men laugh at talk when it is not followed by punishment. The heart of a white man must be very small if he cannot see the necessity of authority by a chief in an Indian camp; and when I loose the use of the whip I loose all power to controll my people. I hope the Chief who has come here from Washington will help us. I am now ready to answer his questions.

Here the investigation and taking of evidence commenced, which I trust will soon lead to the arrest of guilty parties.

In reference to the remarks of Eneas about the use of the whip among the Indians, for the punishment of certain transgressions I would respectfully state that it has always been the rule of the tribes to use it. Captain Marchant made some objection to this as one of their modes of punishment; when the Judges and the policemen notified me that they would resign if they could not continue their own methods of punishment for crime. They claimed, with truth, that they had no good jail, and no other punishment to substitute that would strike terror where young men were guilty of drunkeness, running off with the wives of industrious Indians, debauching young girls of the tribes etc., etc. They also claim that they use the whip with moderation and practice no cruelty, and that the mere disgrace of being publicly flogged, however lightly, has more effect in keeping the young people straight than any other mode of punishment. I must say that I know of no act of cruelty practiced by the Indian Chiefs, Judges or Policemen, and all stories to that effect are mere exagerations. I have promised the Indians to submit the matter to the Hon. Commissioner of Indian Affairs, and if, after Captain Marchants report is received, by his Department, he decides to order the abolishment of the whip altogether I shall so notify the Indians.

I herewith have the honor to enclose vouchers for expenses incurred in calling and feeding the Indians during the council, and have the honor to be

Your obedient servant

Peter Ronan

United States Indian Agent.

Document 83

Missoula Sheriff Posse Kills Innocent Indian

June 24, 1889

Source: Peter Ronan, *Justice to Be Accorded to the Indians: Agent Peter Ronan Reports on the Flathead Indian Reservation, Montana, 1888-1893*, ed. Robert J. Bigart (Pablo, Mont.: Salish Kootenai College Press, 2014), pages 50-52; "The Posse Returns, *The Weekly Missoulian*, June 26, 1889, page 2, col. 3, page 3, col. 4-5.

Editors' note: Two accounts of the shooting of an innocent Indian by a white posse from Missoula on June 24, 1889, have survived. Unfortunately, both tell the story from the white viewpoint. Apparently, Sheriff Daniel J. Heyfron and a posse of white men came on the reservation to arrest two accused Indian murderers. They did not know what the accused looked like, but did shoot an Indian who ran as they approached. The dead Indian was not one of the murderers, and other Indians were understandably upset. The posse members were never punished for this murder. The newspaper account tried to justify shooting the Indian by claiming the Indian fired on the posse first.

United States Indian Service,
Flathead Agency, M.T.
June 27th, 1889.

Thos. H. Ruger
Brigadier General
Commanding Dept. Dakota
St. Paul, Minn.
Sir:

Under date of June 25th, 1889, I received a telegram from you in which it was stated you would be glad to have full statement of facts, including in addition to what was referred to in your telegram of the morning of the same date the facts as to the murder, when it took place, and the circumstances and to wire you at St. Paul. I replied briefly by telegraph but now will give you particulars by letter.

Under date of September 26th, 1888, P. H. Leslie, then Governor of Montana, received the following telegram from Washington:

"Can you give this Department any particulars concerning the alleged murder of Henry William Keys at Flathead, Montana?

(Signed) G. L. Rives
Acting Secretary of State."

Governor Leslie turned the matter over to me and I communicated with the authorities at Ottawa, and was informed by Hon. John Costigan, Minister of Inland Revenue, under the Dominion Government that the man who was reported to have been murdered and whose body was found near the mouth of the Jocko river, Flathead reservation, in July 1887, was reported to be William Henry Keys, of Ottawa. From the description and with the aid of Dr. Hedger, County Corner, I was enabled to report conclusively that the body found was not that of the person sought after by the Canadian authorities.

Recently a desperado, of mixed blood, named Lara Finley, murdered an Indian at the Head of the Flathead Lake, and I succeeded in having him arrested after a chase of several hundred miles and placed him in jail at Missoula.

Here Finley made the following confession which led to the issuance of warrants for the arrest of two Indians, who Killed the man who was supposed to be Keys, and also another man who was encamped with him:

Missoula, Montana,
May 27th, 1889.

Copy of
Statement of Lawrence Finlay relative to
Killing of two whitemen at Jocko river. My true name is Lawrence Finlay. I am 23 years of Age. One year ago last fall, July or later, below Duncan McDonalds, at mouth of Jocko river, I saw three full blood Indians shoot and Kill two whitemen who were in camp there. The whitemen were strangers. The Indians were Pierre Paul and La La See, the name of the other Indian I don't Know. I heard that he was some relative of Pierre Paul; the one whose name I don't Know did not do anything, although he was present. I was walking and heard 5 or 6 shots and when I got there the white men were dead. The Indians made me swear I would Keep it secret. They were going to Kill me at first. They made me swear 5 or 6 times. The Indians wanted me to shoot at the whitemen too so they could say I had a hand in it. The Indians told me they Killed the whitemen for revenge for the Killing of the Indian that Coombs Killed at Arlee.

Would have told Maj. Ronan, but they said they would Kill one of my brothers if I did. I went and told the Chiefs about it but they told me to Keep quiet as it would make trouble for the Indians. Koo-too-lay-uch, a young chief, said stay quiet and only tell it when questioned by proper authorities and then tell a Straight story. I can show spot where whitemen were camped. The Indians said afterwards that they threw the whitemen in the river, that they did not float far so they took them out and buried them (I did not see them). It was just dark when the Killing was done. I understand another Indian by the name of Peter saw Killing. He dresses like a half-breed and lives with a s.... near Horse Plains. He talks good English. I talked with him afterward. He stated that the Indian made him swear too. I did not see him there, I was only about 100 feet away when shooting was done, I only staid a few minutes.

Lawrence (his x mark) Finlay

On Sunday the 23d of June, a large gathering of Indians was expected to be at St. Ignatius to celebrate the feast of Corpus Christi and supposing that the murderers would be there, I informed the sheriff of Missoula County that it would be a good time to arrest the two Indians, that by locating their camps they could be surprised and taken into custody and hustled out of Camp without any trouble providing the plan was properly carried out. The result will show that the Indian culprits and their friends became aware of the sheriff's presence and armed and fixed themselves for a desperate resistance. More men were called for by the sheriff and they boarded a freight train and ran down from Ravalli Station, on the reserve, with the view of heading off the prisoners and some of their backers who had just before proceeded down the wagon road which leads along the railroad track. Overtaking an armed Indian, according to the story of pursuers, the train stopped; A demand was made upon the Indian to surrender and upon showing resistance he was shot and Killed. The posse did not wait to capture the men they were in pursuit of but boarded the train and ran down to Horse Plains which is off of the reservation. I was at Ravalli Station and an Indian runner came flying by on horseback going towards the Mission for a Priest to come down as an Indian had been shot and wounded by the sheriff's posse. Supposing the freight train went on and that the sheriff was making a fight to capture his men, I manned a hand Car with railroad section men and sent them down the road to do what they could to assist the sheriff, but they had hardly got out of sight when I received a telegram that the sheriff and his men were safe at Horse Plains and off of the reservation, but would come back again. Knowing that the Killing of an Indian who was not the one looked for by the posse, and owing to the great excitement among the Indians, I deemed it best to call for troops to overawe any attempt of the murderers and their friends to seize upon the exciting opportunity of attacking the sheriff's posse in force and thus involve the whole nation in war. By your orders Col. [George L.] Andrews, commanding Fort Missoula, sent three companies of the 25th Infantry to Ravalli, on this reservation where they are now encamped. I held a consultation with the chiefs and head men on the 25 and 26th and all deplored the unfortunate circumstances which brought the sheriff's posse and the military upon the reservation. They claimed that they would be more than pleased to have the murderers arrested by the white authorities, but that they were not able to accomplish the arrest themselves, as they feared a conflict with their brethren [sic] which might result in blood shed and a never ending conflict among the relatives on each side.

This is the way the matter stands to-day. I apprehend not the slightest fear of any uprising among the people but the two Indians who have caused the trouble and who are now on the reservation defiant and blood thirsty should be taken at any cost, dead or alive.

I am,

Very respectfully,
(Sgd) Peter Ronan
U.S. Indian Agent.

* * * * * * * *

The Posse Returns
Government Troops Sent to the Scene of the Indian Trouble.
Sheriff Heyfron Determined to Have the Two Indian Murderers.

The situation yesterday regarding the Indian trouble was uninteresting and messages from the scene were very meagre and as a rule were sent to private parties. On information received the day before at department headquarters the troops were ordered out for a little service. Strange as it may seem they actually went to the front, after the citizens posse had been in the field over twelve hours. At 3:20 a special train pulled out of the station bearing 117 men and nine officers, who were well rationed and prepared for a trip.

During the afternoon Mr. McHaffie sent a telegram stating that the situation looked blustery, but the posse felt confident and determined.

The wounded Indian died during the morning, but the effect of his death upon the excited members of the tribe is not known.

After the regular troops left here the opinion was freely expressed that the citizens posse would be relieved from duty and return home during the night some time, while others expressed the opinion that the other Indian murderer would be captured before the return of the sheriff's posse. Thus matters stood at 8 o'clock last night, with the citizens camped at Jocko, or near there.

The citizens posse arrived in Missoula about nine o'clock last night. From Judge Sloane, who commanded, the party the following summary of the affair is gleaned, which covers the ground briefly and faithfully:

When Sheriff [Daniel J.] Heyfron and his men arrived on Sunday night at Ravali it was impossible to do anything in the way of apprehending the murderers. It was known that they were in the vicinity, but the sheriff nor any member of his posse knew the men wanted, and this was a serious draw back. The next morning the sheriff visited McDonald's store and learned that the murderers had gone westward but a short time before. The sheriff and posse boarded a freight train and started to White Pine with the intention of heading them off. When near White Pine two Indians answering the description were seen a distance away. The train was stopped and the Indians ordered to halt. They ran, and when about 300 yards away one of them turned and fired at the posse. The sheriff at first did not want to return the fire, but the Indian peppered at them until Jim Conley fired and winged him. The Indian took the gun in the other hand and continued firing, when Conley fired a second time, hitting him in the chest. Other members of the posse also fired.

While this was taking place none of the posse noticed the approach from the rear a band of Indians numbering about thirty. The train men called out to the sheriff to look out and the posse turned to find the band within thirty yards of them. The train was backed up, the posse taken on board and carried to Horse Plains. The Indians fired several shots as the men were boarding the train, none of them effective, however.

Thus it was that Heyfron realized that with his limited force he was powerless to do anything. He accordingly telegraphed for assistance which was sent as already published in the *Morning Missoulian.*

The posse escorted No. 1 west as far as Duncan. It then returned over the line to Arlee and remained there until morning. There seemed no prospect of apprehending the men there and so the train journeyed back to Jocko, where the dead Indian was, and looked over the field.

No redskins were to be seen there in any considerable numbers, so the posse remained there only a short time. Just before leaving Arlee Sheriff Heyfron had a conference with Agent [Peter] Ronan and it was decided to get the Indian chiefs together and see if an arrangement bould [sic] not be made for the peaceful surrender of the murderers. The plan was followed, and the chiefs notified, but before they reached Arlee a s.... rode out to them and stated that a carload of white police were waiting to take them. The chiefs were finally assured and came in to the council. They were free to state the wounded Indian was "bad," but as to giving up the murderers they claimed they had nothing to do with it, and would take no part in turning over the criminals. If the white police wanted the men they could go and take them, but must expect no assistance from the chiefs.

As a matter of course, this interview was very unsatisfactory and the officers could only await developments.

Soon after this council the regular troops arrived by special train, accompanied by Captain [Henry] Marchant, special agent of the department. Another conference was called and the matter in all its phases discussed, but no agreement could be reached. Captain Marchant explained the matter to the chiefs in a plain way. He told them that when white officers failed in their duty they were deposed, and if the chiefs refused to assist in the execution of the law they would also be reduced to the rank of the average Indian upon the reservation. He produced strong arguments, and when the citizens' posse left Ravalli last evening the prospects seemed fair that the chiefs would order the murderers turned over to the sheriff.

The murderers are not Flatheads, but two Pend d'Oreille renegades, belonging to a family who are all regarded as "bad Indians." The resistance to giving up the men seems to have its foundation in the followers of the renegades on the reservation. The good Indians do not object to the murderers being taken away and punished according to law, but the renegade followers numbers fully a hundred warriors and the effect of a surrender upon this elements is what is feared.

A majority of the armed Indians are now in the brush and on the mountain sides around Jocko. They are in bands of from five to twenty and are watching the movements of the troops from their hiding places. The murderers are in the mountains and it is regarded as next to human impossibility for white men to effect their capture. The friends of the fugitives are especially well armed and it would require almost an army of men to dislodge them from their mountain fastness, and perhaps then with a heavy loss of life. Some of the half-breeds are furnishing the resisting party with ammunition and assisting the murderers to evade the officers. The Indian police have also refused to assist in capturing the outlaws without orders from the chiefs, and thus the matter stood last night — all depending upon the action of the chiefs in regard to giving them up. Should they consent to bring the murderers in and turn them over to Heyfron the trouble is ended, but if they refuse the military must capture them as best it can, which is no small undertaking.

Above: Lalasee, *Below*: Pierre Paul
Source: "Four of a Kind," *Missoula Weekly Gazette*, Nov. 12, 1890,
page 3, col. 1-3.

Document 84

Killing Was in Self-defense

July 17, 1889

Source: "Court House Cullings," *The Weekly Missoulian*, July 17, 1889, page 4, col. 5.

Editors' note: The Missoula court cleared Joe Finley and Baptiste Matt of murdering Seven Pipes or Benoit. The killing had been in self-defense. The archaic spelling of several words in this article are no longer considered correct.

Court House Cullings.

The witnesses who failed to appear on Wednesday, arrived Thursday, and about 3 o'clock the case of the Territory vs. Joe Finley and Baptiste Matt was called before Probate Judge Landers. The men were charged with killing Benoit, alias Seven Pipes, on July 6th, the particulars of which appeared in the *Morning Missoulian.*

The first witness called was Alex Matt. He said that on the day the killing occured Seven Pipes came over drunk. He went to Matt's house and threatened to kill Matt and his son; that they (the Matts) were too thick with the white people and that he (Seven Pipes) was going to make a clean-up and clean out the place of those he did not like. He assaulted Alex Matt, who was crippled with rheumatism, and struck him with a club. Matt tried to raise his gun but could not do so, owing to his weak state. Joe Finley had the gun and was trying to get away from Seven Pipes. Alex Matt called to his brother Baptiste Matt to come to his assistance and not allow him to be killed. Joe Finley was clubbed and stoned by Seven Pipes, and opened fire on his assailant. Steven Pipes ran, and when about 150 yards off Baptiste Matt took a shot at him, evidently with the intention of scaring him off.

Alex Matt's evidence was corroborated by Pierre Finley and others. Harry Lambert testified to the general bad character of Seven Pipes and to his quarrelsome disposition.

County Attorney Webster appeared for the prosecution and F. G. Higgins for the defence. After the argument the court discharged the men on the ground that it was shown conclusively that the killing was done in self defense.

Charlie Finley's Arrest.

A little scheming on the part of the officers landed Charlie Finley in the jail on a charge of violating the game laws of Montana territory. The crimes were committed in Deer Lodge county some time since, and warrents issued for Finley's arrest, but the officers could not catch him off the reservation. While subpœnaes were being made out in the Finley-Matt case it occured to the officials that by strategy they could bring Charley Finley here as a witness. He didn't know anything about the killing, but the bait worked, and after the trial Thursday he was arrested, and jailed. He is the victim of misplaced confidence.

Document 85

Murder of Pend d'Oreille Indians

July 31, 1889

Source: Peter Ronan, *Justice to Be Accorded to the Indians: Agent Peter Ronan Reports on the Flathead Indian Reservation, Montana, 1888-1893*, ed. Robert J. Bigart (Pablo, Mont.: Salish Kootenai College Press, 2014), pages 58-60; "Flatheads in Council," *The Anaconda Standard*, February 19, 1893, page 9, col. 5-6.

Editors' note: The white justice system in Montana Territory vigorously pursued Indian people who murdered — or were accused of murdering — white people, but failed to prosecute with similar energy white men accused of murdering Indians. The Commissioner of Indians Affairs wrote the Secretary of the Interior requesting that the Montana Territorial Governor be instructed to take "appropriate action" to solve the murder of Chief Michelle's relatives. No records have been located indicating anyone was ever tried or punished for these murders. The entire case was further complicated in 1893 when tribal members obtained evidence that Canadian Crees rather than white men may have committed the murders.

United States Indian Service,
Flathead Agency, M.T.
July 31st, 1889.

Hon. Commissioner of Indian Affairs,
Washington, D.C.
Sir:

I have the honor to report that great Excitement Prevails among the Indians of this reservation on account of the discovery of the charred remains of the bodies of some of their missing people.

Last Summer a very respectable Indian, a nephew to Michel, the Head Chief of the Pend d'Oreille Indians of this reserve, accompanied by his wife and his daughter, aged about sixteen years, and another Indian of the Flathead tribe, went out hunting and promised to return before winter. They did not come home at the promised time and no news was heard from them during the winter and spring, which caused great uneasiness among the reservation Indians as the missing ones were popular among all of the tribes.

A half-breed Cree, named Anthony La Course arrived at this Agency some times ago from the Blackfoot country, and brought a horse with him which belonged to the missing Indians. When questioned by myself and the Indians, as to how he got the horse, he told what I considered a straight story: He said that he traded his horse with a white man last fall for the one he rode to the reserve, receiving five dollars to boot. He gave a description of the whiteman and his place of residence, whose named he stated to be Jake Wagoner, and is Chopping wood and making fence rails on Deep Creek, in the Sun River valley, Chouteau County, Montana. Wagoner stated that he got the horse from a party of trappers.

A son and a brother of the missing Indian and other Indian companions started about six weeks ago in search of their missing relatives, and surely enough they found by the Warm Springs, between Sun River and Willow Creek, a mould [sic] of thoroughly buried matter and dirt. Digging a little they found the remains of burned bones; the two stone pipes which they recognized as those of the two missing men, and iron used by the women to dress hides and two pair of rosary beads. The mould and remains found was between the place where some whites had a camp, which the Indians recognized as the camp of whitemen by the signs: namely the Kind of stakes used and the pieces of newspaper scattered around the place.

The searchers came to the conclusion that their Indian relatives were murdered and the bodies carefully burned by some white people. Four days ago the Indian searchers brought in the few remains of the Charred bones, and the few objects found in the mould. They have already come to me and asked for an investigation into this terrible crime, and demand justice for all. If nothing is done in this case it will contribute to embitter more and more the feeling between the whites and Indians, and expose the lives of innocent white people for the future, as the unwritten law among the Indians is life for life from the race they consider guilty of the murder of their Kinsmen.

I have a full description of the horses the murdered Indians had with them, I have one horse that belonged to the murdered Indians, I have the half-breed Cree, Anthony La Course, who traded his horse to a whiteman for a horse which belonged to the murdered party; and La Course is willing to lead me to the camp of said whiteman, whom if not guilty could perhaps give a clue to the perpetrators of the crime. The Indians are greatly in earnest about this matter. They quote the fact that two of their people were hung at the head of Flathead Lake, by a mob of whitemen, on suspicion of having

Chief Michelle
Source: Drawing by Gustavus Sohon, National Anthropological Archives,
Smithsonian Institution, Washington, D.C., 08501400.

Killed three white prospectors, they also quote that two of their Indians were shot by whitemen, one at Arlee station, and another on the hunting grounds down the Mullan road leading through the Coeur D'Alene mountains. They say that the two outlaw Indians whose arrest was recently sought for by the sheriff of Missoula County, and which caused the trouble last month by which a call was made for troops, shot two innocent white travellers in revenge for the two last mentioned Indians Killed by whitemen. They claim that if there is no effort made to ferrit out and punish the perpetrators of this last murder, that the Kinsmen of the murdered ones will be hard to restrain and might try to be avenged according to the traditions of the Indians, that is to take revenge by Killing any person, however innocent, if he belongs to the race suspected of the crime.

This matter might be placed in the the hands of the Sheriff of Choteau County, but the Indians claim and ask that their Agent be instructed to look into this matter, and if necessary go to the country where the bodies were found and there to institute a thorough investigation. I am ready to undertake the investigation for the sake of harmony and good will between the whites and Indians, but shall await instructions and authority before acting. It will

require travel on horseback on an unfrequented trail save by Indians, of about
one hundred and fifty miles over the Cadotte pass and towards the country of
the Sun River. I earnestly desire communication from your office in regard to
my duties in this case soon as possible as the Indians will await with impatience
my orders in this unfortunate affair.

Very respectfully,
Your obd't serv't
Peter Ronan
U.S. Indian Agent.

* * * * * * * *

Flatheads in Council
Reservation Indians Holding Court at St. Ignatius Mission.
The Story of a Crime
A Party of Indians Massacred by Unknown Murderers —
The Reservation Chiefs Investigate the Crime.

Written for the Standard.

On the Flathead Indian reservation for the past week, the Indians have
been holding a council, or rather an investigation, in regard to a murder of
some of their people which was committed in 1888, in the Sun River country,
and at the time of the finding of the remains the Indians of the reservation were
firmly of the opinion that the killing of their people was done by white men.
Events have since transpired which lead the Indians to believe that the British
Crees were the perpetrators of the crime. A general round-up of the Crees
was made last week, and an investigation was ordered. The examination of
witnesses conducted by the reservation Indian judges of the court of the Indian
offenses, is now going on at the council hall, which is a commodious room in
the Indian jail building near St. Ignatius mission. The examination of witnesses
by the Indian judges is said to be conducted in a dignified manner, and if
it should prove that the Crees perpetrated the crime, serious consequences
may follow. Agent Ronan has furnished the *Standard* with some of the details
connected with this Indian tragedy, all the facts in the case having been officially
communicated by him, at the time, to the Indian office at Washington.

It appears that in the spring of 1888, a very respectable Indian, a nephew
of Michel, the head chief of the Pend d' Oreille Indians of the Flathead
reservation, accompanied by his wife and his daughter, a handsome Indian
girl of 16 years, who had previously attended the Sisters' Indian school at the
mission, in company with Pierre Moolman and another Indian of the Flathead
tribe named Baptist Paloo, went out from the reservation on a hunting trip

for furs, and agreed to return before winter set in. They did not come home at the promised time, and no news was heard from them during the winter and spring, which caused great uneasiness among the confederated tribes of the reservation, as the missing family were related to the Pend d'Oreille chief and all were very popular among the Indians.

In June, 1889, a halfbreed Indian named Antoine La Course, arrived on the reservation from the Blackfoot country, and brought a horse with him which was thought to have belonged to Moolman, one of the missing Indians. When questioned by the agent and the Indians as to how he obtained the horse, he told a satisfactory story. He said he traded his horse with a white man, the fall previous, for the one he rode to the reserve, receiving $5 boot. He called the white man Joe Wagoner, and said that he was engaged in chopping wood and making fence rails on Deep creek, in the Sun River valley, in Choteau county. Wagoner stated that he got the horse from a party of trappers. A son and a brother of the mission Indian, Moolman, and some Indian warriors of the reserve started in the spring of 1889 in search of the missing members of the tribes, and they found by the Warm Springs, between Willow Creek and Sun River, a mound of ashes and dirt. Digging a little, they found burned bones; two stone pipes, which they recognized as belonging to the missing men; an iron used by the women to dress hides and two pair of rosary beads. The mound and bones found was near a place where whites had been camped, which the Indians felt sure of by the kind of stakes used, and by pieces of newspapers scattered around the place. The searchers came to the conclusion that their Indian relatives were murdered and the bodies burned by some white trappers. They brought to the agency the remains of the charred bones and the few articles found near the mound before mentioned. To say that there was wild and savage excitement on the reservation and around the agent's office at the time is only putting it mildly.

They asked for an investigation into the terrible crime, and demanded justice of all. They were quieted by the agent, who said he would give the matter prompt attention, and in reporting the case to the commissioners of Indian affairs, he said: "If nothing is done to find out the perpetrators of this crime, it will contributed to embitter more and more the feeling between the whites and the Indians and expose the lives of innocent white travelers or settlers in the future, as the unwritten law among the Indians is life for life from the race they consider guilty of the murder of their kinsmen. The Indians are greatly in earnest about this matter. They quote the fact that two of their people were hanged at the head of the Flathead lake by a mob of white men on a suspicion of having killed three white prospectors; they also quote that two of their Indians were shot by white men, one at Arlee station and another on the hunting ground down the Mullan road leading through the Coeur d'Alene mountains. They say that the two outlaw Indians, Pierre Paul and La-La-Lee [sic], now being sought for by the sheriff of Missoula county, for the murder of a white man, and which occasioned the recent trouble by which a call was made for troops to come upon the reservation, shot two innocent white travelers in revenge for the two last mentioned Indians killed by white men. They claim that if there is no effort made by the white people to find out and punish the perpetrators of this last murder of Indians, that their kinsmen will be hard to restrain. I await instructions in regard to my duty in this affair."

Under date of August 19, 1889, the agent was instructed from Washington to report the matter to the authorities of the territory of Montana, and to urge upon said officers the importance of the matter, and the necessity, in the interest of harmony and good will between the Indians and the whites, for some earnest endeavor on their part to apprehend and convict the parties guilty of the murder complained of. The commissioner added: "By a report of even date herewith, the matter is submitted to the secretary of the interior with the recommendation that the governor of Montana be requested to take appropriate action in the matter under the laws of the territory."

After a lapse of nearly four years, during which time Pierre Paul, La-La-Lee and Pascall, the Indian spoken of as being sought after on the reservation, by both military and civil authority, were captured, tried and executed for murder in Missoula, Mont. The reservation Indians think they have a clue to the murder of the Moolman family. Should their suspicions be sustained by proof there will surely be trouble in the Cree camps in Montana, as well as upon the reservation. One Cree testified that while traveling through the country with his wife and family, he came upon the spot where the relatives and friends of the murdered Indians found the articles and bones described, and being attracted by a stench he proceeded to a small pond in a swampy place a few hundred yards from the old camp and came upon the dead bodies of two Indians and a s...., answering precisely to the description of Moolman and his wife and the Flathead Indian. The body of the girl was not found and this leads the Indians to the belief that she was made a prisoner and is still alive in one of the camps of the British Crees. It is said the investigation will not end with the examination of Cree witnesses on the reservation, but as soon as spring opens the camps of the Crees will be searched for the missing girl, not only on this side of the line, but across the British boundary. The bones found are now supposed to be beaver and other animals, but the pipe and rosary beads were known to have belonged to the murdered Indians.

Document 86

Alcohol on the Reservation

August 1889

Source: "Beligerent Redskins," *Butte Semi-Weekly Miner*, August 14, 1889, page 1, col. 4; "The Indians," *The Weekly Missoulian*," August 21, 1889, page 2, col. 4.

Editors' note: Late 1889 saw frequent news articles about alcohol on the reservation. It was only a small part of what was happening on the reservation, but it got most of the attention.

Beligerent Redskins.
The Mission the Scene of a Big Drunk and a Shooting Scrape.

Mr. Joe Menard returned yesterday from a three days' visit to the Flathead country. He had a very interesting trip and saw the Indians indulge in a series of capers outside of the usual run of things. For several days past the Indians have been getting plenty of whisky, and on Wednesday evening their appetite for the ardent culminated in a grand drunk. During the evening one of the redskins rode a horse into Demers' store, and other acts of recklessness occurred. A row occurred among the intoxicated Indians, and one of the Finleys shot one of the rioters in the leg. Another redskin was clubbed over the head with a gun barrel until he was senseless. In the course of the melee forty or fifty shots were fired.

Pierre Paul was a conspicuous figure among the Indians, says Mr. Menard, and he openly defies the whites to arrest him. He was well mounted and had two six shooters on his saddle and two in his belt, while he wildly waved a short-barrelled repeating rifle in the air. The Indians on the reservation are afraid of Paul, and Mr. Mienard [sic] thinks that the half-breeds would help to capture him. La La See is there but has nothing to say.

There are about twenty lodges of Kootenais there and an unusual number of Cree and Blackfoot Indians are on the reservation.

The liquor is obtained through half breeds who make regular trips to Missoula and other points. Liquor is now causing all the trouble.

* * * * * * * *

The Indians.

Duncan McDonald arrived yesterday from the reservation. When asked about the Indian trouble he said that trouble was reported at Demersville. The Indians, he says, can buy whisky by the pail full at numerous places, and are drunk a portion of the time. It is only when they get drunk that a disturbance occurs and a united raid on the drunken loafers would have a salutary effect. He thinks every Indian on the reservation should be punished under the law, and thinks that the only way to stop the frequent outbreaks. Pierre Paul is defiant and rides around at will generally surrounded by a gang as worthless as himself. He thinks there are a number of Indians who would volunteer to assist in the capture the offenders if led by the right officers.

Document 87

Son of Chief Eneas Murdered at Demersville

August 1889

Source: "The Kootenai Indians Again," *The Inter Lake* (Demersville, Mont.), August 30, 1889, page 4, col. 3; Peter Ronan, *Justice to Be Accorded to the Indians: Agent Peter Ronan Reports on the Flathead Indian Reservation, Montana, 1888-1893*, ed. Robert J. Bigart (Pablo, Mont.: Salish Kootenai College Press, 2014), pages 80-83.

Editors' note: Somehow the local Demersville newspaper was offended that Kootenai Chief Eneas would want justice for the murder of his son. Eneas thought that if Indians were punished for killing white men, white men who killed Indians should also be punished. The killing of Chief Eneas' son, Samuel, in Demersville was a tragic affair and the historical records include many contradictory sources. The local whites seemed to be very anxious to blame an Indian for the killing, but this was possibly a self-serving falsehood. Eneas' statement emphasized his diplomatic efforts to protect his tribe while also avoiding further bloodshed. He controlled his anger, despite the provocations from many of the Upper Flathead Valley whites. Ronan had Eneas' side of the story published in a Helena newspaper and his 1890 annual report to the Commissioner of Indian Affairs. In response to this report, the Commissioner of Indian Affairs decided the killing may have been "totally without justification" and asked the Secretary of the Interior to have the United States Attorney for Montana investigate. He also instructed Ronan to cooperate in the investigation. The Commissioner of Indian Affairs then received various communications from white officials blaming the Indians for the conflict and asking for protection from the Kootenai. The Commissioner requested that the U.S. Army investigate the conflicting claims. A grand jury was convened but there was no record of anyone being punished for Samuel's death.

The Kootenai Indians Again.
Chief Aeneas Accompanied by Fifty or Sixty of His Tribe Visit Us.

Last Wednesday, Chief Aeneas, of the Kootenia tribe, came to Demersville with some fifty or sixty of his followers, all painted and decorated in the latest

Indian style, to find out if possible who killed his son, and who the guilty parties are that have been selling the Indians whiskey. They held a conference at the town hall and two Indians named Louie, and Antwine, swore that certain parties had sold them whiskey. Warrants were at once issued for their arrest. Only one man was arrested however, and he was afterwards released. Chief Aeneas had agreed on Wednesday night that he would be on hand at 10 o'clock a.m. with the two prosecuting witnesses and further, that all who accompanied him should leave their arms behind. After waiting for some time after the hour agreed upon, and no chief showing up, a messenger was despatched for him to come at once. Word was soon brought back that the Indians had all left, and that no signs of their presence were visible. The people of this valley are getting somewhat weary of this continuous outbreak of the Indians, and think its about time that something was done to hold them in check. The Cliff House fed about fifty of these redskins Wednesday noon, and there has never been an Indian excitement here yet, but what has cost Mr. Clifford from $50 to $200.

* * * * * * * *

United States Indian Service,
Flathead Agency,
September 9th, 1889.

Hon. Commissioner of Indian Affairs
Washington, D.C.
Sir:

   With the hope of bringing certain criminals to justice, that live in the settlements at the Head of the Flathead Lake, I shall go to the County Seat of Missoula County, where the Grand Jury is now in session, and bring before them the following statement made to me by Eneas, Chief of the Kootenai Indians of this reservation. It refers to the events and cause of the last sensational reports published through the country of an Indian uprising in that region, and is as follows:

Chief Eneas:

Three Indian boys of my band were gambling near Oust Finley's place on Mud Creek on the reservation. They lost everything they had even to their blankets. They then started for the Head of the Lake going up the East side, and avoiding my home which is on the West side. On the way they passed a creek where there are some white settlers, about one mile from Demersville. At that place a whiteman who was on foot took a horse away from another whiteman who was riding the same. The fellow who was set afoot begged of the Indians to loan him a horse to ride home, which they did and turned back with him. The Man's name is Joe Morant and he is a settler at the Head of the Lake. He gave the Indian boys whisky upon which they got drunk. When they got to Demersville they were drunk from the whisky obtained from Morant. At Demersville, they got into trouble and a whiteman drew a pistol on one of them but a fight was prevented by outsiders. I (Eneas) was camped near Chief Michel's place, and the day after the Indian boys mentioned started for Demersville, I moved my camp to go home. I camped for the night near the Steamboat landing at the Foot of the Lake. My son-in-law, Louie having loaned a horse to the Indian boys he took the steamer to Demersville to get him back. Before getting on the steamer Louie asked my son to take his horse and ride up to Demersville and meet him there. When I got to my home at Dayton Creek, my son and another Indian rode to Demersvill[e]. They had no arms when they left. They camped the first night with some Pend 'd Oreilles and Kootenais on this side of Demersville. In the morning they found the three Indian boys, the party altogether being six Indians. They sat around the

Chief Eneas
Source: Archives and Special Collections, Mansfield Library,
University of Montana, Missoula, photograph number 81-284.

store all day at Demersville. In the evening, two of the boys who previously got whisky from Morant were approached by a whiteman who came out of a saloon, and who is known to the Indians by the name of Jack Sheppard. He asked the boys if they wanted to buy whisky. The Indian boys replied that they had no money; they then reported to their companions that a whiteman offered to sell them whisky. My son-in-law Louie had money and he gave the boys four dollars to buy with. They found Jack and gave him the money. Jack pointed out a place on the bank of the river where he would deliver the whisky. True to agreement Jack returned with two bottles of whisky, which they carried to the other Indians. They all went away from the vicinity of the store to a more secluded spot and commenced drinking. One bottle was drank by six Indians, and my son after drinking said he was hungry and started to the hotel to get something to eat. My son in law Louie followed him. Louie heard a white man talking loud to my son through an upstairs window, ordering him to go away or he would shoot him. Lou[i]e took my son by the arm and tried to take him away. Louie said he heard some one come down stairs who came out the door and while he (Louie) held my son the white man shot him. When my son fell, Louie stated that the man who shot him told him to get away quick or he would be shot. Lou[i]e could not run as he is lame but he turned and saw two white men with guns who told him to get away, and followed him as he hobbled off, for about a hundred yards. Two of the Indian boys who got the whisky started that night after the shooting, for Tobacco Plains, and the other three Indians started back to my home on the reservation. They told me that white men killed my son at Demersville. I sent a whiteman called "Savia" [Francois Gravelle] who is married to a Kootenai woman to get the body of my son. When "Savia" returned with the dead body he told me that the white people at Demersville wanted me to go up there. The morning after the Killing a camp of British Kootenais arrived at Demersville from Tobacco Plains, and they recognized the body as being that of my son. The whitemen told them also to tell me to come to Demersville. I did not wish to go but was advised by a white man who lives in the Lake country to go. It was sixty miles from my home to the Agency and I started for Demersville without letting you (the Agent) know as the distance was so far. I took some of my people along, but sent word ahead that I was coming with no hostile intent, but simply to inquire if my son was killed by whitemen or not. If so to ask that the murder might be punished, and the men who sold the whisky might also be punished, as that was all the cause of the trouble between my Indians and whitemen. I camped on the night of my arrival at the house of Baptist Le Bow [J. B. LeBeau], who is a white settler and lives on this side of Demersville. In the morning I sent another man to let the people know I was coming to talk with them as a friend.

When I got to Demersville the people seemed excited and afraid that I came there for revenge. I assured them through an interpreter as best I could my friendly intentions. I could not get any good council with them. I knew that not one of my Indians who had the trouble had a gun or a pistol with them when they left my camp for the Head of the Lake. I do not know where any of them could have borrowed or purchased a pistol or a gun. I told the people if they could tell me where any one of them got a gun or pistol then I might think my son was killed by an Indian. One of the Indians sold a horse to a white man. I asked that white man if he traded a gun or a pistol for the horse — he said no! I asked to see the ball which killed my son, and was answered that the ball was sent to the Agent (not so it was no[t] sent) and by him it would [be] sent to Missoula. Louie, my son-in-law told the whites at Demersville, in answer to a question that he saw the gun plainly in the hands of a white man which killed my son — that it was not a pistol but a gun which looked like a Winchester. Louie also claimed that he could recognize the man who held the gun, and was asked to do so if he was present. Louie pointed out the man but he was not arrested. That man lives in a house at Demersville, but Louie does not know his name, but can point out the house. Finding that I could not learn anything about who killed my son; whether it was a white man as claimed by the Indians; or by an Indian as claimed by the whitemen. I came home to my place at Dayton Creek. The whites wished me to stay one day longer but I felt it would be useless to do so.

I now leave it in the hands of the white men for investigation, and I trust they will do me the justice to investigate this killing. My Indians claim it was done by whitemen, the white men claim it was done by Indians. God Knows! I do not. I now throw myself upon your sense of justice to all.

A great many of my people have been killed by white men; two of them were hung by a mob. I know of no punishment or even a trial that was ever given to a white man for killing any of my Indians, and I now think it time to show that there is justice to be accorded to the Indians as well as to the whites. If this matter shall be brought before the Court at Missoula I am ready to be there and also to do all in my power to bring in witnesses who might be required.

Eneas Chief of Kootenais
his X mark

Respectfully submitted

Peter Ronan, U.S. Indian Agent.

Document 88

White Travelers Hire Indian Driver

August 3, 1889

Source: "'Yis,' Answered Jim," *The Helena Independent*, August 3, 1889, page 1, col. 8.

Editors' note: The anecdote in this article commented on the language problems in Indian-white dealings on the reservation, but it also emphasized the economic competence of the Indians.

"Yis," Answered Jim.
A Helena Man Has an Experience With a Non-English Speaking Indian.

A member of a party who had just returned from a fishing and hunting trip to the Flathead country, tells a good story on one of the gentlemen which Settles him. There were nine altogether and it was necessary to cross the Flathead reservation to reach their destination. An Indian named Jim, whose only knowledge of the English language was to say "yis," in basso profundo tone of voice, was hired to convey the party across the reserve in an old stage coach. He wanted $10 for the job and this amount was paid. When the stage reached the mission, half the distance, Jim concluded the drive was worth more and getting down from the box he held a conference with a brother Indian, who communicated to the party that Jim said he would take them no farther unless he was paid $2 more. Jim had the bulge on them and the deficiency was promptly paid. One gentleman who rode alongside Jim addressed his remarks to him thus: "Young man, if the condition of the atmosphere was not so sultry and would not cause the perspiration to flow from our sunburnt brows as it does, we would all extricate ourselves from your rib-racking vehicle and walk rather than pay you the money demanded; now, Jim, you know you had the immortal cinch on us, and that's why you made us come down, didn't you?["] "Yis," answered Jim, indifferently. "And do you know what I think of it?" retorted the young man, "It's a mean Irish trick." "Yis," again spoke Jim with that perfect indifference which was aggravating, and the spokesman just then realized that his eloquence was wasted on the winds, as Jim didn't understand a word he was saying.

Document 89

Accused Indian Murderers on Reservation

September 14, 1889

Source: William W. Junkin to Secretary of the Interior, September 14, 1889, U.S. Department of the Interior, "Reports of Inspection of the Field Jurisdictions of the Office of Indian Affairs, 1873-1900," National Archives Microfilm Publication M1070, reel 11, Flathead Agency, 5657/1889; "Wanted to See His Mother," *Butte Semi-Weekly Miner*, September 18, 1889, page 4, col. 1-2.

Editors' note: Junkin gives an account of his side of the story about the attempts to arrest Pierre Paul and La-la-see for the murder of two white men. The manuscript was very hard to read and is reproduced as accurately as possible. The Butte newspaper article gives more details of the same events.

The Indian Murderers.

Flathead Agency, Mon.
Sept. 14, 1889

Sir:

I have the honor to report that shortly after my arrival on this reservation I found apprehension and fear prevailing among the white people at St. Ignatius Mission, as well as among the better class of Indians.

Two years ago two white men were murdered on the reservation, supposed at the time to be the work of Indians. The confession of a half breed now in jail at Missoula and the admission of the men themselves prove that the murders were committed by Pierre Paul and La-la-see, Indians belonging to the Pend d'Oreille tribe, whose habitation is in and around the mission. These murderers are out at large and are to be seen almost any day at the Mission.

Pierre Paul is the boldest and most reckless of the two. La-la-See is quiet and remains at his own house most of the time. He claims that he was led into committing the crime by his companion. Because of the boldness of Pierre Paul the trader and his clerk and their wives are in dread, and the property of the missionaries is in jeopardy. He has threatened to burn down the property of the trader because he was refused credit, and injure the Fathers because they harbored white men.

September 7th I went to St. Ignatius Mission in company with Clerk [Thomas] Adams. Just afternoon we went with Father [Jerome] D'Aste and an Indian policeman to visit the jail, which is utterly unsafe for prisoners. While there an Indian came to the door and finally into the building and commenced abusing the clerk and myself to the policemen. In a short time he left. On our return to the Mission house the Father told us that the Indian was Pierre Paul. When about half way between the jail and the mission Pierre Paul overtook us and began his Indian talk, accompanying it with demonstrative gestures and scowling fuss, pointing frequently to us. We had no arms, and did not understand him. The Father would not interpret, but hurried us into the house. There he told us that the Indian said we had no right on that part of the reservation, that he intended killing the clerk and agent, and then expected to be shot down. We were afterwards told that at his second attack on us he was armed with rifle and pistols.

Believing I had no cause for fear, I marched around the village and tried to salute the Indians pleasantly, but it was a failure. Not half a dozen Indians responded pleasantly. I saw Pierre Paul and passed within a few yards of him, but he did not molest me. He has about fifteen friends and backers among the young men, and the other Indians are intiminidated [sic] by him and his crowd. The only white men at the Mission, outside of the Fathers and teachers, are the trader and his clerk.

On my return to the agency on the 9th inst. I told Maj. [Peter] Ronan that I thought it best to capture Pierre Paul. On the 10th inst. he went to the mission for this purpose, accompanied by farmer Lambert, who is also deputy marshal, and five Indians. Shortly after his arrival three of the Indians met Pierre Paul on the street, while riding, and disarmed and captured him. At the earnest solicitation of his captors and his friends (the latter being quite a crowd) and in the interest of peace, the agent consented that his captors should bring him to this agency. Pierre Paul wanted to bid his mother goodbye. He was permitted to go into the house. In a few moments he came out, jumped on his pony with the agility of a cat and [strove?] for the brush bordering Mission creek. The whole affair occurred so quickly, and I am informed, that the Indian was safe before any one thought of shooting.

Agent Ronan made a talk to the people on the 11th inst. and gave them until 9 a.m. o'clock on the 12th inst. to deliver Pierre Paul. The chief of the Indian's tribe, Michel, counseled his people to make the surrender.

On the 11th inst. at one o'clock Agent Ronan returned to the agency. On the afternoon of that day I went to the mission with Clerk Adams.

On the morning of the 12th inst. I went to the trader's store, where I found four Indians who had been looking for Pierre Paul. They were Indians from this part of the reservation. Not an Indian living in the locality of the Mission, so far as I could learn, had aided in the search. I disbanded the posse. On my return from the Mission I took the cars at Ravalli and met Agent Ronan at Arlee. We proceeded to Missoula and afterwards to Fort Missoula. Finding Col. [George] Andrews absent in camp with the major portion of the troops we returned to Missoula. Agent Ronan sent the following telegram to Gen. [Thomas] Ruger at St. Paul. It explains itself. I herewith attach a copy marked "A."

I endorsed the message to Gen. Ruger because I believe there are grave reasons why troops should be sent to this reservation to arrest these two murderers. Gov. [Benjamin] White has had posted over the country hand bills offering a reward of $500 each for their capture. No one has sought to earn the reward. The longer their capture is delayed, especially Pierre Paul, the bolder they become and the more terrorized will the people be.

If action has not already been taken on the telegram of Agent Ronan I urgently recommend that immediate steps be taken to send troops coming on to the reservation with instructions to capture the murderers and outlaws Pierre Paul and La-la-see. Prompt action is necessary to convince these murderers and their friends that the government will preserve peace. The several efforts to capture them have proven futile, and only the presence of troops will secure the surrender or capture of these fellows and restore strictness to the reservation. The sale of whisky to Indians is at the bottom of all the trouble among the Indians.

Respectfully,
William W. Junkin
U.S. Indian Inspector
Special Disbursing Agent.

To the Hon. Secretary of the Interior.

* * * * * * * *

Exhibit "A."

Missoula, Mont. Sept 13" 1889

Gen. Ruger
Commanding District of Dakota
St. Paul,
Minn.
Sir:

The two Indian Murderers for whose arrest a reward of five hundred dollars each is offered, are yet at large on the reservation, terrorizing the Indians to such extent that they are afraid of death to themselves and relatives, if they assist in arrest. The outlaws threaten to burn the Mission and the Indian Schools and convent. They have followers, that back them against arrest by Indians and have succeeded in over awing the better class of the tribe. The arrest and punishment of the culprits and their backers will settle all difficulty on this reserve, in present condition of affairs Indians will not accomplish this, a company of cavalry on the reserve with orders to arrest the two murderers and their backers will settle matters and bring tranquility among the better Class of Indians. I ordered the Indians yesterday to bring in the outlaws or troops would come. They failed to do so.

I desire to Know from you, if I can have Military aid in this emergency. Answer at Arlee.

(sgd) Peter Ronan
U.S. Indian Agent

Endorsed
(sgd) William W. Junkin
U.S. Indian Inspector.

* * * * * * * *

Wanted to See His Mother.
How Pierre Paul, the Halfbreed Murderer, Gave His Captors the Slip.

Under date of September 13, last Friday, C. V. Carter writes from Arlee concerning the recent capture and escape of Pierre Paul, one of the two halfbreed murderers wanted by the territorial authorities. The other "breed" is La La See, and Governor White has offered a reward of $500 for the capture of each alive.

In his letter Mr. Carter states that the two men have been lurking in the vicinity of the mission near Ravalli station, considerably of late and a week ago last Sunday, September 8, when Indian Inspector Junkin and Clerk Adams, of Flathead agency, were visiting the mission Pierre Paul showed himself to them and finding them unarmed began to utter all manners of threats against them and heaped such abuse and taunts upon them as only a renegade halfbreed Indian can utter. The two gentlemen returned to the agency that evening and informed Major Ronan, the agent, of what had occurred. Bright and early next morning the major gathered together the judges of the Indian court and a posse of Indian police and repaired to the mission and without much trouble succeded in effecting the capture of Paul. The latter cowed completely, although numerous of his friends were present, for they seemed to be equally frightened and offered no resistance to the major and his small force.

While preparing to return to the agency with their prisoner the latter begged most piteously to be allowed to see his old mother. By the advice of the judges and their full assurance that they would not allow the prisoner to escape, Major Ronan finally consented. So persistent and eloquent was Paul in his appeals that several old hunters who despise and hate him, finally also requested the major to grant him the favor asked. With an escort of two of the most trustworthy and reliable members of the police force, Paul was marched to the cabin in which his mother resided. The old lady was not in the house and Paul remarked, "She must be in the yard," thus momentarily throwing the policemen off their guard, and as he said so he stepped to the door as though to look for her, and with a bound leaped onto his horse, which stood within a few feet of the door, and made for some brush and timber near by. In an instant a half dozen policemen were racing after him and soon were joined by other Indians and half-breeds, but the fugitive continued to gain on them and successfully made the brush. Search for him was continued for sometime but without avail.

Major Ronan, after trying his utmost to recapture the murderer, returned to the agency Thursday, but not before he had given strict orders to the police to continue the search, and if possible secure Paul. He also warned the latter's friends not to assist him in any way, and gave the Indians until 9 o'clock the following morning to deliver the man into his custody, being satisfied that Paul was still in the vicinity of the mission.

In case the prisoner was not surrendered at the time set by Major Ronan, so Mr. Carter writes, it was the intention of the major to request Governor White to send out troops to look for Paul, and every Indian suspected of assisting the fugitive to elude the law would be imprisoned and held until such time as Paul would be captured. As the Indians are very much opposed to the idea of troops being camped on the reservation, Mr. Carter thinks they will certainly recapture Paul without assistance from the outside.

Document 90

Charlo and General Carrington Negotiate about Bitterroot Lands October 1889

Source: Excerpt from Henry B. Carrington, "The Exodus of the Flatheads," manuscript, Carrington Family Papers, MS 130, Manuscripts and Archives, Yale University Library, New Haven, Conn., chapter 7, pages 1-12, chapter 8, pages 1-4.

Editors' note: This manuscript is the only detailed description of the negotiations between Charlo and Carrington in 1889. Unfortunately, it only represents Carrington's viewpoint. It would have been very useful to get Charlo's description of the events. Presumably the specific incidents referred to were generally accurate, but Carrington added his own biased interpretation of Charlo's motives and inflated Carrington's skills as a negotiator. "Sic" has not been used except in a few typographical errors.

Chapter VII.
Negotiations with Charlot's Band.

Before leaving Washington, the Commissioner [Henry B. Carrington] obtained from Lieut. General Scofield a letter to the Commanding Officer of the Department having headquarters at St Paul, requesting that the garrison of Fort Missoula, four miles south of the City of Missoula, be authorized to render assistance in case of an emergency requiring military aid. The precaution proved to be unnecessary, but a visit to the post, upon completion of the preliminary investigations at the Jocko Agency, added a moral support to the negotiations that immediately ensued.

The services of blind Michel [Revais] and Eneos Francois, "The Mountain Lion," also a good interpreter as well as one of the patentees of land in the Bitter Root Valley, had been secured, and the journey was made in two days.

A large flag was flying from a tall mast before the Stephensville hotel, upon the arrival of the party, and many citizens as well as Indians had assembled in the vain expectation that a few hours, or possibly a few days, would complete the work prescribed by the Act of Congress. The fact that in addition to the signatures of all Indians interested in the lands, the examination and appraisement of two hundred quarter sections, with their improvements were to be made, did not abate the expectation of many, that the Indians might all be removed before the ensuing winter months of 1889.

On the following morning, early, Michel was called upon to procure suitable transportation to Charlot's cabin, as the first business to be transacted in the valley. To his suggestion that the trip should be made on horseback as the road was bad, or delayed until after Charlot came to town, it was a sufficent reply, that "as Charlot hauled supplies to and from town in a wagon, any other wagon, or a buggy, could make the trip, even if more leisurely, and with some discomfort, but the promise to Charlot must be kept.["] A bright young Flathead, well-painted, well mounted, and well equipped, was enlisted as a guide to the Chief's cabin, and a start was made. Over rocks and bogs, around stumps and fallen trees, through sloughs of uncertain depth, the journey was conducted and after ascending a slight hill confronted by a formidable gate bars, Charlot was seen in *negligee* Indian apparrel, fixing a plow, near a corn stack in front of his home cabin. A few acres of wheat stubble in front, half an acre, perhaps, of corn stumps, and a smaller spot of meadow, with old harrows, wagons, broken wheels, a few farm and garden tools, a very small smoke house, and one half-covered tepee, or lodge, constituted the immediate surroundings, while a rude rack which supported some old harness, three lean horses, a few hogs, some chickens, more dogs, and a cow crumping dry corn fodder in the angle of the fence, constituted the other visible farming resources of the Flathead Chief. It needed no words to confirm his sad refrain, so often repeated at Washington, to Garfield, to Vest, and at Jocko, that "Charlot, was poor."

Close by Charlot's side, as the buggy passed the entrance after Michel had taken down the bars, stood little Victor, his bright grandson, named after the "Great Victor." The introduction, with tender of a cigar and a light, and the assurance that the first thing done upon reaching the Bitter Root Valley, had been in accordance with the promise made at Jocko, and to invite him to a conference in the village, was followed by an invitation to enter his cabin, where acquaintance was made with his family. Beyond this invitation, no business was mentioned and the talk was purely social, or about his farm and crops, and what he had laid up for the coming winter. Upon looking at some photographs, he asked that he might have one for Victor and he placed it upon the shelf above an enormous fireplace. Piles of robes and blankets along the sides of the cabin designated resting places for the entire family at night; and with a parting present of cigars and the request that he send for such bacon, sugar, tea, and tobacco as he needed, the interview closed. Without folling [sic] to the bars, he said to Michel, "Tell the White Chief that he is the first white man from Washington that ever visited Charlot's cabin," that "he promised, when at Jocko, and he did not lie!" He started two sons for Stephensville very promptly, and their return with the supplies promised soon became widely known, so that the next day found Indians from various directions flocking into town, for similar manifestations of the white man's presence and regard.

One incident connected with the visit to Charlot, was so impressively suggestive as not to be omitted. While carefully reining the horse through the roughest part of the journey, as Michel could not drive, and, to follow the mounted guide was of chief concern, a sweet voice, hummed the hymn, "Nearer, my God to Thee: nearer to Thee!" It was Michels. To the inquiry, "Do you know that? Where did you learn it?" and the request "Let us sing it through, together?" he answered, "I forgot! I did'nt know I was singing it aloud! we cant sing it here." The response, "This is the Great Spirit's temple, over head, and these great pines are supporting the arches. It is just the place to sing, as the mockingbirds and whippoorwills all about us are doing," brought a smile and a good hearty outburst of the melody.

Conversation about the death of his wife, and the misconduct of his son who had been put in jail at Missoula for bad conduct when drunk, was followed by an expression of sympathy for him when alone in his cabin near the Agency. He promptly replied, "I am never alone. I say prayers, and sing hymns, and fear nobody; for the Great Spirit who is everywhere, hears me, and if I cant see him, I know he is near, just as I know you are near, but, cannot see you. All the noises in the woods are from the great Spirit, and the birds know just what to do, because he made them, and they cant see him, more than Michel can."

In all subsequent negotiations, and conferences, even when Charlot seemed most obstinate, violent, and threatening, Michel never lost faith in the success of the mission nor that his people would all be gathered at Jocko. He "had prayed for it, all his life, and his father and Francois' father, who helped the white men when they first came to the Bitter Root Valley, would know of it, somehow, and be made happy."

Early on the next day, Michel was busy in giving invitations to all whom he met to come to the appointed place for interviews; and although the Agreement was upon a table by itself, and now and then, a signature was witnessed, no pressure was brought to bear upon any, save the simple announcement of the general purpose of the visit, and the "hope that considerable sums of money would come to the patentees as well as the re-union of all the Flatheads, if all acted together for the good of all." It was known that the visit to Charlot had been simply a friendly call, and before noon, he appeared in person both to return the call and acknowledge the gifts received at his cabin. He came, with hair carefully oiled and braided, wearing the same suit when he wore when visited General Grant [i.e., President Chester A. Arthur] in 1885 [i.e, 1884].

When asked to permit his picture to be taken, in exchange for the one given Victor, he hesitated. When asked to get his people before St Mary's church, and have all taken together, he was pleased with the suggestion and in a very short time more than a hundred assembled. One old man, on crutches, Stephen James, and a very old woman shouldering a pappoose in a cradleboard were among the first to take positions. Other s....s and poappose and several leading men of the tribe, including those who visited Washington with Charlo in 1885, soon completed the effective historic group, while the church in the immediate back-ground, and the three lofty peaks still farther away, supplemented all that was needed to give enduring interest and value to the scene.

Upon return to headquarters, many Indians followed. One brought an "early Rose" potatoe as a present, weighing six pounds and twelve inches in length. Gigantic applies, more than five inches in diameter, were so decidedly extraordinary in size, that two were immediately mailed to the President, as samples of the valley fruit. The gathering of so ma[n]y of the tribe, of all ages, led to the announcement of an early next day service at the St Mary's church. All the benches were filled soon after the bell rang, and nearly every foot of the floor was packed with kneeling forms, intermingled with children of all ages and sizes. The streets and stores had been crowded by Indians, most of them in their best attire, and after the service, the large room at the hotel, set apart for the purpose, and on level with the sidewalk, was filled as closely as men, women and [c]hildren could be squatted together, while the windows were obscured by others whose faces pressed against the glass to see if they could in some degree understand what seemed like some strange patomime occurring within.

From the first, diary notes were taken of these interviews, to be compared, afterwards, with the interpreters recollection, and both questions and answers were written as the interviews progressed.

During the succeding days of constant conference, the citizens generally did all within their power to prevent the idle young men and the weak old men from getting whiskey. The assurance that if a saloon keeper sold or, gave strong drink to an Indian, he would be sent at once to the Missoula jail, and the hire of a wagon for such a possible contingency, may have been an additional inducement to good order; but the citizens generally seemed to feel that the future of the valley might depend on success in this final attempt to effect the removal of the Flathead Indians from their midst. Mr. J. R. Fauds, Editor of the Rocky Mountain Gazette, was most assiduous in his appeals to the public to maintain good order and support of the movement then in progress.

Charlot was constant in his attendance, often passionately demanding the "literal execution of the Stephens Treaty," as "all that he would submit to";

but at every interview some of his people signed the contract, regardless of his protests. Repeatedly, he declared that "he never would sign, but kill himself first." When Vandenberg, his chief companion in the visit to Washington, with his son, stepped to the table and signed, and the immediate approval by the much beloved and worthy Father [Jerome] D'Aste, followed, Charlot seemed impressed by the loneliness of his position. There was a sense of honor in his words and bearing, that was at times almost majestic, as he repeated the fierce threat against his own life, adding "the women will call Charlot a coward and a liar, if he change his promise and sign."

Suddenly, he arose, and thus appealed to his own history, in his own behalf.

"Where is the white man who can say that Charlot is not his people's friend? The Nez Perces went to war with the white man. Chief Joseph filled the mountain passes with his soldiers and then came into my lands, where he never belonged, to kill my brothers the white men. Chief Joseph held out his hand to Charlot, the son of the great Victor, and this is the way he talked. 'The white man is a liar! He talks smooth to get peace and sign papers, and when the Indian lies down to sleep, with no arms, the white man tears up the paper. White man steals the Indian's land and white man lies. He kills all the game, and spoils all the rivers. He hates the red man. We will drive the white man away. We will live as our fathers lived. The white man shall bury his dead, and never come back again.'"

After a few moments pause, Charlos, continued:

"Then I put my hand behind my back, and this is what I said to Joseph. 'Charlot, never lies! Charlot never betrays his friends. You are in the land of the Flatheads, where you never had a home. You want to go through the land of my fathers to kill my friends. If you will go through the valley in peace, Charlot will say, — yes — but will not take your hand, for it is the hand of the white man's enemy. You may go through; but if you steal a calf, or a little chicken from Charlot's friends, Charlot and his soldiers will strike you as his fathers knifed the Blackfeet, on all sides, and spare nobody! Go Joseph! Charlot has no more words for Joseph."

Chief Charlot's account of his services, was not exaggerated in his earnest but calm, recital. Immediately after his interview with Joseph, he organized a full company of his braves, who were armed by the government, and he personally conducted the exposed white families to Fort Owen and other places of security and protected them until additional troops arrived in the valley. Mr. Amos Buck, of Stephensville, who took part in the defense, informed the Commissioner, that "but for Charlot's heroic intervention, and against superior numbers, all the families of the valley would have been massacred."

At one visit, standing in the midst of three encircling groups, all upon the floor, when pipes passed freely and the dense smoke almost obscured recognition, the chief waved before his face a soiled copy of "Governor Stevens Treaty" which he always carried with him, and with aggressive, defiant emphasis, demanded,

"Will the white man, at last, and now, do what this paper says? Is the white man like the Blackfeet, who only steal, and kill, and lie? Charlot will sign no more papers."

Suddenly returning the paper to his bosom he drew forth a white and a red handkerchief. These he spread in silence to his right and left, upon the floor, and with solemn mein continued his appeal.

"See, white Chief. There's no blood, not a drop, there," pointing to the white emblem at his right. The Flatheads never shed the blood of a white man. They shed their own blood to save the white men "Charlot, the son of Victor never lies."

Pointing slowly and scornfully to the red emblem at his left, he raised and wrung it as if soaked with blood, and replacing it upon the floor, again broke forth with a ringing voice that brought crowds from the street to the open windows.

"See there, believe Charlot. That is like the Blackfeet, soaked with the white man's blood. They are liars, thieves, and murderers. I hate the Blackfeet and cut out their hearts." Suiting action towards, he stamped upon the red emblem, in great fury, while every feature betrayed malignant hate, and he made gestures in pantomime, of the sweep of the scalping knife and deadly thrusts. Then he told little Victor to put it in the stove to burn, as the Blackfeet ought to burn.

Then, his face relaxed its sternness as he lifted the white emblem and gently placed it in his bosom, saying in sibfdued [sic] tones, as if only speaking his thoughts, "Charlot, son of Victor, loves the white man, and puts this where the white man is always safe, against Charlot's heart. Charlot, speaks the truth."

The climax of these numerous conferences respecting the removal of his band to the Jocko Reservation, was of peculiar interest, from its semi-religious aspects and deserves [literal?] record. After many interviews, when concession on his part seemed almost hopeless of attainment, and an unusual number of his people crowded the room and adjacent street he again announced, in more excited terms than ever, that "he never, never, signed the Garfield Agreement"; that "whoever said so, was a liar, and he didnt want to talk to liars!"

It seemed for a moment as if the indignant chief had finally resolved to end the interview, whatever his people might individually do. After a brief silence, the Commissioner stepped into the adjoining room, but quickly returned, holding in his hand the *original* "Garfield Agreement," saying, as he approached near the Flathead Chief, "Charlot, I am your friend! Charlot has spoken the truth! I want the interpreter to tell all Charlot's friends that any man who says that Charlot lies, is himself the liar. Here is the paper with Charlot's name written by a white man, but no cross (X) opposite Charlot's name, because Charlot refused to sign the paper when Second Chief Arlee and Third Chief Adolph signed. Charlot is not bound by that paper. The Stephens paper was good, a great while ago, but Charlot needs a new paper, better than either, and the white man and his red brother are old enough to make a new treaty, and let the treaties of dead men be forgotten."

Charlot looked about him and seemed to study the faces of his people. The Indians, for the first time began to talk among themselves, and were not interrupted for several minutes. The vindication of Charlot's statement, that "he never signed the Garfield Agreement" brought exclamations of surprise; and refilling their pipes, they watched his every motion. Suddenly, but with dignity, Charlot again arose and seemed burdened by a sense of injured honor in case he should sign the paper. He spoke, with earnestness, "I said I would never sign the paper" and with a fierce motion as of putting a knife to his breast, added "I would kill myself first. Charlot never changes! The women would call Charlot coward and liar, if he changed. I told you twice, and more than twice that I would kill myself before I would sign, and prove myself a liar. You pinch me too hard. It hurts!"

"But, Charlot," was the reply, "Father D'Aste and myself will, if you kill yourself, be very sorry and mourn for you and your people. But when Charlot's people cry for bread to feed the hungry, or for blankets to keep them warm, can Charlot rise from the grave, when they dig and find him, to answer their cries? When Victor meets him in the spirit land and asks "why Charlot left his people 'can he answer Victor without trembling? No! Charlot will not kill himself! He will stay and lead his people to peace and happiness."

"Charlot, let me ask you something. Think hard, before you answer. Does Charlot, never change?"

"Never," was the impassioned reply.

"But, Charlot, you say that you never change! Once you were a little pappoose, like those in the corner, stretched out on cradle-boards

[Here a page is missing from the surviving manuscript.]

in the Stephensville stores, to come to this room and ordered them to supply nearly sixty families with flour, bacon, coffee, salt, tea, and sugar, with no cost to you and the s....s came and loaded the ponies with all they could carry, you said, "White Chief told the truth and the dream was a lie!"

Charlot, the Great Spirit never tells lies! His whispers are true. To conquer and drive away a bad spirit is a greater victory, according to the good Book, as

Father D'Aste will tell you, than to take your enemy's village and all his braves. Only the Great Spirit — never changes! When Charlot said, I never change! I wondered if the Great Spirit had entered into Charlot's body, and was speaking through Charlot, 'I never change.'"

"Charlot. You tell your young men who gamble, drink fire-water, fight, and steal, that they must change from bad to good. Go now, and think by yourself. To-morrow will be another Sunday, and after the sun rises all will say prayers in the Church. Stay away, and do not come here, until the Great Spirit whispers something to your heart that will bring peace and plenty to all your people. Tell all these people to go away; and Father D'Aste, and your white friend will ask the Great Spirit to give us all the same message because he loves all his children alike, and wants us to be happy in peace and never have war any more. Charlot, our talk is done!"

After a brief pause, Charlot moved his left hand toward the door speaking as if to himself, but understood by his people, and with something like awe in their silent movement, all left. Some went silently to the cabins and tepees near the church. Others mounted ponies and as quietly disappeared.

When the last one had left, Charlot, having wrapped his blanket closely about his person, extended his right hand, and withdrew, with these simple words. "Goodbye! Charlot will think, all night, and do what is right, if he can."

Chapter VIII.
The Flatheads Unite Under Charlot.

It was after 2 O'Clock when Charlot thus dismissed his people and retired to his temporary quarters near St. Mary's church. In addition to the usual Saturday market attendance, the prospect of an early settlement of the Indian land question had attracted farmers, ranchmen, and a few speculators from distant parts of the valley and from Missoula. Several of the poorest Indians from distant tracts, both men and women, squatted themselves on store steps, or on the sidewalk along the course of the bright little stream that ran in the gutter, past the council room, on the way to St Mary's River.

At about 5 O'Clock, Indian women appeared at the door and the windows, evidently in great terror, reporting that "two of the young men who had secured liquor, were cutting each other with knives," and imploring help. An interpreter was at once sent to Charlot with orders to stop the fight and restore order among his people. The gravity of the situation was instantly understood by the Chief. It was a strange episode to occur so soon after the conference of the morning. The offenders were knocked down by him instantly and the flagellation, with his stout whip, was so furious and determined that an appeal from the women and a request to remove them without further punishment, alone suspended the growing excitement. It fitly closed a day of intense and dramatic sensation.

Saturday night passed with unusual quiet in the Indian camp. On the following morning, at a very early religious service, the Indians assembled with peculiar quietness, as if the shadow of some impending calamity rested on the entire congregation. The silence at headquarters was unbroken and the curtains were drawn down. The order of the previous day that "no Indians returns until Charlot should so direct" was observed, although several had sent word by the interpreters that "they wished to sign the paper." It was not until 11 O'Clock that one of the interpreters who had passed through a side door to the hotel office brought word that Charlot was sitting upon the door step without, with no one in company except little Victor, while Vandenburg and others were across the street near Buck's warehouse watching his movements. Presently, a light rap at the door, un-answered, was followed by a second, and then a third more decided rap. Michael partly opened the door and asked Charlot "What he wanted?" Upon his reply that "he wanted to open his heart" he was invited in, and the room was again, almost instantly, packed with his people.

In simple words, with no reference to the incidents of the previous day, he made a full statement of the poverty and wretchedness of the Flatheads of the valley, especially naming several very aged men and women who could not help themselves and whom the young men would not help. He said that "the young men would hunt and sell their game for fire-water, and he could not stop it," that "they followed the words of bad white men and stole what they wanted to eat, without working for it." He dwelt tenderly upon the burial place near the church, asking "if it would be dug up by white men when his people went to Jocko?" Upon being told that "it would be protected, just as well as the other burial places near the white man's churches," he made very explicit inquiry as to what would be their priviliges and holdings at the Jocko." He was informed that "he would have his own choice of land so far as possible, but that good cabins would be built for all and that whatever he thought best for his people would be put upon paper when he was ready to explain their greatest needs."

He then stepped forward, with extended hand, and replied. "The Great Spirit said to me last night, 'Trust the white Chief.' Charlot loves his people! Charlot will change and do right! Charlot will sign the paper, and then, the white Chief can write down what Charlot wants."

A pen was placed in his hand, with the brief word "Charlot is a great Chief. He has conquered the evil Spirit, and will make his people happy! Everybody will be happy!" He then affixed his (X) to his name. His entire demeanor altered, in an instant. Sullen moroseness and passionate action were exchanged for every indication of contentment and peace. A murmur of satisfaction pervaded the room, Blind Michael could not restrain his tears of joy, and Charlot at once spoke again, "Charlot will make everybody sign!"

But he did not lose sight of the promised "List of good things," and seating himself upon the floor began his recital. He "wanted all to be written *twice*, so that he could have a copy and be sure that all was just as the talk had promised." His first inquiry was "if, when his own land was sold, he, and not his people generally would have the proceeds?" *Next*, "He wanted a new wagon and harness." *Next*, "that upon reaching Jocko, every family having young children should have a fresh cow." *Next*, "to have for himself and family the Arlee house and land, which had been improved and were nearest the Agency and the warehouse of supplies." This was promised also, "if just arrangements could be made with Arlee's widow." *Then*, he explained, with pantomimic effect, that, "the sun got very hot over head at noon, and the snow and rain were sometimes very bad," and "he wanted a two-seated, covered, spring-wagaon [sic], for visiting his people and getting them settled at work." This was promised, "conditional upon approval at Washington; but, otherwise, it would be charged to him, because the other Indians who had such wagons had always bought them by sale of stock, or furs." He was also informed that "such groceries as were immediately needed would be furnished them without cost, in addition to such as had been already distributed to the most needy."

Document 91

Banquet of Honor Given by Bitterroot Whites

November 1, 1889

Source: "A Great Banquet," *The Helena Journal*, November 6, 1889, page 2, col. 1-2.

Editors' note: Officially this banquet was given to honor Carrington, Ronan, and Bitterroot Salish leaders. Charlo, Louis Vanderburg, Michel Revais, and Francois Saxa Lamoose were given places of honor. According to Carrington's account, some of the white orators pompously exhibited their arrogance by calling the Salish "savages" in Charlo's presence. Charlo always used an interpreter in his dealings with Carrington, but he knew enough English to visit regularly with white friends and neighbors in the Bitterroot. He understood, and was offended.

A Great Banquet
Tendered to Gen. Carrington and Eaten by Indian Guests.
The Noble Red Man Much Praised.
Speeches at a Stevensville Banquet of a Congratulatory Kind Concerning the Proposed Purchase of the Lands of the Flatheads.
[Special Correspondence of The Journal.]

About two weeks ago General Henry B. Carrington, United States Army, arrived at the Flathead Agency under appointment and instructions of the Indian Department and the Bureau of Indian Affairs, to appraise, for sale, the lands and improvements attaching to fifty-one patents granted to the Flathead Indians in Bitter Root Valley. After consultation and proper preparation the General, in company with Major [Peter] Ronan, proceeded to Stevensville and commenced negotiations with the Indians on the 31st of October. The mission of the General and Major Ronan were successful beyond their expectations. On that date considerably over half the Indian holders signed the agreement to sell their patented land and remove to the Flathead reservation. The citizens of the valley appreciating their obligations, tendered a ball and banquet at the Stevensville Hotel, on Friday evening, Nov. 1st. At least three hundred ladies and gentlemen of the valley dined and danced, while Charlot, the Flathead Chief, Louie La Cook-Sim-Hey, or Grizzly Bear Far Away, and Eneas Francois, occupied prominent seats at the table. The last mentioned are prominent members of the tribe. Geb Norris, the proprietor of the hotel, served up a repast which would do credit to any hotel in Montana. Miss Lida Catlin had charge of the details of receiving, and performed her office in a graceful and charming manner.

When the guests were seated

Major Ronan Was Called

upon to introduce General Carrington, which he did in the following language:

Ladies and Gentlemen: I return to you my sincere thanks for this mark of appreciation, on your part, for humble efforts to settle the land question between the Indians and the white settlers of the Bitter Root Valley — the garden spot of Montana — the home of its earliest settlers, where the log cabin looks out upon a domain which the European palace cannot boast of. Your orchards, pastures, gardens, herds and fields give evidence of thrift and industry. Your churches and schools in the little town of Stevensville are eloquent tributes to your sense of morality, and your sense of obligation to the rising generation. General Carrington who has been entrusted with the important mission of settling and closing up the land relations of the Flathead Indians, with the United States, had command of the Rocky Mountain district from 1865 to 1869, and opened the wagon road around the Big Horn Mountains to Montana. He was the first government official who recognized the immense mineral and agricultural resources, as well as climatic advantages, of this new and vigorous State. He has been foremost in his friendship for the red man, while ever maintaining the value to the white man of a prompt occupation of the rich valleys of the West. In Europe as well as in America he has urged his views in both addresses and published volumes. The white man and the red man alike can feel confidence that all their interests will be safe in his hands, as he designs impartially to advance their interests in perfect harmony toward substantial, peaceful results.

I now have the honor to introduce to the ladies and gentlemen of the Bitter Root Valley your honored guest of this occasion, General Henry B. Carrington, the soldier, scholar and American gentleman.

Response by General Carrington.

Ladies and Gentlemen: — I appreciate your kind welcome to this garden valley. My estimate made more than twenty years ago of the vast resources in store for the emigration to Montana has been more than realized. That report slumbered among valueless miscellaneous papers, when it would have had real value to offset hasty misjudgments if it had been given to the world. One year ago the United States Senate made inquiry as to its fate and published it.

This is not the place to speak of my official duties more than to say that my confidence is [in] your certain prosperity and my intense sympathy with the red man prompted the acceptance of the mission now in my charge. It is equally just to both races that they should have separate homes and industries. If it be my lot to adjust the land problem of this valley acceptably to both I shall count it as sufficient reward for the labor involved and more precious as a legacy to my children than the honors of the field of blood. This social hour, with sparkling water from icy fountain-heads as the medium of our exchanged salutations, is a fit emblem of the purity and peace which I trust will ever be the ornament and glory of our people.

Hon. Luke D. Hatch acted as toast mater, and at the request of General Carrington each sentiment was pledged in water.

The Speech of Welcome

Was delivered by Dr. R. A. Wells, as follows:

General Carrington, in the name of the people of this valley and especially the citizens of this village, I extend to you a hearty welcome and the humble hospitality of the citizens of Stevensville. And permit me to say here, we are not unmindful of the long and illustrious services you have rendered your country as a military officer, having spent the best years of your life in her service, and now being honorably retired on account of advancing age from that arduous and faithful service, you may well, in peaceful seclusion, look back with pride and pleasure upon such a career of usefulness and contemplate the results of that peace which your valor and that of your compatriots in arms so nobly and heroically achieved in the terrible ordeal of battle, not for us alone of this generation, but all posterity; for a nation once rent in twain by a bloody fratricidal war, but now happily reunited and placed on a basis of unity, let us hope, as enduring as the rock-ribbed, snow-capped mountains around us this evening. Nor would we forget your noble services in the peaceful field of literature, where you seem to wield your facile pen with as much grace as you once did your sword, for, "The pen is often mightier than the sword," and "Peace hath her victories no less renown than those of war."

But General, you are here among us on a mission of mercy, in which both we and the Indians are perhaps equally interested. The Indians of the Flathead tribe have ever been at peace with the whites, and it is their boast, and we who know them well believe they have never shed a drop of the white man's blood. As we honestly believe their removal would redound to their interest as well as ours, we wish you great success in the laudable enterprise before you. When the renowned "Kit" Carson was trapping amid the profound solitude of the mountains, upon the head waters of the Missouri River, and fleeing before the bloodthirsty Blackfeet, in a region where no white man had ever ventured, save the hardy trapper and the ubiquitous missionary of the Cross, here in a smiling valley he met the Flatheads who at once knew him and he them, for he spoke their difficult dialect, they at once received him and treated him as a brother, supplied all his wants, and then bid him "god-speed" on his perilous journey.

So, deal gently with our friends, the Flatheads, a remnant of a once powerful tribe — disintegrated by war, and decimated by disease. Place them among their own people where they shall be kindly treated ere they are exterminated by the environments and the inexorable logic of civilization. There may they rest in peace, secure from want and the ravages of war.

Again, General, I extend to you a hearty welcome, and when your mission here is ended we wish you a safe return to the bosom of your friends.

"Our Ladies,

their excellence, and what they have done for the prosperity of our infant industries," was responded to by the Rev. Thomas W. Flowers in choice and eloquent language which won the applause of the assembled guests.

"The Indian Lands

and our appreciation of the legislation on the subject" was responded to by L. J. Knapp. He said:

The most enduring monuments of man's genius soon crumble into dust, are swept away by the storm cloud, and the waves of the sea increasingly chant a requiem to their departed greatness, but laws, principles and institutions, in harmony with God's eternal plan of evolution, must continue to expand as the cycles of time roll on. Nothing in all history is more fully demonstrated than the fact that national development and progress must be commensurate and in harmony with the great law of evolution, and wherever its principles are ruthlessly violated the sins of the fathers have been unrelentingly visited upon the children. Of this no more striking example is found than in our dealings with the Indian race. From the day the campfires of European civilization first lighted our Eastern coast, until within a very recent date this government has persistently pursued a policy of deceit, treach[ery] and dishonor toward the Indians. Disregarding the ancient and sacred right of occupation as an element in their title to the soil, it leveled their dwellings to the ground, desecrated the burial places of their fathers, and drove them from place to place as the caprice and covetousness of the white man might dictate. This policy has borne its legitimate fruits and for more than one hundred years the pioneer has paid the penalty in the dissolution of his home and the blood of his kindred; and on a hundred battle fields the Indian has demonstrated that he cannot and will not be held in subjection. Such was the class of men from which in Mythological days heros were supposed to spring, but we are taught from childhood to look upon the Indian as symbolizing all that is vile and treacherous in mankind and the edict has gone forth from many an orator of our land, that he should be brought to immediate subjection to the laws of our country or exterminated. Those who are blindly influenced by such deceptions should go back fourteen hundred years to the coasts of Jutland, where lived a wild and barbarous people subsisting by hunting, fishing and war. Forced from their native land they crossed to England, where coming in contact with Roman civilization they became in a few hundred years leaders of the world in thought and action. Such is the history of our ancestors, once more barbarous than the red man of America has ever been.

Only a few years ago the government decided to change its policy toward the Indian and treat him as a member of the human race. This new policy too has borne its legitimate results. Wars and massacres are now almost unknown. He is taught to till the soil. Schools and churches are teaching him the benefits of civilization, and it is safe to say if the present wise policy is continued for fifty years every vestage of his barbarous state will be swept away and the Indian will become a useful and honored citizen of this great republic. It seems to me we are met to-night in honor and commemoration of an event of vast importance to this growing commonwealth, for it demonstrates to us that the true spirit of progress, as represented in this government, is not a failure, and that peace may have her victories as renowned as those of war. Of our Indian lands, it is with pleasure we can state that no stain of dishonor rests upon this community because of its dealings with the small band of Flathead Indians now in our midst. But could we see this country just as the Indian sees it we would understand why it is that he hesitates to sign away his treaty rights. From a hundred sunny mountain peaks the spirit of his ancestors long departed beckon him to remain. These hillsides, mountains streams and canyons are peopled with imaginary beings; the dwelling places of heroes and gods in the ages long gone by. The land which Congress has wisely decided to persuade these Indians to dispose of has been held by them many years and the successful consummation of the treaty under consideration will be greatly beneficial to the Indians and to the settlers of this prosperous valley, who are "now but the first low wash of waves, where soon shall roll a human sea." We appreciate most heartily the action of Congress in its efforts to throw open these lands for settlement, but we appreciate above all and far more the disposition of the Government to deal with these Indians in fairness and justice.

"The Early Settlers

and Their Hardships," was responded to by Hon. A. S. Blake, who said:

Ladies and Gentlemen: — The early settlers and their hardships is a theme which would require a full evening to dwell upon. We are here to do honor to-night to two gentlemen whom we class as among our early pioneers. General

Carrington, our honored guest, had command of all the Rocky Mountain district when a number of you were youths, and some not born. Major Ronan, "our Pete," as the old-timers sometimes call him, needs no comment from me; he has been among us from his youth, and his record in every path of life is without a blemish. I look around upon the comrades and partners of my early struggles and greet them with pleasure. To our departed friends, among whom I mention Captain Wiggins [Christopher Higgins], Major [Washington] McCormick, and Frank Worden, God bless their memory! We have not the disposition to dwell upon the characters of our departed comrades, but I ask of you the pledge in silence a draught from the pure waters of the Bitter Root River to their cherished memory.

"The Commercial and Farming Interests of the Valley" was responded to by E. E. Nerstry, and was an eloquent tribute to the locality and industries of Bitter Root.

"The Growth of the Valley as Regards to Lumber and Mineral Interests." was responded to by Dr. R. Gwin, and it is to be regretted that space will not allow, this morning, the publication of the gentleman's valuable statistics and remarks upon this interesting subject.

The festivities closed as the sun arose, tipped and guilded the snow-clad cliffs of St. Mary's Peak, and went down upon the memory of the most pleasing and enjoyable occasions in the history of the valley of the Bitter Root.

Document 92

Salish Elder Remembers Chief Charlo

ca. 1889

Source: Don Matt, "Mary Ann Topsseh Coombs," *Char-Koosta* (Dixon, Mont.), vol. 5, no. 14 (November 15, 1975), pages 8-9.

Editors' note: Mary Ann Coombs witnessed almost a century of Salish history. Her memories of Chief Charlo, the punishments by whipping, and the removal from the Bitterroot to the Jocko Valley in 1891 were especially valuable. As a young woman she worked washing clothes for Agent Peter Ronan's family.

Mary Ann Topsseh Coombs
"From the time my heart first remembers Charlo, he was good man!"
An interview by Don Matt

There is only one left of the Salish band that was forced to give up rich farmlands in Idaho's [sic] Bitterroot Valley and make the trek with Chief Charlo to the reservation. Mary Ann Topsseh Coombs was born in 1884. She remembers Charlo, the Bitterroot Valley, the trek here, and her people's proud religious past. She retold those things for the Char-Koosta, with her grandson, Johnny Arlee, interpreting.

She says that from the time her heart first remembers Charlo, he was a good man. A long time ago a chief was well respected and listened to. He was not chief for nothing, he had to work his way up. He had to be able to see enemies coming and warn his people.

When Charlo was chief, his "children," as tribal members were called, listened to him and he treated them good. Gambling and divorce were forbidden. He had a law that all punishments were to be administered on Sundays, when violators would lie down on a canvas to be whipped. She saw these public punishments and said that after each lash all present would say a Hail Mary to chase the evil out of that person. Charlo's "children" would listen after they were punished. Even those who were divorced would get back together after their public shame. Even her father was whipped. It seems he liked to hide out and gamble in the bushes. But somehow the punishment didn't seem to work in her father's case, he usually got caught. Unfortunately,

Louie and Mary Ann Coombs
Source: Toole Archives, Mansfield Library, University of Montana,
Missoula, photograph number 82-215.

agents, teachers, and priests took these punishment powers away from Charlo. He told the people to to [sic] whip their own children, but many didn't. Here on the reservation things got out of hand.

Mary Ann does not remember there being any hardship in the Bitterroot Valley. They had a garden and her Grandfather had a garden. (She says the soil at her present home is rocky and things do not grow as well.) She remembers eating melons, squash and onions from the gardens. She added that the neighbors were nice to her. She especially remembers a blacksmith who was nice to their family. She said it was the government who made them move out, not the neighbors.

When Charlo refused to give up his lands, he was told the soldiers would bring him if necessary. At first they had not believed they would have to go, and it was about two years before they were forced to leave.

She remembers all the people crying about having to leave. They drug their tipi poles, but not everyone used a travois to carry their things. All the farmer's fences along the way were the old, wooden rail type fence. (She extended her hands with straightened fingers interlaced to show how the fences looked. Her hands were in motion continually throughout the visit, adding emphasis and explanation.) She remembers the spots where they camped. The first one was the other side of Missoula.

Charlo held prayer in the evenings at camp. This helped relieve the agonized gloom that hung over the camp. They camped again on this side of Missoula near Schley. They stayed there for two more days at a place known as Two Creeks in Salish.

Two people were hurt during their journey. Louise Lumphrey, wife of Joe, fell when her horse spooked. Her hip was broken and she was left crippled. A man known in Salish as "Oona Moo" fell near Schley and suffered what was probably a broken shoulder blade. He came out better.

Those people at the [Jocko] church saw shirtless braves in red war paint and best tribal dress galloping up on swift horses. They were firing their rifles in the air and singing. The women came behind crying. The Reverend Phillip Canestrelli (the Indians called him "Pay-leep") got all excited, evidently thinking they were under attack. Mary Ann's future husband. Louis Coombs was there among the crowd awaiting Charlo's arrival. Being young, he panicked and tried to run and hide, but he was stopped and calmed by a woman who was a sister to the chief of the reservation band. Mary Ann felt they were well received by the people on the reservation. The government, however, failed to come through with the promised house for those making the move. Five buildings were built near the Jocko Church for the leaders, but Mary Ann's father was among those left without help. One of her biggest complaints about the way the government handled things here on the reservation was that they evicted Charlo's widow from her home after he died.

Mary Ann says the Bitterroot Salish were a short, well built, good looking people with good clothes and that this drew comments from all who saw them. Mary Ann's grandfather was Salish and she says she has, "a little smell of Salish on me." Later, on the reservation at a wake, Sam Moody, a Nez-Perce, said that all the people there should put their "heads down in shame" because their blood was mixed.

The Salish had the custom of combining two tipis and holding a wake, or big dinner where inheritances were announced and possessions distributed after someone's death. Mary Ann remembers how, as a girl, she and her sister, Ellen Big Sam, used to pretend they were at a wake, inheriting things. Her sister would also announce her under the imaginary name of "Mary Ann, wife of Alexander."

Mary Ann went to the school they had been promised at the Jocko Church. She had a hard time understanding English, although she learned some in her two years of school. The school building was not there long after the Ursulines opened a school at the St. Ignatius mission.

Mary Ann later got a job washing clothes for Peter Ronan's children and one day when she came out of the house there was a man standing there. His name was Louis Coombs. Not much was said during the first conversation, but he was definitely interested. He remembered seeing her that first day she arrived. Mary Ann had always jokingly said that the reason she came to the reservation was to get a husband, and she did. All their children went to the Ursuline's school.

Mary Ann recalled that long ago people believed in gifts through the spirits. Many of the old people had great gifts of healing through the spirits. There was a certain cliff in the Bitterroot where people went to seek a vision and find their powers. People would have a plant's curative powers revealed to them through a dream, or vision. Some people try to use their cures today, but they have "soured out" because the people using them have not received a healing gift through the spirits.

Mary Ann's mind is active and alert, but life today is not easy for her. She lives in a small cabin by herself, with relatives nearby who drop in to check on her from time to time. Although she can walk, she has fallen twice. Both of her hips have been broken and one had to be pinned. She gets tired sitting. She has a VW beetle and tries to talk her relatives into taking her out for a drive in it every chance she gets. She is under regular medical care and takes pills for her heart, but she says she feels okay.

When asked if there was anything that she remembered to give her the courage to keep going all these years. Mary Ann unhesitatingly replied, "really strong prayer" was the thing that kept her going. She told about one time she wondered how she could possibly keep going. "Why am I here? What am I doing here when all the others have gone?" she wondered as she was walking to Arlee. When she met Father [Cornelius] Byrne he said, "It's not yours — its the Father's will." Some how, through prayer, she found the strength to accept that will.

P.S. After the interview, Mary Ann sent word requesting the author to add that she would like to raise her hand and swear that everything she said was the truth.

Index